DREAM IMAGES AND SYMBOLS

DREAM IMAGES AND SYMBOLS

A DICTIONARY

BY KEVIN J. TODESCHI

A Creative Breakthroughs Book

ASSOCIATION FOR
RESEARCH AND
ENLIGHTENMENT

A.R.E. Press • Virginia Beach • Virginia

This edition is reprinted by arrangement with Perigee,
a member of Penguin Group (USA) Inc.

First A.R.E. Press edition: November 2003
2nd Printing, September 2005
ISBN 0-87604-488-7

Library of Congress Cataloging-in-Publication Data
Todeschi, Kevin J.
    The encyclopedia of symbolism / Kevin J. Todeschi for Creative Breakthroughs,
Inc.—1st ed.
p.   cm.
    "A Perigee book."
    Includes bibliographical references.
    ISBN 0-399-52184-4 (pbk. : alk. paper)
    1. Symbolism (Psychology)—Dictionaries. 2. Imagery (Psychology)–Dictionaries.
3. Dream interpretation—Dictionaries. I. Creative Breakthroughs. II. Title.
BF458.T63 1995
154.3—dc20   95-12475
                                                                        CIP
Printed in the United States of America.

Cover design by Richard Boyle

With special thanks to Carol Ann, Karen, and Magaly, the inspirational force behind *Creative Breakthroughs, Inc.,* and their work at helping others tap into the creative potential, which is a part of us all

The language of the brain is symbols; for that reason, they are uniquely individual. The benefits of their exploration include problem solving, creativity, innovation and, most importantly, personal awareness.

Perhaps more than any other tool, images and symbols can provide a deeply personal look into self–discovery and one's search for individual meaning.

Almost like a mirror image, symbols allow individuals the opportunity to glimpse a portion of themselves and their surrounding environment from another (oftentimes objective) perspective.

Because these images are so profoundly and deeply personal, each person is, ultimately, the best interpreter of his or her own symbolism and creative imaginings.

For that reason, these definitions serve as possible explorations into the world of symbols. . . not as definitive answers.

Note: The mythical figures, literary characters, geographical locations, and historical individuals in this volume are provided as a means of developing one's own approach to symbol exploration and discovery. Therefore, the list is not meant to be all–inclusive.

DREAM
IMAGES AND
SYMBOLS

About This Book

Since the dawn of time, individuals have been experiencing dreams that they just couldn't get out of their heads, symbols that possessed a special significance just for them, pictures that seemed to hold them spellbound, or images that occur again and again throughout history and in many different cultures. The world of myth and symbolism has always been an extremely powerful vehicle for human understanding.

This manual can provide you with keys to that world, as well as offer you a complete and refreshing approach to the popular subjects of myth, symbols, dream interpretation, and creative imagery. The thousands of words, symbols, and images in this manual can be used in dreamwork, creativity, counseling, intuition, waking dreams, and personal or professional imagery. Whether you have absolutely no familiarity with imagery and symbolism or you possess a rich history of knowledge and experience, this book will provide you with a thorough and easy-to-use investigation into the realm of creative imagining. In fact, you will find that this text is as easy to use as a dictionary.

For many individuals, the idea of exploring symbols, images, and dreams is immediately set aside because they *don't know how to interpret them*. The important thing to remember is that examining personal symbolism can be extremely helpful, even if you don't yet know how to work with literal interpretation. By simply being interested in the workings of your imagination, your dreams, or your images, by taking the time to write them down, and by wondering about the feelings, the colors, or the personalities that are represented by your mind, you can begin to take advantage of a wealth of untapped insights that are being freely offered by your own subconscious thought processes.

This manual gives you all the symbols you will need in order to examine these insights. Everything from *Abacus* to *Zoroastrianism* is explored within its pages. In addition, most words are cross-indexed with other words. As you explore the world of symbols, you will also find that one symbol can have multiple meanings. The most accurate interpretation depends entirely upon the person having the image. For that reason, each word within this manual has a variety of definitions and examples, allowing you to select the one or ones that feel most appropriate to your current situation. For example, an image of being back in school could be associated with the lessons provided by daily life, it might refer to one's own thirst for knowledge, or it could correspond to the need to expand one's thoughts in a particular situation. Only the individual who had the image will be best able to decide which insight applies most to her life right now.

At times, images can also relate to something that is completely different than what one might first associate with them. In other words, an image could be a metaphor for something else. For that reason, this dictionary of symbols likewise contains literally hundreds of ways in which words can be used as metaphors. For example, *getting in a jam* might mean *being in trouble* (see **Food**), or *I'm all ears* could mean *I'm listening* (see **Ears**). Often, these metaphors hold the very clues you need in order to understand images and symbols that might otherwise appear irrelevant. The keys to these symbols will be found in the issues and activities going on in the current life situation of the one whose subconscious created the image.

Exploring symbols is both rewarding and fun. Everyone can derive immeasurable benefits from looking into the world of his own symbology. For many reasons, you will want to turn to this resource again and again. Throughout its pages, you will find insights into yourself, your life, your surroundings, even your relationships with others. The world of symbology, creative imagery, myth, dream interpretation, and intuition promises to take you on an exciting adventure of self–discovery. It's an adventure that offers personal enlightenment and practical application. It's an adventure that promises nearly limitless uses. It's an adventure that will last a lifetime.

How to Work with Symbols

Even though most people are completely unaware of it, the subconscious mind possesses a remarkable talent for self-exploration, for reviewing life's events, even for practical problem solving. In fact, individuals are much more in touch with themselves, with their relationships with others, and with their surroundings than they are consciously aware. By moving beyond simple logic and exploring an unbounded world of symbology through myth and dreams, the very realm that contains subtle indications of those things that you already know at a subconscious level, you can gain clearer insights into your life, your talents, your frustrations, your shortcomings, your relationships, and even the mission in life for which you may be best suited. Symbols provide mirror images of feelings, situations, fears, experiences, needs, potentials, and desires. The world of myth, imagination, and symbolism is universal, and the possibilities for using this untapped potential for creative expression and problem solving is nearly limitless.

At the very least, creative imaginings and dreams give individuals an objective and safe tool for bringing innermost thoughts and feelings to the conscious level where they can deal with them. Creative imaginings can provide insightful assistance in daily life.

Because there are so many types of symbols, and because a specific symbol can have so many different interpretations, each individual will be the best interpreter of their own images. Thankfully, with a little background, experience, and practice, this process is not at all difficult.

Images that are universal are called *archetypes*. These images have a similar meaning to people across time and culture. Fairy tales, legends, and myths often contain universal symbols and themes. As just one example, more than two hundred legends exist all around the world that tell the story of a Great Flood. Whether or not this story has a basis in fact, because it is so widespread, the tale has a meaning at a subconscious level beyond the story itself. In fact, when one looks closely at these flood stories to see what they have in common, there seems to be a theme of transformation and change. Therefore, to individuals the world over, the story of the Great Flood can be a universal symbol (or archetype) of being overwhelmed by

5

personal transformation and change. In a similar manner, the symbol of an old person is often associated with wisdom and experience, because the more one has lived, hopefully the more one has learned. Even if you are not conscious of it, there are literally hundreds of these universal archetypes of which you are already aware. Water, as the source of all life, can symbolize such things as sustenance, emotions, and even spirituality. A symbol such as a lion, or a great cat, can be associated with power or vitality.

There are also cultural and national symbols that reside in the world of imagery. For example, the symbol of a country's flag often represents patriotism (or nationalism) to citizens of that country. A crucifix is a symbol of faith to many Christians, whereas for many Jews a menorah or a mezuzah might represent the same thing. In the United States, a black cat or walking under a ladder can be considered bad luck. In Egypt, a beetle (or scarab) is symbolic of abundance and good luck. Students of the scriptures may associate a rainbow with a promise or a covenant. Throughout the world, groups of individuals have often given meaning to specific images and symbols based upon their history and experience, and that meaning has been passed along to people sharing a similar cultural background.

Because symbols are so profoundly and deeply personal, however, individuals may also associate their own feelings and thoughts with particular pictures and symbols. When these associations differ from the thoughts and feelings of others, they generally take precedence. For example, people the world over regard the symbol of the Statue of Liberty as representing *the United States, freedom, or independence.* However, to an individual employed as a tour guide for the monument, the statue could simply represent his *work.* Therefore, regardless of whether or not a symbol is universal, cultural, or individual, ultimately each person will be the best interpreter of her creative images because only that person is fully familiar with her current situation, background, experience, and thought processes.

As another example, many individuals have very emotional feelings about their pets. To a pet lover, the symbol of his or her dog could be literally associated with the dog, or it might represent love or faithfulness. Someone without a dog (and no particular feelings one way or another) might be culturally predisposed to associate dogs with man's best friend. Someone who was allergic to dogs, however, might think of dogs as representative of allergies, an irritation, or even the possibility of health problems. The underlying meaning of a specific symbol is usually very closely associated with what one personally equates to that particular image. To the subconscious mind, images contain condensed stories of events, thoughts, feelings, and experiences that mean much more than simply the image itself. By exploring these stories, you can gain valuable insights into your life, your feelings, your thought processes, your current situation, and your future.

Working with personal symbology is like listening to the advice of a trusted friend who acts as a mirror, allowing you to gain a little objectivity. It isn't that the friend's advice is somehow better than your own. It isn't magical. It isn't to be followed blindly. Rather, the process allows for a dialogue between the conscious and subconscious parts of your mind. It allows you to see things a little more clearly. It allows you to stand back and view things from a different perspective. It makes you realize that many answers you have sought have been within yourself all along, but you just never knew how to look for them.

The potential uses for exploring creative imaginings, dreamwork, and personal symbology are nearly limitless. The following sections of this introduction present ways that images might be used for personal problem solving, for gaining insights into life's issues, even for working with children. These examples are merely guides to exploring your own images and symbols.

DREAM BASICS

Perhaps the first lesson to learn about dreams is that they do not necessarily need to be interpreted in order to be helpful to the dreamer. The subconscious mind explores, wrestles with, and often attempts to reconcile every imaginable issue in an individual's life. This occurs in the dream state (and elsewhere), and whether or not an individual is aware of the process does not negate the fact that it is both necessary and extremely helpful.

Yet there can be so much more to dreamwork than just a subconscious process that is forgotten with the light of day. In fact, there is such a wealth of insights and creative experiences available to the conscious mind that it is almost tragic to overlook them. Ignoring the deeper substance of a meaningful dream could be compared with consciously deciding not to open a letter from a trusted personal friend. No one knows an individual better than his own subconscious mind.

Although you may not remember your dreams, science has shown that everyone dreams. Exploring these subconscious insights can be quite simple, and the results of the effort are very rewarding. Even without previous experience, a simple step-by-step approach to dreamwork will enable anyone to begin remembering and working with her dreams immediately. These steps are intended for individuals who wish to begin an ongoing program of personal dream exploration, but they can be helpful to anyone.

Step One: *Write down your dreams immediately upon awakening.* Although you may only remember a color, a scene, or a feeling, write it down. If you wake up in the middle of the night, keep a dream notebook near your bed and write down a few scenes you recall so that you can write down the entire dream upon awakening the next morning. Even if you only have the feeling of a good night's sleep, write it down. Let the subconscious mind know that you are serious.

Step Two: *Realize that the feeling you had about the dream is every bit as important as any one possible interpretation.* What is the emotional response you have to the dream, to other characters in the dream, or to the action taking place in the dream? Note the actions, feelings, emotions, and conversations of each of the characters in your dream, as well.

Step Three: *Remember that every character in the dream usually represents a part of yourself.* Other people may reflect aspects of your own personality, desires, and fears. Even if the character in the dream is a real person who you know, generally the dream character represents an aspect of yourself in relationship to that person.

Step Four: *Watch for recurring symbols, characters, and emotions in your dreams, and begin a personal dream dictionary.* Write down these symbols and what their importance is to you. As you observe what is going on in your life and then look at a particular dream, you'll begin to have an idea of what individual symbols may mean to you, especially if the symbol appears in later dreams. If the symbol had a voice, what would it be telling you? The symbol won't necessarily mean the same thing to other people, because personal symbols are as individual as the dreamer. For example, dreaming of your teeth falling out may be symbolic of gossip to some people, but an individual who has just been fitted with new dentures may have an entirely different interpretation.

Step Five: *Practice, practice, practice!* This final and perhaps most important aspect of exploring your dreams is one of the easiest ways to begin to correlate your dream images with actual experiences in your waking life. After your dreams have been recorded, make a habit of exploring them a few weeks later. Look for themes, situations, emotions, and symbols that are repetitive. One individual found that her cat, who she dearly loved, frequently appeared in dreams that dealt with personal relationships; another discovered that a watch or a clock was a recurring symbol in precognitive dreams about his personal future. These types of personal insights are only possible with ongoing practice.

As you begin to explore your dreams, the first thing you might get a sense of is their overall *feeling.* Does it feel like a positive dream, a frustrating dream, a frightening dream, or an inspiring dream?

After getting a sense of your overall feelings about the dream, you may next wish to explore the essential *symbols and activities* within the dream. One of the easiest ways to do this is to describe what is happening to whom in the image. In order to arrive at the elementary symbols and activity, try describing the dream in no more than two or three sentences.

Look for the theme displayed by your subconscious images. Interestingly enough, multiple dreams in one night (or during the course of a particular experience in one's conscious life) may explore essentially the same theme. Therefore, you may gain insights into a particular dream by looking at other dreams you had during the same time frame.

Once you have reflected upon the dream's feelings, established the essential dream images, and contemplated the theme, look up these essential images in the *dictionary* section of this book. Find interpretations that best reflect a meaning and a tone similar to the one provided by your conscious thought processes. The best interpretations—and there are always more than one—are those that correlate the dream images and feelings to the activities and experiences of your waking life. There is a reason you had that specific dream at that particular time.

Sometimes you may wish to consider a dream as being largely literal. For example, seeing yourself eat a salad in a dream may indicate the need for specific nutrients or a change in your personal diet. You may dream of someone you have not heard from in a very long time and then actually run into that person a short while later. Dreams about future events or experiences may also be literal and precognitive. These dreams provide individuals with foreshadowed insights into the future in order to provide inspiration, to promote personal preparation, or to serve as a warning about the resulting effects of current activities.

In other cases, dreams are more psychological or symbolic of what is happening in waking life. For example, to dream of a person you have not heard from in a long time could be symbolic of an activity that you associate with that individual. Dreaming about different rooms in your house that are locked or have yet to be opened could be pointing to the unexplored portions of your talents or personality. A car may symbolize the physical body and the need to make a change or correct a physical condition. Dreams of birth and death are often symbols of transition or change in your life. A dream will use any image or metaphor that best suits the *idea* that the subconscious mind is trying to bring to your awareness.

Dreams possess many levels of meaning and insight, and they can be extremely helpful even if you don't recognize immediately what they mean. Generally, dreams have more than one meaning due to the multiple levels of the subconscious mind, but even a recognition of the simplest insight can be extremely helpful to the dreamer. For example, a wish fulfillment dream (a dream in which the subconscious mind essentially plays out your personal desires) can contain elements of personal guidance, it may address your emotional feelings or fears, and it might even contain precognitive information. Other dreams may serve primarily as a means for the individual's subconscious to wrestle with issues, concerns, or feelings that have been on the dreamer's conscious mind.

There is a world of exploration just waiting for your discovery—one that has been available to you since the day you were born. Perhaps the time has come for you to embark on your personal journey.

CREATIVE IMAGINING BASICS

Your imagination holds marvelous insights into your current situation and experience. Regardless of whether you are taking part in personal or professional reveries, word association imagery, or simple daydreaming, the symbolism generated by the imagination can provide a unique reflection into your own subconscious thought processes.

Perhaps the easiest approach to working with these various *creative imaginings* is for the individual (the imaginer) to decide what he associates with that image or what appears to be the basic theme. For example, one woman visualized a friend of hers. In the image she saw the moon glowing brightly overhead, illuminating the darkness around them. Upon questioning, the woman associated the moon with her friend because this individual was extremely insightful, often providing the very same illumination in response to a problem or a difficult circumstance.

Sometimes, in an extended image, considering *what is happening to whom* can be extremely helpful. These longer imaginings can be interpreted in the same manner you might use to interpret a dream. In one instance, a man visualized he was being driven somewhere by an individual in a *Model A* Ford. Since, in waking conscious‑ness, he was concerned with his current life's direction, he felt that the image was responding to that question. In the image, the road they were traveling was blocked by various gates along the way. At the first gate, the driver got out and opened it before climbing back into the car and driving through. When the driver got back into the car, the man having the image recognized the driver as Father Ralph de Bricassart of *The Thorn Birds*, and the road they were traveling was heading toward Drogheda. Since this identity had not been established immediately, it can be seen how, in an attempt to assign meaning to random images, the subconscious mind often tries to associate indiscriminate information to symbols and images with which the conscious mind is already familiar.

Although the meaning of the various symbols of this particular image might be analyzed indefinitely, the imaginer decided that the essential theme was that some‑one of professional authority was helping him travel through the obstacles and challenges of life. Since this man had just become professionally involved with a person he greatly respected, he felt as though that particular business relationship was going to be very helpful in establishing his current life's direction.

In addition to the dream state, one of the easiest ways to become open to the wealth of information stored in the subconscious mind is through relaxation rev‑eries. Since the stresses of daily life often block individuals from insights they already possess, this process can be very helpful. Essentially, all an individual must do is to become relaxed, and then pose whatever question has been on her mind in a way that will allow for an objective response. To demonstrate, you may wish to try the following personal experiment.

> **Step One:** Become comfortable and relaxed and begin focusing your attention on your breathing. Notice how cool the air feels as you inhale and how warm it feels as you breathe out. After a few moments, bring your attention to your feet and ankles. Continue to breathe in, imagining the breath flowing through your feet, making them feel totally relaxed. Gradually bring this peaceful awareness up into your legs, remaining conscious of your breath. Notice how your breath is very soothing and relaxing, and that you are beginning to feel very much at peace.
>
> Next, let your awareness move to your hips and your stomach. Your breath flows freely to that area. Consciously breathe in deeply and exhale slowly. Imagine that your breath is a beautiful golden (or white) light, constantly filling your body and bringing you into a deeper sense of peace. When your hips and stomach feel relaxed, move your attention next to your arms. Feel the light spreading through them, making them lighter and free from any strain.

Your breath (and the sense of peace and relaxation) moves across your shoulders and up into your neck. Breathe in and feel its gentleness release any tension you might have in that area. Slowly, it travels up your spine into your head. Your facial muscles become totally at peace and relaxed. You feel very calm, quiet, and free from stress.

Repeat *step one* (the relaxation technique) until you actually feel calmer and possess a greater sense of personal peace.

When you have become totally relaxed read *steps two through four once through in their entirety before continuing.* Then, and only after you understand what it is you are supposed to imagine, go on to *step two*, close your eyes, and attempt the reverie.

Step Two: *Imagine yourself in a place where you feel totally happy, relaxed, and at peace. It might be in your home, a favorite place in the mountains, at the ocean, or even in a different country. Perhaps it's a secluded spot with trees or shade or water or rolling hillsides. Perhaps there's a wonderfully cool breeze blowing, or maybe the sunlight is shining warmly on your face. Visualize yourself in that perfect place and when you're there, meet someone that you haven't seen in a very long time, someone who loves you dearly, someone who you trust. Keep your eyes closed until you see that person clearly. Enjoy your friend's presence for a few moments.*

Step Three: *Once you feel that individual's presence, in your mind ask this person something you have wanted to know, or see if this person might have insights into a problem or a question you have recently faced. Perhaps your friend has an object to give to you and you have something to offer in return. Relax, and enjoy this special time with this special person.* (You should allow yourself from five to fifteen minutes to thoroughly imagine this meeting.)

Step Four: Return your awareness to your body. Become conscious of your feet and your torso and your arms. Become conscious of the room around you and its furnishings. Become aware of your activities for the day. Become aware of being here in the moment but perhaps a little more peaceful than you were only a few minutes before.

Often, these types of experiences allow individuals the ability to get in touch with information that might otherwise be overlooked, forgotten, or beyond immediate conscious reach. The imaginative forces are extremely eager to share unconscious perceptions with the conscious mind. This process can access boundless creativity and limitless possibilities for problem solving. The imaginative forces contain a world of unexplored insight.

IMAGES OF BIRTH, DEATH, SEX, NIGHTMARES, AND OTHER SIGNIFICANT EVENTS

Some of the most frequently recalled images are those we consider nightmares, scenes that depict significant change in one's life, or dreams that explore the themes of birth, death, and sex. These images may remain in the conscious mind far longer than other less memorable symbols. Perhaps one way to approach each of these events is to consider the possibility that the subconscious mind may use these types of symbols in order to process information, attempt resolution, or bring a certain degree of awareness to one's conscious mind.

From this perspective then, there is really no such thing as a bad dream, because all dreams have the potential to be helpful to the dreamer. Nightmares, as well as significant recurring dreams, may simply be a response to information that has been neglected, overlooked, or intentionally ignored. For example, one woman had the frequently occurring dream that her home was being destroyed by earthquakes. She would awaken in terror, wondering if the dream was a warning that she and her family should move from the area. Later, when her husband surprised her with the request for a divorce, she realized that the dream was trying to get her to pay attention to the instability of their relationship—information that she already knew consciously but had chosen to ignore.

Frequently, nightmares are in response to what one has eaten (or even done, or thought) prior to the dreaming episode. In this respect, then, these horrible images are simply an indication that one's physical systems are turbulent. When an individual eats something that he is allergic to or something that is difficult to assimilate (such as a big, thick pizza just before bedtime), his dream life will often portray the conflict that is occurring within his body. Nightmares may also reveal situations or information that has been overlooked or even ignored consciously. For example, one man had a nightmare in which he was being chased through a building and shot at by little dark men with guns who were systematically trying to kill him. Consciously, he had been trying to quit smoking for years but without success. When he awoke from the nightmare, he thought that the building symbolized his own physical body, and that the dark men represented renegade cancer cells. The dream gave him the final encouragement he needed to give up cigarettes.

Images of disastrous events may be anything from a release of the pent-up emotions of a person's life to precognitive insights into the future. When these scenes occur, the imaginer should first ask, *"What is the theme of this event, and how does it apply to my present life experience?"* Often, other images or symbol fragments may contain similar information to guide the individual, as well. Generally, dreams of disaster indicate the disastrous consequences that may occur if the dreamer doesn't change her attitudes, belief systems, relationships, or even diet. Only after the imaginer has attempted to correlate the image with waking, conscious life should she even ask the question, *"What if this is precognitive?"* On the possibility that the dream is a valid insight into the future, we can only be expected to follow through on that which is practical, realistic, and feasible. Even unpleasant dreams can become invaluable tools of personal guidance if an individual attempts to work with them.

Symbols of birth and death are often symbolic. For example, the image of being pregnant often suggests the birth of a new idea or a new beginning. Dreams of death could represent the end of a situation or an experience, a change from doing things a certain way, or the death of a part of one's personality. If an individual dreams that he (or even another person) is being murdered, the first question should be: *"Is there anything in my life that is stifling or killing a part of myself?"*

Sexual symbolism is also very common in imagery. As one of the primary drives of the human species, sexual images are portrayed both literally and figuratively. The female sexuality of the womb can be represented by such symbols as a cave, a box, or even a pocket. Male sexuality corresponding to the phallus can be depicted by an image such as a banana, a snake, or even a hammer. All thoughts, feelings, and desires that the conscious mind dwells upon must be processed, even if only subconsciously. Therefore, the more often an individual consciously daydreams, fantasizes, or even suppresses sexual imagery, the more frequently these same images find their way into the world of dreams.

Just like nightmares, sex dreams can be utilized as a means of blatantly bringing information to the conscious awareness of the dreamer. For example, one gentleman dreamed that he was in bed with his wife on the second floor of their home. In the midst of lovemaking, he suddenly remembered that there was something he had to do on the first floor. Leaving his wife alone, he went down the stairs. Once there, he decided the task was not all that important after all. Unfortunately, however, he could not find the staircase back to the second floor, even though he felt very much like having sex. He awoke, feeling a great deal of frustration. Upon questioning, the dreamer and his wife both stated that impotence or any other sexual problem was not an issue. Therefore, the symbolism was simply trying to point out that the dreamer had the frequent habit of starting projects that he never finished—a trait that created immense frustration for his wife, even though she had never confronted him with it.

Many individuals have found that nothing of major importance ever happens in their lives without it first being *foreshadowed* in a dream. Therefore, this is perhaps the most important insight offered through significant dreams. Part of the reasoning behind this fact is that our conscious and subconscious minds are constantly gathering information, insight, and subtleties. In an attempt to give meaning to this random collection of data, this material is somehow assembled into various potential realities. People know far more about themselves, their lives, their relationships, their jobs, and even their futures than their conscious minds can possibly fathom.

IMAGES AS METAPHOR

Fairy tales, legends, and stories have somehow captured human interest throughout history. Oral traditions, centuries of theater, countless literary volumes, and modern-day movies literally take us away from the real world into a realm inspired by the imagination. Sometimes these stories have managed to encapsulate universal truths, or archetypes, and have become *mythic* in proportion.

A myth is a story, a symbol, or an archetype that has a symbolic meaning greater and richer than its literal or historic truth. These myths often serve as patterns of human experience. The story of Job in the Old Testament is a good example.

Whether or not Job was a historic figure is not important from the perspective of symbolism. What is important is that individuals across time and in many cultures have had similar experiences of frustration, defeat, and failure yet, in spite of everything, they, like Job, have found the determination, faith, and courage to move forward. Job's story somehow describes this particular human condition, becoming an archetype of faith and perseverance in the face of adversity. A twist on this very same theme is personified in Scarlett O'Hara of *Gone with the Wind.*

In the same way that individuals are fascinated by the transformation of the caterpillar into the butterfly, the process of human metamorphosis is also a popular archetypal theme. It is a story depicted in such tales as *Pygmalion (My Fair Lady), Cinderella, Aladdin, Great Expectations,* and even the Old Testament account of Joseph and his rise in authority to become second only to the pharaoh. This ideal of coming into one's own in spite of one's birth, the environment, or those who would stand in the way is a goal for every individual, even if only subconsciously. These universal goals are often depicted in the most popular works of legend and literature.

The gods and goddesses of ancient civilizations also describe patterns of human experience. It doesn't matter whether they were inspired by historic personages; what matters is that these images serve as important psychological metaphors. The attainment of physical beauty is an example of an enduring human desire. To the Romans, the goddess Venus and the god Apollo best described these perfect images. In present times, people often think of movie stars and other glamorous prominent figures as embodiments of the male or female ideal. Regardless of their present-day names, however, fans of these stars are simply admiring the archetypal Venus or Apollo. Famous people become metaphors for the images associated with them. If such people act outside of the parameters created for them or the archetype the public assigns to them, it can be truly disturbing to the human psyche.

Stories frequently repeat archetypal patterns that are important to the human experience. Dorothy in *The Wizard of Oz,* Christian in *Pilgrim's Progress,* Bilbo in *The Hobbit,* Pinocchio in the *Adventures of Pinocchio,* and the eldest son in *The Parable of The Prodigal Son* all describe an individual's personal experiences that eventually lead to self-realization and fulfillment. Therefore, in one .respect, each character represents an archetype of one's search for meaning. The archetype of human perfection is embodied in such figures as Clark Kent of *Superman,* Valentine Michael Smith of *Stranger in a Strange Land,* Jesus of Nazareth, and Joan of Arc. The archetype of betrayal is embodied in Lancelot of *Camelot,* Brutus of Rome, and Judas Iscariot. One can see the tragedy of "forbidden love" played out in such works as *Romeo and Juliet, The Front Runner, West Side Story, Lady, Howard's End,* and *The Thorn Birds.* The number of archetypes is limited only by the varieties of human experience and history.

When symbols and images and tales and legends act as true metaphors for patterns of behavior, emotion, and desire, their impact upon the public and personal consciousness is immeasurable. The closer a story, a character, or a situation can come to describing a valid universal archetype of human experience, the more it captures human imagination for all time and in every circumstance.

CHILDREN AND DREAMS

Children's dreams correlate to the activities of their day as well as to their developing mental abilities. Since one purpose of dreams is to make individuals more consciously aware of what they are experiencing in life based upon the thoughts, feelings, and actions portrayed in the image, children's dreams can show you the motivating influences in their lives. In addition, they can help you gain a clearer sense of your child's needs, allowing you to correlate this information with what you already know at a conscious level. As an adult, you can help your child explore her own dreams in a number of easy ways.

Encourage your child to talk about dreams over the breakfast table. Don't be too quick to dismiss dreams or brush them aside, or you may miss important insights into your child's current experiences and thought processes. When listening to a child's dream, ask yourself, "If I were to have that dream, how would it make me feel or what would I think about it?" Ask your child what he thought about the dream. Ask about the different characters. Do the characters remind your child of anyone in waking life? Did he enjoy the dream, or did he wish that something else would have happened?

Perhaps the best way of working with a child's dreams is to have her draw a picture of the dream and explain what it means. Even if you don't know how to interpret the imagining itself, you can often catch a glimpse into your child's world simply by getting a sense of your own feelings about what she has drawn. A child will often express her world through a creative endeavor. Look at the colors used and the emotions expressed. Is this a house you yourself would feel comfortable in? Is it a happy place? Is there joy in the drawing? On the other hand, is the scenery ominous and foreboding? Are the characters sad, joyful, or scary? Are the colors those of happiness, fear, or worry?

For example, black is often associated with depression or fear (darkness). Red can contain energy or anger. Yellow implies warmth or intellect (the sun). Blue is hope or joy (the sky is the limit). Green is growth and healing (the grass). Pink is warmth and compassion. When you can associate the colors in a drawing with where those same colors may be found in everyday life (especially the everyday life of your child) you will have added insight into your child's world, assisting you in furthering his welfare.

The normalcy of having dreams should also be discussed. You might have your child watch the sleeping family pet to see if the dog moves its legs or barks while asleep. Let your child know that everyone dreams, and that working with dreams can be fun and a great adventure. This can be done with stories or through movies with which the child may already be familiar. For example, Dorothy awakens at the end of the *Wizard of Oz* to discover that everything she has just been through was a dream. Luke Skywalker in *The Empire Strikes Back* has a waking dream in which he must fight Darth Vader. *Sleeping Beauty, Snow White,* and *Rip Van Winkle* all fall asleep as part of the story. The obvious question is, "Did they dream?"

As your child tells his dreams, you may begin to sense that sometimes the stories being related are not dreams at all but are instead the product of an active imagination. This does not matter. The worth of dreams—whether from your child's waking or sleeping mind—is the same.

Children's Nightmares

Children's dreams often explore their own fears (for example, the fear of being left alone, the fear of the dark, the fear of monsters, the fear of being lost). Working with your child's nightmares can assist her in resolving her fears and provide you with insights into the situation that may be troubling your child. One of the best ways to examine nightmares with a child is through the imagination, using creative expression. Make this explorative experience fun.

In addition to discussing the dream, provide your child with paper and crayons or finger paints. The more actively he can participate in expressing the nightmare, the better he will feel about its resolution. After hearing your child tell about the bad dream, you may wish to suggest exercises such as these:

1. Provide a practical possibility to help your child face the nightmare. For example, if the dream was one of being afraid in the dark, have her paint a huge sun or a bright night light.
2. Ask your child why he was afraid, and then suggest drawing a person (a parent, a teacher, a friend, or a superhero) who can help him overcome or get through that fear.
3. If a monster was after your child, suggest that she draw herself bigger than the monster and then turn to chase the monster.
4. Have your child draw both what he did in the dream as well as what he would like to have done. Stress that your child can do anything he wants.
5. Ask your child if there is something in waking life that makes her just as afraid. Ask her to draw it.

Although it is certainly reasonable to stress that dreams cannot hurt your child, you do not want to end this process of resolution too quickly. The purpose of exercises like these is to help your child see that he can be apart from the dream—an objective observer—while resolving the fear generated by it. After he has finished, ask him to say what he will do the next time he has a scary dream. The answer may indicate how well your child now feels. For example, "I will kill the monster" shows much better resolution than "I don't know."

IMAGES AS PROBLEM SOLVERS

The imagination, daydreaming, and dreams themselves often explore the challenges we are faced with consciously, even though the images may appear to have no direct connection with daily life. Unfortunately, when we ignore these images as simply the ramblings of the subconscious mind, we lose the insights and creativity that might otherwise be made available to us. .

Perhaps one of the most famous examples of the creative use of dream images has to do with the inventor of the sewing machine, Elias Howe. He was trying to create a machine that would automatically do what until that time could only be done manually with a needle and thread. In spite of numerous attempts, he was unsuccessful. One night, still struggling with his conscious problem, the inventor had a dream. In the dream he had been captured by enemies holding lances. He noticed that one of the lances had a hole near the end of the point. There was not much to the dream, but even this prompted his own creative expression.

When he awoke, the solution came to him. He had the brilliant idea of placing the thread hole near the point instead of at the head of the needle. It was not that the dream gave Elias Howe a definitive answer to the question he had been seeking, but his creative use of the imagining provided by his own subconscious led the inventor to the solution. It was not that the dream needed to be interpreted, but that the images provided Howe with insights he could apply on the conscious level.

IMAGES AS SUBCONSCIOUS INSIGHT

One young woman was finding herself more and more dissatisfied with all areas of her life. She no longer liked her job. She didn't really want to go back to school. She had no real direction she wished to pursue. She had no enthusiasm to do much of anything. All she knew was that she was becoming more and more unhappy with her life and she really didn't know why.

In response to her apathy, confusion, and sadness, her subconscious mind provided a dream. In the dream, a childhood friend showed the young woman a container of goldfish that had long been neglected. The friend had tried to take care of this young woman's fish, but they still appeared unhealthy and neglected. The young woman awoke, feeling very badly about having ignored her responsibility toward her fish and wanted to resolve the situation immediately.

Upon questioning, the young woman stated that this particular childhood friend had been more involved in spirituality and religion than any of her other friends. Since fish frequently serve as metaphors for *faith and spirituality*, one meaning of the young woman's dream become quite obvious: much of her dissatisfaction was due to the fact that her life lacked spiritual direction. The dream portrayed the fact that she had long overlooked her spiritual needs. Therefore, by beginning to discover her personal philosophical beliefs, she could begin to address this area of her life that had been neglected. Perhaps, in the process, she might even find a renewed sense of satisfaction for her life as a whole.

PRECOGNITIVE IMAGES AS PROBLEM SOLVERS

In another instance of subconscious problem solving, a man was becoming very disillusioned with his job. Long involved in accounting, he wanted a change of pace. Although employed in his present occupation for only a year, he felt he had learned all he could in the financial offices of his medium–sized company. He truly liked the company and the work with which they were involved, but in his dissatisfaction and frustration, his paperwork was being neglected. He desperately wanted to be doing something else. Almost in response, one night he had a dream.

He found himself as a waiter in a restaurant where he had worked long ago as a student. In the dream he was very conscious of the fact that his particular side station (an area filled with plates, cups, saucers, and utensils for setting the tables) needed to be thoroughly cleaned and restocked. He worked at the task with enthusiasm and vigor because he knew that he would be getting a new job in six weeks' time. He awoke on a Monday morning with the dream vividly imprinted upon his mind.

He decided that the dream was suggesting he get his current work in order *and caught up* because his job would be changing soon. With eagerness, he began to bring his paperwork and files up to date. It was surprising to him that his work, which had been so dissatisfying before, now could be accomplished with such enthusiasm. He also resolved to update a listing of job procedures and functions for his current position in response to the dream images.

A few weeks passed. He continued to work, possessing a new sense of optimism. Finally, three weeks after the dream, a long-term employee in the education offices of his company gave notice. The job was posted, and the dreamer applied. Even though his background was completely different from the job posting, he felt the change was something he would really enjoy, and he would be successful. The company management agreed, and the dreamer started his new position in education exactly six weeks after he had his dream. It was not that the dream gave him a new job, but the images renewed him with a sense of purpose in the present and gave him hopefulness for the future.

Perhaps, just as importantly, the dreamer was inspired to follow through on guidance he had received from his own subconscious mind—guidance that made him all the more prepared for the events in his life that would follow.

1. The first letter of the alphabet. 2. The best; first-rate. 3. Associated with schooling: ABCs. 4. May represent the ace in cards. 5. Associated with anno (year) from A.D. (anno Domini, year of our Lord). 6. In logic, an abbreviation for affirmative. 7. Chemically, the symbol for argon. 8. Musically, the sixth note. 9. In literature, associated with adultery: The Scarlet Letter. *10. Metaphysically, the beginning. 11. Numerologically, equivalent to one. 12. Scholastically, outstanding achievement. 13. In Greek, alpha.*

ABACUS 1. Symbolic of calculating the worth of an idea, an activity, a relationship, or one's own self. 2. Can represent an old debt that is owed or due. 3. May indicate the need to take into account or to take stock of the situation or the activity. 4. Could be symbolic of karmic memory. See **Karma**. 5. You may also wish to see **Mathematics**.

ABANDONED 1. That which is neglected, forsaken, renounced, or relinquished. 2. Can be associated with the act of letting go. 3. To surrender to one's feelings or impulses. 4. Corresponds to being rejected by the situation, one's environment, or one's associates. 5. Represents that which is discarded or disinherited. 6. You may also wish to see **Emotion**.

ABBEY 1. A spiritual haven, resting place, or place of safety. 2. That which is free from the outside material world. 3. A place of worship. See **Church**. 4. A spiritual community. 5. May be associated with religious vows: chastity, poverty, obedience, and service. 6. You may also wish to see **Nun**.

ABDUCTED 1. That which is taken unlawfully. See **Thief**. 2. Being moved from one's position by force. 3. Can correspond to that which is under complete control by another.

ABEL 1. Liturgically, corresponds to the offering of oneself. See **Sacrifice**. 2. Rabbinically, associated with nature and God's Creation. 3. Metaphysically, symbolic of right breath and right mind. 4. That which is martyred or killed. See **Kill**.

ABORTION 1. Associated with that which is intentionally neglected, cut short, or abandoned (i.e., an idea, a project, a belief system, etc.). 2. Corresponds to anything that does not reach maturity, or that which is lost in the process of development. 3. May represent one's fears of pregnancy. 4. Could be associated with a literal abortion or a warning of a potential miscarriage. 5. You may also wish to see **Kill** or **Death**. 6. Might correspond to killing one's inner child. 7. You may also wish to see **Birth**.

ABRAHAM 1. Corresponds to the first biblical patriarch and ancestor of the Hebrews. See **Judaism** and **Father**. 2. Associated with being the father of all seekers. 3. The source from whom Judaism, Christianity, and Islam trace their roots. See **Islam** and **Christianity**. 4. Metaphysically, associated with the foundation of faith. 5. May represent one who gives a sacrifice. See **Sacrifice**.

ABYSS 1. May be associated with a trap or a warning. 2. Could indicate a pitfall (i.e., a danger). 3. Suggestive of troubling circumstances that must be gone around or over. 4. Might represent female sexuality. See **Womb**. 5. The feeling of being surrounded or hemmed in. See **Box**. 6. You may also wish to see **Prison, Earth,** and **Mountain**.

ACADEMY AWARD 1. Associated with a reward, an honor, or an accomplishment. 2. Can correspond to being recognized by one's peers. 3. Might be in response to acting the part in a particular situation. See **Acting**. 4. An outstanding performance. 5. You may also wish to see **Movie Star**.

ACCIDENT 1. Corresponds to a disaster, a problem, a bad situation, or a horrible experience. 2. The type of accident has a great deal to do with the symbolism; for example: a car wreck is often associated with a warning about one's body, diet, stress level, or situation (see **Automobile);** a plane wreck might indicate a spiritual problem (see **Airplane);** a shipwreck could indicate a problem with one's current life journey (see **Boat** and **Journey)**. 3. May be a literal warning suggesting alternate plans, doing what one can do to prevent the incident, etc. 4. Metaphorically, she's an accident waiting to happen = she's in very bad shape, physically, mentally, emotionally, or spiritually.

ACORN 1. Can be symbolic of small things that lead to great and powerful outcomes. 2. Associated with something that is hard and impenetrable, or that which surrounds the inner self. 3. An untapped potential just waiting to spring forth. See **Seed**. 4. You may also wish to see **Tree** and **Plant**.

ACROBAT 1. Associated with agility and strength. 2. Can correspond to a wonderful performance or a crazy stunt. 3. One who may accomplish the difficult, the daring, or the seemingly impossible. 4. You may also

wish to see **People** and **Circus**.

ACTING/ACTOR/ACTRESS 1. That personality we present to the world. See **Performance/Performers**. 2. Associated with the role we play in life. See **Drama**. 3. May indicate insincerity on the part of another. 4. May be symbolic of taking on (or the need to take on) the duties of someone else and acting the part. See **People**. 5. The male or female aspects of one's self. See **Phallus** or **Womb**. 6. Associated with one's performance. 7. You may also wish to see **Movie Star**.

ADAM 1. Liturgically, relates to temptation and the Fall. 2. Can represent paradise. 3. The first or the beginning. 4. Metaphysically, associated with spiritual consciousness made flesh; a descent in consciousness. 5. Biblically, associated with Jesus (I Corinthians 15:22).

ADRENALS 1. Glands in the body. 2. Associated with the third endocrine center or chakra. See **Chakras.** 3. Relates to the instinct to either fight or flee. 4. Metaphysically, corresponds to Mars; symbolized by the image of a lion. 5. May be symbolic of anger. 6. In Revelation, it is represented by the Church of Pergamos.

AFFAIR 1. A secret union or partnership. 2. May be associated with a desirable new venture or business. 3. Can correspond to an unexpected alliance. 4. You may also wish to see **Marriage**. 5. That which is clandestine, forbidden, or intriguing.

AFGHAN 1. That which corresponds to personal security or warmth. See **Blanket**. 2. Associated with that which covers the situation.

AFRICA 1. As the central landmass of the earth, it represents the continent of the body. 2. Can symbolize the primitive, the mysterious, or the unknown. See **Unconscious**. 3. Can be representative of the deeper reaches of knowledge or the soul. 4. Associated with slavery or the relinquishment of personal will. See **Slave**. 5. The second largest continent. 6. May be associated with foreign travel.

AGE 1. Associated with the personal awareness and experience of the passage of time. See **Time**. 2. The age of the person or the symbol in the dream may be representative of an activity, a person, or an idea of about the same age that is known to the conscious mind. 3. Can correspond to a cycle or a phase. 4. You may also wish to see **Old Man/Old Woman, Young/Youth, Child,** or **People**.

AIDS 1. That which destroys or wars with itself. 2. Metaphor for something that is eaten away or being destroyed from within (i.e., that which is eating you). 3. Can correspond to negative thoughts and emotions. 4. Can be a literal warning of illness. 5. You may also wish to see **Ill/Illness** and **Body**.

AIR 1. The breath of life. 2. Can correspond to the realm of spirit or that which is unconscious. 3. The activity of the air may be symbolic of one's state of mind. See **Weather**. 4. Can symbolize breath and therefore speech. 5. The sky is the limit. See **Sky**. 6. Might indicate an incoming message. See **Message/Messenger**. 7. One of the four elements (air, earth, fire, and water). See **Elements**. 8. Can correspond with the astrological air signs (**Aquarius, Libra,** and **Gemini**). See individual signs for traits.

AIR-CONDITIONING 1. Associated with one's breath, lungs, or air capacity. See **Automobile** or **House**. 2. Might be associated with emotional feelings. 3. Could indicate the temperature of the situation.

AIR FORCE 1. May be associated with a lofty ideal or principle. See **Airplane**. 2. Might represent service of the highest kind. 3. Can correspond to order, power, discipline, or the relinquishment of personal will. 4. Associated with placing oneself subservient to a greater goal or good. 5. Can represent a warlike environment or situation. See **War.**

AIRPLANE 1. A lofty idea or project. 2. Can correspond to a message from another realm or another level of the mind. See **Message/Messenger**. 3. May literally represent a trip. 4. One's own thoughts/feelings regarding airplanes will be very significant; for example: could represent unresolved fear if one has a fear of flying; may suggest the need for a vacation or an important business trip. 5. *A landing airplane* is associated with an incoming idea, an experience, a relationship (or visitor), or the grounding of oneself. See **Landing**. 6. *An airplane that cannot fly* can correspond to plans that never got off the ground or plans that may be faulty. See **Parked**. 7. *An airplane taking off* may represent an idea or plan whose time has come, or it might represent the end or departure of a relationship. See **Takeoff**. 8. Could be symbolic of the material world trying to dominate the spiritual. 9. Might represent one's physical body or exterior self. See **Automobile**. 10. Depending on imagery, you may also wish to see **Sky**.

AIRPORT 1. A place of high ideals or incoming messages. See **Airplane**. 2. A transformational journey that may be taken with others (physically, mentally, or spiritually). 3. See also **Building**.

AKASHIC RECORDS 1. The complete record of the soul journey. See **Journey**. 2. Associated with one's life experiences, memories, thoughts, and activities. 3. Often symbolized by a library (see **Library**), books (see **Book**), a museum (see **Museum**), or interactions with a wise old figure (see **Old Man/Old Woman**). 4. You may also wish to see **Reincarnation**.

ALADDIN 1. Could be associated with magic and genies. See **Genie**. 2. May represent the process of self–realization through one's life journey. See **Journey**. 3. Might be associated with Arabia and the desert. See **Desert**. 4. Could indicate a dry spell prior to personal fulfillment.

ALARM CLOCK 1. May indicate the need to wake up and pay attention to surroundings, or could be a message of danger. 2. That which is alarming or surprising. See **Clock**. 3. Could indicate the appropriate timing. See **Time**.

ALCOHOL 1. May represent the inclination to escape or to lose control. 2. Could literally refer to too much drinking. See **Drunk**. 3. Can be associated with fire water. See **Water**. 4. Symbolic of that which is intoxicating or tempting. 5. May be a symbol of the spirit (spirits) and the need to quench one's spiritual thirst. 6. Might be a literal message regarding what one is ingesting (i.e., too much alcohol, or overindulgence of starches and sweets). See **Food**. 7. You may also wish to see **Bar**.

ALIEN 1. Corresponds to that which is out of place, or from another environment. 2. May be associated with a foreign or an unknown part of one's self. See **Shadow**. 3. Could indicate an unusual or alien idea. 4. Acting in a way or manner that is out of

keeping with one's normal behavior. 5. Might be a literal indication of a foreign visitor or travel to a foreign locale. 6. Associated with someone or something that is not understood. 7. Depending upon the symbology, could correspond with facing one's fears. 8. That which is unfamiliar. 9. See also **People**.

ALLERGY 1. That which causes irritation. 2. Can correspond to being overly sensitive. 3. You may also wish to see **Ill/Illness**.

ALLEY 1. A narrow pathway or road. See **Road**. 2. May indicate a closed–in portion of one's journey. See **Journey** and **Wall**. 3. Metaphorically, that's right up your alley = that's in your area of interest or expertise.

ALLIGATOR 1. Can indicate something with a tough exterior. 2. Often symbolic of harsh or dangerous words one has spoken. 3. Can be associated with fears or the unknown realms of the subconscious. 4. May be symbolic of a spiritual truth that has been misused. 5. You may also wish to see **Fish** and **Animals**.

ALTAR 1. The offering of self; selflessness. 2. Corresponds to ritual and faith. 3. Biblically, associated with sacrifice and thanksgiving. 4. Metaphysically, that place where the lower self becomes subservient to the higher self. 5. Can represent purification. 6. Associated with what we worship in life (i.e., God, money, desires, etc.). 7. Liturgically, represents the sacrificial nature of Jesus' life and ministry. See **Christ**. 8. See also **Church** or **Temple**.

AMBULANCE 1. Symbolic of an emergency situation. See **Emergency**. 2. Corresponds to the fact that help may be on its way. 3. Represents the need for fast and immediate action. 4. See also **Automobile**.

AMULET 1. Can correspond to good luck. 2. May indicate that which is charmed. 3. That which can protect you from harm. 4. You may also wish to see **Magic/Magician**.

ANCHOR 1. Stable or well-balanced. 2. Tied down by the situation. 3. Refusing to move beyond the current level of understanding. However, taking up anchor represents the willingness to learn or to change. 4. The desire to or fear of having to settle down. 5. May be associated with marriage or childbearing. 6. Corresponds to the power of determination and inner resolve. 7. You may also wish to see **Boat**.

ANCIENT 1. Associated with wisdom, age, or mysticism. 2. Could correspond to instinct or karmic memory. See **Karma**. 3. That which has been in use or has been available for a long time. 4. An old figure in a dream is generally a symbol of wisdom or guidance. See **Old Man/Old Woman**. 5. You may also wish to see **Antique**. 6. Depending on imagery, you may also wish to see **Historical Clothing/Settings**.

ANGEL 1. Representative of spirituality. 2. A messenger of spirit. See **Message/Messenger**. 3. Can correspond to truth, wisdom, or guidance. 4. Sometimes is symbolic of a coming birth or death in relation to an individual or a situation/opportunity. 5. Might be associated with one's higher self. 6. Metaphorically, she's an angel = she's a wonderful person. 7. You may also wish to see **People**.

ANIMALS 1. Represents emotions, instinct, or types of experiences. 2. Generally, whatever the individual thinks of or associates with that particular animal has a great deal to do with the symbolic meaning. 3. See specific type of animal for additional information; for example, see **Horse**. 4. You may also wish to see **Pet**. 5. May correspond to various levels of the mind. 6. The appearance of the animal, its skin or hide, color, and its disposition all represent different aspects of the situation, environment, or oneself; for example: a tame animal could represent those aspects of oneself that have been brought under control; a wild animal may symbolize those emotions one has yet to face or resolve. 7. Different animals symbolize different energies or emotions, and one's own animal nature; for example:

Alligator/Crocodile: That with a tough exterior, or harsh or dangerous words one has spoken.

Badger: To irritate or to badger. Could be associated with hostility and aggression.

Bat: Associated with something that is a little batty. Might indicate that which feeds off others.

Bear: May represent that which is grumpy or overprotective. Can indicate a bear market or a burden.

Beast: Can correspond to animal instincts, or one's shadow. See **Shadow**.

Bird: A bearer of a message.

Bobcat: May be associated with a wild or an aggressive situation.

Buffalo: Can represent intimidation.

Bugs: Irritants or pests.

Bull: May represent stubbornness or nonsense. Can indicate a bull market or a success.

Camel: Having someone (or something) on one's back. Could symbolize a dry spell.

Cat: May be associated with independence. Might suggest that which is catty or malicious. See also **Pet**.

Chameleon: Associated with change, flexibility, betrayal, or inconsistency.

Chicken: Can be associated with one who is afraid.

Clam: May represent being withdrawn, or closed to emotions.

Cow/Cattle: May symbolize one's feminine nature, or a herd of people.

Crab: Associated with negativity or a bad temper.

Deer: Independence and the wild; could represent money (i.e., a buck or doe/dough).

Dinosaur: That which is extinct or outdated.

Dog: Associated with loyalty. Might indicate that which is deteriorating (i.e., going to the dogs). See also **Pet**.

Donkey/Jackass: That which is stubborn. Can symbolize one who is an ass.

Dragon: The mysterious or the magical. Could symbolize temptation or fear.

Duck: Being a sitting duck. Might correspond to avoiding an issue or a person.

Eagle: Associated with vision and clarity. That which soars.

Elephant: Symbolic of memory. Might refer to someone who is nosy.

Fish: Often represents spirituality. Could suggest something that is fishy.

Fox: Can be associated with being sexy or cunning.

Frog: That which is enchanted, unclean, or unconscious. Might indicate having a hard time speaking up.

Giraffe: Could be associated with the throat or the neck. One whose intellect is separated from his emotions.

Goat: May represent stubbornness, an old goat, or a scapegoat.

Horse: Can be associated with a message, one's sexuality, being overbearing, or not being serious enough.

Kangaroo: That which travels by leaps and bounds. Might be associated with a false proceeding.

Lamb/Sheep: Symbolic of innocence, purity, spirituality.

Lion: Often associated with aggression, dominance, danger, or courage.

Mole: One who digs up dirt. May indicate one who hides from emotions or the environment.

Monkey/Gorilla: That which is playful, foolish, or irrational.

Mouse: Can represent timidity, or that which is underfoot.

Ox: Symbolic of hard work and strength.

Pig/Hog: May represent being greedy, filthy, stubborn, gluttonous, or immoral.

Platypus: That which is silly and ridiculous.

Rabbit: Often corresponds to sexuality. May indicate an attentive listener.

Raccoon: Could be symbolic of a hidden thief.

Ram: Associated with power, leadership, sexuality, and drive. That which is forced.

Rat: Symbolic of one who is not nice. May be associated with filth and disease.

Rooster/Cock: Represents a wake up call. May symbolize one's male nature.

Skunk: Often symbolic of a stinky or an unpleasant situation.

Snake: May represent wisdom, energy, temptation, or power.

Squirrel: Could symbolize that which is speedy and agile, or that which is wimpy.

Tiger: Associated with aggression and ferocity.

Turkey: Represents something not very positive or desirable. Could be symbolic of Thanksgiving.

Turtle: Associated with longevity. May indicate that which withdraws into itself.

Unicorn: Symbolic of purity, virginity, and the mysterious.

Whale: An enormous story, endeavor, or undertaking. See also **Fish**.

Zebra: Could be symbolic of that which is imprisoned by its environment.

8. Groups of animals may be symbolic of those groups in which we presently find ourselves (i.e., a school of fish could represent one's spiritual community, church, or school; see **Fish**). 9. Birds are often symbolic of messengers. See **Bird**. 10. You may also wish to see **People**. 11. See **Clothes** and **Colors** if you need to interpret the animal's appearance. 12. Metaphorically, having animal magnetism = possessing a strong, hypnotic quality over others.

ANKH 1. The symbol of life. 2. Represents religion or spirituality. 3. Corresponds to Egypt or ancient wisdom. See **Egypt/Egyptian**. 4. Sometimes associated with Christ. See **Christ**. 5 . You may also wish to see **Cross**.

ANT 1. Corresponds to that which is continuously productive or working. See **Bug**. 2. Can represent that which is little or insignificant, or the seemingly trivial that may disrupt one's plans (i.e., ants may ruin a picnic). 3. Symbolic of those who persevere for the good of the group or the community. 4. May indicate the need to stop being a workaholic.

ANTARCTICA 1. That which is cold, unchanging, and isolated. See **Cold**. 2. May indicate unchanging emotions or a cold heart. 3. Associated with the seventh continent. 4. May be associated with travel or a move to a very cold and unfriendly locale. 5. You may also wish to see **Snow**.

ANTICIPATION 1. May correspond to something advantageous or wonderful in the offing. 2. That which is foreseen. 3. Can be associated with something that causes eager anxiousness. 4. Might be symbolic of precognition. 5. You may also wish to see **Emotion** or **Wait**.

ANTIQUE 1. May be symbolic of that which is valuable and lasting, or that which is obsolete and outdated. 2. Could correspond to ancient wisdom. See **Book** and **Library**. 3. Might indicate karmic memory or unresolved issues from the past. See **Karma**. 4. Whatever is antiquated in the dream will have a great deal to do with the symbolism; for example: an antique bed could be associated with an old-fashioned approach to sex. 5. Can relate to inner urges or instincts. 6. Might represent one's upbringing, opinions, or biases. 7. You may also wish to see **Old** and **Museum**.

ANXIETY 1. May represent another situation with which one is concerned. 2. Associated with restlessness and worry. 3. Might be associated with eager anticipation. 4. You may also wish to see **Emotion**.

APARTMENT 1. One's place of residence. See **House**. 2. Often associated with the physical body, one's personality, or one's current situation or experience. 3. Different portions of the apartment portray different aspects of oneself (see **House** for listing). 4. Depending on one's literal housing situation, might indicate a temporary lodging or condition. 5. You may also wish to see **Building**.

APPLAUSE 1. Corresponds to receiving recognition, a reward, or appreciation. 2. To praise or to encourage. 3. You may also wish to see **Hand** and **Performance/Performers**.

APPLE 1. Associated with health and long life (i.e., an apple a day keeps the doctor away). 2. Biblically, corresponds to temptation; the forbidden fruit. 3. Relates to that which is worthy of consumption or use. 4. Liturgically, represents the Fall of man. See **Adam**. 5. Metaphorically, the apple of one's eye = one's greatest treasure. 6. Can be a literal indication to watch one's diet or to eat apples. See **Fruit** and **Food**. 7. Might be associated with intrigue, magic, or that which is mysterious.

APRON 1. That which one uses to cook. See **Cook**. 2. May indicate that which keeps one clean from a messy situation. See **Clothes**. 3. Corresponds to being shielded or protected. 4. Depending upon one's personal imagery, may be symbolic of one's mother, grandmother, or childhood.

AQUARIUS ♒ 1. Eleventh sign of the zodiac, corresponding to January 20–February 18. 2. Associated with the following positive traits: idealistic, progressive, humanitarian. 3. Associated with the following negative traits: unpredictable, opinionated, eccentric. 4. Astrologically, ruled by Saturn and Uranus. See **Saturn** and **Uranus**. 5. See also **Man (Pouring Water)**. 6. Associated with the New Age, enlightenment, and humanitarianism. 7. An air sign. See **Air**. 8. See also **Astrology**.

ARCH 1. That which spans, brings together, or supports. See **Bridge**. 2. That which sits atop a doorway (i.e., a new direction or an opportunity). See **Door**. 3. Metaphorically, an archvillain = a cunning enemy. 4. In contemporary use, golden arches may be symbolic of dietary eating habits (i.e., McDonald's). 5. Biblically, associated with the rainbow. See **Rainbow**.

ARCHAEOLOGY 1. Can correspond with the need to dig within one's own self for the answers. 2. May be symbolic of the subconscious mind. 3. Can represent that which is ancient or old. See **Antique**. 4. Could indicate ancient wisdom. 5. Might be associated with Karmic memory. See **Karma**.

ARCHETYPE 1. Associated with a pattern or symbol of human experience that is significant across time and cultures. 2. Psychologically, identified as the collective unconscious: a ready–made system of images, emotions, fears, instincts, and beliefs attached to the human psyche from birth and influencing an individual's perception. 3. Metaphysically, the third–dimensional manifestation of that which was formerly in the realm of thoughts and ideas. 4. The most significant kind of symbol. 5. You may also wish to see **Symbol/Symbolism** and **Metaphor**.

ARCHITECT 1. Associated with one who designs, builds, or oversees the construction of new ideas or plans. 2. May represent the creative part of oneself. See **People**.

ARGUMENT 1. A conflict between others or portions of oneself. See **Shadow**. 2. An environment of hostility, aggression, and oppression. 3. Can correspond to an internal struggle. 4. Often associated with retaliation for previous thoughts, words, or actions. 5. May indicate the need to consciously deal with problems that are struggling at the unconscious level. 6. Arguing in a particular location or room could correspond to a conflict in those areas of one's life; for example: a bedroom argument could indicate a sexual conflict or problem; arguing in the kitchen may symbolize a problem with one's diet, etc. 7. Could be associated with the need to fight for what's right. 8. Depending on imagery, you may also wish to see **People** and **War**.

ARIES ♈ 1. First sign of the zodiac, corresponding to March 21–April 19. 2. Associated with the following positive traits: courageous and energetic, direct in approach, and freedom-loving. 3. Associated with the following negative traits: selfish, quick-tempered, and impatient. 4. Astrologically, ruled by Mars. See **Mars**. 5. See also **Ram**. 6. A fire sign. See **Fire**. 7. See also **Astrology**.

ARK 1. Corresponds to the Great Flood. See **Flood**. 2. Symbol of protection. 3. Metaphysically, represents personal transformation. 4. Associated with being overwhelmed by transformation and change. 5. Liturgically, associated with the church and salvation. 6. The spiritual part of oneself. 7. Psychologically, may represent portions of one's inner being. See **House**. 8. Symbolic of personal rebirth. 9. You may also wish to see **Animal** and **Boat**.

ARK OF THE COVENANT 1. Rabbinically, the meeting place of God. 2. Represents a spiritual promise or covenant. See **Covenant**. 3. Metaphysically, relates to humankind's inner divinity. 4. Symbolic of peace or that which is lasting and imperishable. 5. Can relate to a spiritual message.

ARM 1. Identified with the self. See **Body**. 2. Ability to reach out toward others, or ability to give expression or service to others. 3. Work, duty, or responsibility. 4. Metaphorically, may be used as follows: at arm's length = kept at a safe distance; to bear arms = to be readied for battle; arm in arm = united with another individual. 5. Might be symbolic of wearing one's emotions on one's sleeve.

ARMOR 1. Barriers we put up for protection or self-defense. See **Wall**. 2. May represent spiritual, emotional, mental, or physical protection or aid. 3. Could be symbolic of keeping oneself emotionally apart, detached, or protected from the surrounding environment. 4. Might correspond to resistance. 5. You may also wish to see **War** and **Clothes**.

ARMY 1. Can correspond to order, power, discipline, or the relinquishment of personal will. 2. Associated with placing oneself subservient to a greater goal or good. 3. Can represent a warlike environment or situation. See **War**. 4. Metaphorically, there's a whole army of them = there's many of them.

ARROW 1. An incoming message. 2. Associated with something purposeful, powerful, and intentional. 3. Could indicate an aim, a direction, or a course of action. 4. Can correspond to anger, opposition, or vengeance. 5. May represent Cupid's arrow and being overcome by love. 6. Depending on the state of mind of the individual using the arrow (i.e., for sport, for battle), you may also wish to see **Sports** or **War**.

ART/ARTIST 1. Relates to one's creative ability or untapped potential. 2. Associated with creative self-expression. 3. The externalization of an inner emotion, thought, purpose, or idea. 4. Looking at art may indicate one who watches life rather than participates in the process. 5. An artist may be symbolic of one who has strong feelings or emotions. 6. You may also wish to see **Colors** or **People**.

ARTHRITIS 1. That which inflames one's joints. 2. Could be associated with the repression of one's feelings, anger, or emotions. 3. May be literal indication of a potential health problem. 4. That which ties one in knots (i.e., causes anger and frustration). 5. You may also wish to see **Ill/Illness** and **Body**.

ARTIFACTS 1. Associated with history and ancient wisdom. See **Museum**. 2. That which remains from the past. 3. Might correspond to that which is no longer useful. 4. A past project, idea, or experience. 5. You may also wish to see **Antique**.

ASCEND 1. Associated with making progress in one's life journey. See **Journey**. 2. To climb to a higher level of awareness or understanding. 3. May indicate the act of overcoming a situation or a difficulty. 4. Might correspond to a promotion or rise in social or worldly position. 5. You may also wish to see **Mountain** and **Ladder**.

ASCENDANT 1. Corresponds to that which is rising at the moment of one's birth. See **Astrology**.

ASHTRAY 1. May indicate that which goes up in smoke or that which is in ashes. 2. Could correspond to one's smoking habit. See **Cigar/Cigarette**. 3. A literal suggestion to quit smoking. 4. That which holds one's bad habits. 5. You may also wish to see **Smoke/Smoking** or **Fire**.

ASIA 1. Corresponds to the largest continent. 2. May symbolize the Orient. 3. Might indicate that which comes from the East. 4. May be associated with a foreign visitor or travel.

ASTROLOGY 1. Associated with the belief in the study of the stars, planets, Moon, and Sun as they influence or foretell human events, reactions, or experience. 2. Corresponds to the twelve signs of the zodiac:

>*Aries*: March 21–April 19
>*Taurus*: April 20–May 20
>*Gemini*: May 21–June 20
>*Cancer*: June 21–July 22
>*Leo*: July 23–August 22
>*Virgo*: August 23–September 22
>*Libra*: September 23–October 22
>*Scorpio*: October 23–November 21
>*Sagittarius*: November 22–December 21
>*Capricorn*: December 22–January 19
>*Aquarius*: January 20–February 18
>*Pisces*: February 19–March 20

3. Each astrological sign is associated with particular meanings and influences. See individual signs. 4. Metaphysically, the signs of the zodiac correlate to specific archetypes, or patterns of human emotion and experience. 5. The zodiac is separated into twelve astrological houses. The placement of a planet within a particular house is associated with specific traits and human experiences. The influence of the houses are divided as follows:

>*First House*: Corresponds to the individual's personality, appearance, health, and disposition. It is associated with an individual's true self.
>*Second House*: Corresponds to personal possessions, finances, material resources, and income potential.
>*Third House*: Corresponds to modes of communication, education and intellect, travel, and family relationships.
>*Fourth House*: Corresponds to the home and family life. It is associated with an individual's parental instincts, as well as one's relationship with his or her mother.
>*Fifth House*: Corresponds to recreation and pleasure, romance, creative expression, and speculative ventures. An

individual's children are often represented by this house.

Sixth House: Corresponds to health, work, and service. It is also associated with pets and animals.

Seventh House: Corresponds to a person's close personal associations: business partners, marriage, and emotionally intense relationships (positive or negative). It is also associated with agreements and contracts.

Eighth House: Corresponds to an individual's feelings of death and the afterlife. It is also associated with big business, inheritance, shared resources, and insurance.

Ninth House: Corresponds to higher education, religious philosophy, publishing, foreign affairs, and long-distance travel. It may also correspond to an individual's relationship with a partner's relatives.

Tenth House: Corresponds to professional ambitions, public standing, and social prestige. It can also be associated with an individual's parental instincts, but more specifically one's own relationship with his or her father.

Eleventh House: Corresponds to an individual's friends, as well as the organizations with which she wishes to be connected. It is also associated with one's hopes and wishes.

Twelfth House: Corresponds to seclusion, private matters, karmic responsibility, and self-sacrifice. It can also indicate individuals who are prone to escapism.

6. Further described by the following configurations:

Ascendant: Refers to the astrological sign rising on the eastern horizon at the moment of birth. The position of the ascendant creates the start of the first house. It is also called the rising sign. It describes personal characteristics, temperament and personality.

Moon: Refers to one's emotional nature. Next to the Sun sign, it is generally the most important aspect of a birth chart. It is associated with how an individual responds to and relates to people, situations, and experiences. See **Moon**.

Sun Sign: Refers to the individual's astrological sign based upon his date of birth. It is associated with an individual's ego and defines creativity and self-expression. The Sun sign, along with the Moon and the ascendant, best describes the individual. See **Sun**.

7. Astrologically: all signs can be categorized into one of the four elements (see individual signs for traits), as follows:

Air Signs: Aquarius, Libra, Gemini
Earth Signs: Taurus, Virgo, Capricorn
Fire Signs: Aries, Sagittarius, Leo
Water Signs: Pisces, Cancer, Scorpio

ATHLETE 1. Associated with agility, strength, and speed. 2. Can correspond to one who is well trained. 3. One who may accomplish the difficult, the daring, or the seemingly impossible. 4. May correspond to one's activities or sportsmanship in the game of life. See **Sports**. 5. You may also wish to see **People**.

ATLANTIS 1. Can correspond to ancient mysteries, wisdom, and enlightenment. 2. Depending on one's personal association, may correspond to advanced technology, communication, all-encompassing inundation, destruction, or the ultimate struggle between good and evil. 3. An enormous island. See **Island**. 4. You may also wish to see **Historical Clothing/Settings**. 5. Depending on imagery, you may also wish to see **Flood** or **Earthquake**.

ATTACK 1. A conflict between oneself and others or portions of oneself, 2. Associated with feeling inferior, weak, or criticized. 3. May represent an environment of hostility or oppression. 4. Can correspond to an internal struggle. See **Shadow.** 5. You may also wish to see **War** and **Chase**.

ATTIC 1. Symbolizes higher consciousness or the subconscious. 2. Often represents the soul. 3. Corresponds to ideas or internal wisdom. 4. A storehouse of forgotten talents, memories, or dreams of youth. 5. See **House**.

AUDIENCE 1. May correspond to the fact that you are being closely watched or scrutinized in a situation. 2. Might be associated with one's own concerns regarding public opinion. 3. Those in one's own surroundings or environment. 4. You may also wish to see **People**.

AURA 1. Corresponds to the vibratory energy that is emitted by all living things. 2. The color of the aura is associated with different emotional responses; for example: green often symbolizes healing; red represents anger; blue is associated with spirituality. See **Colors**. 3. May also be associated with the halo. See **Halo**.

AUSTRALIA 1. Corresponds primarily to whatever an individual thinks of Australia or Australians (i.e., associated with that which is down under, south, kangaroos, barbecue, etc.). 2. May be indicative of a foreign visitor or travel. 3. Might also symbolize the unconscious.

AUTOGRAPH 1. Associated with the self. See **Self**. 2. Could correspond to ownership or acceptance. 3. One's personal identity. See **Name**. 4. Depending on imagery, you may wish to see **Writing.** 5. Might suggest a prescription or a course of action. 6. For a famous autograph, see **Famous People**.

AUTOMOBILE 1. Symbolic of oneself, one's work, or one's current situation. (*See also individual portions of the automobile below.*) 2. Associated with the external vehicle (personality/occupation) we use to travel life's journey. 3. A car accident may be symbolic of a dangerous situation or simply being accident prone. See **Accident**. 4. A speeding automobile is associated with traveling too fast in life and needing to slow down. See **Speed**. 5. Could correspond to self-control, self-indulgence, or the lack of either (i.e., how is one driving the car?). 6. The driver may be associated with an individual who is helping you on your life's journey. 7. The style and the appearance of the car may represent what one normally associates with that type of vehicle; for example: a station wagon could indicate a family situation; an ambulance might suggest an emergency; an old car one recognizes from one's personal past may symbolize memories or experiences from that time; a car that has a poor appearance may suggest one is not taking care of oneself; an expensive car might indicate one's ego, one's outer personality, or one's social status. 8. Different parts of the car often represent different parts of .the body, as follows:

> *Air-Conditioning*: Associated with one's breath, lungs, or air capacity. The temperature of the situation.
> *Backseat*: Corresponds to the back of the body or the back of the mind (subconscious thoughts). Left side is feminine

(or past), right side is masculine (or future) .

Brakes: Having restraint or lacking it. Sometimes the inability to brake suggests going too fast, or too much fuel (food, sugar, ideas, etc.) in the system. Loss of brakes may also indicate the loss of one's willpower. The inability to move because the brakes are on, or stuck, could represent too much restraint or stubbornness.

Engine: The torso or running systems of the body. Could symbolize the heart, nervous, or electrical systems.

Exhaust: Associated with the elimination systems. Often refers to bowels, skin, kidneys, or lungs.

Front Seat: May represent the front of the body, or the front of the mind (conscious thought). Left side is feminine (or past), right side is masculine (or future).

Headlights: Associated with vision. The ability or inability to see where you're headed.

Heater: Blowing hot air. One's emotions or the temperature of the situation.

Horn: Associated with a message, a warning, or one's own words.

Steering Wheel: Corresponds to that which is determining one's direction. Having someone else drive your vehicle might be associated with giving the control of your life to another.

Tires: Associated with one's foundation and direction.

9. May also indicate one's life journey or direction. See **Journey** and **Direction**. 10. Depending on the imagery, you may also wish to see **Road**.

AUTUMN 1. Associated with the fall, the end of a season, experience, or age. See **Seasons**. 2. May represent the pinnacle of maturity and harvest. 3. Often associated with the onslaught of change or age.

AVALANCHE 1. That which is overwhelming. 2. Can correspond to a shattering experience or a problem situation. 3. Could symbolize the breakup of internal forces. 4. May indicate the falling apart of a situation or an experience. 5. An emotional upheaval. 6. Metaphorically, an avalanche of problems = many problems. 7. You may also wish to see **Weather** and **Mountain**.

AX 1. That which chops or splits apart. 2. A weapon used to create havoc and destruction. 3. Associated with the abuse of power. 4. Could represent that which is two-edged. See **Sword**. 5. Can indicate extreme anger, aggression, or conflict within oneself or with others. 6. Might be associated with an aggressive male nature. See **Phallus**. 7. You may also wish to see **Tool**.

B

1. *The second letter of the alphabet.* 2. *The Roman numeral for 300.* 3. *Associated with schooling; ABCs; second best.* 4. *Not top quality, as in a B-movie.* 5. *Chemically, the symbol for boron.* 6. *Musically, the seventh note.* 7. *Numerologically, equivalent to two.* 8. *Scholastically, good achievement.* 9. *In physics, a symbol for magnetic induction.* 10. *In Greek, beta.*

BABY I. A new beginning, an idea, or a possibility. See **Birth**. 2. Could be associated with a new relationship, or literally a new child. 3. Associated with that which is full of potential though not yet developed. 4. May require further direction, nurturing, encouragement, insight, or guidance. 5. Often represents a creative endeavor or project; whatever is happening to the baby in the imagery is very significant of what one is doing with one's project (i.e., dropping the baby = dropping the project). 6. That which needs to be nurtured. 7. Could suggest the need for a change. See **Diaper**. 8. Biblically, may be associated with innocence and faith. 9. Can represent total vulnerability. 10. Could indicate immaturity, youthfulness, or that which is in the early stages of development. See **Child**. 11. One's inner child. 12. Corresponds to one's own infant self. 13. Metaphorically, can be used as follows: he's such a baby = he acts so immature; it's my baby = it's my project; what a babe = what a sexy woman. 14. You may also wish to see **Pregnancy** and **People**.

BACK/BACKBONE I. Associated with strength and the ability to carry one's load. 2. Where one gets support (the condition of the back may be very symbolic of the kind of support one is getting). 3. Metaphorically, can be used in the following ways: to be on someone's back = to give someone constant criticism; she's flat on her back = she's ill/incapacitated; behind one's back = treachery or secrecy; doing something without the person's knowledge; to turn one's back = to ignore an individual or to turn against her; he's spineless = he's unable to speak up or take a position about anything; she goes back and forth = she's unable to make a decision; to go back on one's word = to lie; to back down (out) = to change one's mind. 4. A backbone is often symbolic of courage. 5. May represent the back of something, the other side of the situation, or the unconscious. 6. See also **Body**. 7. You may also wish to see **Skeleton**.

BACKPACK I. Symbolic of what one has on one's back. See **Back/Backbone**. 2. Could correspond to a sense of or the need for adventure. 3. May be associated with a new journey or experience. See **Journey**. 4. That which one takes with one. See **Luggage**. 5. Might correspond to one's issues or problems that he carries with him.

BADGE 1. Associated with one's occupation, duty, affiliation, or responsibility. 2. Can correspond to an honor, a symbol, or a distinction. 3. May symbolize that which is lawful, moral, or correct. See **Police/Police Station**. 4. You may also wish to see **Work** and **Insignia**.

BADGER 1. May correspond to the act of

being irritating or irritated (i.e., badgered). See **Animals**. 2. Might be associated with hostility and aggression.

BAG/BAGGAGE 1. That which one possesses and may utilize. See **Luggage**. 2. Metaphorically, can be used as follows: having something in the bag = planning on a successful outcome; packing one's bags = getting ready for departure; having excess baggage = having personal problems. 3. Could contain ideas, attitudes, or emotions. 4. The type of bag is very significant; for example: a trash bag could signify that which needs to be thrown away, or that which one has discarded. 5. May represent female sexuality. See **Womb**. 6. Might represent one's personal baggage, issues, or problems.

BAG LADY 1. Corresponds to that which is subjected to the elements or to the environment. 2. May be associated with the abandoned, forgotten, or homeless part of oneself. 3. Might symbolize simplicity. 4. Could indicate that which resides in nature. 5. See also **People**. 6. You may also wish to see **Bag**.

BAIT 1. May be associated with a trap or an enticement. 2. Associated with fishing (i.e., for an answer). See **Fisherman/Fishing**. 3. May correspond to temptation. 4. Depending on imagery, you may also wish to see **Worm**.

BALANCE 1. Symbolic of justice. 2. Associated with weighing the consequences of particular actions. 3. Liturgically, represents Judgment Day. 4. Could correspond to bodily equilibrium and physical, mental, and spiritual well-being. 5. Can correspond to that which still needs to be paid. 6. Metaphorically, a balance of power or trade = the attempt to keep things equal. 7. Astro-

logically, could indicate Libra. See **Libra**.

BALD 1. Could be associated with the loss of one's strength, vitality, or creative ideas. See **Hair**. 2. Might be associated with asceticism and the renouncement of materiality or sexuality. See **Monk**. 3. Depending upon personal associations, could indicate virility and masculinity. 4. May correspond to one's fears of losing one's hair.

BALL 1. Associated with wholeness or oneness. 2. Holding a ball often symbolizes that you have the entire picture or outcome in your hands. 3. What one is doing with the ball is of major importance; for example: dropping the ball could mean making a mistake; playing ball represents being involved (or relaxed) in the experience. 4. Sometimes symbolic of the universal forces manifested in the third dimension. 5. Corresponds to childhood or a time of relaxation. 6. May relate to games, competitiveness, or the sporting instinct. See **Game**. 7. A well-rounded approach to a particular subject. 8. Represents a circle of relationships you possess within your hands: friends, relatives, etc. 9. Metaphorically, can be used as follows: let's play ball = let's work together; don't drop the ball = don't fail; to ball = to have sex; keep your eyes on the ball = pay attention to what you are doing. 10. You may also wish to see **Circle**.

BALLET 1. Depending on personal association, may correspond to balance and preparedness. 2. Associated with dancing. See **Dance**. 3. May indicate fluid motion or orchestrated movement.

BALLOON 1. Often associated with high ideals, thoughts, or dreams. 2. Could correspond to being full of hot air. 3. That which floats on air. 4. May indicate a celebration. 5.

Could suggest a buoyancy or joyfulness. 6. Might represent independence. 7. That which is able to soar on its own. 8. That which is not bound by earthly parameters. 9. You may also wish to see **Air** and **Airplane**.

BALLROOM 1. May correspond to the dance of life. See **Dance**. 2. Associated with formality and one's best appearance to the outside world. 3. Could represent a formal relationship or partnership. 4. A place for a cooperative venture. 5. Might be slang for a place where one takes part in a sexual relationship. 6. You may also wish to see **Building**. 7. Depending on the imagery, you may also wish to see **Orchestra** and **Music**.

BANANA 1. May correspond to the literal need for more fruit in one's diet. See **Fruit** and **Food**. 2. Associated with male sexuality. See **Phallus**. 3. Metaphorically, she's bananas = she's a little crazy or foolish.

BANDAGE 1. That which is or needs to be healed, nurtured, or attended to. 2. Could indicate a portion of oneself that has been hurt or is ill. See **Ill/Illness**. 3. The act of covering one's wounds or emotions. 4. You may also wish to see **Body**.

BANK 1. Corresponds to one's finances or financial condition. See **Building**. 2. Can represent power or material means. 3. Metaphorically, you can bank on it = you can depend on it. 4. You may also wish to see **Money**.

BANQUET 1. Associated with that which may be food for thought. 2. What one may be eating or feasting upon. See **Food** and **Eat**. 3. Can indicate an honor or a ceremony, especially in regard to an idea, a plan, or a situation (i.e., an honorable idea). 4. May be

a dietary warning regarding filling oneself with too much food and drink.

BAPTISM 1. Can correspond to an initiation or a test. 2. Associated with spiritual conversion and/or exploration. See **Water**. 3. Metaphorically, a baptism of fire = an experience that tests one's abilities. 4. Could correspond to a rebirth. See **Rebirth**. 5. You may also wish to see **Christianity**.

BAR 1. Associated with spirits, public socializing, and alcohol. See **Alcohol**. 2. Whatever thoughts one has about being in a bar or drinking will have a great deal to do with the imagery; the condition of the dreamer in the dream is also significant (i.e., joyful, exuberant, or drunk). 3. Metaphorically, may correspond to the law; or, being barred = excluded or denied entrance. 4. See also **Drunk** and **Building**.

BARE FEET 1. Can be associated with relaxation and comfort, or that which is unprepared. 2. Could correspond to the state of one's foundation or present standing. See **Foundation**. 3. Might indicate pregnancy (i.e., barefoot and pregnant). 4. See also **Feet**.

BASEBALL 1. Corresponds to one's ability to play the game of life (i.e., teamwork, cooperation). See **Sports**. 2. May symbolize hitting a home run (i.e., a successful outcome). 3. The activity in the game will have a great deal to do with the associated symbolism; for example: striking out = missing an opportunity or experiencing a failure. 4. You may also wish to see **Ball**.

BASEMENT 1. Can correspond to the unconscious or subconscious mind. See **Unconscious** or **Subconscious**. 2. May represent one's lower self, sexuality, or primal urges. 3. Might correspond to untapped wisdom, information, or intuition. 4. See also **House**.

BASKET 1. That which carries one's ideas, resources, attitudes, or emotions. 2. A full basket could symbolize having many ideas or abilities, or having one's hands full. 3. An empty basket could be associated with being out of ideas or being receptive to one's next responsibility. 4. May represent female sexuality. See **Womb**. 5. You may also wish to see **Bag**. 6. A basket in basketball could indicate scoring or a successful achievement. See **Sports**.

BAT (ANIMAL) 1. Metaphorically, can correspond to being a little crazy (batty) or short-sighted (blind as a bat). 2. May also correspond to the night, the dark side of the unconscious, or hidden fears. 3. An individual represented as a bat may refer to someone who hears everything but is prone to be sneaky. 4. A vampire bat corresponds to that which sucks one's life, emotions, energy, or patience. See **Vampire**. 5. You may also wish to see **Animals** and **Bird**.

BAT (BASEBALL) 1. Can correspond to how one is playing the game of life. See **Game**. 2. May be symbolic of male sexuality. See **Phallus**. 3. That which was designed for sport and teamwork but individually may be used as a weapon. 4. Metaphorically, going to bat for someone = supporting them; your turn at bat = your turn to take charge or your turn as the center of attention. 5. Whatever happens with the bat is significant; for example: striking out = missing the opportunity. 6. You may also wish to see **Ball**.

BATH 1. To be cleansed of old ideas or experiences. 2. The need to be cleansed of one's current situation or state of mind. 3. Corre-

sponds to getting rid of prejudices or that which is no longer necessary. 4. Associated with the inner individuality of the person. See **Nude**. 5. Could be a literal symbol of the need for or the act of some type of physical, mental, or spiritual release or cleansing. 6. Metaphorically, to take a bath = to suffer a heavy financial loss. 7. See also **Water**.

BATHROOM 1. Associated with cleansing oneself, or eliminating something from oneself. 2. Could represent the need for a cleansing: physically, mentally, or spiritually. 3. May indicate the need to literally improve one's eliminations. 4. Can represent one's lower self. See **Toilet**. 5. Could be associated with a place of personal release of feelings or privacy. See **House**. 6. Going to the bathroom in public may symbolize the need to release or confess old ideas, grudges, or emotions, or it may suggest that one feels as though one doesn't have enough privacy. 7. May simply be the subconscious mind acting out the body's desire to go to the bathroom. 8. See also **Body**.

BATTERY 1. Can correspond to one's enthusiasm or energy level. 2. That which provides energy or power to a situation. See **Electricity**. 3. May be associated with one's heart. See **Body**.

BATTLE/BATTLEFIELD 1. A conflict between others or portions of oneself. See **Fight**. 2. An environment of hostility, aggression, and oppression. 3. Can correspond to an internal struggle. 4. Often associated with retaliation for previous thoughts, words, or actions. 5. May indicate the need to consciously deal with problems that are at the unconscious level. 6. Could be associated with the need to fight for what's right. 7. Depending on the time period and imagery, you may also wish to see **Historical Clothing/Settings, People,** or **Shadow**.

BEACH 1. The edge of consciousness between emotions or spirit (water) and the physical world (sand). 2. A time of joyfulness or solitary reflection. 3. See **Sand**. 4. You may also wish to see **Water**.

BEAR 1. That which can be grumpy, overprotective, overbearing, or dangerous. 2. Financially, corresponds to economic sluggishness or fallen prices, as in a bear market. 3. Can correspond to something or someone with two sides: one destructive and the other playful. 4. May indicate the burden that is currently being carried (i.e., borne). 5. Metaphorically, may be associated with the following: he will bear the expenses = he will take care of the costs; to bear witness = to testify; let's bear in mind = let's remember; to bear with or through = to put up with; she bore up under pressure = she was able to handle the stress; bear me out = wait for confirmation, or listen. 6. Might represent that which is dormant or in hibernation (in the situation, in oneself, or in others). 7. Might be symbolic of Russia. See **Russia**. 8. See also **Animals**.

BEARD 1. Can correspond to virility and sexuality. 2. May indicate the proliferation of ideas or creativity. See **Hair**. 3. Might be associated with facing oneself in the mirror. See **Face**. 4. That which one hides behind. See **Mask**. 5. Protecting oneself from the external environment or emotions.

BEAST 1. Corresponds to the animal instincts. 2. Represents irrational thought or behavior. 3. Associated with uncontrolled anger or rage. 4. A repressed or ignored portion of oneself. 5. Psychologically, an individual's shadow. See **Shadow**. 6. Can

represent one's own fears. 7. The outer personality attempting to cover one's inner self. 8. Metaphorically, a beast of burden = that which is forced to carry or transport. 9. See also **Animals**.

BED/BEDROOM 1. Associated with sexual activity, intimacy, and passion. 2. Can represent sleep, rest, or the unconsciousness. 3. To be in bed with an individual often implies being connected, close, or having the same concerns, opinions, and goals. 4. Can be symbolic of a forthcoming marriage or partnership. See **Marriage**. 5. Metaphorically, used in the following ways: you made the bed, now sleep in it = you created the situation that must now be dealt with; a bed of roses = a very favorable experience or situation; bed and board = a place to eat and sleep; strange bedfellows = an unexpected or unusual partnership or relationship; let's put it to bed = let's finish the project; they went to bed = they had sex. 6. A place of security, safety, and comfort. 7. See also **House**.

BEDSPREAD 1. Associated with something that covers the situation, especially one's relationship. See **Blanket**. 2. The appearance of one's personal relationship. 3. Might indicate a marriage or a partnership. See **Bed/Bedroom**.

BEE 1. Associated with one who is always working or busy. 2. That which is irritating or that which stings. See **Bite**. 3. A gathering for a specific purpose, such as a spelling bee. 4. Metaphorically, to be as busy as a bee = to work without resting; to have a bee in your bonnet = to have a problem or a situation in mind that is causing irritation. 5. Might suggest confusion or overwork. 6. See also **Bug**.

BEEF 1. Often associated with one's own attitudes toward beef (i.e., may indicate prosperity, or putting unhealthy substances into one's body). See **Food**. 2. Metaphorically, associated with beefing it up = making things appear or sound better than they are; to beef = to complain; an individual who is beefy = someone who is strong and stout. 3. You may also wish to see **Cow** and **Animals**.

BEEHIVE 1. Symbolic of those who work together for the good of all. 2. A close-knit and interdependent community. 3. Associated with the state of Utah. 4. May indicate the environment of one's work or homelife. 5. See **Bee**.

BEEPER 1. Associated with incoming information, a message, or an insight. 2. Can correspond to a warning. 3. May represent telepathy or intuition. 4. Symbolic of communication or the need to communicate. 5. Might be predictive of someone about to call. 6. Represents someone or something you need to deal with. 7. You may also wish to see **Bell**.

BEER 1. That which provides relaxation, or that which allows escape. See **Alcohol**. 2. Drinking beer with others could symbolize the need for more relaxation and socializing. 3. Being drunk on beer might represent being overpowered by one's own laziness. 4. You may also wish to see **Drunk** and **Food**.

BEETLE 1. Can correspond to tiny or harmless nuisances or irritants. 2. That which destroys or devours slowly. 3. In ancient Egypt, associated with rebirth, prosperity, resurrection, abundance, and good luck. See **Scarab**. 4. You may also wish to see **Bug**.

BEHEADING 1. Associated with losing one's head in a situation. See **Headless**. 2. May indicate losing control or losing one's self. 3. You may also wish to see **Body**.

BELL 1. A message. 2. Represents the fact that the time is now. See **Time**. 3. A call to prayer or to pay attention to that which is near or that which comes after. 4. Announces changes, transformation or, on occasion, death. 5. Associated with automatic responses (as in Pavlov's dogs). 6. Metaphorically, saved by the bell = saved just in time or released from obligation due to another happening. 7. The location of the bell is significant. For example, you may also wish to see **Church** or **House**.

BELT 1. Associated with that which controls, pulls in, or restrains. 2. May be associated with the need for dietary, sexual, or mental restraint. 3. Could represent a literal desire to appear more attractive. 4. Can correspond to being punished or reprimanded. 5. Metaphorically, can be used as follows: they belted each other = they fought each other; that was below the belt = that was unfair or uncalled for; the need to tighten one's belt = the need to conserve, to budget, or to restrain oneself. 6. You may also wish to see **Clothes** and **Pants**.

BENCH 1. Can correspond to one's attitudes, position, stature, thoughts, foundation, or belief system. See **Furniture**. 2. Could symbolize taking a break or resting. 3. Metaphorically, to be benched = to be taken out of the game. 4. You may also wish to see **Chair**.

BIBLE 1. Can correspond to the word of God, or universal laws. 2. Associated with that which contains spiritual wisdom or insight. See **Library**. 3. May represent the history of humankind's development, and/or one's own relationship with God. 4. Associated with sacredness or spirituality. 5. You may also wish to see **Book, Torah, New Testament, Old Testament,** or **Revelation, Book of.**

BICYCLE 1. Movement or motion. 2. Can indicate the attainment of or the need for balance. 3. Associated with an independent journey. 4. Could symbolize an inadequate diet (i.e., a bicycle corresponds to a skinny automobile). See **Automobile.** 5. Riding on a bicycle with another person may indicate a journey, a relationship, or a project together. 6. See also **Journey.**

BIG BEN 1. Symbolic of England. 2. That which counts the passage of time or experiences. See **Time.** 3. May be associated with a foreign visitor or travel. 4. Might symbolize a big message. See **Clock.** 5. You may also wish to see **Building.**

BIKINI 1. Depending on imagery, can correspond to one's desire for attention, an attractive body, or the condition of being under close scrutiny. 2. Losing one's facade or having doubts about one's self-worth. See **Clothes** and **Naked.** 3. One's personal fears regarding one's appearance. 4. Might be associated with swimming. See **Swim.**

BILL 1. Corresponds to a debt owed, that which must be paid, or a reckoning. 2. May be associated with taking stock of the situation, or viewing it from an analytical perspective. 3. May be associated with a financial message. See **Message/Messenger.** 4. Could indicate a memory or a karmic debt. See **Karma.** 5. You may also wish to see **Money.**

BIRD 1. May indicate the bearer of a message. See **Message/Messenger.** 2. Differ-

ent types of birds represent different symbols, for example: a **dove** is indicative of peace or spirituality; **canaries** may imply idle talk; an **eagle** is power or majesty; a **blackbird** or crow may deliver a bad omen, a message, or even death; a **robin** is associated with spring; a **stork** often indicates the birth of a new idea or a literal pregnancy; an **owl** connotes wisdom; a **goose** could indicate that which is a silly goose; a **phoenix** represents a rebirth or a new start; a **hen** might represent being henpecked; a **duck** could indicate ducking the issue; a flock of birds might be associated with a group setting such as work. 3. See also various birds; for example: see **Chicken.** 4. Can be associated with freedom from the material world. See **Airplane.** 5. May represent one's own higher ideas or aspirations. 6. Biblically, the Holy Spirit symbolizes a message from God or from one's own higher wisdom. 7. May be associated with the soul or higher self. See **Soul.** 8. See also **Animals.** 9. Metaphorically, can be used as follows: a birdbrain = someone with very little or no common sense; the early bird catches the worm = the one to arrive early or first is rewarded; birds of a feather flock together = people who are alike (qualities and/or faults) support or join one another. 10. Can represent joy, music, or song. See **Music.** 11. In golf, a birdie is one stroke under par.

BIRTH 1. Corresponds to a new beginning, a fresh idea, or a rebirth (second chance). See **Baby.** 2. That which has been brought forth for others to see. 3. Can indicate that which is awakening or springing to life. 4. Preventing birth (or taking birth control) may be symbolic of suppressing one's own creativity. See **Abortion.**

BIRTH CONTROL 1. May suggest the potential for a literal or figurative pregnancy.

See **Pregnancy**. 2. The act of preventing creativity. 3. Associated with preparedness, the proper precautions, or safe sex. 4. Depending on imagery, you may also wish to see **Sex**.

BIRTHMARK 1. Associated with one's personal mission, destiny, or journey. See **Journey**. 2. Can correspond to a past situation or karmic memory. See **Karma**. 3. The location of the birthmark may have a great deal to do with its symbolic meaning. See **Body**.

BITE 1. Can symbolize that which is gnawing, irritating, or bugging one. See **Bug**. 2. Metaphorically, can be used as follows: don't bite the hand that feeds you = don't spite yourself; he bit off more than he could chew = he took on a bigger project than he could handle; biting words = harsh or sharp words (see **Teeth**); he bit the dust = he died; she bit the bullet = she went ahead and confronted the situation; bite your tongue = don't speak, or maintain silence. 3. Might be associated with one's diet or eating. See **Eat**. 4. That which is sucking the life out of you or another. 5. You may also wish to see **Mouth**.

BLACK 1. Associated with the unknown, the unconscious, or the suppressed. 2. See **Colors**. 3. Could represent the shadow side of one's personality. See **Shadow** and **People**. 4. May correspond to that which is feared. 5. Sometimes associated with death. See **Death**.

BLADE 1. That which cuts or divides. See **Knife**. 2. Could correspond to aggressive male sexuality. See **Phallus**. 3. May indicate an activity that needs to be cut out. 4. You may also wish to see **Cut**.

BLANKET 1. Associated with personal se-

curity and comfort. 2. Can correspond to that which covers the situation. 3. Associated with that which one uses as a cover (outer appearance) at home. 4. Metaphorically, a blanket insurance policy = that which will cover any emergency or situation. 5. May be associated with a relationship or a partnership. See **Bed/Bedroom**.

BLESSING 1. A statement of divine meaning, or a message from one's higher self. See **Pray/Prayer**. 2. Biblically, associated with receiving one's inheritance or destiny.

BLIND 1. Corresponds with the inability or refusal to see, comprehend, or understand. 2. That which lacks insight. 3. Metaphorically, can be used as follows: to do something blind = doing it without the necessary background or insight; she's as blind as a bat = she has very poor eyesight; he was blind in the situation = he was careless or reckless. 4. Might indicate one's biases or attitude. 5. See also **Eyes**.

BLINDFOLD 1. Associated with the inability or the refusal to see. 2. Could represent the attitudes or biases that are preventing clear insight. 3. Might be associated with carelessness. 4. You may also wish to see **Blind** and **Eyes**.

BLISTER 1. Can correspond to that which has been burned or irritated. See **Burn**. 2. May indicate holding on to one's emotions. 3. Metaphorically, associated with a tongue lashing (i.e., criticizing another). 4. Could represent those blemishes in oneself that one has refused to part with. 5. See also **Body** and **Wound**.

BLOOD 1. Represents the physical forces of life itself. 2. Can correspond to the ideas and ideals flowing through a person's body. 3.

Bleeding in a dream may indicate that you are pouring too much of yourself into whatever you're doing. 4. Can be associated with family line or lineage. 5. May be symbolic of the life force. 6. Depending upon the imagery, might be associated with old wounds or that which is occurring to one. See **Body**. 7. Metaphorically, may be used as follows: in cold blood = without feeling or remorse; blood is thicker than water = family relationships are stronger than any other kind; there is bad blood between them = there is animosity or anger between the two; blood brother or blood ties = bound together through physical or metaphorical kinship. 8. Liturgically, symbolic of the sacrifice of Christ. See **Christ**. 9. Rabbinically, associated with Passover. See **Passover**. 10. Because of the color, you may also wish to see red in **Colors**. 11. Depending upon the imagery, you may also wish to see **Wound**.

BLUE 1. Often associated with spiritual truth or insight. 2. See **Colors**. 3. Could correspond to that which is causing depression, i.e., feeling blue.

BLUEBIRD 1. A spiritual messenger. See **Bird**. 2. Associated with joy and happiness, i.e., the bluebird of happiness. 3. Might correspond to summer or spring. 4. The arrival of that which will make you happy.

BLUEPRINTS 1. The plans, outlines, or overview of a new situation, experience, relationship, or idea. 2. That which is in the process of being built. See **Construction**. 3. Might be associated with insight or intuition into an experience. 4. Could correspond with the ability to see the inner workings (i.e., things as they really are).

BOARD 1. May be associated with what one is building, or a new idea. 2. Seeing a board in a particular location might indicate that one finds that aspect of their life or situation boring (i.e., because they are bored). 3. Metaphorically, to sweep the board clean = to start over; to go overboard = to have done more than was necessary; being on board = being involved in the group activity or being ready for the journey. 4. Depending on the imagery, you may also wish to see **Contractor**.

BOAT 1. Corresponds to one's life or soul journey. See **Journey**. 2. Associated with a spiritual voyage or experience. 3. Can represent a talent, a thought, or an idea that is available for one's use. 4. Literally, may be symbolic of a real journey, vacation, or trip. 5. Metaphorically, can be used as follows: we're in the same boat = we're in the same situation; missing the boat = not taking advantage of an opportunity; I'm waiting for my ship to come in = I'm waiting for good fortune (see **Ship**). 6. That which is to be carried abroad. 7. In ancient Egypt, a boat was used for the journey into the afterlife. 8. Might be associated with one who is beginning to explore the realms of spirit or the unconscious. 9. Notice who is captain of your ship (i.e., who you are letting control your destiny). 10. See also **Water**.

BOBCAT 1. Corresponds to a wild or aggressive situation. See **Animals**. 2. May correspond to someone who makes aggressive or spiteful comments. 3. You may also wish to see **Cat**.

BODY 1. Symbolizes the self. 2. Can correspond to one's situation or the environment in which one lives. 3. Portions of the body are often associated with their own symbolic meaning (see various body parts for additional information); for example:

Arms: Duties, emotions, or the ability to reach out to others.

Brain: Thoughts, ideas, state of mind, or beliefs.

Ear: Listening to others for harmony or for a message.

Eyes: Vision, or the ability to see.

Face: Self-esteem, or how one appears to others.

Feet: Direction, journey, personal stance, foundation, or being on one's feet.

Fingers: That with which one is involved, or pointing the finger:

Gonads: Sexuality, energy, or power.

Hair: Thoughts or ideas.

Hands: Service, participation, or work.

Head: Ideas, or one's state of mind.

Heart: Love, stamina, or energy.

Heel: One's callousness, vulnerability, or foundation.

Lap: To care for, or a situation with which one is suddenly involved.

Legs: One's foundation, principles, or morals.

Lips: Speech, or the ability to speak up.

Lungs: One's breath, one's emotions, or that which one holds inside.

Mouth: Speech, or assimilation.

Muscle: Strength, stability, force, balance or beliefs.

Neck (or Throat): Personal will, self.

Nose: Nosiness, or personal involvement.

Phallus: Masculinity, male attributes, sexuality.

Skeleton: Support, belief systems, or personal strength.

Stomach: Assimilation, digestion, or personal constitution.

Teeth: Words spoken; one's diet.

Thumb: Being controlled; an affirmative or negative expression (i.e., thumbs up or thumbs down).

Toes: One's principles, stance, to toe the line, or to become involved.

Waist: Associated with personal image, or stomach.

Womb: Femininity, female attributes, sexuality.

Wrist: Associated with a personal obligation.

4. May also represent the soul. 5. Could indicate the state of one's health, growth, or development physically, mentally, and spiritually. 6. The health of the body or different portions of the body is very significant; for example: a wart could correspond to that which is irritating, unsightly, or feeds off itself; a blister might indicate holding on to a problem, an emotion, or a bad situation; a broken foot may suggest that one has lost his direction. 7. Other individuals often represent ourselves in relationship to that person. See **People**. 8. Different types of individuals represent particular types of encounters; for example: an old man or woman symbolizes wisdom or experience; a child might mean playfulness or inexperience. 9. What one is wearing corresponds to one's state of mind, situation, or how one presents oneself to the world. See **Clothes**. 10. You may also wish to see **Man**, **Woman**, and **Shadow**. 11. If the body is deceased, see **Corpse**.

BOMB 1. That which is explosive or disruptive. See **Explosion/Explosive**. 2. May indicate one's emotional outbursts or temper. 3. Symbolic of aggression or war. See **War**. 4. Metaphorically, she dropped the bomb = she said something very surprising and/or shocking. 5. Might represent an aggressive male nature. See **Phallus**.

BONAPARTE, NAPOLEON 1. May be symbolic of France. 2. Can correspond to aggression or hostility. 3. May be associated with a foreign visitor or travel.

BONDAGE 1. Corresponds to that which has one all tied up. See **Rope**. 2. Might symbolize a disagreeable or difficult responsibility. 3. Can represent servitude or slavery. See **Slave**. 4. Associated with attitudes and beliefs that has one captured. See **Emotion**. 5. Might indicate sexual apprehensions, morals, fears, hang-ups, or fantasies. See **Sex**.

BONE 1. Associated with strength and the ability to carry one's load. See **Back/Backbone**. 2. Metaphorically, can be used as follows: just give me the bare bones = just give me the facts; she has a bone to pick with you = she's upset about something; bones = dice; he's a bonehead = he thinks or studies too much. 3. You may also wish to see **Skeleton**.

BONNET 1. An attitude, opinion, or an idea. See **Hat**. 2. Depending upon the type of bonnet, could symbolize a baby (see **Birth** and **Baby**), Easter (see **Resurrection** and **Easter**), or spring (see **Rebirth** and **Spring**). 3. Represents what one has on her mind. 4. You may also wish to see **Head** and **Clothes**.

BOOK 1. Associated with knowledge or lessons that may be gained or that are already in one's possession. See **Library**. 2. Ideas that are available to one who seeks. 3. Memories to be recollected or used. 4. Metaphorically, by the book = in the usual or customary way or according to the rules. 5. Could be symbolic of that which is booked: an event that is scheduled to occur. 6. Metaphysically, may represent God's Book of Remembrance, the Akashic Records, or one's soul journey. See **Akashic Records**. 7. Biblically, corresponds to the Bible. See **Bible**. 8. A subject for study. 9. May be symbolic of self-expression. 10. The type of book in the imagery could be very significant; for ex-

ample: a law book may indicate that which one is lawfully or unlawfully pursuing; an address book could correspond to social interaction or reconnecting with an old friend; old books might symbolize ancient wisdom.

BOOMERANG 1. Corresponds to an activity, a project, or a situation that will or has come back to you. 2. Could be associated with a karmic situation. See **Karma**.

BOOT 1. May represent an individual's beliefs, ideas, occupation, foundation, principles, direction, or perspective. See **Shoes**. 2. Associated with one's current journey. See **Journey**. 3. Metaphorically, may be used as follows: to give someone the boot = to fire them from employment; to lick someone's boot = to give overindulgent or false praise; to die with one's boots on = to die in the middle of what one is doing. 4. See also **Clothes**.

BORDER 1. Associated with the perimeter or surroundings of a situation, a thought, or a relationship. 2. The imagery of the border will have a great deal to do with the symbolism; for example: crossing the border may suggest that one is delving into new areas or experiences; crossing the border illegally could indicate you are doing something illegal, immoral, or unhealthy. 3. May delineate between levels of consciousness or specific time periods. 4. Depending on imagery, you may also wish to see **Fence, Gate, Earth, Wall**, and **Water**.

BOSS 1. Corresponds to one who is in authority. 2. May be associated with one's higher self or God. 3. The driving force in one's life. 4. Could indicate a disciplinary or parental figure. See **People**. 5. You may also wish to see **Work**.

BOTTLE 1. That which one feeds oneself. See **Food**. 2. The type of bottle (what is in it and what one is doing with it) is very significant; for example: drinking out of a baby bottle could imply taking in that which is childish; a capped bottle may imply that emotions are being bottled up; pouring from a bottle is associated with sharing one's emotions with others. 3. If the bottle is filled with alcohol, see **Alcohol**. 4. Metaphorically, one who took to the bottle = one who began drinking too much.

BOTTLE CAP 1. Could symbolize the letting go or holding in of bottled-up feelings or emotions. See **Bottle**. 2. Might be associated with a literal dietary suggestion; for example: putting a bottle cap on carbonated beverages could indicate that one drinks too much soda; taking a cap off milk could represent the need to drink some milk or to get more calcium.

BOW 1. Corresponds with subservience or service to another person or a situation. See **Servant**. 2. Who is bowing to what is very significant (i.e., could indicate that which one is worshipping). 3. May indicate the need to allow another to have their way.

BOX 1. The conditions surrounding one's life. See **Wall**. 2. That which is hemmed in by circumstances, the environment, or one's state of mind. 3. A container holding an idea, an experience, or a lesson; a gift. 4. Might indicate female sexuality. See **Womb**. 5. In literature, opening Pandora's box is associated with bringing all kinds of difficulties into one's experience. 6. You may also wish to see **Pit**. 7. Could indicate one's emotional insulation from the world or external environment.

BOXING 1. Corresponds to fighting or pro-

tecting oneself. 2. Associated with one who fights for sport or in order to be proven superior. See **Sports**. 3. Metaphorically, to box = to spar (oftentimes verbally) for fun.

BOY 1. May correspond to the male counterpart of one's youthful self. See **Child**. 2. Might symbolize an idea, a project, or a person of about the same age. 3. Could indicate one's own age physically, mentally, or spiritually. 4. Metaphorically, an exclamation of surprise or pleasure: Oh boy! 5. May represent the masculine aspects in oneself that are still immature. See **Man**. 6. The type of boy and how he is dressed may be significant; for example: seeing a boy scout may indicate looking at a well-meaning but immature part of oneself. 7. You may also wish to see **People**.

BRACELET 1. Can correspond to that which one has in one's possession. 2. Associated with what one is doing (arms/wrists) in relationship to others. 3. May symbolize that to which you are cuffed. 4. See **Jewels/Jewelry**. 5. You may also wish to see **Hand, Arm,** or **Wrist**.

BRAG 1. That which is boastful or flaunting. 2. May indicate a message from one's own ego. 3. Associated with the need for self-examination. 4. Might represent the need to be less bashful about one's own talents and abilities. 5. You may also wish to see **Emotion**.

BRAHMA 1. In Hinduism, the god of all that exists, the absolute, the creator. See **Hinduism**. 2. One of the Hindu trinity (i.e., Brahma, Shiva, and Vishnu). 3. Often symbolized by a red individual possessing four arms and four heads.

BRAIN 1. Corresponds to one's thoughts,

ideas, state of mind, or beliefs. See **Head**. 2. Metaphorically, can be used as follows: she's a brain = she's very intelligent; I have you on the brain = I constantly have you in my thoughts; he got his brains beat out = he was beat up. 3. You may also wish to see **Body**. 4. Might be associated with the pineal and the pituitary or sixth and seventh chakras. See **Pineal** and **Pituitary**.

BRAKE 1. Associated with the need for restraint. 2. Can indicate that which is holding one back. 3. See **Automobile**. 4. Might be a message to slow down.

BRANCHES 1. Can correspond to ideas or talents from oneself. 2. Associated with subdivisions of the whole. 3. Metaphorically, to branch out = to extend one's activities. 4. See also **Tree**. 5. Liturgically, may represent faith (i.e., "I am the vine, ye are the branches"; John 15:5).

BRASS 1. Corresponds to that which is inexpensive and showy. 2. Associated with something tarnished or false. 3. See **Colors**. 4. Metaphorically, down to brass tacks = down to the basics.

BREAD 1. Sustenance; the most basic source of life (i.e., the staff of life). 2. That which is needed (kneaded) or used for one's physical, mental, or spiritual well–being, development, or success. See **Food**. 3. Can correspond to a half–baked or perfectly baked idea or plan. 4. Metaphorically, used as follows: bread and butter = a person's source of income; to break bread = to come together (especially for a meal); biblically, to cast your bread upon the water = to do good without expecting a return; know where your bread is buttered = know who is responsible for your livelihood; he has a lot of bread = he has a lot of money. 5. Might be associated

with masculine energy. See **Phallus**.

BREAK 1. That which divides, separates, scatters, or disperses. See **Cut**. 2. To cause to be unusable or unsuitable. 3. What is broken is highly significant; for example: a broken picture may symbolize a broken relationship with that individual; a broken toilet could indicate problems with one's elimination systems; a broken faucet might relate to one's overpowering emotions. 4. Metaphorically, can be used as follows: to break from = to disassociate oneself from; to break off = to make someone stop talking, or to leave a relationship; to break down = emotional collapse; to be broke = to be out of money.

BREAKFAST 1. What one takes into oneself physically, mentally, or spiritually. See **Eat**. 2. Could indicate the start of something new. 3. May correspond to the need to eat breakfast. 4. See **Food**. 5. Literally, to break fast; could symbolize cheating on one's diet.

BREAST 1. Can correspond to nurturing or loving. See **Mother**. 2. May represent female sexuality. See **Womb**. 3. You may also wish to see **Genitals**. 4. See also **Body**.

BREATH 1. To take in spiritual insight or wisdom. See **Air**. 2. Having problems breathing may represent having a difficulty with one's spiritual life. 3. Metaphorically, under one's breath = something voiced in a low tone; in the same breath = at the same time; to catch one's breath = to take a rest; don't breathe a word = be silent about the subject.

BRICKS 1. Words, deeds, or activities that may grow into a larger plan. 2. May symbolize conditions or experiences we have built and must now live with. See **House and Wall**. 3. An idea or an emotion that has solidified and is unchanging. 4. In literature the yellow brick road symbolizes the path to knowledge and enlightenment through personal experience. 5. Biblically, the making of bricks is associated with slavery. 6. That which can be built upon, or used individually as a missile to destroy.

BRIDGE 1. A transformation or journey in understanding. See **Journey**. 2. A new experience, path, or adventure. See **Road**. 3. Can correspond to that which may pass over any obstacle. 4. Associated with a transition of some kind, perhaps even death. See **Death**. 5. Can be symbolic of the connection between two extremes. 6. May represent the meeting place of parts of one's own self; for example, may be symbolic of the link between the conscious and subconscious mind.

BRIDGE (CARDS) 1. May symbolize how one plays the game of life. See **Game**. 2. Might indicate the situation or experience one has been dealt. See **Cards**. 3. Could be associated with a partnership.

BRIEFCASE 1. Often associated with one's occupation. 2. Could be symbolic of taking a trip or getting a new job. 3. Represents the baggage (experiences, beliefs, burdens) an individual takes with him, either necessary or unnecessary. 4. Material, information, or experience that is available to the bearer; that which one has in hand. 5. You may also wish to see **Luggage**.

BROKEN 1. Something that was neglected, broken, or ignored. See **Break**. 2. May be a literal prediction or warning of that which is to come. 3. Could correspond to being out of money. 4. Associated with something that is no longer of use. 5. Metaphorically, brokenhearted = being emotionally crushed.

BROOM 1. Corresponds to that which needs to be swept away or cleaned (i.e., a clean sweep of thoughts, patterns, habits, etc.). 2. May correlate with small chores or ideas that need to be dealt with. 3. Might symbolize male sexuality. See **Phallus**. 4. Might indicate the need for literal housework.

BROTHER 1. Often represents one's own relationship or feelings toward a brother (literal or symbolic). 2. Can indicate a youthful part of oneself (younger brother) or a wiser part (older brother). See **Boy**. 3. A close relationship with one who is like a brother. 4. Could indicate a suggestion or a warning in terms of your brother's welfare. 5. An elder brother may symbolize Christ. See **Christ**. 6. A younger brother might correspond to one's inner child (see **Child),** or one's shadow (see **Shadow)**. 7. You may also wish to see **People**.

BROWN 1. Associated with the earth or the material world. 2. See **Colors**.

BRUSH 1. If brushing one's hair, could be associated with getting one's ideas in order. 2. Could represent the need to clean your mind (hair), your words (teeth), or your outward appearance (clothes or body). 3. Metaphorically, to brush up on something = to rehearse, study, or practice. 4. Depending upon the imagery, see also **Hair, Paint,** or **Mouth**.

BUBBLES 1. That which is buoyant or joyful. 2. May indicate that which appears nice but is unstable or transitory. 3. Could represent useless or trapped thoughts, words, emotions, or ideas. 4. You may also wish to see **Air**.

BUCK 1. May represent a masculine relationship or the masculine side of oneself. See **Animals** and **Man**. 2. Associated with independence and the wild. 3. Metaphorically, a young buck = a young, carefree, independent male; a buck = a dollar (see **Money)**; to pass the buck = to give the blame to someone else.

BUDDHA 1. Corresponds to the realization of selfhood, or one who is conscious (i.e., Buddha said, "I am awake!"). See **Christ**. 2. Associated with divine wisdom and virtue. 3. The founder of Buddhism. See **Buddhism**.

BUDDHISM 1. Religion founded by Buddha in the sixth century B.C. See **Buddha**. 2. Associated with the Four Noble Truths (life is suffering, suffering is caused by satisfying human cravings, suffering will stop as one detaches from cravings, and in order to achieve Nirvana one must follow the Noble Eightfold Path: right understanding, right purpose, right speech, right conduct, right livelihood, right endeavor, right thought, and right meditation). 3. Ignorance of one's proper direction causes suffering; therefore by walking a path of complete morality, suffering will be eliminated. 4. Also corresponds with Buddhism's Five Precepts of moral conduct: abstain from taking life, abstain from taking what is not given, abstain from sexual immorality, abstain from speaking falsehoods, abstain from liquor and that which intoxicates one's mind.

BUFFALO 1. Metaphorically, to buffalo someone = to intimidate them, or to force an individual to do something. 2. Can correspond to that which roams wild and free. 3. May be associated with strength or stubbornness. 4. You may also wish to see **Bull** or **Animals**.

BUFFET 1. Associated with that which may be food for thought. 2. What one may be eating or feasting upon. See **Food** and **Eat**. 3. Can correspond to a variety of choices or opportunities. 4. May indicate an honor or a ceremony, especially in regard to an idea, a plan, or a situation (i.e., an honorable idea). 5. May be a dietary warning regarding filling oneself with too much food and drink.

BUG 1. Associated with parts of oneself (or others) that crawl, creep up on you, gnaw, irritate, get under your skin, or devour. 2. That which is a real pest. 3. The movement, activity, color, and species are all symbolic; for example: a *tick* may indicate something ticking you off; a *roach* could symbolize an area of one's life that is dirty (literally or metaphorically); a *mosquito* might represent that which is sucking the life out of you; an *ant* may indicate something insignificant or industrious; a *spider* can be associated with one who spins a web of deceit, intrigue, or falsehood; bugs eating a plate of food may be associated with the fact that one's diet isn't healthy; a *butterfly* could be the sign of freedom or rebirth. 4. Metaphorically, to bug someone = to bother or to irritate them, or to eavesdrop. 5. Might be associated with personal uncleanliness (physically, mentally, or spiritually). 6. That which is biting you. See **Bite**. 7. Individual bugs might represent individual people in one's life. See **People**. 8. See also names of specific types of bugs, for example: see **Beetle**. 9. The color of the bug may have a great deal to do with the symbolism. See **Colors**.

BUILDER 1. Associated with that which creates one's life or experience. 2. If building a house, could represent the need to care for oneself. See **House**. 3. Might symbolize that which refurbishes or strengthens the situation. 4. You may also wish to see **People**.

BUILDING 1. Associated with one's habits, patterns, beliefs, situations, even particular relationships. 2. A house usually symbolizes one's physical body or current life situation. See **House**. 3. The structure often represents a particular phase or activity in one's life. 4. The situation being depicted may be dependent upon the type of building in the imagery; for example: a library could mean learning, wisdom, or experiences; an office could relate to work or relationships and activities at work; a church would be symbolic of one's spiritual or moral life; the Empire State Building might suggest New York, finances, or work; Fort Knox might symbolize finances; the White House suggests government, politics, or the President; the Eiffel Tower might be associated with Paris, romance, or travels. The condition of the building represents the condition of that portion of your life. 6. Depending upon the imagery, you may also wish to see different portions of the building; for example: see **Door, Roof, Window,** etc.

BULL 1. Associated with stubbornness. 2. Corresponds to financial strength, as in a bull market. 3. Metaphorically, can be used as follows: that's bull = that's nonsense or B.S.; taking the bull by the horns = handling the situation; he's like a bull in a china shop = he creates disorder and chaos. 4. Rabbinically, symbolic of atonement. 5. Liturgically, a papal announcement. 6. Astrologically, one of the twelve signs of the zodiac. See **Taurus**. 7. Metaphysically, relates to the first chakra or endocrine center; sexuality. See **Gonads**. 8. May correspond to aggressive male sexuality. See **Phallus**. 9. You may also wish to see **Animals** and **Cow**.

BULLET 1. Corresponds to aggression, hostility, or forced dominance. See **Gun**. 2. Might indicate an aggressive male nature. See **Phallus**. 3. Could indicate killing or harsh words, criticism, or insult. See **Kill**.

BULLETPROOF VEST 1. That which protects you from insult or harm. 2. Might symbolize one who is untouchable. See **Coat**. 3. Could indicate an emotional barrier or wall that one presents to the world. 4. You may also wish to see **Clothes**.

BULLFIGHT/BULLFIGHTER 1. Associated with the struggle between one's higher (man) and lower (animal) natures. 2. May indicate an argument, a struggle with one's emotions, or perhaps a conflict with someone who is represented by the bull (i.e., a person full of B.S. or someone who is a Taurus). 3. See also **Bull** or **People**.

BULL'S-EYE 1. On the mark, or right on target. 2. Headed in the right direction. See **Direction**. 3. Can correlate to attunement. 4. The attainment of a goal, or a successful accomplishment.

BURGLAR 1. Can correspond with trying to take something illegally. 2. Associated with taking advantage of or being taken advantage of. 3. Something that is stealing one's ideas, energy, emotions, or vitality. 4. Someone who takes what is not theirs by force. 5. See also **People**.

BURIAL 1. May be associated with being overwhelmed. 2. Can correspond to being involved with something that is over one's head. 3. That which has been hidden. See **Funeral**. 4. Associated with the death of an experience or an idea. See **Death**. 5. Might indicate the disposal of that which is no longer necessary. 6. You may also wish to see **Corpse** or **Body**.

BURN 1. Associated with extreme anger, frustration, or irritation. 2. May indicate suppressing one's emotions. 3. Metaphorically, can be used as follows: a burning issue = that which is very important; money burns a hole in his pocket = he has the urge to spend any money he has; don't burn your bridges = don't alienate people or past experiences in your life; she got burned = she got mistreated or she got into trouble; burning the candle at both ends = wearing oneself out; burning the midnight oil = to study late or to work too hard. 4. Depending on the imagery, you may also wish to see **Fire** or **Wound**.

BUS 1. Corresponds to a group of individuals all headed in the same direction, or an experience shared with others. 2. Different types of buses may symbolize different meanings; for example: a school bus may be associated with schooling or life's lessons; a chartered bus might indicate the need for a vacation; being on a nondescript bus could symbolize allowing others to control your direction. 3. Metaphorically, she missed the bus = she missed the opportunity, or she was mistaken in her assumptions. 4. May represent one's physical body or current situation. See **Automobile**. 5. Could symbolize being taken for a ride.

BUTLER 1. Associated with the masculine aspect of oneself that is subservient to oneself or to others. See **Servant**. 2. That which waits on something (i.e., time, others, until the condition is right). 3. Could indicate a helpful suggestion, the need for help, or the need to help others. 4. May be symbolic of the need to place someone in charge of the small details or to take charge yourself. 5. Might correspond to being of service to an idea, a person, or an experience. 6. See also **Man** and **People**.

BUTTERFLY 1. A symbol of freedom or transformation. 2. Can correspond to triviality, changeability, or superficiality. 3. See also **Bug**. 4. Liturgically, another symbol of the resurrection and eternal life. See **Phoenix (Bird)**. 5. May be a symbol of the soul or of rebirth. See **Rebirth**.

BUTTON 1. That which fastens, connects, or joins together. 2. What one is buttoning or unbuttoning is very significant; for example: buttoning a sweater may simply be the need to keep warm; unbuttoning one's pants may correspond to sexuality (see individual clothing articles; for example: see **Coat**). 3. Metaphorically, can be used as follows: hold your button = wait for a moment; button it up = telling someone to be quiet. 4. You may also wish to see **Clothes**.

C

1. *The third letter of the alphabet; 2. The Roman numeral for 100. 3. Associated with schooling; ABCs; third rate. 4. Chemically, the symbol for carbon. 5. Musically, the first note. 6. Numerologically, equivalent to three. 7. Scholastically, fair achievement. 8. In physics, a symbol for coulomb (measures electrical current). 9. In Greek, gamma.*

CAB 1. Corresponds to that which one is allowing to drive one's life. 2. May indicate one feeling disassociated or disconnected from oneself, a particular situation, or life in general. 3. May represent one's physical body or current situation. See **Automobile.** 4. Could symbolize being taken for a ride.

CABIN 1. Can correspond to humility or poor self–esteem. 2. May represent a temporary situation or problem. See **House.** 3. Could indicate a small condition that has surrounded you. 4. You may also wish to see **Building.**

CABINET 1. May be associated with a small part of oneself. 2. Can indicate a storage place for memories, emotions, or experiences. See **Closet.** 3. To hide or conceal oneself or a portion of oneself (i.e., emotions) from others. 4. Depending on the imagery, you may also wish to see **House.**

CACTUS 1. That which is prickly and may stick you. 2. Can represent a hot or dry situation. See **Desert.** 3. Could indicate a situation that appears dangerous but may be sweet once you get inside. 4. See also **Plant.**

CAFÉ 1. Associated with the self, or where one might meet different aspects of oneself. 2. Might represent what one is eating. See **Food.** 3. Could suggest the need for refreshing entertainment, socializing, or relaxation. 4. See also **Building.**

CAGE 1. Associated with a loss of one's personal freedom. 2. Represents the feeling or fear of being trapped. 3. That which is holding you back (ideas, perceptions, beliefs, other people, situations, etc.). 4. Metaphorically, to be caged up = to be confined or jailed. 5. See **Box.** 6. You may also wish to see **Prisoner.**

CAIN 1. Biblically, associated with selfishness. 2. Symbolic of jealousy. 3. Metaphysically, represents the possessive side of human consciousness.

CAKE 1. Corresponds to a celebration, a reward, or an accomplishment. 2. Metaphorically, can be used as follows: that takes the cake = that's really something (either seriously or cynically); to have your cake and to eat it too = to get the best of everything; that was a piece of cake = that was easy; he even got icing on the cake = his situation was even better than expected. 3. May correspond to bad habits or overindulgence of physical appetites. 4. Could indicate receiving one's just desserts. 5. See also **Food.**

CALENDAR 1. That which systematically arranges the situation, schedule, or one's life. 2. Associated with time. See **Time.** 3. Might correspond to one's life journey. See **Journey.**

CAMEL 1. Can represent that which you carry with you. 2. May indicate that you have something or someone on your back. 3. Could be associated with a dry spell in one's life. See **Desert**. 4. Might represent an inner spiritual source. 5. May be associated with a foreign visitor or travel. 6. See **Animals**. 7. You may also wish to see **Egypt/ Egyptian.**

CAMEO 1. Holding an image (situation, experience, or person) in one's own hands. 2. May correspond to memories of experiences, ideas, or relationships. 3. You may also wish to see **Statue** or **Photograph**.

CAMERA 1. The need to focus or to get a clearer picture. 2. Corresponds to memories of experiences, ideas, or relationships. 3. Associated with recalling events with a more detached or objective perspective. 4. Holding a representation of the picture (situation, experience, or person) in one's own hands. 5. To re-experience a situation that has transpired previously. 6. One's dreams coming to life. 7. May also be associated with karmic memory. See **Karma**.

CAMP 1. Could indicate a temporary situation. 2. Could represent your current perspective or opinion. 3. Associated with the need for a vacation or relaxation. 4. Metaphorically, in the same camp = on the same side; to break camp = to depart. 5. You may also wish to see **Tent/Tepee** or **House**.

CAMPUS 1. A learning situation or environment. See **School**. 2. May symbolize any situation or experience that involves the activities of others (i.e., work, home, school, a project, etc.).

CANADA 1. Corresponds primarily to whatever an individual thinks of Canada or Canadians (i.e., associated with the north, cold, a haven of safety, etc.). 2. May be indicative of a foreign visitor or travel. 3. Might be associated with crossing the border (i.e., going out of bounds or over the line).

CANCER (ILLNESS) 1. Metaphor for something that is eaten away or being destroyed from within (i.e., that which is eating you). 2. Associated with warring with one's own self. See **Body**. 3. Corresponds to negative thoughts and emotions. 4. Can be a literal warning of illness unless there is personal physical and emotional change.

CANCER (ZODIAC) ♋ 1. Fourth sign of the zodiac, corresponding to June 21–July 22. 2. Associated with the following positive traits: sensitive, imaginative, maternal/paternal, a homebody. 3. Associated with the following negative traits: overly emotional, moody, prone to self-pity. 4. Astrologically, ruled by the Moon. See **Moon/Moonlight.** 5. See also **Crab**. 6. A water sign. See **Water.** 7. See also **Astrology.**

CANDELABRA 1. Associated with illuminating the darkness. See **Candle/Candlestick.** 2. May represent wisdom or insight. See **Light.** 3. Insight or information that is old, ornate, or unchanging. 4. You may also wish to see **Torch.** 5. The number of points on the candelabra may have significance; for example: a seven-pointed candelabra might represent the chakras. See **Numerology.**

CANDLE/CANDLESTICK 1. Represents a light in the darkness; to illuminate. See **Light.** 2. An answer to a problem; enlightenment. 3. Could indicate a singleness of purpose, if one candle. 4. Metaphorically, burning a candle at both ends = working too hard. 5. Can correspond to male sexuality. See **Phallus.** 6. Liturgically, a symbol of the Church. See **Church.** 7. You may also wish to see **Fire.**

CANDY 1. Can correspond to one's own personal desires, indulgences, satisfaction, or physical appetites. See **Food.** 2. Literally, may be suggestive of too much sugar in the system. 3. An experience that tastes sweet but may not be good for you. 4. May symbolize temptation. 5. That which is sweet. 6. Depending on the imagery, you may also wish to see **Teeth.**

CANE 1. That which provides assistance on a journey or through an experience. See **Direction** or **Road.** 2. Can correspond to a warning of physical injury. 3. How one walks may be symbolic of how the world perceives one's journey/occupation/personality. See **Journey.** 4. May correspond to male sexuality. See **Phallus.** 5. Depending on imagery, you may wish to see **Old Man/Old Woman.** 6. You may also wish to see **Clothes.**

CANOE 1. Associated with a primitive boat. See **Boat.** 2. May indicate a solitary journey or being on your own in the situation. See **Journey.** 3. Could symbolize a personal and private spiritual experience. 4. Might represent the possibility of romance (i.e., especially if the canoe looks like a gondola) or a spiritual relationship. 5. You may also wish to see **Water.**

CAPE 1. That which covers one's emotions. See **Coat.** 2. Depending on the imagery, may represent one who will provide extraordinary help and assistance (i.e., a superman). 3. Could indicate that which is mysterious or partially concealed. 4. You may also wish to see **Clothes.**

CAPRICORN ♑ 1. Tenth sign of the zodiac, corresponding to December 22–January 19. (Represented by either the figure of a goat, or the forepart of a goat with the hind part of a fish.) 2. Associated with the following positive traits: reliable, humorous, patient. 3. Associated with the following negative traits: rigid, pessimistic, cheap. 4. Astrologically, ruled by Saturn. See **Saturn.** 5. See also **Goat.** 6. An earth sign. See **Earth.** 7. See also **Astrology.**

CAPTAIN 1. Corresponds to the one in charge of the journey. See **Journey.** 2. Could be associated with the higher self or soul. 3. Represents the one responsible for the experience/livelihood of those in the same situation. 4. The source of power and authority. 5. May be associated with a parental figure. 6. See also **People.**

CAPTIVE 1. Associated with being trapped, detained, or confined. 2. Might represent that which has you captivated. 3. Could symbolize that to which you have surrendered your personal freedoms. 4. See also **Prisoner.**

CAR 1. The physical body. See **Automobile.** 2. Symbolic of yourself, your work, or your current situation. 3. Associated with the external vehicle (personality/occupation) we use to travel life's journey. 4. A car accident may be symbolic of a dangerous situation or simply being accident prone. See **Accident.** 5. A speeding car is associated with traveling too fast in life, and needing to slow down. See **Speed**. 6. Could correspond to self–control, self–indulgence, or lack of either (i.e., who is driving the car). 7. The driver may be associated with an individual who is helping you on your life's journey. 8. The style and the appearance of the car may represent what one normally associates with that type of vehicle; for example: a station wagon could indicate a family situation; an ambulance might suggest an emergency; an old car one recognizes from one's personal past may symbolize memories or experiences from that time; a car that has a poor appearance may suggest that you are not taking care of yourself; an expensive car might indicate the ego, the outer personality, or social status, etc. 9. You may also wish to see **Journey.**

CARDINAL 1. May indicate a messenger. See **Bird.** 2. Can be associated with virtue, spirituality, or authority. 3. Might correspond to red. See **Colors.**

CARDS 1. Can indicate good luck or fate. 2. Could represent the current situation you're dealing with (i.e., the hand you've been dealt). See **Game.** 3. Metaphorically, can be used as follows: she's a real card = she's a joke; to put one's cards on the table = to express oneself in the situation; it's a house of cards = it's unstable or a little shaky; having a card up your sleeve = having additional resources or a plan; it's not in the cards = it's not likely to happen. 4. Associated with four suits (spades, hearts, diamonds, clubs) of thirteen cards (ace, king, queen, jack, 10, 9, 8, 7, 6, 5, 4, 3, and 2), totaling 52. 5. Depending on the imagery, you may wish to see **Gambling.** 6. You may also wish to see **Tarot.**

CARNIVAL 1. Associated with wild entertainment, eating, rides, games, and attractions. 2. What one is doing in the situation is highly significant; for example: going for a ride may indicate being taken for a ride or going around in circles; playing a game could symbolize how you're handling a certain situation or experience in your life (see **Game**); eating might symbolize what's giving you nourishment, or is tempting you

(see **Food**). 3. You may also wish to see **Circus.**

CARPENTER 1. Associated with that which creates one's life or experience. See **Contractor.** 2. Can symbolize the need for repairs or inspection, physically, mentally, or spiritually. 3. Liturgically, associated with Jesus. See **Jesus Christ.** 4. You may also wish to see **People.**

CARPET 1. A foundation. 2. Something that is under consideration. 3. A state of subservience (i.e., being walked upon). 4. Insulation against worldly influence. 5. To hide or to cover something. 6. Softness, rest, luxury, or comfort. 7. Associated with the feminine. 8. Types of carpets are symbolic of different meanings; for example: a magic carpet may mean a journey, a mysterious adventure, or an experience; a torn carpet signifies a hole in your foundation or belief system; a wet carpet could indicate soggy principles, etc.; the color of the carpet may be significant. See **Colors.** 9. Metaphorically, he got called on the carpet = he got into trouble. 10. You may also wish to see **Floor** and **House.**

CARRIAGE 1. That which delivers, transports, or conveys. 2. The type of carriage may be symbolic of what is being delivered. For example, a baby carriage may indicate a new birth or a new idea being delivered (see **Baby**); a horse carriage may be symbolic of a message (see **Horse**). 3. May be associated with external behavior or attitudes; what you present to the world. 4. See also **Automobile**.

CASINO 1. Associated with taking a risk or participating in an uncertain venture. 2. Often corresponds to taking foolish or wasteful actions. 3. To win at gambling may imply that the risk is worth taking; to lose advises caution or a different course of action. 4. That which is chancy. 5. Depending on the imagery, you may wish to see **Game** and **Cards**. 6. Might indicate good luck. 7. See also **Las Vegas** and **Building**.

CASSETTE TAPE 1. Associated with hearing and the need to remember or to recall verbal communication. See **Ears**. 2. Can correspond to memories of experiences, ideas, or relationships. 3. Associated with recalling events or the need to recall events with a clear picture of what transpired. 4. To re-experience a situation that has transpired previously. 5. May also be associated with karmic memory. See **Karma**.

CASTLE 1. A well-developed or fortified psyche. See **House** and **Building**. 2. May denote protective barriers against outside individuals and the environment or from within one's own self. 3. Represents dominion, stability, and wealth. 4. In chess, associated with a protective movement (castling).

CASTRATE 1. May represent the act of being emasculated or belittled. 2. Might be associated with a loss of sexual desire or impotence. 3. Symbolic of fears of relationships or sex. 4. Can indicate being overwhelmed by the situation or overwhelming and dominating someone. 5. May be a literal indication of prostate problems. 6. Associated with male sexuality. See **Phallus**.

CAT 1. Cats are often symbolic of what you associate with them, or how you feel about them in general (the color may also be important; see **Colors**). See **Pet**. 2. Associated with independence, aloofness, and self-sufficiency. 3. May represent immature sexuality. 4. Since they roam at night and can see in the dark, cats can represent intuition or

the subconscious. 5. Metaphorically, can be used as follows: being catty = being sneaky, malicious, a gossip, or making hateful remarks toward another; as playful as a cat = having a good time or fun with whoever or whatever is available; letting the cat out of the bag = disclosing a secret. 6. A black cat is often symbolic of bad luck. 7. You may also wish to see **Lion** and **Animals.**

CATALOG 1. Can correspond to choices. 2. Associated with the need to make a decision. 3. The type of catalog may symbolize the area in life where the decision needs to be made; for example: a catalog of bedroom furniture may be associated with a relationship; a catalog of children's toys could correspond with decisions related to children, etc. 4. You may also wish to see **Book** or **Shop.**

CATCH 1. May be associated with being thrown the ball. See **Ball.** 2. Could represent taking hold of the situation. 3. Corresponds to the ability to play the game of life (i.e., teamwork, cooperation, etc.). See **Sports.** 4. You may also wish to see **Baseball.**

CATERPILLAR 1. May represent something that is about to or needs to undergo transformation or be changed. See **Butterfly.** 2. Could symbolize something that is creeping up on you. See **Bug.** 3. Might indicate a minor irritant or something that is causing a little destruction. 4. Might symbolize something that appears to be troublesome but holds great promise.

CATFISH 1. May be associated with a partial spiritual insight (i.e., half mammal and half fish). See **Fish.** 2. Could correspond to the unconscious.

CATTLE 1. Metaphorically, can be used as a

derogatory term meaning human beings en masse. 2. May correspond to a specific group of people. See **People.** 3. Might represent the animal instincts. 4. See also **Cow** and **Animals.**

CAVE 1. Something hollow or without substance. 2. A temporary shelter. 3. Metaphorically, to cave in = to collapse or to disintegrate. 4. May indicate the primitive part of the self or the subconscious. 5. Might be associated with female sexuality. See **Womb.** 6. Something enclosed or concealed. 7. A dark situation, experience, or passage. 8. May indicate tunnel vision. See **Tunnel.**

CAVE-IN 1. One's principles, beliefs, ideas, or a project being undermined or experiencing failure. 2. Associated with losing one's support. 3. You may also wish to see **Mountain, Floor,** and **Back/Backbone.**

CAVITY 1. Often associated with words that should not have been spoken. See **Teeth.** 2. Could represent a cause of decay. 3. May indicate a sweet tooth. 4. Depending on the imagery, you may wish to see **Candy.**

CAYCE, EDGAR 1. Associated with Christian mysticism and intuition. 2. May correspond to prophecy, dreams, reincarnation, holistic health, or personal spirituality. 3. Might represent one's higher self. 4. You may also wish to see **Psychic.**

CD/CD ROM 1. Associated with memories of experiences, ideas, or relationships. 2. A storehouse of wisdom and insight. See **Library** and **Book.** 3. May be associated with music, harmony, and song. See **Music.** 4. Can correspond to the mind, rapid intellect, or brilliance. See **Computer.** 5. May also be associated with karmic memory. See **Karma.**

CEILING 1. Protection; covering. 2. Could be associated with something that is over one's head. 3. Metaphorically, can be used as follows: that's the ceiling = the highest limit or price; he hit the ceiling = he lost his temper. 4. Can correspond to mentality and ways of thinking. 5. See also **Roof** and **House.**

CELLAR 1. May indicate the subconscious or the unconscious. 2. Could represent one's lower nature. 3. See also **House.**

CELLULAR PHONE 1. Associated with gaining information or insight. 2. Corresponds to a message. See **Message/Messenger.** 3. Can represent telepathy or intuition. 4. Symbolic of how one communicates with others. 5. Literal prediction of someone about to call or someone you need to call. 6. Might be associated with a relationship, an idea, or spoken words.

CEMENT 1. Associated with a firm foundation. See **Floor.** 2. Something that holds things together. 3. Could represent a state of permanence. 4. Metaphorically, to cement something (i.e., a relationship) = to make it lasting. 5. Depending on the imagery, you may also wish to see **House.**

CENTAUR 1. Mythologically, a creature with the head and trunk of a man and the body of a horse. 2. Astrologically, one of the twelve signs of the zodiac. See **Sagittarius.** 3. Metaphysically, can represent the spiritual nature of man forced to exist in the material world. 4. Could represent a dual nature or a struggle with the higher and lower aspects of one's own self. 5. You may also wish to see **Horse** and **Man.**

CHAIN 1. That which ties, restrains, connects, or enslaves. 2. May be associated with habits, patterns, or beliefs. 3. Could correspond to unified strength or be something that pulls things together. See **Rope.** 4. May represent bondage. See **Prisoner.** 5. Metaphorically, a chain of thought = the process of thinking, or increments of ideas.

CHAIR 1. Can correspond to one's attitudes, position, stature, thoughts, foundation, or belief system. See **Furniture.** 2. Depending upon the appearance of the chair, it could indicate authority or ego (i.e., throne), indecision or rest (i.e., rocker), etc. 3. May be associated with one's rightful place. 4. Metaphorically, to chair the meeting = to run the meeting.

CHAKRAS 1. Associated with seven physiological endocrine glands (centers) of the body. 2. In Eastern philosophy, considered the seven connecting links or spiritual centers between one's physical body and one's soul. 3. The chakras and their basic motivating influences are as follows:

> *Gonads*: First spiritual center; associated with sustenance and physical survival.
> *Lyden (Cells of Leydig)*: Second spiritual center; associated with sexuality and propagation.
> *Adrenals*: Third spiritual center; associated with self-preservation and physical energy.
> *Thymus*: Fourth spiritual center; associated with self-gratification and human love.
> *Thyroid*: Fifth spiritual center; associated with life and personal will.
> *Pineal*: Sixth spiritual center; associated with light and the higher mind.
> *Pituitary*: Seventh spiritual center; associated with universal love and oneness.

4. Metaphysically, the progression of these centers is associated with the opening of the seven seals in Revelation. See **Revelation, Book of.** 5. See also the individual chakras, for example: see **Thymus**.

CHALICE 1. Represents a mission, a duty, a higher purpose, or a journey. See **Journey**. 2. Receiving a cup can be associated with receiving or taking charge of a situation, for it is now in one's own hands. See **Cup**. 3. Liturgically, associated with the blood of Christ, or that which holds the soul. See **Christ**. 4. Might correspond to the Holy Grail. See **Holy Grail**.

CHAMELEON 1. May be associated with change, flexibility, or inconsistency. See **Animals**. 2. Might indicate betrayal. 3. You may also wish to see **Two–Faced**.

CHAMPAGNE 1. Can correspond to success or luxury. 2. May indicate the need for relaxation. 3. See also **Alcohol**. 4. Bubbles may indicate one's thoughts, emotions, or words.

CHANDELIER 1. Could be associated with lofty principles, thoughts, insights, or ideals. See **Ceiling**. 2. Something that is over one's head. 3. Can represent something that illuminates the situation. See **Light**. 4. Depending on the imagery, you may also wish to see **House**.

CHANT 1. Associated with worship or spiritual attunement. See **Pray/Prayer**. 2. May correspond to spiritual harmony. See **Sing/Singer**. 3. You may also wish to see **Meditation**.

CHAOS 1. May be symbolic of the challenges one is currently facing. 2. Could be associated with emotional problems and upsets. 3. Might indicate the need to become more organized physically, mentally, or spiritually.

CHARACTERS 1. Generally associated with parts of oneself. 2. May indicate aspects of individuals we associate with that characterization. 3. See also **People.** 4. Metaphorically, the strength of character = the moral standing of the individual. 5. Whatever is distinguishing about the situation or an individual. 6. Foreign characters may be associated with a foreign visitor or travel.

CHARCOAL 1. That which may be used as a purifier or for fuel. 2. A crude writing instrument. 3. May be associated with the color black. See **Colors.**

CHARM 1. Can correspond to good luck. 2. May indicate something that is charmed. 3. Something that can protect you or others from harm. 4. You may also wish to see **Magic/Magician.** 5. Metaphorically, can be used as follows: he's charming = he's a delight to be around; she's led a charmed life = she's been very lucky and protected.

CHASE 1. Can represent something that is chasing you (i.e., fears), that you are running from, or that you are pursuing. See **Run/ Runner.** 2. May be associated with anxiety, apprehension, inferiority, and uneasiness. 3. The inability to handle one's current experience. 4. The object of fear is often associated with something that needs to be faced in yourself. See **Shadow.** 5. A conflict between others or portions of oneself. 6. Can correspond to an internal struggle. 7. You may also wish to see **Attack.**

CHEAT 1. Being dishonest with yourself. 2. Not living up to your best potential. 3. Associated with deceiving or being deceived. 4. Metaphorically, he cheated on his wife = he had an affair with another person. 5. Trying to get out of one's current lessons or situation. See **School.**

CHEEK 1. Metaphorically, associated with the following: he was cheeky = he was racy or rude; to speak with tongue in cheek = to speak without sincerity. 2. May indicate saving or losing face. 3. See also **Body.** 4. Biblically, associated with forgiveness and turning the other cheek.

CHEERLEADER 1. Corresponds to receiving recognition, a reward, or appreciation. 2. To praise or to encourage. 3. May correspond to the need to be of good cheer. 4. Associated with providing encouragement or support for others. 5. You may also wish to see **People.**

CHEF 1. Something that provides rich nourishment and sustenance. See **Cook.** 2. May correspond to a creative endeavor or plan. 3. Might suggest literal dietary changes or recommendations. 4. You may also wish to see **Food** and **People.**

CHEW/CHEWING GUM 1. Associated with something kept in the mouth (i.e., words not spoken). 2. Metaphorically, to chew upon = to repeatedly think something over again and again. 3. That which must be slowly assimilated or understood. 4. You may also wish to see **Teeth.**

CHICKEN 1. Metaphorically, associated with the following: being chicken = being afraid; don't count your chickens before they're hatched = don't expect something that may not happen. See **Animals** or **Bird.** 2. Could indicate something that is foul (fowl) or someone who is henpecked.

CHILD 1. Represents one's inner self or one's inner child. See **People.** 2. Corresponds to playfulness or youth. 3. May be associated with inexperience. 4. Biblically, symbolic of perfect belief and faith (Matthew 18:3). 5. Associated with hope and simplicity. 6. Being full of potential, though presently undeveloped. 7. Needing additional guidance or direction. 8. The child's age may symbolize or represent a particular situation or experience of the same age in your life (i.e., a project, a business, or a memory). 9. Could correspond to immaturity. 10. A new beginning or a fresh start. 11. Metaphorically, she's with child = she's pregnant. 12. See also **Baby.**

CHIN 1. May indicate one who is obstinate or stubborn. 2. Could be associated with personal pride. 3. Metaphorically, can be used as follows: to keep one's chin up = to stay optimistic in spite of the situation; she's up to her chin = she's very busy. 4. A clenched face may indicate someone who is upset or holding emotions in. See **Face.** 5. See also **Body.**

CHINA (COUNTRY) 1. May be associated with ancient wisdom. 2. Could indicate something mysterious or unknown. 3. May symbolize the direction east. 4. Corresponds primarily with whatever an individual thinks of China or the Chinese (i.e., associated with mystery, fast food, oppression, etc.). 5. May be indicative of a foreign visitor or travel.

CHINA (DISHES) 1. Can indicate whatever is on one's plate. 2. May represent what you are serving yourself or others. See **Food.** 3. Can represent ideas. 4. Might signify something that is easily broken. 5. You may also wish to see **Dishes.**

CHOCOLATE 1. That which is sweet or tempting. 2. May indicate personal indulgences. See **Candy.** 3. Could be associated with the body's craving for natural sugar or love. 4. If chocolate is an individual's favor-

ite flavor, could correspond to that which is satisfying, desirable, or pleasurable. 5. You may also wish to see **Food.**

CHOP 1. Associated with a steady, repeated, rhythmic movement. 2. Metaphorically, chop–chop = hurry or act more swiftly. 3. Depending on the imagery, you may wish to see **Wound.**

CHOPSTICKS 1. Could be associated with a foreign idea or project. 2. Something that provides food for thought. 3. May symbolize the Orient or a foreign visitor or travel. 4. You may also wish to see **Food.**

CHRIST 1. A spiritual messenger. 2. Associated with the manifestation of divinity on Earth. See **God.** 3. A spiritual or higher ideal made real. 4. The pattern (or archetype) of one's own ultimate potential. 5. Can correspond to the soul, mind, or higher self. 6. That which is symbolic of love, kindness, service, etc. 7. Associated with higher consciousness. 8. The realization of divine wisdom and virtue in the flesh. 9. Might represent selflessness. 10. Could correspond to a spiritual rebirth. See **Phoenix (Bird).** 11. You may also wish to see **People** and **Jesus Christ**.

CHRISTIANITY 1. Associated with those who follow the teachings of Jesus. 2. Emphasis of the religion is primarily upon faith and secondarily upon good works. 3. Corresponds to individuals who believe in God incarnate on Earth through Jesus. See **Christ**. 4. Associated with the Ten Commandments (see **Judaism** for listing), and the Two Great Commandments (Matthew 22: 37–39): Thou shalt love the Lord thy God with all thy heart, and with all thy soul, and with all thy mind. Thou shalt love thy neighbor as thyself. 5. Primary religious text is the Bible. See **Bible**.

CHRISTMAS I. Symbolic of joy, love, family gatherings, or youthful memories. 2. Can be associated with spiritual ideas or beliefs being born through oneself. 3. Could indicate the arrival of a gift, a special message, or a rebirth. 4. An individual's own recollections of Christmas will have the greatest impact on the symbolic meaning; for example, the theme of those memories could be the very same theme in the symbolism. 5. Corresponds to the birth of Jesus. See **Jesus Christ**.

CHURCH 1. Associated with spiritual forces; the dwelling place of spirituality, the soul, or higher wisdom. 2. May correspond with safety and security from the outside world. 3. May represent spiritual community. 4. Symbolic of religious or personal beliefs or a childhood association with religion. 5. Can represent your entire being: physically, emotionally, mentally, and spiritually. 6. The condition of the building may give indications into your present life, beliefs, or condition. See **Building**. 7. The spiritual facade we present to the world. 8. Corresponds to something that gives assistance in your own spiritual life. 9. Place of worship. 10. Where spiritual forces impinge upon the conscious mind or the material world. 11. May indicate spiritual initiation. See **Initiation**.

CIGAR/CIGARETTE 1. Something that goes up in smoke. See **Smoke/Smoking**. 2. Could indicate something smelly. 3. Personal associations will greatly determine the symbolism; for example: someone who quit smoking could see it as temptation. 4. Could be a warning regarding the inadvisability of smoking. 5. Might be associated with male sexuality. See **Phallus**.

CINDERELLA 1. Associated with personal transformation. 2. Change from poverty and neglect to personal fulfillment. 3. The realization of one's highest self. 4. The story of human metamorphosis, transformation, and rebirth. See **Phoenix (Bird)**. 5. See also **People**.

CIRCLE 1. Wholeness and completeness. 2. Something without beginning or end. 3. Symbolic of eternity. 4. To protect or to surround. 5. Representative of a group. 6. In logic, an argument that proves itself and is therefore inconclusive. 7. Metaphysically, symbolic of the higher or whole mind. 8. A colored or decorative circle may be symbolic of one's inner self or mandala. See **Mandala**. 9. Might be associated with oneness or God. 10. A circle around one's finger could indicate a memory or a relationship. See **Ring**.

CIRCLES (THREE INTERTWINING) 1. Liturgically, represents the Trinity, or equality, unity, and eternity. 2. Metaphysically, symbolic of wholeness: spiritually, mentally, and physically. 3. See also **Circle**.

CIRCUMCISION 1. A right of passage or initiation. See **Initiation.** 2. May represent the act of being emasculated or belittled. 3. Might be associated with a loss of sexual desire or impotence. 4. Symbolic of one's fears (i.e., fears of relationships or fears of sex). 5. Can indicate being overwhelmed by the situation. 6. May be a literal indication of prostate problems. 7. Associated with male sexuality. See **Phallus.** 8. Biblically, associated with a covenant. See **Covenant.**

CIRCUS 1. Can correspond to various parts of one's own self: personality, talents, ideas, putting on a show, etc. 2. May represent those wild portions of an individual that are viewed publicly. See **Animals.** 3. A three-ring circus may be symbolic of a balanced and orderly integration, a multifaceted activity or project, or it may represent the total chaos of same. See **Circle.** 4. Metaphorically, this place is a circus = a state of disorder, wild entertainment, disarray, and/or chaos. 5. Something providing release and/or entertainment. 6. Might indicate having one's animal instincts all under control.

CITY 1. One's community, environment, or current situation. 2. Could be associated with various aspects of the self. 3. Depending upon the imagery, might be representative of group activities (i.e., work) and teamwork or the lack of it. See **Work.** 4. The place where one acts out their game in life. See **Game.**

CIVIL WAR 1. May represent something that wars against itself. See **War.** 2. Could indicate an inner struggle. 3. An environment of aggression and hostility. See **Fight.** 4. You may also wish to see **Historical Clothing/Settings.**

CLAM 1. Could represent spiritual food or food for the soul. 2. That which is unfeeling, cold, or damp. 3. Metaphorically, to clam up = to withdraw or to stop talking. 4. Could symbolize one who is withdrawn or closed emotionally. 5. See also **Animals** and **Food.**

CLASSICAL MUSIC 1. Corresponds to being in or out of harmony. See **Music.** 2. Associated with an idea or an experience that is in tune with the self, the environment, or the universe. 3. Cooperation with others. See **Orchestra.** 4. Can correspond to the harmony of one's own emotional outpourings.

CLAW 1. May symbolize anything that en-

snares, hooks, or traps. 2. A weapon (i.e., words, actions, etc.) to hurt or wound. 3. Metaphorically, she had her claws out = she was speaking angrily. 4. You may also wish to see **Hand.**

CLAY 1. Something from which new things spring forth. 2. Something that can be molded, shaped, and formed. 3. Biblically, associated with the creation of man (Genesis 2). 4. Something that is soiled. See **Dirt.** 5. You may also wish to see **Earth.**

CLEAN 1. Depending upon the activity (i.e., if something is clean, if it needs to be cleaned, or if it is being cleaned), may indicate the need to clean up one's life. See **Housework.** 2. Symbolic of putting things in order. 3. Could symbolize purity or flawlessness. 4. May indicate a thing that is free from criticism or limitation. 5. Metaphorically, to come clean = to confess; my hands are clean = I am innocent; he cleaned out = he took all there was. 6. Could be associated with the process of or the need for a spring cleaning physically, mentally, or spiritually. 7. You may also wish to see **Maid.**

CLIFF 1. May indicate an obstacle, a difficulty, or a hurdle. 2. Could suggest a dangerous situation. 3. Associated with a fear of failing or a fear of falling in stature. 4. Could symbolize being on the edge. 5. You may also wish to see **Mountain.** 6. Jumping off a cliff may represent a current fear, a danger, or a tremendous leap of faith. 7. You may also wish to see **Ascend** and **Descend.**

CLIMB 1. Associated with making progress in your life journey. See **Journey.** 2. To ascend to a higher level of awareness or understanding. 3. May indicate the act of overcoming a situation or a difficulty. 4. Might correspond to a rise in social or worldly position. 5. You may also wish to see **Mountain** and **Ladder.**

CLOCK 1. Counts the passage of time or experiences. See **Time.** 2. The type of clock is symbolic of the message; for example: an alarm clock signifies a warning; a stopped clock indicates the end or death; a fast clock suggests that time is running out, or you are wearing yourself out. 3. May also be associated with the circle. See **Circle.**

CLOSET 1. May be associated with a small part of oneself. 2. May indicate a storeroom for memories, emotions, or experiences. 3. To shut oneself out from others. 4. To hide or to conceal. 5. Metaphorically, can be used as follows: they were closeted together = they were in consultation; he came out of the closet = he revealed something private about himself (i.e., his sexual orientation). 6. See also **House.**

CLOTHES 1. Can represent the physical, material body as a whole. 2. The outer personality, attitudes, and behaviors. 3. What you show to the world. See **Costume.** 4. One's present state of consciousness or belief systems. 5. Associated with ideas, talents, or occupations. 6. Habits you have made a part of yourself. 7. The style and type of clothing is very significant; for example: striped clothes may symbolize feeling like a prisoner in your current situation; being barely clothed could correspond to being unprepared or feeling exposed (see **Naked**); maternity clothing might indicate a pregnancy; wearing armor could represent the fact that you put up emotional or protective barriers. 8. Tight clothing may suggest that one is no longer suited for the present situation. See **Tight.** 9. Loose clothing could indicate that you have grown too big for yourself. See **Loose.** 10. Frequently, the clothing can be associated with whatever one thinks about that particular piece or brand, or with what one usually does while wearing that particular article of clothing. 11. Different pieces of clothing are symbolic of different meanings. See particular items of clothing (i.e., see **Gloves**), or different portions of body being covered (i.e., see **Hand**) for additional information.

Apron: Can correspond to a messy situation, cooking, or to one's childhood memories.

Armor: Associated with barriers (emotional or physical), protection, or self-defense.

Belt/Girdle: that which controls, restrains, or punishes.

Button: that which fastens, connects, or joins together.

Cape: that which conceals, disguises, or provides assistance (e.g., Superman).

Coat/Jacket: Thoughts and attitudes. May represent the outward personality one shows to the world.

Costume: Associated with the roles one plays in life.

Diaper: that which needs a change. A messy situation or something that needs to be pampered or babied.

Dress: Can correspond to one's image, one's appearance, or a particular experience.

Eyeglasses: Associated with things that enhance comprehension, understanding, or vision.

Foreign Clothing: Can be associated with an unusual or foreign idea. Might indicate the possibility of foreign travel.

Formal: Something showy, expensive, or superior.

Gloves: Can represent anything that one has their hands into. A source of protection.

Hat: Associated with an idea, an opinion, or an attitude.

Jeans: Can be associated with relaxation and comfort.

Life Jacket: Represents personal protection or the need for it.

Mask: Conceals or disguises the truth; the image one presents to the world.

Naked: Being exposed, losing one's facade, or having doubts about one's self worth.

Pants: One's personal identity, philosophy, or direction.

Purse: Associated with one's personal resources, security, or identity.

Raincoat: Protection from one's emotions or the emotions of others. May also be indicative of weather.

Shoes/Boots: May represent an individual's beliefs, principles, direction, or perspective.

Shorts: one's identity; that which is developing; relaxation or being unprepared.

Suit: Duty, occupation, or state of mind.

Tie: Associated with one's appearance, a close connection, or even a karmic tie.

Tuxedo: Can be associated with formality, a celebration, weddings, or funerals.

Vest: Outward personality, appearance, or emotions.

Wallet: Associated with one's personal resources, security, or identity.

Zipper: Might indicate sexual desires. That which fastens or joins together.

12. You may also wish to see **Colors.** 13. If historical or period clothing, could correspond to an antiquated idea or karmic memory. See **Historical Clothing/Settings.** 14. See also **Body.**

CLOUDS/CLOUDY 1. Can represent the inability to see clearly due to one's own mental state or emotions. See **Weather.** 2. May also be associated with freedom, independence, and buoyancy. 3. You may also wish to see **Sky.**

CLOVER 1. Corresponds to growth, freedom, and luxury. 2. That which develops in a balanced way (i.e., physically, mentally, and spiritually). 3. A four-leaf clover may indicate good luck or destiny. 4. You may also wish to see **Garden** and **Grass.**

CLOWN 1. Associated with playfulness or horseplay. 2. Could represent being a fool. 3. Metaphorically, to clown around = not to take things seriously. 4. See also **People.** 5. Might indicate a joke.

CLUB 1. Something that can be used as a weapon or for sport. See **Bat (Baseball).** 2. May be associated with a group of people who have joined together for a common interest. 3. Associated with a suit in playing cards. See **Cards.**

COACH 1. Corresponds to the one in charge of the experience, situation, or environment. 2. Could be associated with the higher self or the soul. 3. The one who provides encouragement, structure, discipline, or feedback. 4. The source of power and authority. 5. May be associated with a parental figure. 6. See **People.**

COAST 1. Symbolic of the border between two worlds, i.e., mental and physical or material and spiritual. 2. Associated with a division of people, time frames, or ideas. 3. See also **Beach** and **Sand.**

COAST GUARD 1. A patrol of the various levels of oneself, one's environment and boundaries, or one's consciousness. 2. Might represent service or a spiritual journey. See **Boat, Journey,** and **Water.** 3. Can correspond to order, power, discipline, or the relinquishment of personal will. 4. Associated with placing oneself subservient to a greater goal or good. 5. Can represent a warlike environment or situation. See **War.**

COAT 1. Thoughts and attitudes. 2. Often indicates the outward personality one shows to the world. See **Clothes.** 3. Different types of coats are symbolic of various experiences; for example: wearing a raincoat could mean you are protecting yourself from the emotions of others, or from your own emotional upset; wearing a colored coat suggests the types of emotions or attitudes one is dealing with (see **Colors**); wearing a fur coat symbolizes being insulated from your own or others' emotions. 4. Particular types of coats might be predictive of upcoming experiences, emotions, or literal weather patterns. 5. Might be a literal indication to dress more warmly.

COBWEB 1. Associated with the webs that one spins (i.e., deception, lies). 2. Can represent a little trouble that covers the situation. 3. Could indicate a possible snare or trap. 4. Confusion or uncertainty. 5. May literally be a suggestion to clean house. 6. You may also wish to see **Spider.**

COCK 1. Associated with a male chicken; one who is afraid. See **Chicken.** 2. Metaphorically, can be used as follows: he was half-cocked = he was almost ready to explode; that's a cock and bull story = an unreal, impossible story; to cock one's head = to listen, or to appear menacing; she's a little cocky = she's too self-assured. 3. You may also wish to see **Animals.** 4. May be symbolic of male sexuality. See **Phallus.** 5. Liturgically, symbolic of Peter's betrayal. (See Matthew 26:33–75.)

COCKROACH 1. Symbolic of a little irritation. 2. Can represent something dirty or contaminated. 3. See **Bug.**

COFFEE 1. Could indicate the need to stay awake (i.e., alert) in the situation. 2. How the coffee is pictured is very significant; for example: receiving a very tiny cup could indicate that one needs *to* cut back on daily consumption. 3. May represent the need to become more energized. 4. Whatever one's personal associations are with coffee are significant (i.e., relaxation, socializing, hospitality, a stimulant, etc.). 5. You may also wish to see **Food.**

COFFIN 1. Something passing; the experience of significant change. See **Funeral.** 2. Associated with the mysterious, or the unseen spiritual world. 3. Possible symbol of death. See **Death.** 4. Lacking in consciousness, vitality, or awareness. 5. Something filled with decay or uselessness. 6. May represent a container that holds one's beliefs of the afterlife. 7. Metaphorically, those kids are trying to put a nail in their mother's coffin = the kids are always giving her stress.

COLD 1. Associated with frozen emotions. See **Ice.** 2. Frigidity. 3. Could indicate being unwelcome. 4. See also **Weather.** 5. Metaphorically, may be used as follows: cold-blooded = heartless or without emotion; to catch a cold = to become sick; to throw cold water on = to discourage. 6. You may also wish to see **Ill/Illness.**

COLLAR 1. May be symbolic of willpower, or something that is around one's neck. See **Neck.** 2. Could be associated with employment (i.e., white collar, blue collar). See **Work.** 3. Metaphorically, he was collared = he was reprimanded, restrained, or spoken with. 4. You may also wish to see **Shirt** and **Clothes.**

COLLEGE 1. A place of higher learning. 2. Associated with the lessons and education provided by daily life. 3. Can correspond to the need or the opportunity to expand one's own thoughts, education, or consciousness in a particular situation. 4. What one has to teach to others or what one needs to learn from others. 5. Awareness or knowledge from a higher level. 6. May be symbolic of unresolved issues or experiences from the past. 7. A means to provide discipline to the untrained mind. 8. A situation that brings unrelated individuals together for a common goal (i.e., work may be seen as a university where one might learn cooperation, human interaction, and teamwork). 9. Can symbolize a thirst for knowledge. 10. You may also wish to see **Building, Test**, and **Teacher**.

COLLISION 1. Corresponds to a disaster, a problem, a bad situation, or a clash of viewpoints. 2. The type of collision has a great deal to do with the symbolism; for example: a car wreck is often associated with a warning about one's body, diet, stress level, or situation (see **Automobile**); a plane wreck might indicate a spiritual problem (see **Airplane**); a shipwreck could indicate a problem with one's current life journey (see **Boat** and **Journey**). 3. May be a literal warning suggesting alternate plans, doing what one can do to prevent the incident, etc.

COLORS 1. Symbolic of our experiences, our emotions, our surroundings, our consciousness, or our state of mind. 2. Something colored may be associated with a thing that is not being seen clearly. 3. Different colors have specific meanings.

Black: 1. That which is unconscious, subliminal, or subconscious. 2. The deep, mysterious, or feminine. 3. Associated with negativity, sin, or evil. 4. Can represent depression, illness, or disease. 5. Metaphorically, knowing black from white = knowing wrong from right; being in the black = having a financial gain; seeing everything in black and white = limited vision; seeing things only as true or false, right or wrong. 6. May be associated with ignorance. 7. Might indicate death. 8. Something both black and white may be symbolic of that which is good and evil, right or wrong. 9. A black aura can correspond to depression, serious illness, or even the possibility of death.

Blue: 1. Truth or insight. 2. Spiritual values, wisdom, or healing. 3. The inner voice or higher self. 4. Associated with tranquillity and calm. 5. May represent the young masculine. 6. Metaphorically, feeling blue = being depressed. 7. Corresponds to the fifth endocrine center or chakra (see **Thyroid**), and personal or divine will. 8. Metaphysically, associated with the planet Uranus. 9. The fifth color of the rainbow. 10. Corresponds to the fifth note of the musical scale (sol). 11. A blue aura can correspond to spirituality, idealism, imagination, or wisdom.

Brass: 1. Can represent a false or tarnished truth. 2. Metaphorically, can be associated with rudeness or being too forward. 3. May correspond to something that is not as worthwhile as it appears. 4. A brass aura can correspond to earthiness or to falsehood.

Brown: 1. Relates to the material, the earthy. 2. Can represent the common side of human nature. 3. Extreme practicality. 4. Might indicate passion. 5. If a rich, beautiful brown, could represent growth or the desire for accomplishment. 6. If a dull brown, might correspond to depression or negativity. 7. A brown aura can mean earthiness or low energy.

Gold 1. Usually represents spiritual truth or an insight of tremendous value. 2. Can be associated with something invaluable. 3. Relates to powers of the soul. 4. May be associated with royalty. 5. Could correspond to money or riches (though usually riches of the soul). 6. May be a message or a gift from God. 7. Might be associated with the sun or the masculine principle. 8. Sometimes symbolic of intuition. 9. Metaphorically, as good as gold = that which can be depended upon; a gold digger = one who is interested only in personal material gain. 10. A gold aura can correspond to a spiritual presence, higher awareness, or intuition.

Gray: 1. Often indicates depression or an emotional problem. 2. Can indicate cloudiness or lack of clarity. 3. Can be associated with the mysterious. 4. May indicate twilight. 5. May also be associated with the brain, age, or depression. 6. A gray aura can correspond to fear, boredom, repressed emotions, or confusion.

Green: 1. Often associated with healing and nurturing. 2. Can indicate development, growth, and vitality. 3. Metaphorically, green with envy = jealousy. 4. Related to the heart, especially in terms of human relationships and emotions. 5. Corresponds to the fourth endocrine center or chakra (see **Thymus),** and human love. 6. Metaphysically, associated with the planet Venus. 7. The fourth color of the rainbow. 8. Corresponds to the fourth note of the musical scale (fa). 9. A green aura can correspond to healing, compassion, or growth. 10. May also be associated

with money or prosperity.

Indigo: 1. Often associated with the higher mind or the soul. 2. Can correspond to spiritual fulfillment. 3. May indicate philosophy or deep science. 4. The color of calm. 5. Corresponds to the sixth endocrine center or chakra (see **Pineal**); selfless service. 6. Metaphysically, associated with the planet Mercury. 7. The sixth color of the rainbow. 8. Corresponds to the sixth note of the musical scale (la). 9. An indigo aura can correspond to spiritual development or the presence of great spirituality.

Ivory: 1. Somewhat clouded from the truth. 2. May be associated with resources or ideas that were obtained through negative means (i.e., ivory tusks). 3. A metaphor for detachment and aloofness: an ivory tower. 4. An ivory aura can correspond to something partially revealed or that which possesses some degree of spirituality.

Orange: 1. Associated with creativity. 2. Can symbolize temptation. 3. Might be associated with activated wisdom, hidden power, or vigor. 4. Could symbolize sexuality. 5. Corresponds to the second endocrine center or chakra (see **Lyden**). 6. Metaphysically, associated with the planet Neptune. 7. The second color of the rainbow. 8. Corresponds to the second note of the musical scale (re). 9. An orange aura can correspond to vitality, energy, sexuality, or a focus on the physical and mental realms.

Pink: 1. Associated with higher or divine love. 2. Can correspond to the young feminine. 3. Symbolic of happiness and generosity. 4. Metaphorically, in the pink = being in fine health; tickled pink = very happy; seeing through rose-colored glasses = always seeing things in a favorable or optimistic light. 5. A pink aura can correspond to love, optimism, or joy.

Purple: 1. May be associated with royalty. 2. Can relate to mystical or sacred vision. 3. May represent an honor or privilege of the highest order (i.e., a Purple Heart). 4. Symbolic of spiritual development. 5. Can also be associated with selflessness or personal suffering. 6. A purple aura can correspond to spiritual power.

Red: 1. Anger or rage. 2. Trouble or misunderstanding. 3. Associated with human lust and desire, identity, or base creativity. 4. Associated with energy or power. 5. The life force. See **Blood.** 6. Corresponds to the first endocrine center or chakra (see **Gonads**), and sexuality. 7. Might be symbolic of evil or aggression. 8. Metaphorically, she saw red = she was very angry. 9. Metaphysically, associated with the planet Saturn. 10. The first color of the rainbow. 11. Corresponds to the first note of the musical scale (do). 12. A red aura can correspond to anger, lust, or energy.

Silver: 1. Often associated with resources, money, or something of material value. 2. May represent a spiritual message or insight. 3. Associated with recognition (i.e., a silver anniversary). 4. Metaphorically, refers to a persuasive and eloquent individual: a silver tongue. 5. Could correspond to the silver cord (i.e., the connection between one's soul and physical body). 6. A silver aura can correspond to spirituality or intuition.

Violet: 1. Associated with great spirituality or spiritual dedication. 2. Usually considered the highest spiritual color (sometimes substituted for white). 3. Associated with being at one with God.

4. Corresponds to the seventh endocrine center or chakra (see **Pituitary**), and perfect attunement and unity. 5. Metaphysically, associated with the planet Jupiter. 6. The seventh color of the rainbow. 7. Corresponds to the seventh note of the musical scale (ti). 8. A violet aura can correspond to spiritual dedication or mastery.

White: 1. Associated with purity, innocence, virginity, and holiness. 2. Often corresponds to the presence of Spirit. 3. Can represent the highest spiritual color since it contains all the rest. 4. Indicates that which is complete unto itself. 5. May be associated with the conscious or known. 6. Something both black and white may be symbolic of that which is good and evil, right and wrong. 7. A white aura can correspond to spiritual dedication or mastery.

Yellow: 1. Associated with great intelligence and wisdom. 2. May symbolize personal power. 3. Could correspond to the sun, brightness, or a cheery disposition. 4. Metaphorically, may correspond to cowardice (i.e., a yellow streak) or cheap sensationalism (i.e., yellow journalism). 5. Corresponds to the third endocrine center or chakra (see **Adrenals**). 6, Metaphysically, associated with the planet Mars. 7. The third color of the rainbow. 8. Corresponds to the third note of the musical scale (mi). 9. A yellow aura can correspond to intellect, wisdom, or creativity.

4. Depending on the imagery, you may also wish to see **Light** or **Dark.**

COLUMN 1. Something upright, supportive, and sturdy. See **Concrete.** 2. Could represent ancient knowledge or wisdom. See **Library.** 3. Might be associated with being straitlaced or narrowly focused. 4. Depending on imagery, you may also wish to see **Historical Clothing/Settings.**

COMA 1. Associated with being unconscious to the external environment. See **Sleep.** 2. Symbolic of not paying attention to the situation. 3. Metaphorically, she puts me in a coma = she is extremely boring. 4. May be a literal warning to see a doctor.

COMB 1. Associated with getting one's ideas in order. 2. Could represent the need to clean your mind. 3. Metaphorically, to comb the house = to look everywhere. 4. See also **Hair.**

COMET 1. An incoming insight, experience, opportunity, or obstacle. 2. A thing that is brilliant or exceptional. 3. A falling comet could indicate a problem, a demotion, or a descent, or it might symbolize a death. See **Descend** and **Death.** 4. A meteor shower could suggest confusion, lots of activity, or conflicting ideas. 5. See also **Star.**

COMPASS 1. A source of direction, information, or guidance. See **Direction.** 2. The need for direction or the capacity to give it. 3. Metaphysically, a compass can symbolize the whole. See **Circle.** 4. Enclosing or drawing together. 5. May be associated with one's soul journey. See **Journey.**

COMPLIMENT 1. Can represent the need to give or receive praise. 2. Might indicate congratulations or success. 3. Could represent your feelings about yourself.

COMPUTER 1. Associated with the mind, rapid intellect, or brilliance. 2. Could correspond to memory, knowledge, or insight.

See **Book.** 3. Might symbolize one's work situation. See **Work.** 4. Meaning may have a great deal to do with one's personal association with computers (i.e., playing computer games, or the fear of new technology).

CONCRETE 1. Something real, stable, or unyielding. 2. Associated with a firm foundation. See **Floor.** 3. Something that holds things together. 4. Could represent a state of permanence. 5. Metaphorically, to make something concrete = to make it real or specific. 6. Depending on the imagery, you may also wish to see **House.**

CONDOM 1. May suggest the potential for a literal or figurative pregnancy. See **Pregnancy.** 2. The act of preventing creativity. 3. Associated with preparedness, the proper precautions, or safe sex. 4. Depending on imagery, you may also wish to see **Sex.** 5. See also **phallus.**

CONDUCTOR (MUSICAL) 1. The individual responsible for people or activities working together in harmony. See **Boss.** 2. May correspond to the need or the ability to control one's emotional nature. 3. Could refer to the importance of music in life. See **Music.** 4. Might indicate the desire or the need for relaxation. 5. You may also wish to see **Hear** and **People.**

CONDUCTOR (TRAIN) 1. Corresponds to the one in charge of the journey. See **Journey.** 2. Could be associated with the higher self or soul. 3. Represents the one responsible for the experience or livelihood of those in the same situation. 4. The source of power and authority. 5. May be associated with a parental figure. 6. You may also wish to see **Train.** 7. See also **People.**

CONFEDERACY/CONFEDERATE 1. Can

represent those who are united in conspiracy. 2. May indicate seceding from a group or an activity. 3. Those who are joined together in a losing battle. 4. May be associated with the South. See **South.** 5. You may also wish to see **Historical Clothing/ Settings.**

CONFUCIANISM 1. The philosophy of Confucius (sixth century B.C.). 2. Corresponds to wisdom, benevolence, devotion, peace, and respect for all human life. 3. His philosophy was summed up by, "What you do not want done unto yourself, do not do to others." 4. Associated with striving to respond ideally in each of life's situations.

CONSTRUCTION 1. A situation, idea, experience, or relationship that is being built or is under review. See **Contractor.** 2. Could be associated with work. See **Work.**

CONTAINER 1. Receptivity; associated with the feminine. See **Womb.** 2. What one is currently holding in mind. See **Box.** 3. Associated with the physical body or the soul.

CONTRACTOR 1. Associated with a creator of one's life or experience. 2. Whatever is being built will have a great deal to do with the symbolism; for example: building a house could represent the need to care for oneself. (See **House** or **Building.**) 3. Might symbolize something that refurbishes or strengthens the situation. 4. You may also wish to see **People.**

CONVENT 1. A spiritual haven, resting place, or place of safety. 2. A place that is free from the outside material world. 3. A place of worship. See **Church.** 4. A spiritual community. 5. May be associated with religious vows: chastity, poverty, obedience, and service.. 6. You may also wish to see **Nun.**

CONVICT 1. Associated with one who is being controlled or trapped by circumstances, conditions, feelings, others, or the environment. 2. One who no longer enjoys personal freedoms. 3. Metaphorically, being a prisoner of love = losing independence because of your feelings toward another. 4. That part of yourself that is unable to see the outside world. See **Shadow.** 5. See also **People.**

COOK 1. May indicate something that is under a lot of heat (i.e., questioning, inspection). 2. Something being devised or planned. 3. Metaphorically, what's cooking = what's going on; let's get cooking = let's get started; plans that are half-baked = plans only partially thought through or prepared. 4. Cooking itself may indicate how ideas are being prepared, or may suggest literal and specific dietary changes. 5. You may also wish to see **Food** and **People.**

COP 1. Corresponds to the law (manmade or universal). 2. Can represent one's own conscience. 3. That which provides regulation, safety, and moral guidelines. 4. Associated with keeping (or the need for) order and control. 5. Introducing into the situation some element to bring order out of disorder. 6. The clothing of the police officer may be important; for example: a plainclothes officer may indicate man-made laws; a uniformed police officer may be symbolic of spiritual, karmic, or universal laws. 7. A police station indicates a place where law and order are maintained; could correspond to moral beliefs or the higher self. See **Building.** 8. You may also wish to see **People.**

CORN 1. Associated with the harvest. 2. Could indicate kernels of truth, wisdom, or important ideas for consumption. 3. Metaphorically, can be used as follows: corn = simple and basic humor; that was corny = that which was supposed to be funny and wasn't. 4. See **Food.** 5. You may also wish to see **Plant.**

CORNER 1. Can correspond to being cornered or unable to escape. 2. Metaphorically, to cut corner = to take shortcuts; to turn the corner = to have survived the situation 3. Might suggest a meeting place or where two divergent points come together. 4. Could suggest the need for a change of directions. 5. You may also wish to see **House.**

CORNERSTONE 1. The foundation. 2. That from which all else springs forth, or that which holds everything together. 3. See **Building.** 4. You may also wish to see **Cement.**

CORPSE 1. Could represent a mistake that has been found or something an individual wishes had remained dead and buried (or hidden). 2. Something that has come to an end. 3. Metaphorically, he's a corpse = he's lifeless or useless. 4. See also **Death** and **Funeral.** 5. You may also wish to see **Body.**

COSTUME 1. The roles one plays in life. See **Drama.** 2. Also associated with ideas, thoughts, and experiences. 3. See **Clothes.** 4. How one wishes to appear to others. 5. Something that a person hides behind. See **Mask.**

COUCH 1. Associated with rest, relaxation, sleep, or laziness. See **Furniture.** 2. Metaphorically, can be used as follows: a couch potato = one who wastes time by watching television; it was couched = it was hidden. 3. If on the couch with another person, may indicate togetherness (i.e., a love seat). 4. You may also wish to see **Chair** or **Bed/Bedroom.**

COUNTERFEIT 1. Something that is false. 2. Can correspond to the need to look more closely at the situation. 3. May be associated with worthlessness. 4. You may also wish to see **Money**.

COUPLE 1. May represent a joining, a union, or the agreement to work with another. 2. See **Wedding**. 3. A promise or a commitment. 4. Might be a literal indication of a relationship that will come to pass. 5. Could be a reconciliation with oneself or shadow. See **Shadow**. 6. You may also wish to see **People**.

COURT 1. Represents a place where an individual is put on trial. 2. To be judged or criticized by one's current activities, thoughts, or emotions. 3. The place where one is tried against man-made, moral, or spiritual laws. 4. Associated with focusing on past deeds or behaviors. 5. You may also wish to see **Building, Judge,** or **Police/Police Station**.

COVENANT 1. The most lasting type of promise. 2. Associated with your true spiritual nature and your relationship with God. See **God**. 3. Biblically, associated with God's promises of his covenant with humankind, including the rainbow (Genesis 9: 12–17), the rite of circumcision (Genesis 17: 11–13), the Sabbath (Exodus 31:16), the Ten Commandments (Exodus 20 and 34: 28), etc.

COW 1. May represent the earthy side of the feminine. See **Womb**. 2. Can be associated with passivity or nature. 3. That which gives nurturing. 4. In India, representative of the source of life itself (food, fuel, and warmth). 5. In ancient Egypt, the symbol of love and joy; the goddess Hathor. 6. Might refer to human beings en masse (i.e., like a group of cattle). 7. Metaphorically, she's a real cow = she's very matronly and unappealing. 8. Biblically, associated with famine and plenty (Genesis 41). 9. You may also wish to see **Animal**. .

COWBOY 1. Associated with one who herds livestock or people. See **Executive**. 2. Could correspond to one's driving instinct. 3. You may also wish to see **Cattle**. 4. You may also wish to see **Historical Clothing/Settings**.

CRAB 1. Metaphor for a negative or bad temper. See **Animals**. 2. Associated with complaining or finding fault. 3. Corresponds to withdrawing from a situation; to back out. 4. Possessing a hard exterior or impenetrable emotions. See **Shell**. 5. Astrologically, one of the twelve signs of the zodiac. See **Cancer (Zodiac).**

CRACK 1. May indicate either a potential opening or a possible negative condition. 2. If a crack appears in a building, it may represent the condition of that symbolic portion of your life. See **Building** or **House**. 3. A crack in a roadway or path could symbolize a potential problem in your current direction. See **Road**. 4. A crack in a wall may indicate that stubborn old patterns, emotions, or belief systems are crumbling. See **Wall**. 5. Metaphorically, crack = drugs.

CRADLE 1. Associated with a new beginning, a new project, or a literal baby. See **Birth** and **Baby**. 2. Might be associated with a small or immature bed. See **Bed/Bedroom**. 3. That which one nurtures, relishes, or cradles.

CRASH 1. Corresponds to a fall, an unexpected problem, or a disaster. 2. May indicate a financial collapse. 3. What's crashing is highly significant; for example: an automobile crash could suggest that the individ-

ual is headed for a physical problem (see **Automobile**); an airplane crash might suggest a spiritual emergency or difficulty (see **Airplane**). 4. May be a literal warning of an upcoming crash, suggesting that one make alternate travel plans. 5. See also **Accident.**

CRAWL 1. Something that just barely creeps along. 2. May indicate one who is lazy, lax, or incapable, especially if a person is crawling. 3. See **Bug**. 4. Could suggest humility or the need for it. 5. May represent something that has just gotten moving or started. 6. You may also wish to see **People.**

CREDIT CARD 1. Something borrowed, bestowed, or given unto another. 2. Can be associated with heavy spending, personal debt, and extravagance. 3. Borrowed Money. See **Money.** 4. Metaphorically, can be used as follows: to give credit = to give recognition, approval, or commendation; she gets the credit = it was her idea. 5. To pay something back in time or in a timely manner.

CRIB 1. Associated with a new beginning, a new project, or a literal baby. See **Birth** and **Baby**. 2. Might be associated with a small or immature bed. See **Bed/Bedroom**. 3. That which one nurtures, relishes, or cradles.

CRIME/CRIMINAL 1. The act of doing something one should not have done. 2. Something unlawful, immoral, or out of character. 3. Might be associated with the villainous parts of oneself. 4. Could correspond to intrigue, deception, or actual criminal activity. 5. Metaphorically, that's a crime = that's too bad (cynical or serious). 6. The hidden portion of oneself. See **Shadow.** 7. You may also wish to see **People.**

CRIPPLED 1. Hindrance, disadvantage, or weakness. 2. Corresponds to something that cripples or cages. See **Cage.** 3. If a physical handicap, you may wish to see the portion of the body that is affected or see **Body.** 4. Metaphorically, he crippled the situation = he damaged or stopped the situation.

CROCODILE 1. Because they have a very prominent mouth, crocodiles are usually associated with dangerous or biting words that have been spoken. See **Teeth.** 2. Also symbolic of a tough hide. 3. See also **Alligator** and **Animals.**

CROOK 1. Can correspond to trying to take something illegally. 2. Associated with taking advantage or being taken advantage of. 3. Something that is stealing one's ideas, energy, emotions, or vitality. 4. The villainous aspects of oneself. See **Villain.** 5. Someone who takes what is not his by force. 6. Metaphorically, by hook or by crook = to achieve one's goals at any cost. 7. Might indicate something bent, unsavory, or immoral. 8. See also **People.**

CROSS 1. May indicate a surrender or crucifixion. See **Crucifix/Crucifixion.** 2. Suggestive of anger or irritation. 3. Could represent spirituality or the need for spiritual discipline. 4. A cross on a document might symbolize a signature or a personal commitment. 5. A spiritual journey. See **Journey.** 6. Metaphorically, can be used as follows: to be cross = to be angry; to cross someone = to go against them; to cross one's fingers = to wish for luck; to cross one's heart = to tell the truth; to cross someone's palm = to bribe someone; to take up one's cross = to begin to fight for one's perspective; to cross someone's path = to meet a person by accident; to cross over = to cooperate with another's viewpoint, also to die. 7. Associated with the surrendering of one's lower self to the higher self. See **Christ.** 8.

Might suggest the crossroads of a situation (i.e., the end or the moment of choice). 9. Can represent one's burdens, problems, or difficulties.

CROW 1. Might be associated with change, trial, or even death. See **Bird.** 2. Metaphorically, can be used as follows: as the crow flies = as directly as possible (i.e., a straight line); she crowed over the new baby = she was very expressive and joyful about the new baby.

CROWD 1. Often representative of work or family life or wherever one may be involved in a group situation. 2. Depending on the imagery; you may wish to see **Work, School,** or **Church.** 3. Can represent a busy mind, a crowded schedule, or something that is complicated or uncontrollable. 4. See also **People.**

CROWN 1. May indicate a brilliant idea, a crowning achievement, one's ego, or success. See **Hat.** 2. Associated with power and authority. 3. Might represent a reward or an honor. 4. Mastery over oneself or the situation. 5. Could symbolize the crown or seventh chakra (pituitary). See **Chakras.** 6. You may also wish to see **King** or **Queen.**

CROWN OF THORNS 1. Liturgically, a symbol for humiliation and suffering. 2. Corresponds to a mission or journey of selfless service. See **Journey.** 3. Associated with Jesus and Christianity. See **Christ.**

CRUCIFIX/CRUCIFIXION 1. Associated with Jesus and Christianity. See **Christ.** 2. A sign of faith. See **Christianity.** 3. Could represent selflessness or the need to surrender one's ego. See **Cross.** 4. Might correspond to being publicly humiliated or ridiculed. 5.

Associated with pain and suffering. 6. May suggest torture or a tormenting situation.

CRUISE 1. Associated with a spiritual journey or experience. See **Boat** and **Journey.** 2. An easy, enjoyable experience. 3. May be associated with the need to enjoy life rather than racing through it; going with the flow. 4. Could indicate the need for more relaxation and recreation. 5. You may also wish to see **Water.**

CRUST 1. Something that is hard to get through. 2. May indicate that the outer exterior is harsher or harder than it is once you get inside. 3. Could correspond to the parameters that hold everything together. 4. You may also wish to see **Food.**

CRY 1. Corresponds to the release of emotions. 2. May indicate a severe disappointment. 3. Might symbolize a cleansing. 4. Metaphorically, to cry out = to complain; a far cry = something very different than expected; an outcry = a loud protest. 5. Could be associated with feeling sorry for what you have done. 6. You may also wish to see **Eyes**.

CRYSTAL/CRYSTAL BALL 1. Associated with clarity, purity, and higher energies. 2. May indicate spiritual insight or vision. See **Eyes**. 3. Can correspond to being a receiver of energies, information, or insights (especially a crystal ball). 4. Metaphorically, seeing things crystal clear = having perfect insight. 5. A crystal ball may symbolize the ability to foretell future trends or experiences. 6. Associated with the gift of vision. 7. You may also wish to see **Jewels/Jewelry.**

CUBA 1. Corresponds primarily to whatever an individual thinks of Cuba or Cubans (i.e., associated with revolutionary change, poverty, illegal activities, oppression, an island, the tropics, etc.). 2. May be indicative of a foreign visitor or travel.

CUP 1. Represents a mission, a duty, a higher purpose, or a journey. See **Journey.** 2. Receiving a cup can be associated with receiving or taking charge of the situation for it is now in one's own hands. 3. Might indicate that which is one's share or portion. 4. Liturgically, associated with the blood of Christ, or that which holds the soul. See **Christ.** 5. Might correspond to the Holy Grail. See **Holy Grail.** 6. Liturgically, associated with Communion and the words of Jesus (Matthew 26:27–29 and 39–42).

CUPBOARD 1. May be associated with a small part of oneself. 2. May indicate a storage place for memories, emotions, or experiences. See **Closet.** 3. To hide or conceal the self or a portion of the self (i.e., emotions) from others. 4. Depending on the imagery, you may also wish to see **House.**

CURB 1. Can correspond to the need for restraint. 2. Something that hems in the situation. 3. Might indicate the need for careful and close scrutiny. 4. Could indicate a minor obstacle or barrier. 5. See also **Road.**

CURTAIN 1. Associated with the beginning or the end of something. See **Drama.** 2. Something that conceals, cloaks, hides, or obscures vision. 3. May indicate the need for privacy; one who is too private; encouragement to be more private about one's personal matters. 4. Ideas, experiences, or attitudes that cover one's environment or surroundings. 5. Could indicate a separation or a joining together, depending on whether the curtains were opened or closed. 6. Metaphorically, a drawn or black curtain indicates death or the end of something; a raised curtain implies a new beginning or a new revelation.

CUT 1. Disconnection or separation. See **Knife.** 2. Could symbolize the opening of something (i.e., emotions that have been held in). 3. May be something that affects or hurts deeply. 4. Metaphorically, associated with the following: to cut something or someone = to ignore or to skip out on; to cut (liquor) = to dilute; to cut something out = to stop or omit; to cut across = to take a shorter route; to cut back = to reduce; to cut off = to intersect, to stop someone in mid-sentence, to stop speaking to an individual; to cut short = to bring to an end quickly; to cut loose = to become less guarded, more outgoing; to cut up = to play around; it's a cut above = it's better than the rest; it's cut and dried = simple and straightforward; a cutting remark = a hurtful statement. 5. Depending on the imagery you may also wish to see **Wound.**

CYMBALS 1. May represent the need for music and harmony. See **Music.** 2. Depending on imagery, could be used as a message, an announcement, or warning.

CYST 1. Something that has gotten under one's skin. 2. Can correspond to something irritating, unsightly, or that feeds off itself. 3. May indicate holding on to a problem or a bad situation. 4. Might represent self-criticism or punishment, or negative aspects of yourself that you have refused to part with. 5. See also **Body.** 6. May symbolize emotional distress or pressure. 7. Could indicate a literal health problem. 8. You may also wish to see **Wound.**

D

1. *The fourth letter of the alphabet.* 2. *The Roman numeral for 500.* 3. *Chemically, the symbol for deuterium.* 4. *Musically, the second note.* 5. *Numerologically, equivalent to four.* 6. *Scholastically, poor achievement, barely passing.* 7. *Associated with Domini, (Lord) from A.D. (anno Domini, year of our Lord).* 8. *In physics, a symbol for density.* 9. *In Greek, delta.*

DAGGER 1. Something that cuts, divides, separates, or wounds (i.e., words, aggression, anger, opposing viewpoints, etc.). 2. Can correspond to aggression, hostility, or forced dominance. 3. Could indicate something with a sharp point. 4. Metaphorically, to stare daggers = to look at with hatred. 5. Can represent an aggressive male figure. See **Phallus.** 6. May indicate evil. 7. Might be associated with an activity that needs to be cut out. See **Cut.** 8. Depending on imagery, you may also wish to see **Wound.**

DALMATIAN 1. May be associated with one's need to see things in black and white. 2. Because of their association with firemen, Dalmatians may indicate a hot situation or literally be a warning sign of a potential fire. See **Fire.** 3. See also **Dog.** 4. You may also wish to see **Animals.**

DAM 1. Associated with repressing one's feelings or emotions. 2. Can indicate a possible emotional outburst. 3. Something confined or restrained. 4. Might symbolize a reservoir of hope or spiritual depth. 5. See also **Water.**

DANCE 1. Corresponds to a rhythmic movement; to step out with precision. 2. May suggest the dance of life. See **Journey.** 3. To join in partnership with an individual or a group. 4. To work together harmoniously; may suggest the need for harmony and cooperation. 5. May symbolize the need to watch your step. 6. Depending on the imagery, you may wish to see **Music.**

DANGER 1. A warning of injury, danger, or risk. 2. May indicate the need for caution. 3. That which is at risk. 4. Often a literal warning of possible dangers, suggesting alternative plans or choices.

DARK 1. Devoid of light or spirit. 2. Suggestive of the unknown. 3. Where one meets oneself; coming in contact with one's fears. See **Shadow.** 4. Unable to see or think clearly. 5. That which is gloomy or disheartening. 6. Might symbolize the mysterious, the unknown, or the unconscious. 7. Could correspond to something evil or to illness. 8. To be without wisdom, knowledge, or insight. 9. Metaphorically, to be in the dark = to be kept unaware; to darken one's door = to visit without welcome. 10. Depending on the imagery, you may also wish to see **Colors.**

DARTH VADER 1. Associated with the embodiment of evil. See **Evil.** 2. Could correspond to the dark side of one's own nature or self. See **Shadow.** 3. Might represent an evil or an undesirable father. See **Father.**

DATING 1. May represent a joining, a union, or the agreement to work with another.

2. That with which one is becoming involved. 3. Might be a literal situation that will come to pass. 4. You may also wish to see **Wedding.**

DAUGHTER 1. Often suggests aspects of the relationship you possess with your own daughter (i.e., how your daughter appears may be symbolic of your attitude or feelings toward her). 2. Could indicate a suggestion or a warning in terms of your child's welfare. 3. Associated with that childish part of oneself. See **Child.** 4. May be symbolic of youthful femininity. See **Woman.** 5. That part of yourself that may still need direction. 6. See also **People.**

DAVID 1. Biblically, symbolic of victory over tremendous obstacles and odds. 2. Associated with possessing dominion. 3. Representative of a forerunner of Christ. 4. Metaphysically, corresponds to divine love manifested in the earth. 5. Can correspond to a promise of the inevitable. 6. See **Star of David.**

DAWN 1. Associated with the start of something new or the awakening of a fresh perspective. 2. Symbolic of growing awareness or enlightenment. 3. Can correspond to the appearance and growth of light. See **Light.** 4. Metaphorically, it finally dawned on him = he finally understood. 5. The awakening of new forces, healing, a fresh idea, or a new beginning. 6. Something that gradually becomes clear to the mind's eye. 7. You may also wish to see **Sun/Sunlight.**

DAY 1. Associated with a fresh start or a new beginning. See **Dawn.** 2. Metaphorically, the difference between day and night = complete opposites (i.e., good and evil). 3. Could suggest clarity, truth, or insight. See **Light.** 4. Depending on imagery, you may wish to

see **Sun/Sunlight** and **Clouds/Cloudy.**

DEAD BODIES 1. Associated with ideas, experiences, biases, or attitudes that are dead weight, or no longer useful. See **Death.** 2. That which is lifeless. 3. Something that needs to be buried or put behind oneself. See **Funeral.** 4. You may also wish to see **Body.**

DEAD END 1. Could indicate you are going nowhere in the situation. See **Sign.** 2. Associated with the need for a new direction. 3. Might symbolize obstacles in one's life journey. See **Journey.** 4. The need to make a new choice. 5. Corresponds to traveling a path to nowhere. 6. You may also wish to see **Road.**

DEAD SEA SCROLLS 1. Can correspond to secret mysteries or ancient wisdom. See **Book** and **Library.** 2. An important message, especially from the past. See **Message/Messenger**. 3. May be associated with religious doctrines or sacredness. 4. Could correspond to the scriptures. See **Bible**. 5. May represent laws or customs. 6. Might be associated with knowledge or wisdom that is no longer applicable or understood. 7. Might correspond to soul memory or the Akashic Records. See **Akashic Records**. 8. You may also wish to see **Ancient**.

DEATH 1. Represents the end of an idea, an experience, a project, or a relationship. 2. Symbolic of a transition or a change. 3. Could correspond to the approach of a condition or an experience that will tremendously challenge your current understanding of yourself. 4. An awakening of the subconscious mind. 5. A literal announcement of an event that may come to pass. 6. Loss of a characteristic or talent in your own life that is often symbolized by the individual who died. 7. That which makes all things equal. 8. Could be symbolic of your own current understanding of the afterlife. 9. Could correspond to the need to show greater love and compassion toward the one who died or else they may die emotionally. 10. May represent the state of feeling separated from oneself, others, or one's relationship with God. 11. Metaphorically, he's at death's door = he's very sick. 12. Associated with thirteen in the tarot. See **Tarot**. 13. You may also wish to see **Funeral**.

DE BRICASSART, RALPH, OF *THE THORN BIRDS* 1. May symbolize desire or forbidden love. 2. Associated with the church or a professional authority. See **Priest**. 3. The pursuit of spirituality. 4. Might correspond to heartbreak, unrequited love, or love that is painful.

DEER 1. Associated with independence, nature, and the wild. 2. A female deer may represent a female aspect or relationship; a male deer may represent a male aspect or a male relationship. See **Animals** and **Woman** or **Man**. 3. Metaphorically, both a buck and a doe (dough) may represent money. 4. See also **Buck** and **Doe**.

DEFECATE 1. To spoil with a part of oneself. 2. To cleanse one's impurities physically, mentally, or spiritually. 3. Done in public, it is often associated with showing off, making a mistake, or doing something one shouldn't have done. 4. See also **Bathroom**. 5. Could indicate the need to release toxins or impurities from one's physical, mental, or spiritual systems. 6. Something in the feces might correspond to a health problem. 7. May be a literal need to defecate.

DEPRESSION (ERA) 1. May correspond to financial difficulties, unemployment, or problems in business activities. 2. Can represent sadness, gloominess, low energy, or personal hardships. See **Depression (Mental State)**. 3. Might suggest the possibility of tough or hard times. 4. That which is lower in value. 5. Might be associated with one who suppresses, controls, or dominates another. 6. You may also wish to see **Money**. 7. You may also wish to see **Historical Clothing/Settings**.

DEPRESSION (MENTAL STATE) 1. Associated with sadness, moodiness, gloominess, or personal hardships. See **Emotion**. 2. Depending on the imagery, can symbolize actual problems that need to be dealt with consciously. 3. You may also wish to see **Depression (Era)**.

DESCEND 1. Might correspond to failure, a demotion, or no longer being in control. See **Fall**. 2. May be associated with the completion of a hurdle or an obstacle successfully overcome. See **Mountain**. 3. Depending on imagery, could represent an obstacle, dark times, or the completion of something in one's life journey. See **Journey**. 4. To lower one's level of awareness, understanding, principles, or morals.

DESERT 1. That which is not fertile, is bleak, or is abandoned. 2. Being caught without the proper insight or equipment. 3. May correspond to a wasteland. 4. Uncharted territory. 5. Could suggest desertion, abandonment, or failure. 6. Lacking water (insight or spirit). 7. Could be symbolic of hopelessness or pessimism. 8. Might correspond to a dry spell in one's own life. 9. You may also wish to see **Egypt/Egyptian** and **Earth**.

DESK 1. Can correspond to one's work situation and environment. See **Work**. 2. May indicate one's attitudes, position, stature, thoughts, foundation, or belief system. See **Furniture.** 3. The appearance of the desk will have a great deal to do with the imagery (i.e., clean, disorganized, broken–down, etc.). 4. Can correspond to study or education. See **School.** 5. Might suggest putting one's desk (work, thoughts, etc.) in order. 6. You may also wish to see **Table.**

DESSERT 1. Something that is tempting. 2. Can correspond to one's own personal desires, indulgences, satisfaction, or physical appetites. See **Food.** 3. Can indicate a reward or some merit. 4. Something that comes at the end. 5. Literally, may be suggestive of too much sugar in the system. 6. Metaphorically, she received her just desserts = she got what she deserved. 7. That which is sweet. 8. Depending on the imagery, you may also wish to see **Teeth.**

DETECTIVE 1. Can correspond to the act of or the need for close inspection, scrutiny, and investigation. 2. Could indicate some unseen activity, a sense of intrigue, or mystery. 3. The curious part of oneself. 4. Might suggest the need for additional information or insight. 5. See also **People.**

DETOUR 1. Might be a warning sign regarding the need for another direction. See **Sign.** 2. Could be associated with unforeseen obstacles or experiences in one's current journey. See **Journey.** 3. You may also wish to see **Road.**

DEVIL 1. Associated with temptation. 2. That which is evil. See **Evil.** 3. Could represent the dark side of one's nature (i.e., hatred, jealousy, immorality, etc.). 4. The shadow part of yourself. See **Shadow.** 5. Wickedness. 6. That part of you or that aspect of the environment that threatens to possess you. 7. Metaphorically, he's a poor devil = he's an unlucky individual; between the devil and the deep blue sea = between two negative choices or conditions; give the devil his due = to acknowledge that good exists even in a person one doesn't like; gone to the devil = it's in bad shape or disrepair. 8. Something one fears. 9. Associated with fifteen in the tarot. See **Tarot.** 10. You may also wish to see **People.**

DIAMOND 1. Information, insight, or an idea of great value. See **Jewels/Jewelry.** 2. Could correspond to spiritual vision or understanding. See **Crystal/Crystal Ball.** 3. Metaphorically, a diamond in the rough = having great worth or talent that needs to be developed. 4. May be symbolic of marriage or the start of an important relationship or union. See **Marriage.** 5. Something that is hard, stable, and nearly indestructible. 6. Might indicate spiritual or material treasure. 7. Associated with a suit in playing cards. See **Cards.**

DIAPER 1. Something that needs a change. 2. Can correspond to a need to be pampered or babied. See **Baby.** 3. Could indicate a messy or unpleasant situation. 4. You may also wish to see **Clothes.**

DICE 1. Associated with taking a risk or participating in an uncertain venture. See **Gambling.** 2. Often corresponds to foolish or wasteful actions. 3. Something that is chancy. 4. Metaphorically, no dice = no deal. 5. Depending on the imagery, you may wish to see **Game.** 6. Might indicate good luck.

DIG 1. That with which you are involved or becoming involved. 2. Associated with a search or the act of mining for something (i.e., information, insights, etc.). 3. Metaphorically, he dug up a lot of dirt = he uncovered a lot of unfavorable information. 4. Depending on imagery, you may also wish to see **Dirt** and **Earth.**

DINING ROOM/TABLE 1. Corresponds to what one is feeding the body, mind, or soul. See **House.** 2. May represent literal suggestions of dietary changes or recommendations. 3. A place where people come together to share community, experiences, and ideas. 4. What you eat becomes a part of you. See **Food.** 5. See also **Furniture.**

DINOSAUR 1. Associated with the extinct or the outdated. See **Antique.** 2. Metaphorically, he's a dinosaur = he is out of touch with contemporary thought. 3. May indicate one's own primitive nature. See **Beast.** 4. See also **Animals.**

DIPLOMA 1. Often corresponds to some type of graduation or a successful accomplishment. 2. May indicate learning a particular lesson. 3. See also **School.**

DIRECTION 1. Getting direction (guidance). 2. Could represent the ability to give guidance or counseling or the need to accept it. 3. Turning to the right can be associated with the future, that which is conservative, or it may indicate a proper choice. See **Right** 4. Turning to the left can be associated with the past, that which is liberal, or it may indicate a wrong choice. See **Left.** 5. See other specific directions; for example, see **North.** 6. See also **Journey.** 7. Depending on imagery, you may also wish to see **Road.**

DIRIGIBLE 1. Often associated with high ideals, thoughts, or dreams. 2. Could correspond to being full of hot air. 3. Something that floats on air. See **Air.** 4. You may also wish to see **Zeppelin.**

DIRT 1. Associated with things that are common, filthy, or improper. 2. Can correspond to something that needs to be changed in a person or situation. 3. May represent the need to become more appropriate in the ways in which the world sees you. See **Clothes.** 4. Metaphorically, to get the dirt on someone = to hear gossip or information that is unfavorable; to eat dirt = to regret one's own words. 5. May be symbolic of something illegal or immoral. 6. Biblically, God made man from the dust of the ground (Genesis 2). See **Clay.** 7. You may also wish to see **Earth.**

DISABLED 1. Something that hinders, causes a disadvantage, or weakens. 2. Corresponds with being crippled or in a cage. See **Cage.** 3. If a physical handicap, you may wish to see the portion of the body that is handicapped or see **Body.**

DISAPPEAR 1. Can correspond to something that is out of sight. 2. Unable to comprehend or to understand. 3. Something that ends or dies. See **Death.** 4. Could indicate that something has been forgotten.

DISASTER 1. May be symbolic of a disaster or a misfortune. 2. Might be a literal warning encouraging a different course of action. 3. A bad idea. 4. Suggests cautionary measures. 5. Depending on imagery, you may also wish to see **Accident.**

DISHES 1. Can correspond to ideas (i.e., food for thought). See **Food.** 2. Something on one's plate. 3. Washing dishes could indicate cleaning out old ideas; eating off of someone else's plate may symbolize cooperation, stealing their ideas, or a relationship. 4. Metaphorically, can be used as follows: to dish it out = to mistreat or to ridicule another individual; she's a real dish =

she's very desirable. 5. May represent what you are serving to others. 6. Something easily broken. 7. You may also wish to see **Kitchen.**

DIVE 1. To completely plunge into a relationship, experience, or an attitude. 2. Metaphorically, a dive = a place that is substandard; to dive into something = to forge ahead, sometimes with reckless abandon. 3. A diving board may indicate an idea on which you are about to take a stand. 4. You may also wish to see **Swim.**

DIVORCE 1. The ending of an experience or a relationship. See **Death.** 2. The separation or dissolution of an agreement, a bond, or an idea. 3. Can represent the act of getting rid of something. 4. May be symbolic of new independence or regained freedom or of one who is desiring freedom.

DIZZY 1. Associated with feeling giddy, foolish, confused, or unstable. See **Emotion.** 2. Metaphorically, to be dizzy = to lack common sense, balance, or maturity. 3. May correspond to being overcome by an experience or by emotions. See **Faint.**

DOCK 1. Associated with the arrival of an important insight, a new situation, or a visitor. 2. May indicate a spiritual activity or an experience. See **Boat** and **Water.** 3. Depending on the imagery, might suggest that one's ship has come in. 4. Metaphorically, can be used as follows: that which is docked = something which is shortened, lowered, or lessened. 5 . You may also wish to see **Shore** and **Journey.**

DOCTOR 1. Might indicate a literal health message and the advice to see the doctor. 2. The physician within one's own self. 3. May be associated with one's ability to help or to

heal others. 4. Could correspond to a physical (health), a mental (emotional/counseling), or a spiritual (minister) doctor. 5. Metaphorically, to doctor the evidence = to falsify the evidence. 6. See also **People.**

DODO 1. Symbolic of extinction. 2. A way of the past. 3. Represents something out of place or no longer appropriate to the current situation. 4. Might relate to worthlessness (i.e., a flightless bird). 5. You may also wish to see **Bird** and **Animals.** 6. A foolish person or a dumb idea.

DOE 1. May represent a feminine relationship or the feminine side of yourself. See **Animals** and **Woman.** 2. Associated with independence and the wild. 3. Metaphorically, dough (doe) = money. See **Money.**

DOG 1. May be symbolic of loyalty and faithfulness or aggressiveness and territorialism. See **Animals.** 2. Often associated with man's best friend. 3. Metaphorically, can be used as follows: the company's going to the dogs = it's deteriorating, falling into disarray; she put on the dog = she put on a real show of class; letting sleeping dogs lie = leaving something alone; it's a dog's life = it's a bad (or a lazy) life; he's in the doghouse = he's in trouble; dog eat dog = aggressive and competitive; every dog has his day = everyone gets a turn at success; being dog-tired = being exhausted. 4. Dogs are often symbolic of what the individual associates with them or how one feels about them in general; for example: may be symbolic of anything from love and loyalty to allergies and irritants. 5. May also represent what the individual associates with the particular breed in the image. 6. You may also wish to see **Pet.**

DOLPHIN 1. May be associated with great

spiritual wisdom or insight. See **Fish.** 2. May correspond to the unconscious mind. 3. Dolphins may have a great deal to do with what one associates with them (i.e., intuition, communication, intelligence, playfulness, etc.). 4. You may also wish to see **Animals** and **Water.**

DONKEY 1. May be symbolic of stubbornness or obstinance. 2. May be metaphor for an ass. 3. Biblically, associated with humility (i.e., Jesus entering the city on a donkey). 4. Could correspond with bearing a heavy load or possessing a subservient position. 5. You may also wish to see **Animals.**

DON QUIXOTE 1. Associated with the inability to see things clearly. 2. Could suggest a state of personal confusion. 3. Might represent the noble part of oneself. See **Knight.**

DOOR 1. Opportunities, openings, directions, or new pathways to personal expression. 2. Associated with deeper reaches or unexplored regions of the self. See **House**. 3. A transition to another state of mind or place. 4. Sometimes could refer to death. See **Death**. 5. Biblically, can correspond to spirituality or Christ ("I stand at the door and knock," Revelation 3:20). 6. A barrier that needs to be removed. See **Wall**. 7. Different doors often represent different activities or experiences:

> *Back Door:* The desire to retreat, or relax; possibility of escape; informal opportunity.
>
> *Closed Door:* Being closed off from opportunities, either through your own activities or the actions of another; anticipation or a surprise as to what lies beyond.
>
> *Front Door:* Meeting a new experience; awaiting what comes next in life.

> *Locked Door:* Refusing to face a particular experience or avoiding unpleasant conditions; not knowing how to deal with a situation; feeling unworthy to explore what resides beyond.
>
> *Opened Door:* Wide-open opportunity; obvious direction; new experience.
>
> *Trapdoor:* The unexpected; a surprising development; traps, pitfalls, or potential obstacles.

8. Metaphorically, it lies at his door = it's his fault.

DOORKNOB 1. Associated with a new direction or opportunity. See **Door**. 2. Often symbolic of the fact that the next move is in one's own hands.

DOORPOST 1. Entryway. 2. Associated with a new direction. 3. Rabbinically, corresponds to the Passover; God's intervention and protection. 4. See also **Door**.

DORMITORY 1. Associated with the lessons of life, learning, or schooling. See **School**. 2. Might be associated with one's home or work situation. See **Work** and **House**. 3. You may also wish to see **Building**.

DOROTHY OF *THE WIZARD OF OZ* 1. Symbolic of every soul's journey. See **Journey**. 2. The individual seeker in life. 3. A literary counterpart to the Biblical prodigal son.

DOVE 1. Peace, harmony, innocence, and tranquillity. 2. The bearer of a message. See **Bird**. 3. Biblically, relates to the great Flood. See **Flood**. 4. Denotes spirituality, forgiveness, and new life. 5. Liturgically, corresponds to the Holy Spirit and the presence of God.

DRAFTED 1. The act of being called into duty or service. 2. Corresponds to being recruited for a project or an activity. 3. One who has no choice but to participate. 4. Might correspond to the presence of aggression and war. See **War.**

DRAGON 1. Represents something mysterious or magical. 2. Symbolizes the deeper reaches of the unknown or the unconscious. See **Unconscious.** 3. Possibly associated with metaphysics or the paranormal. 4. In China, it is a symbol of the highest spiritual reality. 5. Might represent the material side of spirituality. 6. Could symbolize fears. 7. Repressed feelings or emotions. 8. Liturgically, representative of Satan, sin, and temptation (i.e., a dragon under the feet of religious figures is symbolic of their victory over evil). See **Devil.** 9. You may also wish to see **Shadow** and **Animals.**

DRAIN 1. Associated with the body's elimination systems or one's emotions. 2. Depending on imagery, can correspond to the need to release toxins or emotions or problems with such a release. 3. Metaphorically, his money went down the drain = his money was wasted. 4. You may also wish to see **Plumbing.**

DRAMA 1. Refers to the drama of one's life. See **Journey.** 2. Associated with acting out roles. See **Acting/Actor/Actress** and **Costume.** 3. Often symbolizes a particular situation or scene you are experiencing. 4. Could refer to the need to become more or less dramatic or emotional. 5. Depending on the imagery, you may also wish to see **Movie Star.**

DRAPERIES 1. Something that covers, hides, or obscures vision. See **Curtain.** 2. Could be associated with the need for pri-vacy, or one who is too private. 3. Ideas, experiences, or attitudes that covers the environment or surroundings. 4. See also **Window.**

DREAM 1. Associated with the subconscious storehouse of symbols and images. See **Symbol/Symbolism** and **Imagery.** 2. The act of correlating one's mental processes with the events, the dreams, the fears, and the hopes, etc., of one's life. 3. A symbolic representation of an experience, an image, an activity, a thought, or an individual. See **Metaphor** and **Archetype.** 4. Can correspond to a wish fulfillment or an escape from mundane reality. 5. To know that you are dreaming while you are dreaming is a lucid dream. See **Lucid Dream.** 6. Dreaming of actual events that may happen in the future is known as a precognitive dream. See **ESP.**

DRESS 1. An idea or experience. See **Clothes.** 2. Putting on a new dress = trying on something new (i.e., occupation, experience, etc.). 3. What one shows to the outside world; one's personal image or personality. 4. Metaphorically, to dress down = to put on informal clothes or to reprimand someone; putting on one's best dress = to give one's best appearance. 5. Associated with feminine energy or qualities. See **Womb.**

DRIFT 1. Associated with a lack of personal direction (i.e., being adrift). See **Journey.** 2. Something that is carried out of one's control. 3. Can indicate a tendency to be in error. 4. See whatever is causing the drifting activity; for example: see **Automobile, Boat,** or **Wind.**

DRINK 1. Something one thirsts for. 2. Could be a literal indication of the need for more fluids (especially water) in your diet. 3. You may wish to see what it is that you are drinking (i.e., see **Water** or **Alcohol**). 4. Metaphorically, to drink in the experience = to absorb and reflect upon the experience; to drink like a fish = to drink too much alcohol.

DRIVE 1. Associated with one's journey or direction. See **Journey.** 2. An automobile is associated with the physical body or the current situation. See **Automobile.** 3. Something that impels or directs. 4. How one drives (directs) oneself or others. 5. Indicates what or who is driving your life (i.e., your motivation or your dominating influence). 6. Depending on imagery, could correspond to self–control, self–indulgence, or the lack of either. 7. Represents how one maneuvers in a situation or through life. 8. The activity while driving will have a great deal to do with the symbolism; for example: a speeding automobile is associated with traveling too fast in life and needing to slow down. See **Speed.**

DROWNING 1. Associated with being in something over one's head. 2. Being over-inundated by an experience. See **Flood.** 3. To be overpowered by (i.e., work) or over involved in (i.e., sexuality) a situation or activity. 4. Might correspond to being overcome by one's emotions or mental stress.

DRUGS/DRUGSTORE 1. May be associated with either a source of healing or a source of escape. 2. Associated with that which overtakes the self; the relinquishment of personal will. 3. To be drugged = to be out of one's normal state of mind, usually through artificial and external means. 4. Could correspond to one's overreliance on medication. 5. A drugstore might represent a place of healing. See **Hospital.**

DRUM 1. Something that makes noise for attention or in order to emphasize one's message or point of view. 2. May be symbolic of one's own heartbeat or emotional connection. 3. Metaphorically, can be used as follows: to drum up interest = to follow one's own life path or personal calling. 4. You may also wish to see **Music.**

DRUMMER 1. Can correspond to an announcement or an important message. See **Message/Messenger.** 2. One who seeks attention or tries to emphasize his point of view. See **Drum.** 3. You may also wish to see **People.**

DRUNK 1. Could literally refer to too much drink. 2. Associated with becoming overwhelmed or losing control. 3. Too much toxicity in the system; could correspond to too much sugar in the diet. 4. Being overwhelmed by the spirit. 5. You may also wish to see **Alcohol.**

DUCK 1. Metaphorically, can be used as follows: ducking an issue or a person = to avoid the issue or the person; to duck something = to lower it into water or to move very quickly; a queer duck = that which is very unusual; he's a sitting duck = he's in a very vulnerable position; she took to it like a duck takes to water = it was very natural for her. 2. Depending on the imagery, might be associated with a lofty idea or one's hunting instinct. 3. See also **Bird.** 4. You may also wish to see **Animals.**

DUEL 1. Symbolic of a fight, challenge, or argument between two individuals or opposing viewpoints. 2. May be associated with an internal struggle within one's own self. 3. You may also wish to see **Fight, Shadow,** or **War.**

DUMMY 1. Can be associated with that which is controlled by external forces or individuals (i.e., a puppet). See **Puppet.** 2. Metaphorically, a dummy = one who lacks common sense or experience. 3. Can represent a false image or belief. 4. See **People.**

DUST 1. Associated with something that is being overlooked or neglected. 2. Can correspond to something improper, common, or filthy. See **Dirt.** 3. Might suggest something old, no longer necessary, or worthless. See **Old.** 4. Depending on the imagery, you may also wish to see **Antique.**

DWARF 1. Can correspond to that which may be overlooked or considered small or insignificant (i.e., an idea, a person, etc.). 2. Might represent something that is under-developed or that is in the formative or ger-minating stages. See **Child** and **Size.** 3. May symbolize that which is in miniature. 4. Something stunted or kept from further growth. 5. Can be associated with the enchanted or the realm of the unconscious. See **Magic/Magician.** 6. Could represent mischief. 7. In literature, the seven dwarfs = order and symmetry in union or the ultimate self-realization of the individual aspects of self when in harmony, cooperation, and balance (see seven in **Numerology).** 8. See also **People.**

DYNAMITE 1. A powerful experience, message, or idea. 2. Could be symbolic of explosive feelings or emotions. See **Explosion/Explosive.** 3. Metaphorically, that was dynamite = something incredibly overpowering (generally positive).

1. *The fifth letter of the alphabet.* 2. *The Roman numeral for 250.* 3. *Chemically, the symbol for erbium.* 4. *Musically, the third note.* 5. *Numerologically, equivalent to five.* 6. *Scholastically, unacceptable achievement, failure; might correspond to excellence.* 7. *In physics, a symbol for elasticity or electromotive forces.* 8. *In logic, an abbreviation for negative.* 9. *In Greek, epsilon.* 10. *A prefix meaning* without.

EAGLE 1. Associated with wisdom, clarity of vision, nationalism, freedom, and strength. 2. Could indicate a lofty ideal or insight. 3. May symbolize the ability to soar above the material world; one's own soul qualities. See **Flying**. 4. Might correspond to a bird of prey. See **Bird**. 5. Metaphorically, one who is eagle-eyed is sharp sighted or able to see every detail. 6. In golf, a score of two strokes under par. 7. Metaphysically, relates to the fourth chakra or endocrine center; human love. See **Thymus**. 8. Might symbolize the United States of America.

EARRING. 1. Corresponds to something that has hold of one's ear. See **Ears**. 2. Who or what one is listening to. See **Hear**. 3. You may also wish to see **Jewels/Jewelry**. 4. May indicate one's talent for listening.

EARS 1. Associated with listening or the need to be heard. See **Hear**. 2. Might correspond with the need to listen for harmony, cooperation, or a message. See **Message/ Messenger**. 3. Metaphorically, can be used as follows: to give someone your ear = to listen to someone; she's up to her ears = she's overwhelmed (with work, bills, etc.); I'm all ears = I'm listening; he has the boss's

ear = the boss listens to everything he says; he turned a deaf ear = he didn't want to be involved. 4. Could indicate personal openness and receptivity or the lack of it. 5. May suggest the need to listen to another or one's higher self. 6. You may also wish to see **Body**.

EARTH 1. May correspond to that place where one resides or the situation one is in the midst of. See **Hear**. 2. Might be associated with something usual, mundane, material, earthly, or sensual. 3. Can represent the Great Mother. See **Mother**. 4. Metaphorically, can be used as follows: come back down to earth = be sensible or practical; she'd move heaven and earth = she'd use every effort to make something happen; he's down to earth = he's practical. 5. Third planet from the Sun; fifth largest planet in our solar system. Has a rotation year of 365.41 days. 6. One of the four elements (air, earth, fire, and water). See **Elements**. 7. Can correspond with the astrological earth signs (**Taurus, Virgo, Capricorn**). See individual signs for traits. 8. Considered the observation point in astrology. 9. Might be associated with a firm foundation or solid ground. 10. You may also wish to see **Dirt** or **Clay.**

EARTHQUAKE 1. May indicate a warning or a message. 2. Could symbolize the breakup of internal forces or of a situation. 3. Can correspond to a shattering or problem situation. 4. An emotional upheaval. 5. Might be a literal foreshadowing of an earthquake. 6. You may also wish to see **Weather.** 7. Something that shatters one's values, stance, principles, or belief systems.

EASEL 1. Something upon which one's work is displayed. See **Work.** 2. Could be associated with getting the picture. See **Photograph.** 3. See also **Artist.** 4. You may also wish to see **Platform.**

EAST 1. Associated with the rising sun or the beginning of a cycle. 2. Often represents a new situation or experience. 3. The place of new birth or rebirth. 4. See also **Direction.** 5. Might be associated with Asia or the Orient. 6. Might be associated with the left. See **Left.**

EASTER 1. Associated with resurrection and rebirth. See **Resurrection** and **Christ.** 2. Can correspond to new beginnings and spring. See **Spring.** 3. May be associated with one's burdens or crosses in life. See **Cross.**

EAT 1. May symbolize what is being devoured, consumed, or contemplated. 2. Something you put in your mouth. See **Chew/Chewing Gum.** 3. An unawakened potential. 4. Metaphorically, can be used as follows: I had to eat my words = I had to take back what I said; eat your heart out = feel jealous or disheartened; she ate it up = she enjoyed every part of it. 5. May correspond to literal dietary suggestions. 6. Might be associated with personal appetites or self-gratification. See **Food.** 7. Something that must be digested physically or mentally. 8. You may also wish to see **Teeth.**

ECLIPSE 1. That which shadows or overpowers the situation. 2. May correspond to a lack of insight or clarity. 3. Metaphorically, to eclipse someone = to surpass them. 4. Depending on the imagery, you may also wish to see **Sun/Sunlight** and **Moon/**

Moonlight. 5. Something that is in darkness. See **Dark.** 6. Might be associated with an ending, a decrease, or a death. See **Death.**

EEL 1. Corresponds to something being slippery. 2. Something that is difficult or dangerous to get one's hands on. 3. See **Fish.** 4. You may also wish to see **Snake.** 5. Might be associated with male sexuality. See **Phallus.**

EGG 1. The birth of a new idea. See **Birth.** 2. Metaphorically, can be used as follows: they egged him on = they prodded him; she has egg on her face = she's embarrassed; don't put all your eggs in one basket = don't have all your hopes in one place; the boss laid an egg = the boss made a real mistake; she's a good egg = she's a good person, or she's really smart. 3. Something whole or complete unto itself. See **Circle.** 4. Might be associated with female sexuality. See **Womb.** 5. May correspond to being in or coming out of one's shell. 6. Painted eggs could be associated with Easter. See **Easter.** 7. Ornamental eggs may represent something fragile, beautiful, or valuable. 8. You may also wish to see **Food** and **Seed.**

EGYPT/EGYPTIAN 1. Often symbolic of ancient or sacred wisdom. See **Book.** 2. Could represent a legacy, antiquity, severity, or even slavery. 3. Could be associated with a dry spell in one's life. See **Desert.** 4. Metaphysically, represents ancient teachings, mysteries, and temples. 5. Biblically, associated with plenty and famine (Genesis 41) or slavery. 6. See also **Mythology (Egyptian).** 7. May be associated with a foreign visitor or travel. 8. See also **People.** 9. You may also wish to see **Historical Clothing/Settings.**

EIFFEL TOWER 1. Symbolic of France. 2.

See **Building**. 3. May be associated with a foreign visitor or travel. 4. Metaphorically, may relate to an eye full.

EIGHT 1. Associated with balance or infinity. 2. See **Numerology**. 3. Metaphorically, she's behind the eight ball = she's in a very difficult place or position.

EINSTEIN, ALBERT 1. Corresponds to genius or a bright idea. 2. Might represent eccentricity or creativity. 3. Could indicate a message from one's higher mind. 4. Might symbolize the brain. See **Brain**.

ELBOW 1. Associated with one's ability to reach out, to bend, or to serve. See **Arm**. 2. Metaphorically, can be used as follows: she elbowed her way in = she forced her way; just use a little elbow grease = just use a little force; it's at my elbow = it's within arm's reach; he rubbed elbows with them = he got very near some famous or important people; she's up to her elbows = she's very busy. 3. See also **Body**.

ELECTRICITY 1. A provider of energy, force, or power to a situation. 2. Can correspond to a source of information or insight. See **Light**. 3. May be associated with the flow of ideas or intuition. 4. Could represent strong emotional ties toward a situation or individual. 5. Electric or power lines can be symbolic of one's personal connection or of the physical nervous system. 6. You may also wish to see **Lightning**.

ELEMENTS 1. Associated with the four elements that were once thought to constitute all matter: air, earth, fire, and water. 2. See individual elements; for example: see **Air**. 3. Astrologically, all signs can be categorized into one of the four elements (see individual signs for traits), as follows:

Air Signs: Aquarius, Libra, Gemini
Earth Signs: Taurus, Virgo, Capricorn
Fire Signs: Aries, Sagittarius, Leo
Water Signs: Pisces, Cancer, Scorpio

4. You may also wish to see **Earth**.

ELEPHANT 1. Associated with memory, wisdom, cunning, power, and age. See **Animals**. 2. Can correspond to something that is thick-skinned or nosy. 3. In India, symbolic of great spirituality and wisdom. 4. Could be associated with carrying something valuable but illegal (i.e., ivory). 5. Might correspond to one's inner self. 6. Symbolic of one of the Hindu gods (Ganesh). See **Hinduism.**

ELEVATOR 1. Corresponds to the ups and downs in life's journey. See **Journey.** 2. Could be associated with levels of the mind or different states of consciousness. 3. Can be symbolic of an experience, idea, or situation that may lift things to another level. 4. You may also wish to see **Stairs.** 5. Depending on the imagery, you may wish to see **Building** or **House.**

ELEVEN 1. The first master number; mastery in the physical dimension. 2. Associated with courage and power. 3. See also **Numerology.**

ELF 1. Associated with enchantment, the mystical, or mischief. 2. The active force in nature. See **Man.** 3. See **People.** 4. You may also wish to see **Dwarf.**

ELIJAH 1. The forerunner of Christ. See **John the Baptist.** 2. Can be symbolic of someone with spiritual power but only human wisdom.

EMERGENCY 1. An urgent situation. 2.

Could correspond to a literal warning. 3. Something that has reached crisis proportions. 4. May be a precognitive warning of a possible situation, advising a different or a precautionary course of action. 5. Depending on imagery, you may wish to see **Doctor** or **Accident.**

EMOTION 1. Generally, can be categorized into one of four basic emotions: mad, sad, glad, or scared. 2. The emotion within the image often symbolizes an actual situation or experience within one's conscious life (i.e., an experience that evokes the same type of emotion being portrayed). 3. Might correspond to the need for self-examination, the urge to confront an issue or a person, the need for a change, the desire for more joy in one's life, etc. 4. The imagery itself may symbolize various emotional responses; for example: something broken may suggest a broken heart or an emotional collapse; something burning could indicate extreme anger, frustration, or irritation; balloons in the air might be joyfulness; a dam could represent suppressed emotions. 5. If a fearful emotion was evoked, you may wish to see **Nightmare.**

EMPIRE STATE BUILDING 1. May be symbolic of finances, work, or the stock market. See **Building.** 2. Associated with New York. 3. May indicate a domestic vacation or travel. 4. You may also wish to see **City.**

EMPLOYEE 1. Associated with work. See **Work.** 2. Can correspond to those parts of oneself that are working together. 3. See also **People.** 4. Depending on the imagery, you may also wish to see **Boss.**

EMPTY 1. Can correspond to a loss or something that is missing. 2. Might indicate something being stolen. See **Thief.** 3. Something that is removed, transferred, or deprived. 4. Metaphorically, an empty promise = a meaningless statement or a lie.

ENDOCRINE CENTERS 1. Associated with the physiological glands of the body that produce secretions; they are as follows: gonads, lyden, adrenals, thymus, thyroid, pituitary, and pineal. 2. Metaphysically, associated with the spiritual centers, or the connections between one's physical body and one's soul. See **Chakras**. 3. You may also wish to see individual glands; for example, see **Thymus**.

ENEMY 1. Can symbolize those portions of yourself that are at war or those aspects of yourself that are injurious. See **Shadow**. 2. Something that is hostile or in opposition. 3. Depending on imagery, you may also wish to see **War**.

ENGAGEMENT 1. May represent a joining, a union, or the agreement to work with another. 2. See **Wedding**. 3. A promise or a commitment. 4. Might be a literal situation or a relationship that will come to pass. 5. Could be a reconciliation with oneself or shadow. See **Shadow**.

ENGINE 1. Associated with one's energy, enthusiasm, or drive. See **Automobile**. 2. Could symbolize the torso or running systems of the body (i.e., the heart, the nerves, or the electrical systems). See **Heart**. 3. A bad engine may suggest the need to see a mechanic (if literally applicable to one's car) or a doctor (if symbolic of one's heart). 4. You may also wish to see **Drive**.

ENTRANCE 1. The way into a situation. 2. Can correspond to an opportunity. See **Door**. 3. A new beginning. 4. Metaphorically, to be entranced = to be in great awe. 5. See also **House**.

ENVELOPE 1. Associated with a message. See **Message/Messenger**. 2. The arrival of a new idea, an opportunity, a communication, or an insight. See **Letter**. 3. Something that surrounds or protects the internal contents. 4. Might correspond to one's body. See **Body**.

EPSTEIN BARR 1. Associated with something that sucks or drains one's life, emotions, energy, or patience (i.e., the situation, another person, current thoughts, etc.). 2. Can correspond to something that destroys itself. 3. The suppression of one's emotions, will, desires, or higher self, leading to physical collapse. 4. You may also wish to see **Ill/ Illness** and **Body**.

ERASE/ERASER 1. May correspond to a mistake or an error. 2. Symbolic of starting over. 3. To rub out, destroy, stop, kill, or get rid of. See **Kill**. 4. Might indicate the need to release or to let go of habits, faults, emotions, or thoughts. 5. Depending on imagery, you may also wish to see **Letter**.

ERRAND 1. Associated with a task. 2. Can correspond to a short trip or a project. 3. Might represent the need for personal examination in a new light. 4. You may also wish to see **Work**.

ESCAPE 1. Represents one's desire for a way out. 2. To free oneself from confinement. See **Prisoner**. 3. Metaphorically, can be used as follows: his name escapes me = I can't remember; she escaped getting sick = she remained well. 4. Could indicate the need for better conditions or a change.

ESP 1. Associated with expanded sense per-

ception. 2. The ability to gain insights or awareness that transcend the basic information of the five senses (i.e., seeing, hearing, tasting, smelling, and touching). 3. ESP in dreams is usually associated with clarity, warnings about loved ones, situations with which one is emotionally involved, or repeated images that may appear in one's precognitive dreams. 4. Types of ESP are as follows:

Clairaudience: Receiving information through one's own hearing faculties. .

Clairvoyance: Mind-to-object (or mind-to-event) knowing. Realizing information without the involvement of another mind (i.e., telepathy is the relay of information from one person to another; clairvoyance does not necessarily involve information coming from the mind of another).

Precognition: Foreknowledge of events (literally, preknowing).

Psychokinesis: Ability to move objects by thought.

Psychometry: Ability to derive information about a person or an event by holding an object that was involved in the situation or belonged to the person.

Retrocognition: Ability to see events of the past with clarity.

Telepathy: Mind to mind communication.

ESTATE 1. One's place of residence. See **House.** 2. Associated with an individual's environment at home or at work. See **Work.** 3. May correspond to one's state of mind or current situation. 4. Might indicate the talents, abilities, resources, or material goods that one has available. 5. One's personal fulfillment.

EVE 1. Corresponds to womanhood and motherhood. See **Woman.** 2. Can represent suffering. 3. Liturgically, relates to temptation and the Fall. See **Adam** and **Apple.** 4. Associated with paradise. See **Heaven.** 5. Metaphysically, associated with earthly desire.

EVENING 1. Associated with the closing of a period in one's life, the end of an experience, or the end of a relationship. 2. May correspond to the autumn of one's life. See **Seasons.** 3. Might correspond to a literal death. See **Death.** 4. Can represent rest, completion, retirement, or sleep. 5. Might correspond to the presence of darkness. See **Dark.** 6. Depending on imagery, you may also wish to see **Sky, Moon/Moonlight,** or **Sun/Sunlight.**

EVIL 1. Bad, immoral, or harmful. 2. Something that is wrong or may cause injury to another. 3. The dark side of life. See **Devil** and **Shadow.** 4. Metaphorically, to give someone the evil eye = to wish them harm. 5. Might correspond to ill health (physically, mentally, or spiritually). 6. Could be associated with one's feelings of guilt or low self-esteem.

EXCREMENT 1. A waste product. 2. Could correspond to the need to eliminate poisons or thoughts from one's system. 3. Might be associated with one's negative habits, thoughts, or prejudices. 4. You may also wish to see **Bathroom.** 5. To spoil with a part of oneself. 6. Done in public, it is often associated with showing off, making a mistake, or doing something one shouldn't have done. 7. Something in the feces might correspond to a health problem. 8. May be a literal need to defecate.

EXECUTIVE 1. Corresponds to one who is in authority. 2. May be associated with one's

higher self or God. 3. The driving force in one's life. 4. Could indicate a disciplinary or parental figure. See **People.** 5. You may also wish to see **Work.** 6. Depending on the imagery, may suggest a literal promotion.

EXERCISE 1. Can correspond to the literal need for more exercise. 2. That which is carried out in daily life (i.e., a duty, work, an obligation, etc.). See **Journey** and **Work.** 3. Might indicate an overemphasis on one portion of an individual's body or activities. 4. May be associated with the need to exercise a portion of one's being physically, mentally, or spiritually. 5. You may also wish to see **Body.**

EXPLOSION/EXPLOSIVE 1. Associated with disruption, violence, and noise. 2. Could represent emotional outbursts; temper. 3. Something that bursts after being repressed. 4. Metaphorically, to explode something = to discredit or to prove false. 5. Could represent a sudden and dramatic change. 6. Can be symbolic of things breaking or the experience of flying to pieces. 7. You may also wish to see **Dynamite.** 8. Depending on imagery, you may also wish to see **Accident.**

EXTRATERRESTRIAL 1. Corresponds to something that is out of place or from another environment. 2. May be associated with a foreign or unknown part of oneself. See **Shadow.** 3. Could indicate an unusual or alien idea. 4. Acting in a way or manner that is out of keeping with one's normal behavior. 5. Might be a literal indication of a foreign visitor or travel to a foreign locale. 6. Associated with someone or something that is not understood. 7. Depending upon the symbology, could correspond with facing one's fears. 8. Something that is unfamiliar. 9. See also **People.**

EYEGLASSES 1. Associated with enhanced comprehension, understanding, or vision. 2. The ability to clearly see through the experience. 3. Something that aids inner vision. See **Vision.** 4. Seeing through rose–colored glasses = seeing things better than they really are, or seeing them as one wishes them to be. 5. See **Eyes.**

EYES 1. The ability to see; vision. See **Vision.** 2. The windows to the soul; one's own individuality. See **Window.** 3. May correspond to one's outlook on life. 4. An all–seeing eye = spiritual vision, intuition, or God.

5. Metaphorically, may be used in the following ways: to shut one's eyes = to ignore what is happening; an eye for an eye = an equal punishment or reaction; giving an eye to detail = paying close attention; to give someone the evil eye = to wish them harm; to feast one's eyes upon = to look with admiration and longing; making eyes at = to flirt; catching one's eye = to draw attention to; they were able to see eye to eye = they were able to agree; in the public eye = brought to the world's attention. 6. See also **Body.**

F

1. *The sixth letter of the alphabet.* 2. *The Roman numeral for forty.* 3. *Chemically, the symbol for fluorine.* 4. *Musically, the fourth note.* 5. *Numerologically, equivalent to six.* 6. *Scholastically, unacceptable achievement or failure.* 7. *In physics, a symbol for farad (electromagnetic measurement).* 8. *In mathematics, a symbol for function.* 9. *In printing, a symbol for folio.* 10. *In genetics, a symbol for filial generation.* 11. *In Greek, digamma.* 12. *May be associated with father.*

FACE 1. Associated with self–esteem or how one appears to others. See **Body**. 2. Corresponds to one's own self; one's personal identity; or, one's facade. 3. May indicate one's qualities, faults, and thoughts. 4. How we see ourselves or how others see us. See **Mirror**. 5. Metaphorically, can be used as follows: face the facts = deal with reality; she had to face the music = she had to deal with the consequences; he faced up to his involvement = he dealt with and/or confessed to his involvement; to fly in the face of something = to ignore or to disregard it; to lose face = to be humiliated. 6. You may also wish to see **Mask**.

FACTORY 1. May correspond to regularity or predictability. 2. Associated with hard work. See **Work**. 3. Might indicate tedium or boredom. 4. You may also wish to see **Building**.

FAINT 1. The act of being overwhelmed, depressed, weak, or cowardly. 2. Metaphorically, to be fainthearted = to be unable to express one's true inner feelings. 3. You may also wish to see **Dizzy**. 4. Could be a literal indication of a health condition.

FAIRY 1. Can correspond to enchantment or magic. See **Magic/Magician**. 2. A small messenger or angel. See **Angel**. 3. Metaphorically, he's a fairy = he's gay, or he's overly effeminate; that's a fairy tale = that's a lie. 4. You may also wish to see **Dwarf** and **People**.

FAIRY TALES 1. Stories, fables, and myths that demonstrate universal themes of human experience. 2. Through the story's theme, characterization, and symbolism, one can discover the essential purpose or moral intent. 3. Metaphorically, that's a fairy tale = that's an exaggeration or a lie. 4. See also **Fairy**.

FAITH/FAITHFUL 1. A belief or inner awareness based on personal experience. 2. Corresponds to spirituality. See **God** and **Prayer**. 3. Metaphorically, can be used as follows: he's a faithful husband = he doesn't cheat on his wife; in good faith = with total trust. 4. You may also wish to see **Worship**.

FALCON 1. A predatory bird. See **Bird**. 2. Can correspond to preying upon others or the fear of being preyed upon.

FALL 1. Associated with not being in control. 2. Could represent falling conditions: physically, financially, or emotionally. 3. Feeling no support. 4. Associated with failure or making a mistake. 5. Could represent fallen morals or reputation. 6. Losing a position, reputation, or an experience of importance. See **Descend**. 7. Metaphorically, can have the following meanings: falling in love = losing control of one's own feelings and emotions; the plan fell through = it didn't work out; to fall in with = to become a part of, or to be associated with; to fall in battle = to be wounded or killed; to fall behind = to get behind in an activity or financially; he fell flat on his face = he made a fool of himself; to fall on your feet = to end up in the right place. 8. Financially, for something to be worth a decreased value. 9. Corresponds to autumn; the end of a season, experience, or age. See **Seasons**. 10. Biblically, associated with the Fall of man. See **Adam**. 11. Losing one's state of innocence.

FAMILY/FAMILY MEMBERS 1. Often corresponds to the relationship one possesses with that individual (i.e., feelings toward the person, areas of the relationship that one remembers or that still need to be worked on, etc.). 2. See specific family relationships; for example, see **Mother**. 3. Can correspond to various aspects of oneself. See **Self**. 4. May represent aspects of oneself in relationship to that person or talents, qualities, or experiences that one associates with that person. 5. A deceased relative may indicate a message from another realm. 6. A parental figure can represent the need to look after one's activities. 7. Might indicate a literal suggestion or a warning in terms of the person's welfare. 8. See also **People**. 9. You may also wish to see **Child**, **Man**, or **Woman**, depending upon the individual's age and sex.

FAMINE 1. Associated with hunger and yearning physically, mentally, or spiritually (i.e., food, education, and spirituality). 2. To be deprived of what is necessary for survival. 3. Not getting enough food. See **Food**.

FAMOUS PEOPLE 1. Often associated with the quality we think most about in regard to that person. See **People**. 2. May be indicative of our own need for personal recognition. 3. Could indicate a talent or an aspect in ourselves that has long been overlooked. 4. If the famous people were in the movies, they may represent some aspect of a role they've played. See **Movie Star**. 5. You may also wish to see **Performance/Performers** and **Acting/Actor/Actress.**

FANG 1. Symbolic of one's sharp words or the cutting things that one has said. See **Teeth**. 2. Can also be associated with snakes. See **Snake**. 3. Associated with aggression and anger.

FARM 1. May be associated with portions of one's animal nature. See **Animals**. 2. Depending on personal association, could indicate simplicity or hard work. 3. One's youth memories. 4. You may also wish to see **Historical Clothing/Settings.**

FAST 1. Something that is rapid, speedy, swift, or reckless. 2. A speeding object may be associated with traveling too fast in life and needing to slow down. See **Speed.** 3. Metaphorically, she's fast = she's promiscuous, or she's very intelligent; he pulled a fast one = he managed to trick us. 4. If a vehicle is traveling too fast, you may wish to see that vehicle; for example: see **Car.**

FAT 1. Something excessive, overweight, overly pronounced, or very productive. See **Size.** 2. Can correspond to one's poor self-image and desire for weight loss. 3. Could indicate an area of yourself that is overused. See **Body.** 4. Metaphorically, can be used as follows: his fat's in the fire = he's in trouble; she has a fat wallet = she has a lot of money; they live off the fat of the land = they have money and live a luxurious life; let's chew the fat = let's talk; fat chance = not very likely. 5. Something that is weighted down by worries, emotions, or problems. 6. Something that insulates you from the world. See **Clothes.**

FATHER 1. Represents authority, leadership, or power. 2. Can represent the masculine aspects of God (energetic, forceful, protective, etc.), whereas the mother is associated with the feminine qualities (receptive, compassionate, nurturing). See **Man** and **God.** 3. Often corresponds to the relationship you possess with your father (i.e., how your father appears may be symbolic of your feelings toward him). 4. A deceased father may indicate a message from another realm; see **Message/Messenger.** 5. Can represent the need for personal discipline. 6. Metaphorically, to be the father of something = the creator, the inventor, or the founder. 7. Could indicate a suggestion or a warning in terms of your father's welfare. 8. See also **People.**

FAUCET 1. Something that controls the flow of one's emotions, ideas, spirituality, or eliminations. See **Water.** 2. The imagery of the faucet has a great deal to do with possible symbolism; for example: a faucet that will not turn could indicate that you are holding in all of your feelings; a faucet covered with moss could symbolize productive ideas that have never been shared with others; a foreign substance (such as pus) dripping from a faucet could indicate a literal health problem. See **Plumbing.** 3. You may also wish to see **House.**

FEAR 1. Associated with anxiety, apprehension, and uneasiness. See **Emotion.** 2. The inability to handle one's current experience. 3. Oftentimes whatever you are fearful of is associated with something that

needs to be faced in yourself. See **Shadow.**

FEATHER 1. Depending on imagery, may be associated with confusion, transformation, ideas, humiliation, or one's outer appearance. See **Clothes.** 2. Metaphorically, can be used as follows: that was a feather in his cap = that was quite an accomplishment; birds of a feather flock together = people who are alike (qualities and/or faults) support or join one another; she feathered her nest = she took care of herself financially; to be tar and feathered = to be humiliated or reprimanded; in fine feather = in great appearance or in one's best condition. 3. Plucking feathers may represent something that needs to be removed from the situation. 4. Flying feathers could indicate a disruptive or confusing condition or experience. 5. Might correspond to wings and spirituality. See **Wings.** 6. Depending on imagery, you may also wish to see **Bird.**

FECES 1. That which is a waste product. 2. Could correspond to the need to eliminate poisons or thoughts from one's own system. 3. Might be associated with negative habits, thoughts, or prejudices. 4. You may also wish to see **Bathroom.** 5. To spoil with a part of oneself. 6. Done in public, it is often associated with showing off, making a mistake, or doing something one shouldn't have done. 7. Something in the feces might correspond to a health problem. 8. May be a literal need to defecate.

FEDORA 1. A showy hat or an idea. See **Hat.** 2. Symbolic of what is on your mind. 3. May indicate an important job, experience, or new state of mind. 4. You may also wish to see **Head** and **Clothes.**

FEED 1. May symbolize what one is giving to others for physical, mental, or spiritual consumption. See **Eat.** 2. Could indicate that portion of one's life that is being nurtured by self (i.e., bad habits, creativity, new ideas, spirituality, etc.). 3. Metaphorically, she likes to get feedback = she likes to have comments about what she has done. 4. You may also wish to see **Food.**

FEET 1. Associated with one's personal direction, mission, or goal. See **Direction, Journey,** and **Road.** 2. Could correspond to one's grounding, understanding, or knowledge. 3. Metaphorically, can be used as follows: to be swept off one's feet = to be carried away by emotion or the experience; to stand on one's feet = to have independence and financial security; she put her best foot forward = she gave her best impression or attempt; one foot in the grave = to be old or near death; to put one's foot down = to make a personal stance; he put his foot in his mouth = he said something inappropriate or out of line; underfoot = in the way; to foot the bill = to pay for everything. 4. Could represent a current position in life or in the situation. 5. You may also wish to see **Shoes** and **Body.**

FEMALE 1. Associated with one's individuality. See **Self.** 2. Corresponds to the feminine side of one's nature. 3. Possibly corresponding to feminine traits, i.e., compassion, intuition, sensitivity, receptivity, and tenderness. See **Woman.** 4. May correspond to the female counterpart of one's youthful self. See **Child** and **Girl.** 5. Might symbolize an idea, a project, or a person of about the same age.

FENCE 1. Something that prevents passage in or out. 2. Could represent being confined or confining oneself through the limits of emotions, beliefs, feelings, or circumstances. 3. Associated with a barrier or an obstacle

between oneself and what is beyond. See **Wall.** 4. Provides protection from the external environment. 5. Metaphorically, can be used as follows: to fence = to avoid a direct reply; she's on the fence = she can't decide; they were fenced = they were stolen. 6. Historically, the art of fencing is a form of self–defense using a sword. 7. You may also wish to see **Gate.**

FEVER 1. Can represent the cause of anger, stress, or frustration. 2. Might literally suggest the need to see a doctor. 3. Something that makes one burn. See **Fire.** 4. Metaphorically, she makes him feverish = she excites him. 5. You may also wish to see **Ill/ Illness.**

FIANCÉ/FIANCÉE 1. A new beginning. 2. A new commitment or experience. See **Marriage.** 3. Something that engages or involves. 4. May represent a joining, a union, or the agreement to work with another. 5. Might indicate a literal situation that will come to pass.

FIELD 1. Associated with one's place of harvest, duty, or mission. See **Garden.** 2. Represents a wide–open expanse. 3. Could correspond to new possibilities waiting to be planted. See **Plant.** 4. May be associated with one's field of work. See **Work.** 5. Metaphorically, to play the field = to not limit oneself to only one person or activity.

FIGHT 1. A conflict between others or portions of oneself. See **Shadow.** 2. An environment of hostility, aggression, and oppression. 3. Can correspond to an internal struggle. 4. Often associated with retaliation for previous thoughts, words, or actions. 5. May indicate the need to consciously deal with problems that are at the unconscious level. 6. Arguing in a particular location or room could correspond to a conflict in those areas of one's life; for example: a bedroom argument could indicate a sexual conflict or problem; arguing in the kitchen may symbolize a problem with one's diet, etc. 7. Could be associated with the need to fight for what's right. 8. Depending on imagery, you may also wish to see **People** and **War.**

FILE DRAWER 1. Associated with the storage of experiences or memory. 2. Can correspond to one's work environment. See **Work.** 3. May contain insights, possibilities, or untapped talents. 4. Could correspond to the need to put things in their place or to become more organized. 5. Might symbolize the Akashic Records. See **Akashic Records.**

FINDING 1. To discover additional insights about oneself, the situation, or another. 2. The act of looking for something. 3. May correspond to discovering unknown parts of oneself. See **Shadow.** 4. Solving a situation. 5. You may also wish to see **Detective.**

FINGERS 1. An extension of one's hands (i.e., self, service, activities, etc.). See **Hand.** 2. That with which one is involved. 3. Whatever is happening with the fingers is significant; for example: seeing a ring on a finger is associated with a relationship or a partnership; having a finger shake itself at you may symbolize an accusation for something you have done. 4. Metaphorically, can be used as follows: he pointed the finger = he told on the individual; stop fingering it = stop touching it; to have your finger in it = to be involved in it; having it at your fingertips = having something readily available; she fingered it = she stole it; he had his fingers all over it = he was very much involved: 5 . You may also wish to see **Body.**

FINISH LINE 1. A successful accomplishment, completion, or finish. 2. The attainment of one's goal. 3. Might indicate the end of an activity or a relationship. 4. Depending on imagery, may suggest one's activities in a competition. See **Sports.** 5. Depending on imagery, you may wish to see **Athlete** or **Car.**

FIRE 1. That which overcomes, purifies, or destroys. 2. Associated with strong emotions. 3. Corresponds to that which inflames the situation. 4. Could represent a burning issue. See **Burn.** 5. May indicate anger and frustration. 6. Metaphorically, can be used as follows: he's playing with fire = he's taking a dangerous risk; to open fire = to begin shooting; going through fire and water, under fire, or trial by fire = great difficulties; to inflame the fires = to arouse desire or sexuality; she set the world on fire = she became very successful; being fired = to be dismissed from the job; fire away = to begin asking questions. 7. Could represent consuming conditions in one's experience environmentally, physically, emotionally, or spiritually. 8. Biblically, associated with the burning bush and a message from God (Exodus 3). 9. One of the four elements (air, earth, fire, and water). See **Elements.** 10. Can correspond to the astrological fire signs (**Aries, Sagittarius,** and **Leo**). See individual signs for traits.

FIRE EXTINGUISHER 1. May indicate the need for caution, relaxation, or to calm one's temper. 2. Associated with things that have become too hot or have gotten out of control. 3. See also **Fire.** 4. Depending on imagery, might indicate one's ability to calm a situation or the need to calm oneself. 5. Might correspond with a literal fire hazard and the need to take appropriate precautions. See **Message/Messenger.**

FIREPLACE 1. Can be associated with purification, warmth, or digestion. See **House**. 2. Could symbolize desire, passion, or romance. 3. Might be representative of the hearth and home and one's family environment. 4. Sparks from a fire may indicate a fight or anger. 5. See also **Fire**. 6. You may also wish to see **Furnace** and **Lightning**.

FIREWORKS 1. Corresponds to a celebration. 2. Could represent personal achievement or public acclaim. 3. May be associated with an outer representation of one's inner joy, emotions, or state of mind. 4. You may also wish to see **Lightning**.

FISH 1. A symbol of faith and spirituality. 2. A secret sign used by the early Christians to denote their belief in Jesus. 3. Liturgically, symbolic of Christ. See **Christ**. 4. Astrologically, one of the twelve signs of the zodiac. See **Pisces**. 5. Metaphorically, a fish can be used in the following ways: to drink like a fish = to drink heavily; he's like a fish out of water = he's out of his own environment or area of expertise; neither fish, flesh, nor fowl = not recognizable; other fish in the sea = additional choices, especially in relationships; having other fish to fry = having additional and more important matters to attend to; being a little fish in a big pond = being just a tiny part of all that occurs in one's environment; she's a cold fish = she's frigid or unemotional; something is fishy = not quite right; fishing for something = looking for the answer. 6. Eating a fish may represent partaking of a spiritual truth or insight, or it may simply be a dietary recommendation from the subconscious mind. 7. Different types of fish may correspond to different meanings; for example: a *goldfish* could indicate great spiritual wisdom; a *trout* might symbolize the need to relax and take it easy; a *catfish* could represent some-

thing that is not spiritually developed; a *whale* might suggest an exaggerated story; a *dolphin* could symbolize communication; an *eel* suggests something that is slippery. 8. You may also wish to see **Water**. 9. Might represent information from the unconscious. See **Unconscious**. 10. See also **Animals**.

FISHERMAN/FISHING 1. Represents those who seek or distribute spiritual insights. See **Fish**. 2. Associated with one who is called into service. 3. Liturgically, symbolic of the apostles. 4. May be representative of Jesus. See **Christ**. 5. Might indicate one who is fishing for answers.

FISHING POLE 1. Associated with the desire to increase one's faith. 2. Could indicate the act of fishing for answers. 3. Might suggest the need for relaxation. 4. See also **Fish**.

FIST 1. Can correspond to power, force, or repressed emotions. 2. Represents anger and tension. 3. Metaphorically, to clench one's fists = to control one's anger, or to prepare to fight. 4. May indicate your own defensiveness. 5. Depending on imagery, you may also wish to see **Fingers**, **Hand**, or **Fight**.

FIVE 1. Associated with change, new beginnings, or the five senses. 2. See **Numerology**.

FLAG 1. Corresponds to national or international affairs. 2. Acceptance or involvement in a particular group or set of ideas. See **Insignia**. 3. Metaphorically, to flag down = to send out a signal. 4. Different colors of flags could be associated with different meanings:

> *Red Flag:* Dangerous or problem situation
> *White Flag:* Sign of surrender or submission
> *Yellow Flag:* Symbol of illness or quarantine

Black Flag: Representative of death

5. Associated with a call to pay attention. 6. Could be associated with self–identity. See **Self**. 7. Patriotism or nationalism. 8. A flag at half–mast is associated with death. See **Death**. 9. A flag of a particular country is associated with the feeling one has for that country or its people.

FLAGPOLE 1. That standard or belief system we wish to raise. 2. What we wish to show others about our identity. 3. See also **Flag**.

FLASHLIGHT 1. Can correspond to the need for or the act of being prepared. 2. Could indicate a small truth or insight. See **Light**. 3. Something under scrutiny or inspection. See **Spotlight**.

FLEUR DE LIS 1. Symbolic of the French monarchy. 2. Associated with Joan of Arc and freedom against oppression. 3. Liturgically, represents the Virgin Mary. See **Virgin Mary**.

FLIES 1. An irritant that is constantly in one's way. See **Bug**. 2. Metaphorically, there's a fly in the ointment = there's a problem that must be dealt with. 3. May indicate erratic thoughts or behavior.

FLOOD 1. Corresponds to an inundation of water, spirit, emotion, or frustration. See **Water**. 2. Something that overwhelms one's situation; a breakdown. 3. A facilitator of personal transformation. See **Ark**. 4. Associated with the need to release one's feelings. 5. Might correspond to one's menstrual flow. 6. Could be a literal indication of a flood. 7. You may also wish to see **Weather** and **Boat**.

FLOOR 1. Principles, a foundation, or a belief system. 2. Something that is under consideration. 3. A state of subservience (i.e., being walked upon). See **Carpet**. 4. The bottom of any building. See **Building** or **House**. 5. Where one gets support (i.e., a job, a relationship, a belief system, etc.). 6. You may also wish to see **Feet**.

FLOUR 1. Provides sustenance or food for thought. See **Food**. 2. Could indicate the staff of life. See **Bread**. 3. Depending upon the imagery, may be associated with a literal food allergy. 4. You may also wish to see **Cook**. 5. May be a pun on something that grows and flowers. See **Flowers**.

FLOWERS 1. Can correspond to something within one's own self about to blossom. 2. May be symbolic of the growth (blossoming) of spiritual gifts, sexuality, or a new insight. 3. Could relate to the inner garden of one's spiritual life. See **Garden**. 4. Represents beauty, hope, and new life. 5. Types of flowers may be symbolic of individual meanings; for example: a lily may symbolize a new beginning or a rebirth; a lotus can represent something beautiful that springs forth from something unworthy or evil; wildflowers may be associated with uncultivated abilities, the natural growth of gifts, or new sexuality. 6. Talents or inner beauty that bursts forth. 7. See also **Plant**.

FLUORESCENT LIGHT 1. Associated with artificial or man–made light. See **Light**. 2. Could correspond to narrow or limited vision. 3. May represent a man–made teaching or law. 4. Symbolic of something that is not as enlightening as a spiritual truth. 5. Can be associated with something that is harmful to the human body.

FLUTE 1. Could suggest the need for harmony and cooperation. See **Music**. 2. In literature, associated with the *Pied Piper*, and being an obedient follower. 3. Something that is high–pitched or shrill.

FLYING 1. To journey freely through understanding. 2. Associated with great joy or euphoria. 3. Associated with rising above or overcoming a situation or experience. See **Ascend.** 4. Can correspond to being in the spiritual realm. 5. May be symbolic of astral or mind travel. 6. Could be predictive of upcoming travel. 7. Often occurs just prior to the awareness within a dream that one is dreaming (a lucid dream). 8. May be associated with a desire to avoid the real world and engage in fantasy. 9. Metaphorically, can be used as follows: to fly in the face of = to oppose consciously; he flew off the handle = he erupted emotionally; there's a fly in the ointment = there's a problem. 10. Associated with success or accomplishment. 11. You may also wish to see **Airplane** and **Sky.**

FLYING SAUCER 1. Could indicate an unusual or an alien idea. See **Alien.** 2. Something that is out of place or from another environment. 3. Associated with a message from another realm or another level of the mind. See **Message/Messenger.** 4. May be associated with a foreign or an unknown activity or experience. 5. A lofty idea or project. See **Airplane.**

FOG 1. Associated with the inability to see or think clearly, often due to cloudy perceptions or emotions. See **Weather.** 2. Can correspond to being in a confused state of mind. 3. Because it is water mist, it could represent being in a state of spiritual bewilderment. See **Water.**

FOGHORN 1. A warning of an impending emotional situation or experience. 2. A warning regarding something that is not currently seen. 3. May be associated with a spiritual message. See **Message/Messenger.** 4. See **Fog.**

FOOD 1. Represents nourishment or sustenance of a spiritual, mental, or physical sort. 2. Can correspond to one's own personal desires, indulgences, words, satisfaction, or physical appetites. 3. Associated with spiritual truths, new ideas, or something that you're feeding or that you need to feed to yourself or another. 4. Dreaming of eating a particular kind of food is often associated with a literal subconscious dietary recommendation. 5. Metaphorically, different types of food often are symbolic of different meanings; for example: being buttered up = being praised falsely or excessively; bread of life = source of all sustenance; a piece of cake = that which is easy; gumming up the works = getting in the way; the spice of life = something that makes things important or worth living; food for thought = another's words or ideas; getting in a jam = being in trouble; receiving only crumbs = receiving very little, or what others have rejected; hamming it up = being overly dramatic; doesn't know a hill of beans = doesn't know anything; milk of human kindness = compassion and understanding. 6. Phallic images in food include: hot dogs, bananas, carrots, etc. See **Phallus.** 7. Frozen food may symbolize talents or thoughts that need to be thawed or brought out into the open. See **Freeze/Freezer.** 8. What one is eating in the dream is highly significant and has its own meaning; for example: eating rabbit in a dream may indicate that one's current diet is stimulating the sex drive; eating a letter may be symbolic of eating one's words; eating lettuce could simply be a suggestion that more vegetables or roughage should be in the diet; drinking coffee out of an aspirin bottle could suggest that one's intake of caffeine is attributing to headaches. 9. You may also wish to see **Fruit.**

FOOL 1. One who is lacking in intelligence, reason, or common sense. 2. Can correspond to possessing bad judgment. 3. May be associated with playfulness or horseplay. 4. Metaphorically, can be used as follows: he's a fool = he doesn't know what he's doing; she played the fool = she pretended she didn't know the answer; they're fooling around = they're having an affair; she's nobody's fool = she's extremely intelligent. 5. Associated with zero in the tarot. See **Tarot.** 6. See also **People.**

FOOTBALL 1. Corresponds to one's ability to play the game of life (i.e., teamwork, cooperation, etc.). See **Sports.** 2. May symbolize having a touchdown (i.e., a successful outcome). 3. The activity in the game will have a great deal to do with the associated symbolism; for example: dropping the ball could represent missing an opportunity or experiencing a failure. 4. Metaphorically, a football might suggest a situation or a problem that may be passed from one individual to another. 5. Could symbolize one's direction or journey. See **Feet.** 6. You may also wish to see **Ball.**

FOOTPRINTS 1. Can correspond to one's direction, mission, goal, or journey. See **Journey.** 2. Associated with your footing or foundation. See **Feet.** 3. Suggestive of where one is headed, where one is going; the act of following or leading. 4. In literature, the name of a poem that suggests the continual presence of God in one's life.

FOREHEAD 1. Associated with confidence and intelligence. 2. Something that is uppermost in one's mind; an idea. 3. You may also wish to see **Head** and **Face.**

FOREIGNER 1. Corresponds to something that is out of place or from another environment. 2. May be associated with a foreign or unknown part of oneself. See **Shadow.** 3. Could indicate a foreign idea. 4. Acting in a manner that is out of keeping with one's normal behavior. 5. Might be a literal indication of a foreign visitor or travel to a foreign locale. 6. See also **People.**

FOREST 1. Associated with growth, nature, or new ideas. 2. May represent thoughts or the unconscious mind. 3. See also **Tree** and **Wood/Woods.** 4. Metaphorically, can't see the forest for the trees = getting caught up in small details at the expense of the overall perspective. 5. May indicate one's current situation or duty. 6. You may also wish to see **Plant.**

FORK 1. May be associated with one's dietary habits. 2. Might symbolize a separation or a division between portions of the whole. 3. Could correspond to a choice or something that one picks out carefully. 4. Metaphorically, can be used as follows: to fork it over = to give it to someone. 5. You may also wish to see **Food.**

FORK IN THE ROAD 1. Associated with a choice in directions. See **Road** and **Journey.** 2. May correspond to two different ideas, experiences, or choices that one must choose between. 3. Might be a representation of choosing good from bad, right from wrong.

FORMAL 1. Something that is polite or superior. 2. Associated with one's outward appearance. See **Clothes.** 3. Could indicate being overdressed, overprepared, elaborate, expensive, or showy.

FORT 1. A place where one can build a defense. 2. That part of oneself that is at war. See **War.** 3. May correspond to creating a wall of protection for one's emotions or from the environment. See **Wall.** 4. May suggest that one is too defensive. 5. You may also wish to see **Building** or **House.**

FORT KNOX 1. Associated with finances and security. See **Building.** 2. Might be symbolic of the financial condition of the United States or the stock market. 3. You may also wish to see **Money.**

FOSSILS 1. Associated with the extinct or the outdated. See **Antique.** 2. Metaphorically, she's a fossil = she is out of touch with contemporary thought. 3. Could indicate past experiences or memories. 4. You may also wish to see **Ancient.**

FOUNDATION 1. Associated with plans, dreams, or basic understanding. See **Building.** 2. Could correspond to the physical body, mental understanding, or spiritual beliefs (i.e., the foundation or different parts of oneself). See **House.** 3. May represent the establishment of something new. 4. One's principles, beliefs, or support (i.e., a job, a relationship, etc.).

FOUNTAIN 1. The source of knowledge, understanding, or spiritual information and insights. 2. Can correspond to a reservoir of help or health. 3. The Fountain of Youth symbolizes restoration of youth and vitality. 4. The water of life. See **Water.**

FOUR 1. Associated with stability, materiality, and something that is of the earth. 2. See **Numerology.**

FOUR–LEAF CLOVER 1. Associated with good luck, fortune, or destiny. 2. See also **Clover.**

FOX 1. Symbolic of one who is sly and cunning. See **Animals.** 2. Metaphorically, can be used as follows: she's foxy = she's sexy; he was foxed = he was tricked.

FRAME 1. Something that surrounds, contains, or displays. 2. An object of attention. See **Picture.** 3. Metaphorically, he was framed = he was set up.

FRANCE 1. Corresponds primarily to whatever an individual thinks of France or the French (i.e., associated with Paris, romance, the city of lights, food, the Riviera, etc.). 2. May be indicative of a foreign visitor or travel.

FRANCIS OF ASSISI 1. Can correspond to one who has become master over the animal instincts. See **Animals.** 2. Associated with personal spirituality and faith. 3. May represent a spiritual messenger or teacher. 4. May be symbolic of the Catholic church or Italy.

FRANKENSTEIN 1. Associated with one's basic instincts or lower nature. 2. Psychologically, may represent an individual's shadow. See **Shadow.** 3. Could symbolize one's own fears. 4. Something that destroys its creator or itself. 5. Might indicate an outer appearance that is misunderstood by others or the environment. 6. You may also wish to see **Beast.** 7. See also **People.**

FRANKLIN, BENJAMIN 1. Can correspond to invention, patriotism, or writing. 2. May be associated with the internal tinkerer, or the youthful spirit in age. 3. Can be indicative of lifelong human desire or the joy of life. 4. May be associated with any of his inventions. 5. May be a symbol for the United States.

FREEZE/FREEZER 1. Something that keeps things frozen, cold, static, impenetrable, or unchanging. 2. Can correspond with emotional detachment. 3. May indicate sexual frigidity. 4. Something melting could represent the release of old patterns, thoughts, or beliefs, or the opening up of emotions. 5. May be associated with unused ideas or dreams (i.e., one put them in cold storage). 6. Metaphorically, a frozen asset = one that cannot be used immediately. 7. See **Weather**. 8. You may also wish to see **Refrigerator**.

FREUD, SIGMUND 1. May be symbolic of the need to seek psychiatric help or to help another. 2. Associated with the Oedipus complex and human sexuality. See **Sex**. 3. Could represent a figure of wisdom or the higher self. 4. Might correspond to Austria.

FRIEND 1. If the person is unknown to you, could indicate an aspect of yourself that needs to be befriended. See **Shadow**. 2. If a known person, could correspond to the relationship one possesses with that individual (i.e., feelings toward the person, areas of the relationship that need to be worked on, etc.). 3. Can be associated with aspects of ourselves in relationship to that person, or talents, qualities, or experiences that we associate with that person. 4. Could indicate a suggestion or a warning in terms of your friend's welfare. 5. Might suggest the need to become more friendly. 6. Could indicate the need to become friends with the person in the image. 7. See also **People**.

FROG 1. Can be associated with enchantment, uncleanliness, or unconscious knowledge. 2. May indicate an enchanted prince. 3. Something that can leap over hurdles. 4. Metaphorically, having a frog in one's throat = having difficulty speaking. 5. You may also wish to see **Water**, **Fish**, and **Animals**.

FRONT DESK 1. Something that is placed before the public. 2. May be associated with how you are viewed by or how you view others. See **Mask**. 3. May indicate one's attitudes, position, stature, thoughts, foundation, or belief system. See **Desk** and **Furniture**. 4. Associated with how you greet your current situation.

FRUIT 1. That which the body, mind, or soul feeds upon or needs to feed upon. See **Food**. 2. Associated with gifts, talents, or ideas that are ready to be harvested. 3. Metaphorically, the fruit of one's labors = the end result or accomplishment; he's a fruit = he's effeminate. 4. In slang, represents something unusual, different, or out of the ordinary. 5. May often correspond to a literal dietary suggestion. 6. Associated with feminine energy. See **Womb**. 7. Might represent an increase in one's fruits of the spirit. 8. You may also wish to see **Flowers**.

FRY 1. A source of heat, torment, or agitation. 2. Can correspond to mental worry or distress. 3. Metaphorically, out of the frying pan and into the fire = from a bad situation into an even worse one. 4. You may also wish to see **Cook**.

FULL 1. Something that is complete or overflowing. 2. Could symbolize being busy or overwhelmed, or a crowd. 3. May be literally connected to having eaten too much food. See **Food**. 4. Might indicate a full emotional condition or experience. 5. Metaphorically, he's had his fill = he's had enough or he can't take any more; she's full of it = she's exaggerating or fooling herself.

FUNERAL 1. Associated with a transition or change. See **Death**. 2. To bury or discard what is no longer necessary. 3. Could represent a loss, an approaching disaster, or an unwelcome event. 4. Might be a literal in-dication of an approaching death. 5. That which has come to an end.

FURNACE 1. Can correspond to a place of extreme heat, anger, or emotional frustra-tion. 2. Associated with severe trials. 3. Can correspond to one's stomach (i.e., heart-burn), assimilation, or digestion. See **House.** 4. Might correspond to one's homelife (i.e., hearth and home). 5. A source of warmth and comfort. 6. See also **Fireplace.**

FURNITURE 1. Something that clutters, decorates, or fills one's mind or environ-ment. 2. May be associated with ideas or opinions. 3. Might indicate beliefs, feelings, or attitudes regarding a certain situation or person. 4. The age and type of furniture will have a great deal to do with the symbolism; for example: antiques could represent wis-dom, one's upbringing, or old biases (see **Antique**); a desk may be associated with work (see **Desk** and **Work**); a chair might be symbolic of one's position or beliefs (see **Chair**); new furniture could represent a new idea, position, or project; baby furniture could indicate a childish situation, an im-mature idea, or a pregnancy (see **Baby**); a loveseat may symbolize a relationship, etc. 5. The condition of the furniture will pro-vide additional insights into the symbology; for example, note whether the furniture is clean, disorganized, broken, etc. 6. You may also wish to see types of furniture; for ex-ample, see **Bed/Bedroom.** 7. Depending on the imagery and placement of the furniture, you may also wish to see **House.**

FUSE 1. Can correspond to one's enthusi-asm or energy level. 2. A source of energy or power in a situation. See **Electricity.** 3. May be associated with one's nerves or blood pressure. 4. Something that is combustible and/or under pressure (i.e., emotions). 5. Metaphorically, don't blow a fuse = don't get so upset.

FUTURE 1. Associated with time. See **Time** and **Calendar.** 2. Dreaming of the future is called a precognitive dream. See **ESP.** 3. Symbols that may be associated with the future are as follows: approaching objects, the right side of a scene, or something that is brand-new.

G

1. *The seventh letter of the alphabet.* 2. *The Roman numeral for 400.* 3. *Musically, the fifth note; G clef, or the treble clef* 4. *Numerologically, equivalent to seven.* 5. *Scholastically, a good achievement.* 6. *Slang symbol for $1,000, as in 100 Gs ($100,000).* 7. *In Greek, gamma.*

GAMBLING 1. Associated with taking a risk or participating in an uncertain venture. 2. Often corresponds to taking foolish or wasteful actions. 3. To win at gambling may imply that the risk is worth taking; to lose advises caution or a different course of action. 4. That which is chancy. 5. Depending on the imagery, you may wish to see **Game** and **Cards.** 6. Might indicate good luck. 7. You may also wish to see **Las Vegas.**

GAME 1. Corresponds to the experience one is currently involved in (i.e., the game of life; current challenges, etc.). 2. Often symbolic of your group activities (i.e., work, family). See **Work.** 3. Associated with personal interactions with others. 4. The activity in the imagery may display your propensity or lack of it for cooperation, teamwork, sportsmanship conduct, winning and losing, etc. See **Sports.** 5. May suggest relaxation or finding nonstressful forms of amusement. 6. Associated with friendly competition. 7. Metaphorically, can be used as follows: the game is up = it's over; play by the game = abide by the rules; his game was off = he wasn't as successful as usual. 8. May be suggestive of a course of action or a game plan. 9. Might also indicate a period in one's life journey. See **Journey.**

GANDHI, MAHATMA 1. Symbol of nonviolence and peace. 2. Associated with India. 3. Represents religious tolerance and cooperation. 4. Corresponds to independence and passive resistance. 5. May be associated with a foreign visitor or travel.

GANESH 1. The Hindu god of wisdom, discretion, and sound judgment. See **Hinduism.** 2. Symbolized by the head of an elephant with the body of a man. 3. You may also wish to see **Elephant.**

GANG 1. Can correspond to portions of oneself. 2. May be associated with group activities with which one is involved. 3. Might represent a criminal element. See **Gangster.** 4. Could symbolize one's combined problems, fears, frustrations, or difficulties. 5. Metaphorically, the girls ganged up against her = they took sides opposing her. 6. You may also wish to see **People.**

GANGSTER 1. Corresponds to the perpetrator of evil, intrigue, deception, or criminal activity. 2. Might be associated with the crooked aspects of oneself (i.e., bad thoughts, negative attitudes, harsh words, etc.). 3. May correspond to those parts of oneself that are hidden or are at war. See **Shadow.** 4. See **Gang.** 5. Depending on the imagery, you may also wish to see **Thief.** 6. See also **People.** 7. Associated with taking advantage or being taken advantage of. 8. Might indicate that which is bent, unsavory, or immoral.

GARAGE 1. Associated with one's automobile, self, personal storage, or one's personal workshop. See **House.** 2. The meaning of the imagery will depend upon what is happening in the garage; for example: fixing one's car could indicate the need for personal healing physically, mentally, or spiritually, or it may suggest that your car literally needs to be examined by a mechanic; cleaning the garage may suggest the need to clean out one's life in those areas that are neglected. 3. Might be associated with old ideas or patterns that need to be discarded or reexamined once again. 4. You may also wish to see **Car.**

GARBAGE 1. Something worthless, offensive, or immoral. 2. Can correspond to those things we have discarded or those things that need to be discarded, i.e., ideas, words, opinions, attitudes, etc. 3. Might also be calling to mind something that you inadvertently threw away and shouldn't have, or the fact that you are wasteful. 4. Could indicate a rotten diet or food that has been wasted. See **Food.** 5. Might be associated with one's own stomach (i.e., especially the image of a garbage disposal). 6. Could also be associated with the lower sex drive. 7. Might indicate a need for cleansing. See **Bathroom.** 8. That which needs to be organized or put in order. See **Clean.**

GARDEN 1. Associated with what one is currently cultivating or neglecting. See **Field.** 2. The place of inner spirituality and peace. 3. The appearance of the garden or what you have planted as a current crop may give clues as to your own inner state. 4. Metaphorically, he led her down the garden path = he misled her. 5. What one is doing in the garden will have a great deal to do with the symbolism; for example: weeding the garden might suggest the need to discard useless or negative ideas; sowing seeds could be associated with sharing your insights with others; watering various plants and flowers might symbolize the need to either nurture some of the things or people in your life or to be more spiritual in your activities. 6. Associated with the mind or unconscious. See **Unconscious.** 7. Biblically, what you sow you reap. See **Karma.** 8. Depending on the imagery, you may also wish to see **Plant** and **Flowers.**

GARDENER 1. Represents the higher self. See **Garden.** 2. Could be associated with Christ. See **Christ.** 3. That which your subconscious mind is planting. See **Plant.**

GAS 1. Can correspond to something that is inflammable or that provides light, energy, or heat. 2. May be associated with volatile emotions or a bad temper. 3. Could symbolize fuel (food, experiences, relationships, or ideas) that can assist in the arrival at the next stage of life's journey. 4. Metaphorically, can be used as follows: step on the gas = hurry up; to pass gas = to physiologically expel air; that show was a gas = that was really funny. 5. Can correspond to one's enthusiasm or energy level. 6. That which provides energy or power to a situation. See **Electricity.** 7. You may also wish to see **Automobile.**

GATE 1. A new opening, idea, or direction. See **Door** and **Road.** 2. A passage to the next experience, idea, or relationship. 3. Associated with the way out of one's current environment, obstacle, or state of mind. 4. Metaphorically, to show an individual the gate = to ask her to leave. 5. You may also wish to see **House, Yard,** or **Fence.**

GELATIN I. That which is wobbly and unstable. 2. Might indicate the state of being easy to shake (i.e., throw off balance, or change one's mind). 3. Could indicate a literal dietary suggestion (i.e., gelatin rather than desserts, etc.). 4. May be associated with compressed emotions or an idea that is solidifying. 5 You may also wish to see **Food.**

GEMINI Ⅱ 1. Third sign of the zodiac, corresponding to May 21–June 20. 2. Associated with the following positive traits: versatile, intelligent, and skilled in any form of communication. 3. Associated with the following negative traits: changeable, inconsistent, and prone to gossip. 4. Astrologically, ruled by Mercury. See **Mercury.** 5. See also **Twins.** 6. An air sign. See **Air.** 7. See also **Astrology.**

GEMS 1. May be associated with spiritual truths, wisdom, mental health, or material success. See **Jewels/Jewelry.** 2. That which is prized for its beauty. 3. Metaphorically, he's a real gem = he's wonderful. 4. Could correspond to one's talents.

GENIE 1. The magical or limitless part of oneself. 2. Represents the ability to do much more than seems possible. 3. Could be symbolic of boundless creativity or the manifestation of ideas. See **Magic/Magician.** 4. Can correspond to help or assistance from the spiritual realm or one's higher self. 5. Might be a positive or a negative influence depending on the type of genie. 6. You may also wish to see **People.**

GENITALS 1. Associated with sexuality. See **Phallus** or **Womb.** 2. May correspond to one's sexual desires or fears. 3. The appearance of the genitals has a great deal to do with the symbolism; for example: extremely small genitals are associated with immaturity; large genitals might indicate an overemphasis on sex. See **Sex.** 4. You may also wish to see **Man** or **Woman.**

GHETTO 1. An impoverished situation or experience. See **House.** 2. A place of darkness, sadness, or little hope. 3. Can correspond to crime and negativity. 4. One's own association with ghettos may have a great deal to do with the symbolism.

GHOST 1. Often corresponds to one's fears, thoughts, the past, or that which keeps haunting you. 2. Could represent seeing only a partial outline of what's there. See **Silhouette.** 3. Might be associated with one's true nature or inner self. See **Soul.** 4. May be a spiritual messenger. 5. Might be associated with one's shadow. See **Shadow.** 6. Could indicate a faint possibility. 7. Might symbolize a death. See **Death.** 8. You may also wish to see **People.**

GIANT 1. That which appears larger than life. See **Size.** 2. People or conditions that are threatening or present themselves as obstacles. 3. Could be associated with power or ego. 4. May indicate that which has the brawn but not the brains (the power but not the insight). 5. A big event. 6. Metaphorically, she's an intellectual giant = she's extremely intelligent. 7. See also **People.**

GIFT 1. Associated with a gift, a present, a quality, or one's hidden talent. 2. Metaphorically, can be used as follows: she's a gifted student = she's more intelligent than the average student; don't look a gift horse in the mouth = don't be overly critical of anything given to you. 3. Might indicate a reward, a celebration, or a surprise. 4. Could correspond to the need to give or to receive praise or encouragement. 5. Depending on imagery, you may also wish to see **Box.**

GIRAFFE 1. Because of the long neck, associated with the throat and therefore the will. See **Animals.** 2. May also symbolize that one has a great distance between their thoughts (head) and their emotions (heart). 3. Might also be a representation of the desire to wring someone's neck. 4. Something that is out of reach. 5. Might indicate a throat condition.

GIRDLE 1. Associated with something that controls, pulls in, or restrains. See **Clothes**. 2. May be associated with the need for dietary, sexual, or any type of restraint (i.e., wearing a girdle around your mouth suggests that you need to control your words or your eating). 3. Could represent a literal desire to appear more attractive. 4. Depending on imagery, you may also wish to see **Fat**.

GIRL 1. May correspond to the female counterpart of one's youthful self. See **Child**. 2. Might symbolize an idea, a project, or a person of about the same age. 3. Could indicate one's own age: physically, mentally, or spiritually. 4. May represent the feminine aspects in oneself that are still immature. See **Woman**. 5. The type of girl and how she is dressed may be significant. 6. You may also wish to see **People**.

GLAD 1. One of the four basic emotions (glad, mad, sad, and scared). See **Emotion**. 2. May be associated with activities or interactions causing one to be cheerful, joyful, delighted, or satisfied.

GLADIATOR 1. Can be associated with fighting with one's own emotions, ideas, desires, or thoughts. 2. Associated with the contest between different portions of oneself (i.e., physically, mentally, or spiritually). See **Shadow**. 3. A struggle with someone or something at work, at home, or in the present situation. 4. May correspond with the struggle between various portions of

one's mind (conscious, subconscious, or higher self). 5. Can correspond to an old battle or a problem that must be conquered. 6. You may also wish to see **Fighting** and **War.**

GLASS 1. Associated with vision. 2. What one is seeing through. See **Window**. 3. The type of glass is symbolic of what one is looking through or with; for example: stained glass suggests spiritual vision; rose-colored glass symbolizes seeing things better than they actually are. 4. Could represent a fragile part of one's life. 5. May correspond to solidified or unchanging emotion. 6. That which holds something to eat or drink. 7. A glass wall can represent emotion or obstacles and situations that you can see through but that still have you feeling trapped. See **Wall.** 8. Depending on imagery, you may also wish to see **Broken.**

GLASSES (EYE) 1. Represents that which enhances comprehension, vision, or understanding. See **Eyeglasses.** 2. May be associated with how one views the world. See **Eyes** and **Window.**

GLOVES 1. Corresponds to something that you put your hands into. See **Hand** and **Clothes.** 2. Associated with taking care of oneself or the need to protect oneself from the elements. 3. Could be a literal indication of weather change. 4. Metaphorically, handle with kid gloves = to be very careful with. 5. That which covers or hides something your hands are doing. 6. What one is involved with. See **Fingers.**

GLUE 1. Something that binds, connects, joins, or holds things together. 2. May correspond to a sticky situation. 3. Metaphorically, they stick together like glue = they're firmly united.

GO 1. Associated with a message. See **Message/Messenger.** 2. Might correspond to an answer to a personal question, encouragement, or the indication that everything is okay to proceed. 3. Depending on imagery you may wish to see **Traffic Light** or **Sign.**

GOAT 1. Associated with stubbornness. 2. Metaphorically, can be used as follows: to get someone's goat = to irritate another individual; he's an old goat = he's a horny old man; scapegoat = one who is forced to take the blame for others. 3. Astrologically, one of the twelve signs of the zodiac. See **Capricorn.** 4. See also **Animals.**

GOD 1. The source of all power, life, light, wisdom, love, creation, and authority. 2. Could be associated with one's higher self or soul. 3. Ultimately, all that can be conceived to exist. 4. May represent the need to pay closer attention to the spiritual side of one's life. 5. Associated with great bliss and joy. See **Heaven.** 6. Dreaming about God telling you his name is symbolic of the need to have a more personal relationship with spirituality. 7. The ultimate authority in all spiritual matters or concerns. 8. A spiritual messenger. See **Message/Messenger.** 9. May be associated with a parental figure. See **Mother** or **Father.** 10. The source of higher consciousness. See **Soul.** 11. May be symbolic of a source of unlimited wisdom: a seer, a sage, a prophet, or Christ. See **Christ.** 12. Might be symbolized by the colors gold or violet. See **Colors.** 13. You may also wish to see **People.** 14. For ancient gods and goddesses, see **Mythology.**

GOLD (COLOR) 1. Something gold is often associated with a spiritual truth or insight. 2. See **Colors.**

GOLD (METAL) 1. Can represent great spiritual wealth or insight. 2. Could be associated with personal riches (i.e., talents) or material wealth. 3. That which is invaluable, precious, or heavenly. 4. Metaphorically, can be used as follows: as good as gold = something that is very worthwhile or that can always be depended upon; she's a gold digger = she's only interested in herself (personal material gain); one's golden years = one's retirement years; the Golden Rule = do unto others as you would have them do unto you; all that glitters isn't gold = everything that appears beautiful is not necessarily worth having; fool's gold = fake gold or a worthless activity. 5. You may also wish to see **Colors**.

GOLDEN GATE BRIDGE 1. May imply a passage through spiritual understanding or insight. See **Bridge.** 2. Associated with San Francisco. 3. May indicate domestic travel. 4. Could represent a golden or advantageous situation or way out of the experience.

GOLDFISH 1. May be associated with great spiritual wisdom or insight. See **Fish.** 2. Something that is important or valuable. See gold in **Colors.** 3. You may also wish to see **Gold (Color)** or **Gold (Metal).**

GOLF 1. Can be associated with the game of life. See **Sports.** 2. Can represent the need for relaxation. 3. A golf ball may indicate the current situation or experience one is playing with. See **Ball.** 4. A golf club could represent what you are doing with your opportunities.

GONADS 1. A gland in the body. 2. Associated with the first endocrine center or chakra. 3. Relates to human survival and sexuality. 4. Metaphysically, corresponds to Saturn; also associated with the symbol of a bull. 5. In Revelation, it is represented by the Church of Ephesus. 6. You may also wish to see **Genitals**. 7. See also **Chakras**.

GONE WITH THE WIND 1. A tale of perseverance and determination. 2. Could be associated with the South. 3. Might correspond to an ending, a parting, or coming to a close (i.e., that which is gone with the wind).

GOOSE 1. Associated with foolishness or stupidity. 2. Metaphorically, can be used as follows: she cooked his goose = she got him in trouble; to get goose bumps = to have an eerie or fearful feeling; that was the goose that laid the golden egg = something unusual that was very successful. 3. You may also wish to see **Bird**.

GOPHER 1. May represent one who does things at the command of others (i.e., a go for). See **Puppet**. 2. One who burrows to protect oneself from emotions, others, or the environment. See **Animals**. 3. Depending on imagery, you may also wish to see **Hole**.

GORGE 1. Can correspond to a narrow pass or troubling conditions or circumstances that must be gone through, around, or over. 2. Metaphorically, may represent overeating. 3. Might represent female sexuality. See **Womb**. 4. The feeling of being surrounded or hemmed in. See **Box**. 5. You may also wish to see **Prison, Earth,** and **Mountain.**

GORILLA 1. The largest type of ape. See **Monkey.** 2. Might be associated with low intellect or irrational behavior. 3. Metaphorically, he's a gorilla = he's strong, hairy, large, apelike, etc., or he's a gangster. See **Gangster.** 4. You may also wish to see **Animals.**

GOSPEL 1. Literally, the good news. 2. Often associated with the teachings of Jesus.

See **Christ**. 3. Corresponds to the first four books of the New Testament: Matthew, Mark, Luke, and John. 4. You may also wish to see **God** and **Bible**. 5. A spiritual message. See **Message/Messenger**. 6. You may also wish to see **Christianity.**

GOURD 1. Might indicate the fact that one is retaining water or emotions. 2. You may also wish to see **Squash.**

GRADUATE 1. The act of completing a situation, a lesson, or an experience. 2. An activity in which one no longer needs to participate. 3. That which one has passed. 4. You may also wish to see **School.**

GRAIN 1. Corresponds to an idea, a plan, or an experience that has the potential to grow. 2. Associated with something that may be planted for later harvest. See **Garden**. 3. Metaphorically, against the grain = in opposition to oneself or others. 4. Biblically, associated with great faith and limitless potential (Matthew 17:20 and Luke 17:6). 5. You may also wish to see **Seed.**

GRANDFATHER/GRANDMOTHER 1. Usually associated with wisdom and insight from personal experience. 2. Often relates to an individual's own higher self or to subconscious information. See **Old Man/Old Woman.** 3. May be a literal symbol of a grand mother or father. See **Mother** or **Father.** 4. That which is kindly and indulgent. 5. Metaphorically, to be grandfathered in = to supersede current regulations or guidelines. 6. Could be indicative of one's own forebears or a karmic memory. See **Karma.** 7. Often corresponds to that relationship one possesses with one's own grandparent. 8. A deceased grandparent may indicate a message from another realm. See **Message/ Messenger.** 9. You may also wish to see **People.**

GRAPES 1. Can be associated with wine and the spirit. See **Wine**. 2. May be associated with fruitfulness. 3. Something that may undergo transformation and become even more desirable. 4. Might be a literal dietary suggestion for more fruit in one's diet. See **Fruit.** 5. Metaphorically, she's eating sour grapes = she's upset (soured) about the outcome. 6. Liturgically, symbolic of Communion. 7. You may also wish to see **Food.**

GRASS 1. Associated with growth, healing, energy, or vibrancy. 2. Can correspond to a healthy foundation. See **Foundation**. 3. Mowing the grass may indicate putting one's thoughts or activities in order. See **Yardwork**. 4. See also **Plant**. 5. Metaphorically, associated with marijuana.

GRAVE 1. Represents the past or that which has been left behind. 2. Can be associated with the unconscious or subconscious. See **Unconscious** or **Subconscious**. 3. Metaphorically, that which is very serious. 4. Something purposefully buried or hidden. 5. See **Death** and **Funeral**. 6. You may also wish to see **Earth** and **Vault**.

GRAY 1. Associated with the mysterious or the emotional. 2. See **Colors**.

GREAT EXPECTATIONS 1. A story of self-realization and human metamorphosis. 2. Coming into one's own in spite of birth, environment, or those who would stand in the way. 3. Great things may be forthcoming. 4. Associated with an unexpected but generally positive outcome.

GREEN 1. Associated with healing, growth, money, or human love. 2. See **Colors**.

GREENHOUSE 1. The inner spiritual garden. See **Garden**. 2. Something that is delicate and being cultivated. 3. Associated with the ability to grow and mature regardless of outside influences or the environment. 4. Might indicate one's own productivity, ideas, or talents. 5. You may also wish to see **Plant** and **Flowers**.

GRIFFIN 1. Mythologically, a creature with the body of a lion and the head and wings of an eagle. See **Lion** and **Eagle**. 2. Metaphysically, symbolic of a strong guardian of truth. 3. Liturgically, associated with the twofold nature of Christ (both human and divine). 4. You may also wish to see **Animals** and **Bird**.

GROCERIES 1. Associated with choices and decisions. 2. May symbolize opportunities or possible directions in one's current situation. See **Shop**. 3. Depending on imagery, might correspond to one's dietary needs or literal dietary suggestions. See **Food**.

GROW 1. Something that becomes more important, larger, a bigger problem, or closer in perspective. See **Size**. 2. Associated with development and maturity. See **Plant** and **Garden**. 3. The meaning of the symbolism will depend upon what is growing; for example: a growing checkbook could suggest that one will be receiving more money or more bills; growing in height at work may symbolize that your stature and importance is about to increase; a growing nose might be associated with telling lies (i.e., *Pinocchio*), or that one has become too nosy; a growing rash on one's body might indicate a health problem, or a growing source of irritation.

GUARD 1. Might suggest the need to be on guard or symbolic of something one wishes kept from others. 2. Could indicate personal protection, security, or lawfulness. See **Police/Police Station**. 3. May be associated with the need to be cautious. 4. Corresponds to one who is keeping a watchful eye on a person, a place, or the situation. 5. May also represent a guardian. See **Angel**. 6. Metaphorically, can be used as follows: he was caught off guard = he wasn't prepared. 7. See also **People**.

GUIDANCE/GUIDE 1. Can be associated with one's higher self, wisdom, principles, or upbringing. 2. Giving direction to one's spiritual journey. See **Journey**. 3. You may also wish to see **Old Man/Old Woman** and **Christ**.

GUINEVERE 1. Associated with beauty and the feminine principle. See **Woman**. 2. Can correspond to yearning or desire. 3. Might be symbolic of temptation. See **Eve**.

GUM 1. Can symbolize an idea or a situation that one is chewing upon. See **Chew/Chewing Gum**. 2. That which is in one's mouth (i.e., words). 3. Depending on imagery, you may also wish to see **Mouth** or **Teeth**.

GUN 1. Can correspond to imposing one's views or will on others. 2. Associated with violence or aggression. 3. Represents something that can cause injury. 4. Could be representative of being overly defensive or the need to become defensive. 5. May represent an aggressive male nature. See **Phallus**. 6. That which causes fear. 7. You may also wish to see **War**.

GYM 1. Associated with fitness, exercise, or the need to get in shape. See **Exercise**. 2. A place for sports and group activities. See **Sports**. 3. Depending on imagery, you may also wish to see **Athlete**.

GYPSY 1. That which wanders from place to place or from one experience to another. 2. May correspond to one who is enchanted, magical, or mysterious. See **Magic/Magician**. 3. Might represent intuition, wisdom, good fortune, or insight. See **Psychic**. 4. You may also wish to see **People**.

1. *The eighth letter of the alphabet.* 2. *The Roman numeral for 200.* 3. *Chemically, the symbol for hydrogen.* 4. *Musically, the German name for B-natural.* 5. *Numerologically, equivalent to eight.* 6. *In physics, a symbol for henry (measurement for inductance) or the horizontal component of magnetism.* 7. *In Greek, eta.*

HAIR I. Corresponds to ideas, thoughts, creativity, intellect, state of mind, or mental processes. See **Head.** 2. May be associated with one's appearance, ego, or image. 3. Metaphorically, can be used as follows: the hair of the dog that bit you = taking a drink to calm a hangover; she took him through a hair-raising experience = she took him through a scary situation; to have someone by the short hairs = to have them completely under control; hair-brained idea = a poorly thought out scheme; splitting hairs = arguing a very minor or meaningless point; don't touch a hair on her head = don't harm her in any way. 4. Having an over-abundance of hair could suggest that you spend too much time in your head (rather than in your heart or emotions) or it might symbolize being oversexed. 5. Blow-drying one's hair could indicate something that blows one's mind. 6. Brushing or cutting your hair could suggest changing your outer appearance or getting your thoughts in order. 7. Coloring one's hair might symbolize the act of or the need for changing your mind. You may also wish to see **Colors.** 8. Knotted hair may symbolize a state of confusion. 9. If losing one's hair, see **Bald.** 10. Associated with how one is viewed by the world. See **Clothes.** 11. Biblically, associated

with great strength and vitality (the story of Samson; Judges 13–17). 12. Depending on imagery, you may also wish to see **Hat.**

HAIRCUT 1. Getting one's thoughts or ideas in order. See **Hair.** 2. The desire or act of changing one's outer appearance. See **Clothes.** 3. Eliminating that which is no longer necessary. 4. Depending on imagery, you may also wish to see **Scissors.**

HALL I. Associated with a passageway in understanding, experience, or consciousness. See **House.** 2. Can correspond to journeying deeper into the experience or one's own consciousness. 3. A direction, a path, or a journey. See **Journey** and **Road.**

HALLOWEEN I. A grand costume party. See **Costume.** 2. Can be associated with allowing one to express one's hidden self or shadow. See **Shadow.** 3. Hiding behind one's true feelings or thoughts. See **Mask.** 4. May be associated with mystery, darkness, or playful magic. 5. You may also wish to see any costumes being portrayed; for example, see **Ghost, Devil,** or **Witch.**

HALO 1. May correspond to spirituality, saintliness, or one's true (higher) self. 2. A fallen halo would suggest that you have not lived up to your spiritual or moral principles. 3. Could symbolize eternity. See **Circle.** 4. You may also wish to see **Mandala.** 5. May be associated with one's aura. See **Aura.**

HAMLET 1. Can correspond to fate, tragedy,

and revenge. 2. May be associated with the Oedipus complex. 3. Might be considered a literary version of the biblical Job.

HAMMER 1. Something that strikes, pounds, or irritates continually. 2. The driving force or something that has impact. 3. Corresponds to building an idea; making a mental concept become material. See **Contractor**. 4. May represent power and aggression. See **Phallus**. 5. The ability to build, shape, or create. 6. You may also wish to see **Tool**.

HAND 1. Identified with the self. See **Body**. 2. Service toward others. 3. Associated with one's work, duty, or responsibility. 4. Metaphorically, can be used as follows: to give a hand = to help out or to show recognition and appreciation; things got out of hand = things were out of control; to force one's hand = to force someone into making a decision or into making their move; biting the hand that feeds you = turning on your own source of supply; he lives from hand to mouth = he spends money as fast as he earns it; eating out of someone's hand = being totally subservient to their wishes or being under their complete control; laying hands on something = to take control, to attempt to injure, or laying-on-of-hands healing; she won hands down = she won without question, effortlessly; to hand over = to deliver or to delegate; she kept a hand in the project = she stayed involved. 5. Depending upon the imagery, you may also wish to see **Fingers** or **Gloves**.

HANDICAP 1. That which hinders, causes a disadvantage, or weakens. 2. Could be associated with balancing the competition between opponents in a game. See **Game**. 3. If a physical handicap, you may wish to see the portion of the body that is handicapped or see **Body**.

HANDKERCHIEF 1. Associated with crying and expressing one's emotions. See **Cry**. 2. Could symbolize one's allergies. 3. May be a literal indication of an emotional experience (i.e., a wedding, a funeral, a birth, etc.). 4. If one is using the handkerchief to wipe a portion of the body (i.e., face or nose), it may indicate focusing one's attention on that area. See **Body**.

HANDSHAKE 1. Corresponds to an agreement, a partnership, or a reconciliation. 2. Associated with a friendship, a desired friendship, or an involvement with whoever or whatever one is shaking hands with. 3. May represent meeting a part of one's self or the need to connect with that part of oneself. See **Shadow**. 4. Depending on imagery, might indicate a departure or an arrival 5. You may also wish to see **Hand**.

HANDWRITING 1. Associated with a message, self-expression, or communication. See **Letter**. 2. May indicate the need to communicate with someone. See **Write**. 3. Metaphorically, one can see the handwriting on the wall = one is aware of what is coming next (usually a negative event). 4. You may also wish to see **Pen**.

HANG 1. Associated with a bad idea, decision, or outcome (i.e., that which will hang oneself). 2. May indicate one's hangups, or attitudes and belief systems that keep hanging on. See **Noose**. 3. Something lacking support, insecure, or dangerously close to falling. See **Fall**. 4. If a hanged man, could be associated with the death of a portion of oneself or a part of one's life. See **Death**. 5. Metaphorically, hang it up = give it up. 6. You may also wish to see **Puppet**. 7. If something is hanging on a wall, see **Wall**.

HANUKKAH 1. A Jewish celebration. See

Judaism. 2. Associated with the rededication of the Jewish temple in the second century B.C.E. (before current era). See **Temple.** 3. A nine-pointed candelabra is associated with Hanukkah. See **Menorah.**

HAPPY 1. Associated with joy, luck, pleasure, or gladness. See **Emotion.** 2. Can symbolize something that will make one happy. 3. Might indicate a wish fulfillment. 4. Metaphorically, he was slap-happy = he was foolish, or intoxicated.

HARBOR 1. Associated with the arrival of an important insight, a new situation, or a visitor. 2. May indicate a spiritual activity or experience. See **Boat** and **Water.** 3. Depending on the imagery, might suggest that one's ship has come in. 4. You may also wish to see **Shore** and **Journey.**

HARP 1. Corresponds to heavenly music or harmony. See **Music.** 2. May be associated with becoming involved in spiritual activities. 3. Could indicate the need to listen to spiritual information or insight. See **Minister.** 4. Metaphorically, he kept harping at her = he continued to nag her.

HAT 1. Associated with an idea, an opinion, or an attitude. 2. Symbolic of your thoughts or what is on your mind. 3. May represent an individual's occupation or that with which they are involved. See **Clothes** or **Work.** 4. The type of hat may indicate the state or the nature of what is currently on one's mind. 5. Metaphorically, can be used as follows: they were passing the hat = they were asking for money; hats off = congratulations; he's throwing his hat into the ring = he decided to participate. 6. You may also wish to see **Head** and **Hair.**

HAWK 1. One that preys on another. 2. A scavenger bird. See **Bird.** 3. Metaphorically, she's a hawk = she's very cunning or she's a cheat; he had to hawk it = he had to sell it.

HAY 1. Associated with fields, horses, and fodder. See **Field** and **Food.** 2. Gathering hay could indicate the need to prepare for a message. See **Horse.** 3. Eating hay might represent the need for more fiber in one's diet. 4. Harvesting hay could symbolize the field one is cultivating. 5. Metaphorically, can be used as follows: let's make hay while the sun is shining = let's use the opportunity that we have right now; it's time to hit the hay = it's time to go to sleep; they made hay = they made love. 6. Might be associated with allergies (i.e., hay fever).

HAZY PICTURE 1. Something that has not been clearly set or determined. 2. Could represent a faint possibility or an uncertain condition. 3. Might symbolize a cloudy memory. See **Photograph.** 4. Depending on imagery, you may also wish to see **Mist.**

HEAD 1. Corresponds to ideas, intentions, or one's current state of mind. See **Body.** 2. The position of the head may be symbolic of one's current mental condition; for example: being headless = losing one's head over the situation; head on backward = not thinking straight; hanging one's head = remorse or shame. 3. Metaphorically, may be used as follows: that's using one's head = that's giving it some thought; it went to his head = he became egotistical; she's out of her head = she's crazy; heading off the problem = stopping the situation; turning one's head, or being head over heels = losing self-control (often in relationship to another); her ability is head and shoulders above the rest = she's more talented than any of the others; heads up = warning of immediate danger; they couldn't make heads or tails =

they didn't understand; it's coming to a head = it's moving toward a confrontation; he's in over his head = his current situation exceeds his ability to handle it. 4. Depending on imagery, you may also wish to see **Hair** or **Hat.**

HEADBAND 1. An idea that is circling one's head. See **Hat.** 2. Something one is thinking or contemplating. 3. You may also wish to see **Hair** and **Head.**

HEADLESS 1. Associated with losing one's head in a situation. See **Head.** 2. Could indicate not thinking straight. 3. May be associated with losing control of oneself. 4. Can correspond to losing one's stature, position, or self-respect.

HEADLIGHTS 1. Associated with vision. See **Automobile.** 2. The ability or inability to see where you're headed. 3. Something that allows sight in the midst of darkness. 4. You may also wish to see **Eyes.**

HEALER 1. The physician within one's own self. See **Doctor.** 2. May be associated with one's ability to help or to heal others. 3. Could correspond to a physical (health), a mental (emotional/counseling), or a spiritual (minister) healer. 4. You may also wish to see **People.**

HEALING/HEALTH 1. That which is made whole or in the process of becoming whole. 2. Corresponds to physical, mental, and spiritual well-being. 3. May represent a reconciliation or the act of cooperation. 4. Might be symbolized by the color green. See **Colors.** 5. Dreaming of doing something in order to become well might be a literal health suggestion.

HEAR 1. Associated with listening. See

Ears. 2. Might correspond to the need to listen for harmony, cooperation, or for a message. 3. Metaphorically, a favorable hearing = a favorable trial or outcome. 4. Could be associated with an intuitive message or extended sense perception through sound. See **ESP.** 5. The act of being receptive and attentive.

HEARSE 1. Symbolic of death or the passing of something. See **Death.** 2. May be a warning associated with someone's physical health and well-being. 3. You may also wish to see **Funeral.** 4. Could indicate a problem with one's car or driving. See **Automobile.**

HEART 1. Corresponds to love, stamina, feelings, desires, or energy. 2. Often considered to be the place of one's emotions. See **Body.** 3. Associated with an emotional experience or situation. 4. Metaphorically, can be used as follows: she didn't have the heart for it = she wasn't interested or didn't have the ability to do it; that's the heart of the issue = that's the main point; you're after my own heart = that's exactly what I want; wearing one's heart upon their sleeve = to be vulnerable to everyone; to lose heart = to give up. 5. Might symbolize a literal health condition. 6. Corresponds to a suit in playing cards. See **Cards.** 7. May be associated with the thymus or fourth chakra. See **Thymus.**

HEAT/HEATER 1. Could indicate the temperature of the situation. 2. Associated with one's breath, lungs, words, or air capacity. See **Automobile** or **House.** 3. Might be associated with emotional feelings. 4. Metaphorically, can be used as follows: the boss turned on the heat = the boss became more intense or focused regarding the situation; their relationship is really hot = they have a very passionate and/or emotional relationship; the dog is in heat = the dog is in a period of sexual arousal.

HEAVEN 1. Associated with spirituality. 2. Corresponds to a message from the higher self or the higher mind. 3. The house of God. See **God**. 4. May be associated with great bliss and joy. 5. Might represent an ideal or idealism. 6. A state of harmony, love, attunement, and oneness. 7. Associated with paradise or perfection. 8. Metaphorically, that's heaven = that's perfect or that's a really advantageous outcome. 9. Could relate to the zodiac. See **Astrology**. 10. Depending on imagery, you may also wish to see **Sky**.

HEDGE 1. That which is fenced in by shrubbery. See **Fence**. 2. May be associated with a defense, one's own independence, or the desire to keep others out. 3. Metaphorically, to hedge one's bet = to wager in various ways in order to cut the chances of losing; he's constantly hedging = he's unable to commit to anything. 4. You may also wish to see **Plant** and **Garden**.

HEEL 1. The hind part of one's foot, understanding, or principles. See **Feet**. 2. Metaphorically, can be used as follows: he's a heel = he's a rotten or callous person; she's head over heels in love = she's totally and uncontrollably in love; to be hot on one's heels = to be very close to another; that's his Achilles' heel = that's what makes him most vulnerable; the boss kicked up his heels = the boss let himself have a good time. 3. Might symbolize that which was behind, or something in one's own past.

HEIGHT 1. Associated with stature, one's appearance, or elevation. 2. May correspond to a ranking when measured against others. 3. How you see yourself or how others view

you. 4. Depending on the imagery, you may also wish to see **Giant** or **Midget**.

HEIR 1. The one receiving an inheritance, traits, or a situation from another. 2. May correspond to the one next in line for succession (i.e., a promotion at work). 3. The part of oneself that is waiting to come into its own (i.e., one's highest potential). 4. Those talents, strengths, or abilities that are part of oneself.

HELL 1. Associated with turmoil, guilt, suffering, and anguish. 2. The house of evil. See **Devil**. 3. Metaphorically, this is hell = this is horrible. 4. May correspond to one's fears. 5. The state of being separated from spirituality or God.

HELMET 1. Protecting your thoughts or protection from other's thoughts. 2. Stubbornness. 3. See **Hat**. 4. May also suggest an impenetrable or untouchable idea or opinion. 5. Depending upon the imagery, might be associated with war. See **War**.

HEN 1. A female chicken. See **Chicken**. 2. Metaphorically, can be used as follows: he's henpecked = his wife nags or dominates him; don't be such a mother hen = don't be so worried. 3. Might symbolize a specific woman in one's life. See **Woman** and **People**.

HERMIT 1. Can correspond to one who is emotionally isolated. 2. Can be associated with people who detach from or think themselves better than others. 3. Could represent spiritual safety or harmony. See **Monk**. 4. One's own conscience or belief systems. 5. Might indicate one's desire to escape from a relationship or the current situation. 6. Associated with nine in the tarot. See **Tarot**. 7. You may also wish to see **People**.

HERO 1. Associated with one's higher self or inner potential. 2. Can correspond to strength, courage, or the representation of ideal qualities. 3. The fully realized self. See **Christ.** 4. Might symbolize the ultimate male or female potentials. See **Man or Woman.**

HEROD 1. Can correspond to aggression, authority, domination, and betrayal. 2. May symbolize the death of innocence. 3. Might represent one who is dominated by one's negative female traits.

HERRING 1. That which is seasoned or salty. See **Fish.** 2. Metaphorically, a red herring = a false belief, clue, or insight that gets one off the track.

HIDE 1. To conceal something about oneself, the situation, or another. 2. The act of seeking safety or protection. 3. May correspond to unknown parts of oneself. See **Shadow.** 4. That which is kept safe from others. 5. Associated with what one is hiding from or refusing to deal with. 6. You may also wish to see **Sneak.**

HIGHCHAIR 1. Associated with childishness or immaturity. See **Child.** 2. May indicate one's feelings about being in a childish position. See **Chair.** 3. Might suggest small-minded ideas, beliefs, or attitudes.

HILL 1. An obstacle, an elevated portion in one's journey, or the next hurdle. See **Mountain.** 2. Can correspond to higher states of mental or spiritual development. 3. May be associated with seeing things from a more objective perspective. 4. Depending on imagery, might be associated with ascending to a higher material level. See **Ascend,** or a demotion. See **Descend.** 5. Metaphorically, can be used as follows: he's over the hill = he's old and out of touch; that's a hill of beans = that's not important.

HINDUISM 1. The religion of much of India. 2. The basic premise of the religion is that each individual is responsible for finding his own relationship with God. 3. Associated with the Perennial Philosophy: All that exists in matter and in consciousness is a part of God; apart from God there is nothing that exists. Human beings may not only know about God, but they may also have a personal and direct awareness, uniting the knower with the known. Human beings have a dual nature: an eternal Self, which is a spark of God, and a phenomenal ego; it is possible for human beings to identify fully with the former and not the latter. The only purpose for being on the earth is to unite fully with the eternal Self and the spirit of God. 4. There are three paths to achieve the liberation promised, by the Perennial Philosophy: the path of knowledge (inana), the path of devotion (bakhti), and the path of good works (dharmas). 5. Primary spiritual texts are the Vedas (hymns, prose writings, scholastic interpretations of scripture, and symbolism; compiled between 1500 and 600 B.C.). 6. To some Hindus, although there is ultimately only one God, that God takes on many different manifestations (i.e., Brahma, Shiva, Vishnu, Ganesh, Krishna, Jesus, etc.).

HISTORICAL CLOTHING/SETTINGS 1. Generally represents whatever one associates with that clothing, those settings, or that historic locale (i.e., upbringing, history, thoughts about specific places, outfits, or countries, etc.). 2. Could represent one's own photographic memories. See **Photograph.** 3. Might be indicative of reincarnation or one's karmic memory regarding a place, an activity, or a person. See **Karma** and **Reincarnation.** 4. Historical or period clothing may also indicate something that is anti-quated or outdated. See **Clothes.**

HITCHHIKER 1. Associated with one who goes along for the ride. 2. If you are hitch-hiking, can correspond to giving control of your life to another. See **Puppet.** 3. Picking up hitchhikers may correspond to picking up unknown parts of oneself. See **Shadow.** 4. Depending upon the imagery, may be a literal warning not to pick up hitchhikers. 5. You may also wish to see **Car.**

HOBO 1. A bum, a tramp, or a wanderer. 2. May correspond to losing one's way in the journey of life. See **Journey.** 3. Might be associated with laziness or detachment from the material world. 4. Could indicate an ex-cessive state of relaxation. 5. You may also wish to see **People.**

HOCKEY 1. A team sport played on the ice. See **Sports.** 2. Often symbolic of one's own group activities (i.e., work, family, etc.). See **Work.** 3. The activity in the imagery may display one's own propensity or lack of it for cooperation, teamwork, sportsmanship conduct, winning and losing, etc.

HOG 1. Symbolizes greed or filth. See **An-imals.** 2. A person who hogs the show becomes the center of attention. 3. Meta-phorically, can be used as follows: pighead-edness = being stubborn; they went whole hog = they went all out (i.e., were extrav-agant); to buy a pig in a poke = to obtain something with very little information or foresight; she was hog–wild = she was very excited. 4. Could be associated with one who is of low class morally or sexually. 5. May be symbolic of a poor diet, gluttony, or making a pig of oneself.

HOLE 1. A dark situation, experience, or passage. See **Cave.** 2. That which is hidden or concealed. 3. May represent female sex-uality. See **Womb.** 4. May be associated with a trap, a warning, or a hole in one's plans, ideas, or thought processes. 5. Depending on imagery, you may also wish to see **Prisoner** and **Earth.**

HOLIDAY 1. A festival, a time of relaxation, a celebration. See **Party.** 2. May correspond to a recognition or a reward. 3. A pleasant day, activity, or gathering. 4. Whatever one associates with holidays in general will have much to do with the symbolism.

HOLMES, SHERLOCK 1. Associated with the act of or the need for close inspection, scrutiny, or investigation. See **Detective.** 2. Could indicate some unseen activity, a sense of intrigue, or a mystery. 3. May be symbolic of England. 4. Depending on one's personal association, might represent substance abuse.

HOLY GRAIL 1. Associated with a spiritual mission, duty, journey, purpose, or goal. See **Journey.** 2. The cup used by Jesus at the Last Supper. See **Jesus Christ.** 3. Liturgically, associated with the blood of Christ or that which holds the soul. See **Chalice.**

HOLY LAND 1. Associated with Palestine. 2. A sacred site of spirituality. 3. The meeting place of God. See **God.** 4. Might correspond to one's higher self. 5. One's ideals, aspira-tions, or dreams. See **Heaven.** 6. Can be as-sociated with the religion of the Jews (Judaism), the Christians (Christianity), and the Moslems (Islam). 7. One's spiritual Jour-ney. See **Journey.**

HOLY MAN/HOLY WOMAN 1. A spiritual presence, authority, or messenger. See **Min-ister.** 2. Might be associated with one's own higher self. 3. Can correspond to a message of truth, wisdom, or guidance. See **Wise Man/Wise Woman.** 4. Might be associated with positive male/female attributes. See **Man** or **Woman.** 5. Might be symbolic of Christ. See **Christ.** 6. You may also wish to see **People.**

HOME PLATE/HOME RUN 1. An accomplishment or a successful completion of one's goal. 2. The finish line. See **Finish Line.** 3. You may also wish to see **Sports** and **Baseball.**

HOMOSEXUAL 1. Can correspond to the opposite–sex attributes in one's own self. See **Man** and **Woman.** 2. Depending upon the imagery, may represent a close possible relationship with an individual of the same sex. 3. Might be associated with one's shadow. See **Shadow.** 4. Facing one's fears, prejudices, or negative attitudes. 5. Might be a literal indication of one's sexuality.

HONEY 1. That which makes things sweet. 2. A term of endearment. 3. Metaphorically, his words flowed like honey = he was overly sweet and diplomatic. 4. To praise another. 5. The sweet result that may come from a labor of confusion and irritation. See **Bee.** 6. Biblically, associated with the Promised Land (i.e., a land flowing with milk and honey; Exodus 33:3). 7. May be associated with spirituality due to its golden color. See **Colors.** 8. You may also wish to see **Food.**

HORN 1. As a growth, can correspond to one's animal nature, stubbornness, aggression, or sexuality. You may wish to see **Animals.** 2. As a sound, associated with a message, a warning, or one's words. See **Automobile.** 3. Can correspond to abundance (i.e., see **Horn of Plenty**). 4. Might be associated with a negative thought. See **Head.** 5.

Metaphorically, can be used as follows: to blow one's horn = to praise one's own accomplishments or to be egotistical; he's horny = he's oversexed. 6. May be associated with music and harmony or disharmony. See **Music.** 7. Biblically, associated with power, might, and honor.

HORN OF PLENTY 1. May represent abundance, good fortune, rewards, good luck, or prosperity. 2. One's talents, abilities, or hidden potentials. 3. Depending on imagery, you may also wish to see **Flowers, Fruit,** and **Food.** 4. In mythology, the horn that fed Zeus. See **Mythology (Roman and Greek).**

HORNET 1. Associated with a cause of irritation or provocation. See **Bug.** 2. Metaphorically, to stir up a hornet's nest = to cause problems. 3. Being stung may be symbolic of problems or obstacles that will affect the individual. 4. Can correspond to an unfriendly environment. 5. That which can sting. 6. You may also wish to see **Bee.**

HORSE 1. A bearer of a message. See **Message/Messenger.** 2. The type and color of the horse may indicate the type of message. For example: a racehorse could symbolize a speedy or important message; a wild horse suggests that which is instinctual or uncontrollable; a white horse or winged horse could bring a spiritual message; a red horse might indicate a warning or a message of desire. See **Colors.** 3. Metaphorically, may be used as follows: he's horsing around = he's not taking things seriously; putting the cart before the horse = not keeping things in their proper order or perspective; horse of a different color = additional information that causes the situation to be reconsidered or different; she's on her high horse = she's egotistical or overbearing; looking a gift horse in the mouth = not being appreciative of something. 4. Unbridled passion, uncontrollable passion. 5. Biblically, associated with the Four Horseman of the Apocalypse, or the writers of the Gospel (Matthew, Mark, Luke, and John). 6. Metaphysically, corresponds to the four lower endocrine centers or chakras: white horse = gonads; black horse = Lyden; red horse = adrenals; pale horse = thymus. See **Chakras**.

HORSE AND BUGGY 1. May be symbolic of that which is obsolete and outdated (i.e., an idea). See **Old**. 2. Could symbolize going back to basics. 3. Might represent Victorian ideas, attitudes, or morality. 4. That which is no longer appropriate. 5. Depending on one's personal association, may also indicate something relaxing, peaceful, or pleasant. 6. You may also wish to see **Antique**. 7. You may also wish to see **Historical Clothing/Settings**.

HOSE 1. Associated with the flow of water, emotions, or eliminations. 2. That which can direct, guide, or control. 3. May be associated with male sexuality. See **Phallus**. 4. You may also wish to see **Water**. 5. Depending upon imagery, may indicate literal problems with one's house, one's body, or one's automobile.

HOSPITAL 1. A place of healing or regeneration. See **Building**. 2. Associated with that portion of one's life or environment that is in need of healing. 3. Could represent the immune system. 4. You may also wish to see **Doctor**.

HOTEL 1. A temporary residence or state of mind. 2. May be associated with one's current situation, experience, or health. See **House**. 3. The appearance of the hotel will have much to do with one's situation (i.e.,

luxurious or worn down). See **Building**. 4. May be associated with business, relaxation, or a discreet (perhaps illicit) relationship.

HOUSE 1. Usually associated with the physical body, one's personality, or one's current situation or experience (i.e., dwelling place). 2. Can correspond to the psyche of an individual, a group, or even a situation. 3. May represent the status of one's state of consciousness (i.e., the condition of the house gives clues to one's mental and emotional condition). 4. The portion of the house being portrayed represents different aspects of oneself (see also individual portions of the house).

Air Conditioner/Heater: Associated with one's breath or words. The temperature of the situation.

Attic: Higher consciousness, the soul, the higher mind, or spirituality.

Backyard (or Back Door): What we keep to ourselves (i.e., secrets from the outside world). A place to retreat or relax.

Basement (or Cellar): Sexuality, the lower self, one's personal storehouse (i.e., memories), or may be associated with the subconscious mind or soul.

Bathroom: Where one cleanses oneself. What needs to be cleansed. Could be associated with a place of personal release (feelings) or privacy.

Bedroom: Associated with sexual activity, intimacy, and relationships. Could represent the need for rest. See **Bed/ Bedroom.**

Carpet: A foundation, a state of subservience (i.e., being walked upon), insulation against worldly influence, or luxury.

Closet: That which is hidden. Could represent something that is in storage and may be utilized at a later date.

Dining Room: What one absorbs publicly. A call to pay attention to one's physical, mental, or spiritual diet.

Door: An opportunity, experience, or an idea.

Fireplace: Associated with purification, warmth, desire, or digestion.

Floor: A foundation or a belief system. Something that is under consideration.

Front of House (or Yard): What we show the world. Awaiting what comes next in life.

Furnace: Corresponds to heat, anger, emotional frustration, or digestion and assimilation.

Furniture: Inner opinions, choices, beliefs, or attitudes. That which clutters one's mind.

Garage: Associated with discarded ideas, or a part of one's self (i.e., the automobile) .

Hall: May indicate a passage in understanding, experience, or consciousness. A journey.

Kitchen: Where one is fed or nurtured physically, mentally, or spiritually. Could be associated with the literal need to become more aware of dietary habits. .

Living Room: Associated with one's state of mind or environment. Could correspond to one's daily activities or a more formal and public life.

Main Floor: Consciousness, the conscious mind, or the place of everyday life.

Plumbing: Corresponds to one's elimination systems or one's emotions.

Porch: A new opportunity or opening. Could suggest a temporary haven.

Roof: Spiritual thoughts; the highest thought. Can correspond to protection and security.

Stairs (or Steps): Rising or descending to another level (i.e., consciousness, awareness). Can correspond to the need to take life one step at a time or the fact that one has missed a step.

Threshold: Same as door. See **Door.**

Windows: What one sees through. Corresponds to vision.

5. Symbolic of what we show to the world. 6. The symbol of any particular part of a house is often associated with one's own personal experience; for example: an individual who dreamed of going swimming in the pool (something that was actually done with the family) may interpret the symbol as being related to relaxation or family unity; for others, the symbol could indicate a spiritual plunge. 7. Metaphorically, can be used as follows: to clean house = to organize; she brought the house down = she was very popular. 8. You may also wish to see **Building.**

HOUSE (ASTROLOGICAL) 1. Associated with twelve aspects of the zodiac. See **Astrology.**

HOUSEWORK 1. May indicate the need to clean one's environment or state of mind physically, mentally, or spiritually. See **Clean.** 2. Might be associated with the arrival of an unexpected guest; therefore the dream is a literal indication to prepare for the visit. 3. The symbology will have a great deal to do with which part of the house one is working in. See **House.**

HUDSON, ROCK 1. Associated with the quality we think most about that person. See **Movie Star.** 2. Could be associated with stability (i.e., rock solid). 3. Might indicate ill health and the need to see a doctor. 4. May represent some aspect of a role he played in a film. 5. Associated with closet sexuality.

HUNGER 1. Associated with a physical, emotional/mental, or spiritual craving. See **Food.** 2. The need for more stimulation or education. 3. Being deprived of one's desires. 4. Might be literally associated with not getting enough food or the proper nutrients.

HUNT/HUNTING PARTY 1. The object of one's search. 2. A quest for meaning or purpose. See **Journey.** 3. Can correspond to the act of or the need for close inspection, scrutiny, and investigation. See **Detective.** 4. May symbolize a group of individuals who work together. See **Work.** 5. The curious part of oneself. 6. Might indicate the need to look into one's own thought processes, talents, or background. 7. Metaphorically, the hunting instincts = one's basic urges, desires, and drives. 8. You may also wish to see **People.**

HURRICANE 1. Corresponds to environmental situation or challenges. 2. Often associated with one's mental state and current emotional experience. 3. See also **Weather.**

HURRY 1. Associated with urgency. See **Speed.** 2. That which is rushed or done in haste. 3. Could be associated with stress and the need to slow down. 4. Might indicate the need to be more careful in what one is doing.

HUSBAND 1. Often suggests literal aspects of the relationship with one's spouse. 2. How your husband appears may be symbolic of your attitude and feelings toward him. 3. Could indicate a suggestion or a warning in terms of your husband's welfare. 4. Can correspond to new insights into your husband's behavior, attitudes, or opinions. 5. May indicate how your conscious interactions are affecting him physically, mentally, or spiritually. 6. Might be associated with the masculine part of oneself. See **Man.** 7. May also represent a close personal relationship with any male (especially if one isn't married). 8. Might be a literal indication of marriage. 9. You may also wish to see **Phallus** and **People.**

HYMN 1. A joyful song of praise. See **Worship, Pray/Prayer,** and **Sing/Singer.** 2. Associated with spiritual harmony. 3. One's aspirations or hopes. 4. You may also wish to see **Music.**

1. *The ninth letter of the alphabet.* 2. *The Roman numeral for 1.* 3. *Biblically, associated with the great I Am (Exodus 3:14).* 4. *In astronomy, the inclination of an orbit.* 5. *Chemically, the symbol for iodine.* 6. *Numerologically, equivalent to nine.* 7. *Scholastically, a mark for incomplete.* 8. *In logic, an affirmative proposition.* 9. *In physics, a symbol for current density, inertia, or magnetic intensity.* 10. *In zoology, a symbol for incisor.* 11. *In Greek, iota.* 12. *Corresponds to one's personal identity. See* **Self.** 13. *May indicate one's qualities, faults, and thoughts.* 14. *See* **People** *and* **Man** *or* **Woman.** 15. *You may also wish to see* **Shadow** *and* **Acting/Actor/Actress.** 16. *How we see ourselves or how others see us.*

I CHING 1. An ancient Chinese esoteric system. The basic premise is that simultaneous and seemingly unrelated events may be causally and meaningfully connected. See **Synchronicity.** 2. A tool for gaining an objective perspective of one's inner reality. 3. A system of sixty-four hexagrams associated with specific meaning and subject to interpretation much like imagery or dreamwork; they are as follows: 1. Creativity; 2. Receptivity; 3. Beginnings; 4. Inexperience; 5. Patience; 6. Conflict; 7. Synergy; 8. Unity; 9. Restraint; 10. Conduct; 11. Prosperity; 12. Stagnation; 13. Community; 14. Leadership; 15. Moderation; 16. Dedication; 17. Acceptance; 18. Rejuvenation; 19. Application; 20. Observation; 21. Determination; 22. Grace; 23. Decay; 24. Rebirth; 25. Purity; 26. Energy; 27. Nourishment; 28. Decisiveness; 29. Danger; 30. Clarity; 31. Attraction; 32. Endurance; 33. Withdrawal; 34. Power; 35. Progress; 36. Perseverance; 37. Family; 38. Opposition; 39. Obstacles; 40. Liberation; 41. Diminishing; 42. Increasing; 43. Resolution; 44. Temptation; 45. Gathering; 46. Ascending; 47. Challenging; 48. Source; 49. Instability; 50. Order; 51. Trials; 52. Introspection; 53. Growth; 54. Propriety; 55. Abundance; 56. Transition; 57. Achievement; 58. Joy; 59. Purification; 60. Limitation; 61. Insight; 62. Responsibility; 63. Equilibrium; 64. Completion.

ICE 1. That which is frozen, impenetrable, or cold. See **Cold.** 2. Can correspond to emotional detachment. 3. May indicate sexual frigidity. 4. Metaphorically, can be used as follows: on thin ice = in a dangerous position; to break the ice = to start the conversation. 5. Might indicate the separation between consciousness or physicality and spirit. 6. Melting ice could represent the release of old patterns, thoughts, or beliefs or the opening up of emotions. 7. You may also wish to see **Weather, Freeze/Freezer,** and **Water.**

IDOL 1. That which one worships or places in awe (i.e., money, fame, individual people, etc.). 2. Can represent a false principle or belief system. 3. An image without substance. 4. You may also wish to see **Statue.**

IGLOO 1. A frozen house. See **House.** 2. Can correspond with a cold, chilly, or detached environment (i.e., house, work life, etc.). 3. You may also wish to see **Ice.**

IHS 1. The first three letters of the Greek spelling of Jesus: iota, eta, sigma. 2. See **Jesus Christ** and **Christ.**

ILL/ILLNESS 1. Associated with physical, mental, or spiritual ailment. 2. Metaphorically, can be used as follows: I feel ill at ease = I don't feel comfortable; it was an ill-fated trip = it was a disastrous trip. 3. Can correspond to a bad temper or situation. 4. Different types of illness are associated with different meanings; for example: dreaming of cancer may suggest that something is eating you up or it could be a literal warning; dreaming of a cold might symbolize an approaching problem, or it could indicate that one is unfeeling, cold, and detached. 5. Depending upon the imagery as to what is ill, you may also wish to see **Body.** 6. May be a literal indication of an approaching illness, advising the dreamer to see a doctor. 7. Depending on imagery, you may also wish to see **Cold** or **Fever.**

ILLEGAL 1. The act of doing something one should not have done. See **Crime/Criminal.** 2. That which is unlawful, immoral, or out of character. 3. May be associated with one's conscience or guilt.

IMAGERY 1. A symbolic representation of an experience, an activity, a thought, or an individual. See **Metaphor** and **Archetype.** 2. Associated with the subconscious storehouse of symbols and images. See **Symbol/ Symbolism** and **Dreaming.** 3. The act and/or process of mental creation. 4. That which is symbolic but able to be correlated with conscious reality.

IN-LAWS 1. Often represents one's own relationship or feelings toward one's in-laws. 2. Associated with a part of oneself that has not been fully integrated. See **Shadow.** 3. Could indicate a suggestion or a warning in terms of your in-laws' welfare. 4. May be associated with one's feelings or a situation with one's spouse. See **Husband** or

Wife. 5. See also **People.**

INCEST 1. May represent a forbidden connection or relationship. See **Sex.** 2. Might correspond to one's fears or memories. 3. Could correspond to a repressed desire. 4. May indicate the presence of nepotism. 5. Could symbolize a conflict (or narcissism) between portions of oneself. See **Shadow.** 6. Might be associated with karmic memory. See **Karma.**

INDIA 1. Can correspond to ancient wisdom and spirituality. 2. Might be representative of the caste system. 3. Associated with Hinduism. See **Hinduism.** 4. May be associated with a foreign visitor or travel.

INDIAN 1. Corresponds to natural spirituality. 2. Associated with nature and a love of the earth. See **Earth.** 3. Represents living in harmony with one's surroundings and environment. 4. Could be symbolic of a spiritual journey, guide, or quest. See **Journey.** 5. Might be associated with the savage part of one's own self. See **Shadow.** 6. Metaphorically, Indian giver = an individual who gives something and then asks for it back; Indian summer = a mild, tranquil period, generally later in the year or later in one's life. 7. See also **People.**

INDIGO 1. Color associated with something that comes from the higher mind or the spiritual part of yourself. 2. See **Colors.**

INFANT 1. A new beginning, an idea, or a possibility. See **Birth.** 2. Could be associated with a new relationship or literally a new child. 3. Associated with that which is full of potential though not yet developed. See **Baby.** 4. Can represent total vulnerability. 5. Could indicate immaturity, youthfulness, or something that is in the early stages of development. See **Child.** 6. One's Inner Child. 7. May correspond to one's own infant self. 8. Depending on imagery, you may wish to see **Boy** or **Girl.**

INFECTION 1. Can correspond to that which is swollen, sore, irritated, or infected. 2. A bothersome situation or condition. 3. Poisons affecting the system (i.e., thoughts, actions). 4. That which has gotten under one's skin. See **Cyst.** 5. Could indicate a specific and literal health condition. 6. Depending upon what is infected, you may also wish to see **Body.** 7. Metaphorically, she has an infectious smile = her smile makes you smile as well. 8. You may also wish to see **Ill/Illness.**

INITIATION 1. Associated with a rite of passage or belonging. 2. Could indicate a probationary or a trial period. 3. Being accepted as a member of the whole. 4. A graduation or an accomplishment. See **School.** 5. That which is introduced, begun, or inaugurated.

INJURE 1. Can symbolize the act of hurting or harming someone or of being hurt by another (literally or figuratively). 2. A portion of oneself that is inflicting personal harm. 3. May be an indication of a possible accident, advising a different course of action. See **Accident.** 4. The part of oneself that is being harmed may have a great deal to do with the symbolism. See **Body.** 5. Depending on imagery, you may also wish to see **Kill.**

I.N.R.I. 1. Liturgically, Latin for Jesus of Nazareth, King of the Jews. (Iesus Nazarenus Rex Iudaeorum; see John 19:19.) 2. See **Jesus Christ** or **Christ.**

INSECT 1. Associated with parts of oneself

or others that crawl, creep up on you, gnaw, irritate, get under the skin, or devour. See **Bug.** 2. See also specific insect; for example, see **Flies/Fly.** 3. Metaphorically, an insect = an insignificant, often irritating person. 4. That which is biting you. See **Bite.**

INSIGNIA 1. Acceptance or involvement in a particular group or set of ideas. 2. Could be associated with self-identity. See **Self.** 3. Associated with one's occupation, duty, affiliation, or responsibility. 4. A sign, a symbol, or an identification. See **Badge.** 5. You may also wish to see **Flag.**

INSURANCE 1. Corresponds to personal protection. 2. May indicate that one is assured of the proper outcome. 3. Might be a literal suggestion to obtain appropriate insurance.

INTERSTATE 1. Can correspond to being in the fast lane. 2. Associated with one's life journey. See **Journey.** 3. The road, situation, or activity with which one is currently involved. See **Road.** 4. Depending on imagery, you may also wish to see **Speed** and **Car.**

INTRUDER 1. Something that breaks into one's experience or environment. See **Burglar.** 2. Corresponds to going where one is not allowed; illegal entry. 3. That portion of the self that is in hiding. See **Shadow.** 4. Associated with people who force their will into the situation or attempt to make their will dominant in relationship to others. 5. Can represent that which is uninvited or unwelcome.

IRON 1. That which is strong, firm, or inflexible. 2. Straightening out oneself or one's appearance. See **Clothes.** 3. Metaphorically, can be used as follows: to iron things out = to straighten things; strike while the iron is hot = act while the time is right; he has several irons in the fire = he has several things (interests) going on at the same time. 4. If ironing clothing, you may also wish to see **Laundry.**

ISLAM 1. The Moslem religion founded by the prophet Mohammed. See **Mohammed.** 2. Associated with five articles of faith: the belief in one God, the belief in angels, the belief in sacred scriptures (including the Bible and the Koran), the belief in ancient prophets (including Abraham, Moses, Jesus, and Mohammed), and a belief in the Day of Judgment. 3. Primary religious text is the Koran. See **Koran.** 4. Also associated with five obligatory duties: the recitation of faith ("There is no God but Allah, and Mohammed is his prophet"); prayer five times per day (before sunrise, right after noon, late afternoon, after sunset, and just before bed); the payment of a purification tax (a 2.5% tithe given to charities, the poor, and the needy); fasting during the month of Ramadan (the month the Koran came into being); and a visit to Mecca (in Saudi Arabia) at least once in a Muslim's lifetime.

ISLAND 1. Associated with something that is isolated (i.e., a person, an idea, etc.). See **Hermit.** 2. Could correspond to a place of safety from the environment. 3. May be symbolic of emotions cut off from others. 4. Depending on imagery, you may also wish to see **Water** and **Earth.**

ITALY 1. Corresponds primarily to whatever an individual thinks of Italy or Italians (i.e., associated with romance, Venice, expressive emotions, the Vatican, etc.). 2. May be indicative of a foreign visitor or travel.

IVORY 1. May be symbolic of teeth or speech. See **Teeth.** 2. An illegal possession. 3. Can correspond to the piano, teeth, or dice. 4. You may also wish to see **Elephant.**

IVORY (COLOR) 1. Can represent that which is not quite clear. 2. See **Colors.** 3. Also associated with something that can be valuable or aloof. 4. Might be associated with purity.

J

1. *The tenth letter of the alphabet.* 2. *Historically (prior to the seventeenth century); a variant of I.* 3. *Numerologically, equivalent to one.* 4. *In physics, a symbol for joule (electrical unit).*

JACK–O'–LANTERN 1. Symbolic of Halloween. See **Halloween**. 2. A method of illuminating the darkness. 3. Could represent carrying a torch or a light through the mysterious. See **Torch**.

JACKASS 1. May be a metaphor for an ass (oneself or another). See **Animals**. 2. Could correspond to that which is stubborn or obstinate. See **Donkey**. 3. One who lacks intelligence or class.

JACKET 1. Often indicates the outward personality one shows to the world. See **Coat**. 2. Thoughts and attitudes. See **Clothes**. 3. How one insulates oneself from the environment.

JACOB 1. The father of the twelve tribes of Israel and therefore the Hebrew nation. See **Judaism**. 2. Biblically, can be associated with Jacob's ladder, the stairway to heaven (Genesis 28:12). 3. Might correspond to trickery (i.e., Jacob tricked his own father, but he himself was also tricked into servitude).

JAIL 1. That which confines, surrounds, or penalizes. See **Wall**. 2. Losing individual freedom and will. See **Prisoner**. 3. That which has caused one to be trapped (i.e., habits, circumstances, or environment). 4. You may also wish to see **Cape**.

JAM 1. Metaphorically, can be used as follows: he's gotten himself into a jam = he's gotten .himself into trouble; the door was jammed = the door was stuck; the signal was jammed = the signal was interrupted. 2. Might correspond to the preservation of the fruits of one's labor. See **Fruit**. 3. Could correspond to feeling pressed or squeezed. 4. You may also wish to see **Food**.

JAPAN 1. Corresponds primarily to whatever an individual thinks of Japan or the Japanese (i.e., associated with industriousness, wealth, cars, overcrowding, intelligence, etc.). 2. May be indicative of a foreign visitor or travel.

JAW 1. May correspond to words spoken. See **Mouth**. 2. Associated with chewing. See **Chew/Chewing Gum**. 3. Thinking an idea over in one's head. 4. Metaphorically, to jaw another person = to talk to, to scold, or to hit someone in the mouth. 5. You may also wish to see **Teeth** and **Body**.

JEANS 1. Associated with relaxation and comfort. 2. May correspond to an easy journey or getting down to work. See **Pants** and **Clothes**. 3. Will often be associated with whatever the individual thinks about jeans or with what one usually does while wearing jeans.

JELL–O 1. That which is wobbly and unstable. 2. Might indicate the state of being easy to shake (i.e., throw off balance, or change one's mind). 3. Could indicate a literal dietary suggestion (i.e., gelatin rather than desserts, etc.). 4. May be associated with compressed emotions or an idea that is solidifying. 5. You may also wish to see **Food.**

JESUS CHRIST 1. The founder of the religion of Christianity. See **Christianity.** 2. Associated with the manifestation of divinity on the earth; the full manifestation of the higher self. See **Christ.** 3. Could correspond to human perfection. 4. Might represent a divine messenger. See **Message/ Messenger.**

JET 1. A lofty idea or project. See **Airplane.** 2. Can correspond to a message from another realm or another level of the mind. See **Message/Messenger.** 3. May literally represent a trip. 4. One's own thoughts or feelings regarding jets will be very significant; for example: could represent unresolved fear if one has a fear of flying; may suggest the need for a vacation or an important business trip. 5. Might represent one's physical body or exterior. See **Automobile.**

JEWELS/JEWELRY 1. May be associated with spiritual truths, wisdom, mental health, value, or material success. 2. Symbolic of those things that facilitate healing and beauty. 3. That which is eternal. 4. Can be associated with promises, agreements, unions, or relationships. 5. May indicate rewards, talents, or spiritual gifts. 6. Different types of jewelry are associated with different meanings; for example:

> **Bracelets:** Can be associated with personal power, service, or something one possesses.
> **Ear Jewelry (i.e., Earrings):** Can correspond to one's ability to listen or to what one is hearing.
> **Hair Jewelry (i.e., Barrettes, Crowns):** Of-

ten correspond to one's thoughts or ideas.
> **Necklaces:** Can represent one's willpower or that which the individual is currently carrying in life (i.e., ideas, problems, etc.). May correspond to one's personal stature, image, or current situation.
> **Rings:** Symbolic of a relationship or a partnership.
> **Watches:** Associated with time. See **Clock.**

7. Various jewels represent different meanings; for example:

> **Amethysts:** Often symbolic of that which possesses great value or importance; the spiritual qualities of loyalty and truth.
> **Crystals:** Associated with clarity, purity, and higher energies. May indicate spiritual insight or vision.
> **Diamonds:** May indicate either a relationship, wealth, or something that is priceless or perfect. Can correspond to that which is eternal.
> **Emeralds:** Can symbolize enlightenment, health, or growth.
> **Hematite:** Can be associated with grounding energy and absorbing negativity.
> **Jade:** May represent healing, power, life, or China.
> **Lapis Lazuli:** Often associated with intuition and insight.
> **Moonstone:** Can correspond to one's emotions or other feminine energies.
> **Opals:** Associated with the higher realms of consciousness and spirituality.
> **Pearls:** Can indicate purity, wisdom, or inner beauty. Also associated with the transformative process of life's experiences.

Rose Quartz: Associated with the heart and healing.

Rubies: Often associated with love, empathy, or compassion.

Topaz: Associated with healing, wholeness, and strength. May correspond to wisdom.

8. The color of the jewelry is highly significant. See **Colors**. 9. Metaphorically, she's a jewel = she's wonderful. 10. In folklore, often associated with mysticism and dragons. You may wish to see **Dragon**. 11. You may also wish to see **Money**.

JOB 1. Associated with one's work. See **Work**. 2. Can correspond to any task, duty, or obligation. 3. That which one makes into a job, suggesting the need to lighten up in the situation.

JOB (BIBLICAL) 1. Associated with faith and perseverance. 2. Often symbolic of one who receives one adverse condition or problem after another. 3. Corresponds to enduring determination even in the midst of adversity.

JOCKEY 1. Depending on one's personal association, may correspond to good luck or gambling. See **Gambling**. 2. One who carries a message. See **Horse** and **Message/ Messenger**. 3. Metaphorically, he's a jockey = he's a cheat, or he's an athlete.

JOG 1. A situation or experience from which one is running or toward which one is headed. 2. Depending on personal association, may indicate a challenge, a commitment, or the act of personal exercise. See **Exercise**. 3. You may also wish to see **Run/ Runner**.

JOHN THE BAPTIST 1. Associated with baptism and religious conversion. See **Baptism**. 2. The forerunner of Christ. See **Christ**. 3. He who paves the way for that which follows. 4. Can correspond to losing one's head. 5. Might be associated with the wilderness.

JOINT 1. Can correspond to an unsuitable establishment or an illegal substance. You may wish to see **Building** or **Drugs/Drugstore**. 2. The place where two or more pieces are joined. 3. Can correspond to an agreement or a cooperative venture.

JONAH 1. Associated with being a reluctant prophet. 2. May be symbolic of something that is swallowed up. 3. Can correspond to bad luck or misfortune. 4. You may wish to see **Whale** and **Fish.**

JOSEPH (BIBLICAL, NEW TESTAMENT) 1. Can be symbolic of wisdom, intuition, and insight through dreams and spiritual messengers. 2. May correspond to being the reluctant husband or the perfect stepfather. 3. Might be symbolic of an older relationship.

JOSEPH (BIBLICAL, OLD TESTAMENT) 1. Symbolic of the favorite son. 2. Associated with one who rises above adversity through one's own initiative. 3. The ability to receive insight through dreams. 4. May correspond to self-realization. 5. Might be associated with feast, famine, or Egypt.

JOURNEY 1. One's life journey. 2. The journey of the soul through time and space. 3. A passage through time, experiences, or awareness. 4. Physically, associated with a journey through health and experiences; mentally, associated with emotions and relationships; spiritually, associated with inner meaning and the discovery of one's relationship with God. 5. May indicate the direction one is pursuing in life. See **Direc-**

tion. 6. Often corresponds to an individual's destiny. 7. May indicate the search for one's talent, calling, or next step. 8. Literally, may be symbolic of a real journey, vacation, move, or trip. 9. The place (i.e., road, street, air, water), the conditions (i.e., bad road, clear skies, a fork in the road, etc.), and mode of transportation (i.e., automobile, airplane, boat, walking, etc.) associated with the journey are important; for example: a fork in the road is symbolic of a choice to make; losing one's headlights can be associated with not watching where one is headed; a boat sinking might symbolize losing one's spiritual direction. See various places, conditions, and vehicles: i.e., **Path, Road, Direction, Weather, Airplane, Automobile, Boat,** etc.

JUDAISM 1. Associated with those who belong to the Jewish heritage or religion. 2. The first great religion of monotheism, recognizing one loving God of humankind. 3. In the Old Testament, God's chosen people (through Moses, Abraham, Isaac, Jacob, and the twelve tribes of Israel). 4. The faith in which much of the modern world has its roots (i.e., Judaism, Christianity, and Islam). 5. Associated with the Ten Commandments (Exodus 20): Thou shalt have no other gods before me; Thou shalt not worship graven images; Thou shalt not take the name of the Lord thy God in vain; Thou shalt keep holy the Sabbath; Thou shalt honor thy father and mother; Thou shalt not kill; Thou shalt not commit adultery; Thou shalt not steal; Thou shalt not bear false witness; Thou shalt not covet. 6. Primary religious texts are the Torah (first five books of the Old Testament), Talmud (Jewish law, folklore, and history), and Midrashim (rabbinical commentary and study).

JUDAS 1. Associated with betrayal. 2. Often corresponds to a lack of wisdom or understanding. 3. Might be symbolic of one who takes a bribe.

JUDGE 1. Can correspond to one's critique and analysis of oneself or others. See **People.** 2. To criticize oneself or others. 3. May be symbolic of one's higher self or inner wisdom. 4. Corresponds to a supreme worldly authority.

JUMP 1. A sudden movement, rise, departure, or transition. 2. Metaphorically, can be used as follows: he makes me jumpy = he makes me nervous; she got the jump on the project = she won out or she was first; to jump the experience = to get over or around an experience; to jump the claim = to take that which belongs to another; his father jumped all over him = his father reprimanded him; they jumped the gun = they acted before they were supposed to; to jump bail = to disappear. 3. That which is neglected or skipped. 4. See whatever is being jumped (i.e., cliff, road, etc.). 5. One's current situation or state of mind. See **Journey.** 6. Depending on imagery, you may also wish to see **Walk** and **Leg/Legless.**

JUNG, CARL 1. Associated with analysis, exploring the unconsciousness, or working with dreams. 2. May be a message from one's own unconscious self. 3. Could represent the need to get or give counseling.

JUNGLE 1. Associated with dense foliage and overgrown vegetation. See **Plant.** 2. That which is thriving and in overabundance. 3. May also correspond to basic instincts, the primitive, or the unruly. 4. Metaphorically, it's a jungle out there = it's a complicated, confusing, or bewildering situation. See **Work.** 5. Can represent the unconscious mind. See **Unconscious.** 6. The image will have a great deal to do with one's own feelings about jungles, as well as what is happening in the situation. 7. You may also wish to see **Animals.**

JUNK 1. That which is worthless, offensive, or immoral. 2. Can correspond to those things we have discarded or those things that need to be discarded, i.e., ideas, words, opinions, attitudes, etc. 3. Might also be calling to mind something that one inadvertently threw away and shouldn't have or the fact that one is wasteful. 4. Could indicate a rotten diet or food that has been wasted. See **Food.** 5. That which needs to be organized or put in order. See **Clean.**

JUPITER ♃ 1. Corresponds to noble purposes, broad vision, and perfected emotions. 2. Associated with the universality of force, benevolence, and supreme kindness. 3. In Roman mythology, symbolic of the ruler of all gods. See **Mythology (Roman and Greek).** 4. Fifth planet from the Sun; largest planet in our solar system. Has a rotation year of 11.86 years. 5. Astrologically, associated with Sagittarius and Pisces. See **Astrology.** 6. Metaphysically, associated with the seventh chakra (pituitary). See **Chakras.**

JURY 1. Associated with those who sit in judgment on others. 2. Can correspond to one's critique and analysis of oneself or others. See **People.** 3. To criticize oneself or others. 4. May be symbolic of one's conscience, higher self, or inner wisdom. 5. Corresponds to a worldly authority.

K

1. *The eleventh letter of the alphabet.* 2. *The Roman numeral for 250.* 3. *In jewelry and precious metals, the symbol for carat.* 4. *Chemically, the symbol for potassium.* 5. *Numerologically, equivalent to two.* 6. *In mathematics, a symbol for a constant.* 7. *In meteorology, a symbol for cumulus (a cloud formation).* 8. *In Greek, kappa.*

KANGAROO 1. That which travels by leaps and bounds. See **Animals.** 2. May correspond to one who is jumpy. See **Jump.** 3. Metaphorically, a kangaroo court = a false legal proceeding. 4. Might be one who is surefooted (i.e., a firm foundation). 5. May also be associated with Australia. See **Australia.**

KARMA 1. That which is only memory, or how one responds to the present based on unconscious memories of the past. See **Reincarnation.** 2. May indicate one's personal destiny or the current cycle of life. See **Journey.** 3. Might represent that which is owed to another. 4. You may also wish to see **Time.** 5. Could be symbolized by ancient locales or historical images. See **Historical Clothing/Settings.**

KENNEDY, JOHN F. 1. Associated with the president; the chief power or authority. See **President.** 2. May represent hope or the creation of visionary dreams. 3. Might be symbolic of infidelity. 4. Whatever one associates with him will definitely have a strong bearing on the symbolism.

KEY 1. The solution or the answer. 2. Can represent a new possibility. 3. Associated with liberation or freedom. 4. Represents knowledge or that which is necessary for knowledge or insight. 5. Associated with the mysterious. 6. Can represent that which provides safety. 7. Metaphorically, can be used as follows: she's all keyed up = she's very tense; holding the key = having the solution. 8. Liturgically, represents the papacy, the church, the keys to heaven, or the apostle Peter. 9. Depending on imagery, you may also wish to see **Door, Lock,** or **Safe.**

KIDNAPPED 1. That which is taken unlawfully. See **Thief.** 2. Being moved from one's position by force. 3. Can correspond to that which is under complete control by another. 4. Might be a literal or symbolic warning.

KIDS 1. Associated with playfulness, youth, inexperience, or immaturity. See **Child.** 2. May represent one's inner self or one's inner child. 3. The age of the kids may symbolize or represent a particular situation or experience of the same age in one's own life (i.e., a project, a business, or a memory). 4. See also **People.**

KILL 1. Associated with that which you are trying to kill or dispose of or that which is trying to do away with you (i.e., aspects of self, a difficult experience, another person, repressed memories, etc.). 2. That which is destroyed or put to death. See **Death**. 3. Can correspond to the prevention or end of something. 4. Metaphorically, you're killing me = you're causing uncontrollable laughter. 5. Could indicate those portions of oneself that are at war or are being denied. See **Shadow**.

KIMONO 1. Associated with an unusual or foreign idea or experience. See **Clothes**. 2. That which covers the situation. 3. May indicate one's insulation from the outside world. See **Coat**. 4. Associated with Japan. See **Japan**.

KING 1. Corresponds to the ruling authority or the higher self. 2. Could represent an authority figure such as a boss, a father, or a dominant male relationship. See **Man**. 3. May be associated with a majestic or high ideal, principle, or a dominant idea. 4. That which may provide protection, guidance, and lawfulness. 5. Associated with the masculine aspects of God. 6. See also **Phallus**. 7. Often that which rules the situation. 8. Corresponds to that which is elevated in stature. 9. See also **People**.

KING ARTHUR 1. May represent the soul's search for truth, enlightenment, or self-realization. 2. An archetype for the journey of life. See **Journey**.

KISS 1. Associated with feelings of affinity, love, or empathy. 2. Could indicate a close personal relationship or a sexual relationship. See **Marriage**. 3. Metaphorically, can be used as follows: to kiss and make up = to ask forgiveness; to kiss off = to give someone the brush-off. 4. Liturgically, a symbol of betrayal (Luke 22:48). 5. You may also wish to see **Lips**.

KITCHEN 1. Where one is fed or nurtured physically, mentally, or spiritually. See **House**. 2. May be associated with the literal need to become more aware of dietary habits. 3. Could represent something you are preparing to take into your body, mind, or

soul. 4. You may also wish to see **Cook** and **Food**.

KNEEL 1. Associated with humility and submission. 2. Can correspond to a state of awe or inspiration. 3. May indicate a need for spiritual discipline and prayer. 4. See **Prayer**. 5. Could symbolize giving into another's demands. See **Bow**.   .

KNEES 1. Can symbolize getting down on one's knees: becoming very involved personally or submitting to another's wishes. See **Body**. 2. Metaphorically, can be used as follows: to bring to one's knees = to dominate or to force into submission; on bended knee = to pray: to fall on one's knees = to ask for forgiveness. 3. Can be associated with using one's own experiences (i.e., standing on one's own). 4. You may also wish to see **Leg/Legless**.

KNIFE 1. That which cuts, divides, separates, or wounds (i.e., words, aggression, anger, opposing viewpoints, etc.). See **Cut**. 2. Can correspond to aggression, hostility, or forced dominance. See **War.** 3. Could indicate that which has a sharp point. 4. Metaphorically, can be used as follows: she's under the knife = she's having surgery; he knifed the guy in the back = he betrayed the guy or killed him. 5. Can represent an aggressive male figure. See **Phallus.** 6. May indicate evil. 7. Might be associated with an activity that needs to be cut out. 8. Depending on imagery, you may also wish to see **Wound.**

KNIGHT 1. Corresponds to a noble male figure or a noble part of oneself. 2. The desire to fight for what one believes in. 3. Metaphorically, a knight in shining armor = a deliverer or the one who saved the situation. 4. Since a knight is often riding a horse, you may wish to see **Horse.** 5. See also **People.**

KNOCK 1. Can correspond to opportunity knocks. 2. Could suggest a message. See **Message/Messenger.** 3. To cause to fall or fail. 4. May indicate criticism. 5. Metaphorically, can be used as follows: to knock something = to criticize it; knock it off = stop what you're doing; she was knocked out = she was made unconscious; she's a knock-out = she's gorgeous; he knocked her up = he made her pregnant; knock yourself out = enjoy yourself.

KNOT 1. Can represent a problem, an entanglement, or a difficult situation. 2. Metaphorically, associated with tying the knot, or marriage. See **Marriage.** 3. Might indicate a relationship or a partnership. 4. That which ties, binds, or secures. See **Rope.** 5. A knot on the body might symbolize stress or a literal health concern.

KORAN 1. The sacred text of the Muslems, associated with the words of God, or God's laws. See **Bible.** 2. Spiritual wisdom, insight, or direction. 3. See also **Islam.**

KRISHNA 1. In Hinduism, the manifestation of God (Vishnu) on the earth. See **Hinduism.** 2. The personification of the fully realized, perfected self. See **Christ.** 3. Often symbolized by a beautiful, asexual individual possessing perfected male and female qualities.

KUNDALINI 1. In mysticism, the energy that rises along one's spiritual centers or chakras. See **Chakras.** 2. Corresponds to pure and creative energy. 3. Often associated with the number seven (see **Numerology**) and symbolized by the snake (see **Snake**).

1. The twelfth letter of the alphabet. 2. The Roman numeral for fifty. 3. Referring to shape, as in an L-shaped building. 4. The symbol for longitude. 5. Numerologically, equivalent to three. 6. In physics, a symbol for heat. 7. In Greek, lambda.

LADDER 1. That which allows one to ascend or to overcome a situation, an obstacle, or an experience. See **Ascend.** 2. Climbing a ladder symbolizes achievement by taking one step at a time, growing in ability and experience, success, or the process of spiritual evolution. 3. Descending a ladder symbolizes going lower than one's previous stature, a demotion, a descent in morals, or the act of giving up. See **Descend.** 4. Missing a rung on a ladder could mean overlooking an important step or idea. 5. Walking under a ladder may be symbolic of bad luck or it may indicate the act of passing beneath an obstacle or experience. 6. Could correspond to journeying into higher states of consciousness. 7. Biblically, associated with an ascent to heaven and with Jacob's ladder (Genesis 28). 8. Might be symbolic of one's journey. See **Journey.** 9. You may also wish to see **Mountain.**

LAKE 1. Associated with rest, peace, and tranquillity. 2. Could correspond to a spiritual reservoir or source. See **Water.** 3. That which reflects one's image or current situation. See **Mirror.** 4. The appearance of the lake is extremely important. For example, a muddy lake could imply soiled spirituality, moral decline, or cloudy insights. 5. Can be associated with spiritual depth. See **Sea.**

LAMB 1. Represents innocence, meekness, purity, and gentility. 2. That which is child-like. See **Child.** 3. Liturgically, the Lamb of God; Christ. See **Christ.** 4. Rabbinically, associated with Passover. See **Passover.** 5. Metaphysically, purity manifest on the earth. 6. You may also wish to see **Animals.**

LAMP 1. Can correspond to an awareness, a light, or an insight. See **Light.** 2. That which is illuminated. 3. Could be associated with putting something under a spotlight (i.e., in plain view of everyone). See **Spotlight.** 4. Turning a lamp on could indicate a new understanding. 5. Turning a lamp off may symbolize refusing to understand or a death. 6. May symbolize one's own light or spirituality.

LANCE 1. That which may cut, pierce, or injure. See **Sword.** 2. Could indicate aggression or hostility. 3. Might symbolize the need for release. 4. Associated with male sexuality. See **Phallus.** 5. You may also wish to see **War.** 6. Might symbolize the need for physical surgery.

LANCELOT 1. Associated with bravery, male beauty, and deception. 2. May be symbolic of temptation or human passion. 3. That which appears without flaw but is only human.

LANDING 1. Associated with an incoming idea, an experience, a relationship, or a visitor. See **Airplane.** 2. May symbolize the act of or the necessity of coming back down to earth, or grounding oneself. 3. That which settles down. 4. In boating, associated with coming ashore, settling down, or resting after one's journey. See **Journey.** 5. You may also wish to see **Airport.**

LANGUAGE 1. May symbolize self–expression or communication. 2. Associated with how one is understood. 3. You may also wish to see **Mouth.** 4. Hearing bad language could indicate that you have said things—often about others—that should not have been said. 5. Hearing garbled language suggests the need to listen or to communicate more clearly.

LAP 1. That which one cares for and nurtures or the situation in which one is currently involved. 2. Metaphorically, she's in the lap of luxury = she has a great deal of material wealth and comfort. 3. You may also wish to see **Body.**

LARGE 1. Can be associated with feelings of greatness or supremacy. See **Size.** 2. That which is important or overwhelming. 3. May indicate that which is developed, mature, or overdeveloped. 4. Could correspond to an obstacle. See **Giant.** 5. Might indicate that which is in the present or in the future.

LAS VEGAS 1. Can correspond to good luck, good fortune, or temptation. 2. Symbolic of the fact that one may be gambling literally or metaphorically. See **Gambling.** 3. May indicate domestic travel. 4. Associated with an overnight relationship.

LAUGH 1. Associated with joy and happiness, or the act of being ridiculed. 2. That which is amusing, foolish, or fun. 3. Might suggest the need for more relaxation or joy in one's life. 4. Could symbolize the desirability of being able to laugh at oneself. 5. Metaphorically, to laugh it off = to not give

the subject much attention. 6. A release. 7. Might indicate a bad idea (i.e., a real joke). 8. You may also wish to see **Mouth.**

LAUNDRY 1. Corresponds to one's personal life or situation. 2. Metaphorically, airing your dirty laundry = telling others about your personal or family problems; the crook laundered the money = he placed it illegally into circulation. 3. May be associated with outer appearances. See **Clothes.** 4. Might indicate that which needs to be cleansed or washed (i.e., attitudes, thoughts, etc.). 5. See also **Wash.**

LAW 1. Rules of conduct, discipline, or expectations. 2. Associated with obedience and conformity. 3. Metaphorically, can be used as follows: to lay down the law = to scold someone; he took the law into his own hands = he acted as judge and jury in the situation (see **Judge**). 4. You may also wish to see **Police/Police Station.**

LAWN 1. Associated with growth, healing, energy, or vibrancy. 2. Can correspond to a healthy foundation. See **Foundation.** 3. See also **Plant.** 4. One's current situation (i.e., homelife) or the field one is tending to. See **Field.** 5. Because of the color, you may also wish to see green in **Colors.**

LAZARUS 1. Associated with resurrection, rebirth, or new beginnings. 2. That which came forth from the tomb. See **Cave.** 3. Corresponds to a healing.

LEAF/LEAVES 1. Growing leaves may represent new growth, fresh ideas, or a rebirth. 2. The appearance and the activity of leaves will be symbolic of their meaning. For example: blowing leaves may indicate too many discarded or unused ideas; tarnished leaves could symbolize things that are no longer worthwhile; raking leaves could represent dealing with one's memories or past experiences; dead leaves are often those things that were once part of oneself that must now be discarded. 3. Metaphorically, can be used as follows: to take leave = to excuse oneself or to depart; to turn over a new leaf = to make a fresh start. 4. You may also wish to see **Tree** or **Plant.**

LEASE 1. That which one obtains for a time. 2. A temporary belonging. 3. Metaphorically, a new lease on life = a new beginning or rebirth. 4. A temporary contract, entanglement, or situation. See **License.** 5. May be an indication of a literal happening. 6. Depending upon what one is leasing in the imagery, you may also wish to see **Car, House,** or **Building.**

LEASH 1. Associated with restraint, control, or ownership. 2. Could correspond to manipulating others or being manipulated by them. See **Puppet.** 3. Might indicate a pet project. See **Pet.**

LECTURE 1. May be the act of lecturing to or being lectured to; nagging. 2. Can be associated with learning and education. 3. You may also wish to see **School.**

LEDGE 1. Could suggest a dangerous situation (i.e., being on the edge or out on a limb). 2. May indicate an obstacle, a difficulty, or a hurdle. 3. Associated with a fear of failing or a fear of falling in stature. 4. You may also wish to see **Mountain.**

LEFT 1. Associated with the past, receptivity, open-mindedness or liberal ideas, and the west. 2. Often associated with unconscious parts of oneself. 3. May indicate a wrong choice or direction. See **Direction.** 4. However, one who is left-brained is generally intelligent, logical, and focused. 5. May be associated with the feminine side of oneself. See **Woman** and **Womb.** 6. Metaphorically, can be used as follows: a left-handed compliment = an insincere compliment; she's out in left field = she's very confused.

LEG/LEGLESS 1. That which is one's foundation, support, principles, or morals. See **Foundation.** 2. Metaphorically, can be used as follows: she pulled his leg = she teased him; shake a leg = hurry or get moving; I need to stretch my legs = I need to go for a walk; he's on his last leg = he's about ready to die. 3. See also **Walk.** 4. To be legless may suggest one is without principles, a backbone, a sense of direction, a job, or self-respect. 5. You may also wish to see **Feet** or **Body.**

LEO ♌ 1. Fifth sign of the zodiac, corresponding to July 23–August 22. 2. Associated with the following positive traits: generous, magnanimous, organized. 3. Associated with the following negative traits: aggressive, intolerant, opinionated. 4. Astrologically, ruled by the Sun. See **Sun/Sunlight.** 5. See also **Lion.** 6. A fire sign. See **Fire.** 7. See also **Astrology.**

LESSONS 1. What one needs for growth, understanding, or enlightenment. See **School.** 2. May suggest that one does not have all of the necessary knowledge or information. See **Test**.

LETTER 1. A message, idea, or insight of value. See **Message/Messenger.** 2. The arrival of a new idea, an opportunity, an insight, or a fresh perspective. 3. Metaphorically, the letter of the law = in accord with exact regulations. 4. Could correspond to information from another source, person, or the intuition. 5. May be suggestive of self-expression or the need to express oneself. See **Write.** 6. Associated with communication or the need to communicate. 7. You may also wish to see **Pen.**

LIBRA ♎ 1. Seventh sign of the zodiac, corresponding to September 23–0ctober 22. 2. Associated with the following positive traits: fair, diplomatic, idealistic, romantic. 3. Associated with the following negative traits: indecisive, changeable, easily influenced. 4. Astrologically, ruled by Venus. See **Venus.** 5. See also **Scales (Method of Weighing).** 6. An air sign. See **Air.** 7. See also **Astrology.**

LIBRARY 1. Corresponds to a place of vast knowledge and information. See **Building.** 2. The higher mind or soul. 3. Metaphysically, may represent the Akashic Records. See **Akashic Records.** 4. Associated with how you use the knowledge or awareness you already possess. 5. See also **Book.**

LICE 1. That which is a pest or an irritant. 2. Could be associated with a destructive or a bad idea. See **Hair.** 3. Metaphorically, a louse = a bad or immoral person. 4. Associated with personal uncleanliness (physically, mentally, or spiritually). 5. See also **Bug.**

LICENSE 1. That which grants authority or permission. 2. Associated with a contract, an entanglement, or permission. 3. Metaphorically, to receive poetic license = to be able to deviate from the facts. 4. Depending on imagery, you may also wish to see **Car** or **Lease.**

LICK 1. Often corresponds to licking one's wounds or feeling sympathetic toward oneself. 2. The act of cleansing oneself. See **Bath.** 3. Metaphorically, can be used as follows: they need to be licked into shape = they

need to be straightened out; he licked it up = he ate every bite; he was licked = he was beaten. 4. You may also wish to see **Tongue.**

LIFE GUARD 1. That which guards the various levels of one's consciousness, one's boundaries, or one's environment. 2. Might be associated with being engulfed in spirituality, emotions, feelings, creative ideas, a goal, or a project. See **Swim.** 3. That which provides safety, protection, or guidance. 4. See also **Water.** 5. You may also wish to see **People.**

LIFE JACKET 1. Can correspond to personal protection. 2. May indicate the appearance of safety or being untouchable *to* the rest of the world. See **Coat.** 3. Survivalist thoughts and attitudes. 4. You may also wish to see **Clothes.**

LIFTING. 1. Could correspond to the act of rising in stature, abilities, or awareness. See **Ascend.** 2. To raise one's goals. 3. Depending on imagery, may be associated with one's arms and therefore the self. See **Body.** 4. May indicate that which needs support or assistance.

LIGHT 1. Associated with great lessons, great truths, or higher knowledge. 2. Could correspond to significant understanding or brilliance. 3. Represents the flash of a spiritual insight or important idea or experience. 4. Associated with the presence of God or Christ. See **God.** 5. A higher directing force or power. 6. Could correspond to conscious intellect or understanding. 7. Hope in the midst of difficulties. 8. That which provides illumination for others. 9. Biblically, associated with creation: Let there be light (Genesis 1). 10. Metaphorically, to make light of = to lessen in importance; to bring into the light = subject to scrutiny; to light into = to attack. 11. Might be a pun on something that is really unimportant or light. 12. That which is placed under investigation. See **Spotlight.** 13. Different colors of light can be associated with different meanings; for example: a white light can represent an affirmative response, God, or spirituality; a dark light can indicate a negative response, the need for caution, or that which is evil or dangerous. 14. Depending on the imagery, you may also wish to see **Colors.**

LIGHT BULB 1. Could correspond to one's own intuition or awareness. 2. Represents that which brings the light of understanding. See **Light.**

LIGHTHOUSE 1. That which rises above the situation, or that which illuminates the environment. See **Tower.** 2. An insight or a spiritual direction. See **Light.** 3. That which borders levels of one's consciousness or the various aspects of an experience. 4. Could correspond with one's direction or guidance upon life's journey. See **Journey.** 5. You may also wish to see **Building.**

LIGHTNING 1. May be indicative of emotional or mental outbursts. See **Weather.** 2. Also associated with vivid flashes of insight or intuition from the higher self. 3. Can act as a warning sign for a forthcoming message or situation. 4. You may also wish to see **Electricity.** 5. Being struck by lightning could indicate an explosive situation (see **Explosion/Explosive**), or being overcome by an experience or another person. 6. Metaphorically, lightning never strikes twice = bad luck or extraordinary good luck doesn't happen to the same person twice; he's a lightning rod = he attracts situations to him.

LILY 1. Associated with that which is beautiful or humble. See **Flowers.** 2. Liturgically,

a symbol of Easter and immortality. See **Easter.** 3. May indicate one's own talents or spiritual enfoldment.

LINCOLN, ABRAHAM 1. Symbolic of freedom and democracy. 2. May be associated with martyrdom. 3. Could indicate the desire for equality, unity, or reconciliation.

LINEN 1. May be associated with sexual activity, intimacy, or the need to rest. See **Bed/Bedroom.** 2. That which covers or improves the appearance of a situation. See **Blanket.**

LION 1. Associated with great courage, power, vitality, and energy. 2. Astrologically, one of the twelve signs of the zodiac. See **Leo.** 3. The king of the forest (i.e., the boss). 4. Metaphorically, can be used as follows: to get the lion's share = to receive the greatest or to take more than any other individual; into the lion's den or putting one's head in the lion's mouth = to place oneself in a position of great danger. 5. Metaphysically, relates to the third chakra or endocrine center; to flee or to fight. See **Adrenals.** 6. Is symbolic of the Christ in C. S. Lewis's *Chronicles of Narnia*. See **Christ.** 7. Associated with one's search for courage and self-respect in *The Wizard of Oz*. 8. Might also be a play on the statement, "You're "lyin'." 9 . You may also wish to see **Cat.**

LIPS 1. Represents speech or speaking up for oneself. 2. Corresponds to passion or romance. 3. Associated with sexuality. 4. Metaphorically, can be used as follows: to keep a stiff upper lip = to hold in one's emotions; bite your lip = hold back what you were about to say; to smack your lips = to express great anticipation or satisfaction; don't give me any lip = don't talk back to me. 5. See **Body** or **Mouth.** 6. You may also wish to see **Kiss.**

LIQUOR 1. May correspond to physical overindulgence or habits. See **Food.** 2. That which causes the loss of physical consciousness or personal inhibitions. See **Drunk.** 3. Can represent something that is making the individual intoxicated or overcome. 4. Associated with the desire to escape reality or to achieve relaxation through artificial means. 5. May be a pun on partaking of the spirit. See **Water.** 6. See also **Alcohol.**

LIVING ROOM 1. Can correspond to a current state of mind or personal situation. 2. See also **House.** 3. Associated with one's environment or surroundings.

LOBBY 1. A place of waiting. 2. The facade or front presented to the public. 3. See also **House.** 4. Associated with how one greets a current situation. See **Front Desk**.

LOBSTER 1. May correspond to one's personal feelings about lobster (i.e., luxury, wealth, allergies, etc.). 2. Associated with a spiritual experience or a spiritual food (food for the mind or soul). See **Fish**. 3. That which possesses a hard exterior or impenetrable emotions. See **Shell**. 4. Depending on imagery, you may also wish to see **Tail**.

LOCK 1. Can represent security, protection, secrecy, or the refusal to deal with a particular situation or emotion. 2. Might be a problem, an obstacle, or a difficulty. 3. Associated with unexplored talents, hidden levels of oneself, or repressed feelings and emotions. See **Door**. 4. The symbolism may depend upon what is locked; for example: a locked door could be associated with refusing to face a particular experience or not knowing how to deal with a situation; a locked treasure chest could indicate one's untapped talents and abilities, etc. 5. That which keeps others out. 6. You may also wish to see **Key**.

LOOSE 1. Associated with loosening, unbinding, releasing, or freeing a portion of oneself (i.e., attitudes, beliefs, morals) or one's connection with or overdependence on something or someone. 2. That which becomes less fixed or more calm. 3. Loose clothing could indicate that you have grown too big for yourself. See **Clothes**. 4. Whatever is loose will have a great deal to do with the imagery; for example: if one is wearing loose clothing, it might also suggest the fact that one's current position is not appropriate or is too large; if the image is of a loose knot, it may symbolize that a connection or a relationship is not all that firm or that a problem or a stressor is being relaxed. 5. Metaphorically, she's loose = she's easygoing; or sexually, she's easy to have. 6. Depending on imagery, might suggest something that is relaxed, stress-free, or unfit.

LOS ANGELES 1. Literally, the city of angels. 2. Corresponds to the individual's own opinions and thoughts regarding the city. 3. Could be literally an indication of a journey or a move to California.

LOST 1. To lose a part of oneself (i.e., hopes, morals, dreams), the situation, or another. 2. May correspond to the feeling that something is missing from one's life. See **Journey**. 3. May be associated with having forgotten to deal with something. 4. Losing track of a portion of oneself. See **Shadow**.

LOTUS 1. A beautiful idea, experience, or something about to blossom. See **Flowers**. 2. Liturgically, associated with rising above evil influences. 3. Metaphysically, corresponds to gradual and personal enlightenment.

LUCID DREAM 1. To know that one is

dreaming while in the midst of the dream. 2. Associated with conscious awareness, lucidity, clear thinking, and the ability to shape one's surroundings, thoughts, or experiences. 3. You may also wish to see **Dream**.

LUGGAGE 1. Symbolic of taking a trip or a journey either literally or metaphorically. 2. Represents the baggage (experiences, beliefs, burdens) an individual takes along, both necessary and unnecessary. 3. Can indicate insights, material, information, or experiences that are available to the bearer. 4. That which one has in hand. 5. You may also wish to see **Bag.**

LUMP 1. Associated with something that has gotten under one's skin (i.e., a frustrating individual or experience). See **Cyst.** 2. A potentially harmful irritant. 3. May indicate a literal physical problem that needs to be addressed by a physician. 4. Could symbolize something that is being held in. 5. You may also wish to see **Body** or **Wound.**

LUNGS 1. Can correspond to one's breath, one's emotions, or that which one holds inside. See **Body.** 2. Associated with the breath of life. See **Breath** and **Air.**

LYDEN 1. Associated with the second endocrine center or chakra. 2. Relates to creativity or temptation. 3. Also referred to as the cells of Leydig; interstitial cells throughout the gonads. 4. Metaphysically, corresponds to Neptune; also symbolized by the image of an androgynous man. 5. In Revelation, it is represented by the Church of Smyrna. 6. See **Chakras.**

1. The thirteenth letter of the alphabet. 2. The Roman numeral for 1000. 3. Chemically, a symbol for an element in electrolysis. 4. Numerologically, equivalent to four. 5. In physics, a symbol for inductance. 6. In logic, the symbol for a middle term between propositions of a syllogism. 7. In Greek, mu. 8. May be associated with mother.

MACHINE 1. That which is mechanical, predictable, or habitual. 2. May represent physiological functioning such as assimilation, elimination, reproduction, or digestion. See **Body**. 3. Could be symbolic of that which has no independent thought or personal will. 4. You may also wish to see **Puppet**.

MAD 1. One of the four basic emotions (glad, mad, sad, and scared). See **Emotion**. 2. May be associated with activities or interactions causing one to be sad, irritated, angry, or rageful. 3. Metaphorically, he's a little mad = he's a little crazy.

MADONNA (BIBLICAL) 1. Represents the feminine aspect of Christ. See **Christ** and **Womb**. 2. Archetypally, the symbol of motherhood. See **Mother**. 3. Corresponds to divine love. 4. See also **Virgin Mary**.

MADONNA (SINGER) 1. The freedom of creative or sexual expression. 2. Symbolic of independence. 3. May represent expressive ego. 4. You may also wish to see **People**.

MAGAZINE 1. That which is of general or everyday interest. 2. A source of information, insight, or opinion. See **Library**. 3.

Could represent a message, a personal insight, or intuition. 4. Reading different articles in the magazine may be associated with different meanings or concerns; for example: reading an advertisement could indicate something you want or a message you need to hear; reading an individual's story might be an analogy of one's own life or situation. 5. You may also wish to see **Book**.

MAGGOT 1. Irritants that feed off oneself or others. See **Bug**. 2. Associated with filth and decay (physically, morally, or spiritually). 3. May indicate that which has sprung from previous actions and choices or the current situation. 4. Might be symbolic of taking that which was left by others. See **Burglar**.

MAGI 1. Associated with the three wise men. See **Wise Man/Wise Woman**. 2. One who possesses mystical or magical powers. See **Magic/Magician**. 3. In ancient Persia, associated with the study of astrology. See **Astrology**.

MAGIC/MAGICIAN 1. Corresponds to the power of thought, creation, or the imagination. 2. May represent untapped and limitless potential. 3. That which can accomplish anything. See **Witch** and **Wizard.** 4. May indicate assistance from a spiritual source or higher levels of one's own consciousness. 5. May correspond to mysticism or ancient knowledge. 6. A hidden or special talent, ability, or gift. 7. Could be symbolic of the conscious mind trying to dominate the unconscious. 8. That which creates illusion from reality. 9. Associated with one in the tarot. See **Tarot.** 10. You may also wish to see **People.**

MAGNET 1. That which attracts, unites, or repels. 2. Metaphorically, she has a magnetic personality = she is very popular with people. 3. Might correspond to temptation or desire.

MAGNIFYING GLASS 1. Associated with something that is placed under close scrutiny, criticism, or inspection. See **Spotlight.** 2. Could symbolize making something appear bigger or more important than reality. 3. Associated with improving one's vision, comprehension, or understanding. See **Eyes.**

MAID 1. Associated with the feminine aspect of oneself, subservient to oneself or to others. See **Servant.** 2. That which waits on something (i.e., time, others, until the condition is right, etc.). 3. Could indicate a helpful suggestion, the need for help, or the need to help others. 4. May be symbolic of the need to clean house physically, mentally, or spiritually. See **Clean.** 5. Might correspond to being of service to an idea, a person, or an experience. 6. See also **Woman** and **People.**

MAIL 1. Messages, ideas, or insights. See **Message/Messenger.** 2. The arrival of a new opportunity or perspective. 3. Metaphorically, the letter of the law = in accord with exact regulations. 4. Could correspond to information from another source, person, or the intuition. 5. May be suggestive of self-expression or the need to express oneself. See **Write.**

MALE 1. Associated with the individuality of oneself. See **Self.** 2. Corresponds to the masculine side of one's nature. 3. Possibly

corresponding to masculine traits, i.e., strength, courage, determination, virility. See **Man.** 4. May correspond to the male counterpart of one's youthful self. See **Child** and **Boy.** 5. Might symbolize an idea, a project, or a person of about the same age.

MALL 1. Can correspond to a place of activity, money, shopping, materiality, or where anything may be obtained. 2. Associated with people, crowds, and being enclosed in one's environment. 3. Whatever one associates with shopping in a mall will have a great deal to do with the symbolism (i.e., a fun outing or a shopping hassle). 4. You may also wish to see **Shop.**

MAN 1. Associated with the individuality of oneself. 2. Corresponds to the masculine side of one's nature. See **Phallus.** 3. Possibly corresponding to masculine traits, i.e., strength, courage, determination, virility. 4. Can represent independence. 5. Different types of men can be associated with different meanings; for example: a wild man could symbolize uncontrollable aspects of oneself; an old man could represent wisdom or experience; a young man might suggest youthfulness, naivete, or inexperience. 6. Metaphorically, can be used as follows: man about town = being socially extroverted; man and boy = an unchanged aspect of the individual throughout life; man in the street = an ordinary or everyday person; man of the world = an experienced and wise individual; being one's own man = having control of oneself; man of God = spiritual person; Oh man = an exclamation of wonderment, excitement, or surprise. 7. Metaphysically, relates to the second chakra or endocrine center; temptation and creativity. See **Lyden.** 8. You may also wish to see **People** and **Boy.**

MAN (POURING WATER) 1. Astrologically, one of the twelve signs of the zodiac, represented by a man pouring water from a watering pot or gourd. See **Aquarius.** 2. Symbol of creativity or emotional outpouring. 3. Can represent being a deliverer of peace, healing, or spirit into a troubling situation. 4. See also **Man.**

MANAGER 1. Corresponds to the one in charge of the activity. 2. Could be associated with the higher self or soul. 3. Represents the one responsible for the experience or livelihood of those in the same situation. 4. The source of power and authority. 5. May be associated with a parental figure. 6. See **People.**

MANDALA 1. A visual symbol that corresponds to a representation of the whole self. See **Christ.** 2. That which contains all aspects of the individual: physically, mentally, and spiritually, as well as all levels of the mind. 3. Different colors in the mandala can represent different qualities in the self. See **Colors.** 4. That which provides insight and integration into one's true nature. 5. See also **Circle.** 6. You may also wish to see **Journey.**

MANGER 1. Associated with simplicity or poverty. 2. Liturgically, represents Christ. See **Christ.** 3. Could indicate going back to basics. 4. A temporary shelter, experience, or condition.

MANSION 1. Corresponds to a big idea, a large project, one's ego, the truth about oneself, or what one thinks of oneself. See **House.** 2. May represent one's current situation or state of affairs. 3. That which is enormous and all-encompassing. See **Size.**

MAP 1. Associated with direction or the need for direction. See **Direction.** 2. Represents seeing or needing to look at an overview of the entire situation. 3. Corresponds to the need to explore new horizons or uncharted territory. 4. Could be symbolic of one's purpose or upcoming experience. 5. Where one is headed. See **Journey.** 6. Can indicate the need to take stock of or reevaluate the current situation or experience.

MARATHON 1. Associated with distance, endurance, and agility. 2. Could correspond to one's competitive nature. See **Sports.** 3. Might symbolize a large distance or an excessive time period. 4. May represent that from which one is running away. See **Run/Runner.** 5. You may also wish to see **Athlete** and **Race.**

MARCH 1. Could correspond to taking orders or following instructions. 2. One's current activities, journey, or state of mind. See **Journey.** 3. Metaphorically, marching to the beat of a different drummer = to follow one's own life path. 4. To move forward or make progress in an orderly manner. 5. You may also wish to see **Walk** and **Military.**

MARIJUANA 1. That which is illegal. 2. Attempting to escape one's current situation. 3. May be a literal indication of taking something internally that is harmful to your system. See **Food.** 4. That which goes up in smoke. See **Cigar/Cigarette** and **Smoke/Smoking.**

MARINES 1. Can correspond to specialized training, a careful selection, or an intense activity or journey. 2. Might represent service of the highest kind. 3. Can correspond to order, power, discipline, or the relinquishment of personal will. 4. Associated with placing oneself subservient to a greater goal or good. 5. Can represent a warlike environment or situation. See **War**. 6. Depending on imagery, you may also wish to see **Water**.

MARRIAGE 1. Corresponds to a union or a partnership. 2. Associated with commitment and responsibility toward another person or duty. 3. May indicate a new venture or proposal. 4. Could be a literal indication of marriage or the start of a close relationship. 5. The unifying of two sides, opinions, or personalities. 6. An indication of harmony and cooperation or the need for it in a particular situation or relationship. 7. The joining together of two parts of one's own self. See **Shadow**.

MARS ♂ 1. Corresponds to the urge for activity and movement. 2. Associated with power, creation, and energy. 3. Positively associated with self-confidence and courage; negatively associated with anger and dominance. 4. In Roman mythology, symbolic of the god of war. See **Mythology (Roman and Greek)**. 5. Fourth planet from the Sun; the red planet. Has a rotation year of 686.9 days. 6. Alchemically, corresponds to iron. 7. Astrologically, associated with Aries and Scorpio. See **Astrology**. 8. Metaphysically, associated with the third chakra (adrenals). See **Chakras**.

MARTYR 1. Could indicate self-sacrifice for a cause. 2. May be associated with self-righteousness or a holier-than-thou attitude. 3. Killing a part of the self, or allowing a part of the self to be killed. See **Kill**. 4. Might indicate that one is stubbornly refusing to submit to the opinions or desires of another or a group. 5. May be symbolic of emotional turmoil or suffering. 6. You may also wish to see **People**.

MARY (BIBLICAL) 1. The divine feminine.

See **Virgin Mary**. 2. The archetypal mother. See **Mother**.

MARY MAGDALENE 1. Associated with forgiveness, personal transformation, and faith. 2. Can correspond to service and selflessness. 3. Might represent human metamorphosis. See **Phoenix (Bird).** 4. You may also wish to see **Prostitute.**

MASK 1. That which conceals or disguises the truth. 2. Can correspond to what we present to the world. See **Clothes** and **Acting/Actor/Actress.** 3. Suggests that one needs to look beyond appearances for reality or the hidden truth. 4. May be symbolic of hiding the real self. 5. See also **Face**. 6. You may also wish to see **Shadow.**

MASSACRE 1. Symbolic of being thoroughly beaten or overwhelmed by the situation. 2. Could indicate portions of yourself or the environment that are destroying you. See **Kill.** 3. Depending on imagery, you may also wish to see **Death** and **War.**

MASTURBATION 1. May represent sexual desires and frustrations. See **Sex.** 2. Can be associated with the abuse of creative talents. 3. Might be indicative of a waste of energy. 4. To excite oneself. 5. Could be associated with the potential energy one has available for use in creativity, healing, etc. 6. You may also wish to see **Phallus** or **Womb.**

MATHEMATICS 1. That which creates order. 2. For specific numbers, see **Numerology.** 3. May represent that which is exact or precise. 4. Could suggest one's opinion that it's only a numbers game (i.e., the only goal is for profit). 5. Might be associated with one who is exacting. 6. Can indicate one's own focus on budgeting or the need to budget time, energy, or resources. 7. That which can calculate the worth of something. See **Abacus.**

MATTRESS 1. May be associated with sexual activity, intimacy, or the need to rest. See **Bed/Bedroom.** 2. Can indicate a relationship, a union, a cooperative activity, or a reconciliation. See **Marriage.** 3. Might symbolize a foundation. See **Foundation.** 4. Depending on imagery, you may also wish to see **Sleep.**

MAZE 1. Associated with confusion or uncertainty. 2. May indicate a loss of direction on one's life path. See **Direction** or **Journey.** 3. Could correspond to a disorganized part of life (physically, mentally, spiritually) or a disorganized situation. 4. Metaphorically, can be used as follows: being a rat in a maze = being ruled by the environment, the experience, or one's surroundings. 5. May be symbolic of various or confusing choices.

MEDALS 1. Associated with one's occupation, duty, affiliation, or responsibility. 2. Can correspond to an honor, a symbol, or a distinction. 3. May symbolize that which is lawful, moral, or correct. See **Police/Police Station.** 4. You may also wish to see **Work** and **Insignia.**

MEDITATION 1. Could symbolize the need for personal introspection, self-analysis, or spiritual pursuits. 2. Corresponds to that which allows integration of the whole self. See **Christ.** 3. May indicate a message from the higher mind or listening to the divine within. 4. See also **Yoga/Yogi.** 5. You may also wish to see **Prayer.**

MELCHIZEDEK 1. Associated with righteousness and peace. 2. Corresponds to the Old Testament figure of Christ. See **Christ.** 3. Metaphysically, associated with the divine

mind or divine will. 4. May represent that which is without beginning or end.

MELTING 1. Melting ice could represent the release of old patterns, thoughts, or beliefs. 2. That which ends or disintegrates. 3. Could represent a softening or an opening up, as in an opening up of emotions. 4. You may also wish to see **Ice** and **Water**.

MENORAH 1. A candelabra associated with the Jewish faith. See **Judaism**. 2. Can represent wisdom, insight, or illumination. See **Candle/Candlestick**. 3. A seven-pointed candelabra might represent the chakras. See **Chakras**. 4. A nine-pointed candelabra is associated with Hanukkah. See **Hanukkah**. 5. You may also wish to see **Numerology**.

MERCURY ☿ 1. Corresponds to high mental abilities, judgment, and criticism. 2. Associated with communications, reason, and calculation. 3. In Roman mythology, symbolic of the messenger of the gods. See **Mythology (Roman and Greek).** 4. Closest planet to the Sun; smallest planet in our solar system. Has a rotation year of 88 days. 5. Astrologically, associated with Gemini and Virgo. See **Astrology**. 6. Metaphysically, associated with the sixth chakra (pineal). See **Chakras**.

MERLIN 1. Represents inner wisdom, guidance, or insight. 2. One who is capable of the magical or the mysterious. See **Magic/Magician.** 3. Could correspond to a guiding or fatherly influence.

MERMAID 1. Can correspond to the integration of the spiritual with the physical. 2. See also **Fish**. 3. The feminine energy that arises from the unconscious. See **Water** and **Womb**. 4. Might indicate the need to submerge oneself into a creative project. 5. See also **Swim**.

MESSAGE/MESSENGER 1. Associated with information, insight, inspiration, or intuition from oneself, from one's surroundings, from another person, or from another realm. 2. Can correspond to that which one needs to hear or that which one needs to act upon; for example: guidance, a decision, a direction, a choice, etc. 3. May symbolize one's own inner or higher self. 4. Messages and messengers come in many shapes and sizes; for example: a spiritual message could come in the form of a minister; a mental message could come in the form of insight or sudden knowledge; a physical message could be portrayed in different portions of one's physical body, etc. 5. Could provide a literal warning suggesting alternate plans, doing what one can do to prevent a problem, or to make a better choice, etc. 6. Spoken or written words are generally highly significant and may sometimes be taken literally. 7. Might be a literal telepathic communication from a loved one (living or deceased). 8. You may also wish to see **People** and **Letter**.

METAL 1. May be associated with strength, endurance, resiliency, etc. 2. Depending on imagery, could indicate one's flexibility, emotional openness, or personal foundation and stability. 3. If the metal is deteriorated or neglected, you may wish to see **Rust**.

METAPHOR 1. A symbolic representation of an experience, an image, an activity, a thought, or an individual. 2. That which represents something else entirely; for example: an image of animals fighting may simply be a metaphor for an area in one's life where there is argument or discord; a smooth, sparkling lake might be a metaphor for in-

ner tranquility and emotional calm, etc. 3. You may also wish to see **Symbol/ Symbolism** and **Archetype**.

METEOR I. An incoming insight, experience opportunity, or obstacle. 2. That which is brilliant or exceptional. 3. A falling meteor could indicate a problem, a demotion, or a descent, or it might symbolize a death. See **Descend** and **Death**. 4. A meteor shower could suggest confusion, lots of activity, or conflicting ideas. 5. See also **Star**.

METHUSELAH I. That which is extremely old, ancient, or wise. See **Old Man/Old Woman**. 2. Metaphysically, associated with renewal or quick thought. 3. May indicate that which will not die.

MEXICO 1. Corresponds primarily to whatever an individual thinks of Mexico or Mexicans (i.e., associated with vacation, food, siestas, illegal activities, etc.). 2. May be indicative of a foreign visitor or travel. 3. Might be associated with crossing the border (i.e., going out of bounds or over the line).

MEZUZAH 1. A sign of Jewish faith. See **Judaism**. 2. A rolled scroll attached to the doorpost of Jewish homes, containing verses from Deuteronomy 6:4–9 and II: 1321: "Hear 0 Israel: The Lord our God is one Lord: and thou shalt love the Lord thy God with all thine heart, and with all thine soul, and with all thy might. . ." etc.). 3. You may also wish to see **Door**.

MICKEY MOUSE 1. Associated with joy, optimism, and enthusiasm. 2. The personification of happiness. 3. Metaphorically, a mickey mouse operation = a disorganized activity. 4. Could indicate a vacation or a relaxing escape from the real world.

MICROSCOPE I. Associated with something that is placed under close scrutiny, criticism, or inspection. See **Spotlight**. 2. Could symbolize making something appear bigger or more important than it is in reality. 3. Associated with improving one's vision, comprehension, or understanding. See **Eyes**. 4. Might correspond to that which is very insignificant or small. See **Small**.

MICROWAVE 1. Corresponds to that which is modern, quick, and speedy. 2. That which accomplishes something without putting on the heat (i.e., force, anger, or frustration). 3. Might suggest a great deal of agitation with very little effort. 4. Depending upon imagery, could be associated with dietary suggestions. 5. You may also wish to see **Cook**.

MIDGET 1. That which is underdeveloped or in its germinating phase. See **Size.** 2. That which may be overlooked or considered insignificant. 3. That which is a miniature. 4. See also **Dwarf.**

MIDNIGHT 1. Can correspond to something that is eerie, mysterious, or magical. See **Magic/Magician.** 2. Could be associated with the unconscious. See **Unconscious.** 3. May suggest the close of an experience, a relationship or a dark or gloomy experience. See **Evening.** 4. Can be a very positive or a very negative image depending on the feelings associated with the experience. 5. Metaphorically, she's been burning the midnight oil = she's been studying or working very hard and/or late. 6. Depending on imagery, you may also wish to see **Moon/Moonlight.**

MILITARY 1. Corresponds to order, power, discipline, or the relinquishment of personal will. 2. Associated with placing oneself subservient to a greater goal or good. 3. Can represent a warlike environment or situation. See **War.**

MILK 1. Associated with nurturing or what one is feeding the body, mind, or soul. See **Food.** 2. Could represent a literal dietary suggestion for milk or calcium. 3. Could correspond to one's mother. See **Mother.** 4. Metaphorically, associated with the following: to cry over spilt milk = to be upset over something that cannot be changed; to milk dry = to drain of resources or talents; the milk of human kindness = the highest human feelings of compassion and empathy.

MILK OF MAGNESIA 1. Represents the need to become more relaxed. 2. Corresponds to stress reduction. 3. Could be related to poor dietary habits and an excess of stomach acid.

MIME 1. Associated with one who mimics, copies, or acts like another. 2. Might correspond to people who refuse to speak up for themselves or for their opinions. 3. Could indicate one who imitates, takes credit, or steals another's ideas. See **Thief.** 4. Might be suggestive of one who is clowning around. See **Clown.** 5. You may also wish to see **People.** 6. To pretend one is something one is not. See **Acting/Actor/Actress.**

MINISTER 1. A spiritual presence, authority, or messenger. See **Message/Messenger.** 2. Could represent spiritual safety or harmony. 3. Metaphorically, to minister unto others = to serve or to take care of others. 4. One's own conscience or belief systems. 5. The appearance of the minister may be symbolic of your own feelings toward religion. 6. One who is involved in spiritual matters or concerns. 7. May represent the need to pay closer attention to the spiritual side of one's life. 8. Might symbolize the state of being spiritually self-realized. See **Christ.** 9. See also **People** and **Church.**

MIRROR 1. That which reflects one's own image, experience, or the situation. 2. The reflection may have a great deal to do with the symbolism; for example: a poor self-image, a split personality, etc. See **Body.** 3. That which is imitation or illusory. 4. Could correspond to egotism and thinking only of oneself. 5. May indicate the need for self-reflection and examination. 6. One's individuality. See **Self.** 7. Breaking a mirror might be associated with bad luck.

MISCARRIAGE 1. Corresponds to anything that does not reach maturity or that which is stopped in the process of development. 2. Losing something or having to let go of something important. 3. May be associated with one's own fears of pregnancy. 4. Metaphorically, a miscarriage of justice = a failure to reach a just decision. 5. Might be a literal warning of a potential miscarriage. 6. You may also wish to see **Kill** or **Death.** 7. Might correspond to a miscarriage of one's inner child. 8. You may also wish to see **Birth.**

MIST 1. Often refers to emotional or mental depression. See **Weather.** 2. Associated with seclusion and introspection. 3. May correspond to ancient or mythical information. 4. Can relate to a personal mystical or spiritual experience. 5. You may also wish to see **Water** and **Clouds/Cloudy.**

MOAN 1. Can be symbolic of a complaint, grief, or a regret. 2. That which invokes pity and sorrow. 3. See **Cry.**

MOB 1. Can correspond to unruly portions of oneself. See **Shadow.** 2. May symbolize groups with which one is associated (i.e., work). 3. Might represent a criminal element. See **Gangster.** 4. Could symbolize one's combined problems, fears, frustrations, or difficulties. 5. Metaphorically, mob rule = individuals combining their efforts to overthrow authority. 6. You may also wish to see **People.**

MOCKINGBIRD 1. That which imitates or takes the ideas of another. See **Mime.** 2. Could indicate a false message. 3. Associated with the fear of being criticized. 4. That which mocks. 5. See also **bird.**

MODEL 1. That which is patterned after the real image. See **Statue.** 2. Associated with that shown to the outer world. See **Acting/Actor/Actress.** 3. May be symbolic of the self. See **Self.** 4. An imitation of reality.

MOHAMMED 1. Associated with human contact with the divine. 2. See **Message/Messenger.** 3. May be symbolic of Islam. See **Islam.** 4. One who brings order out of chaos. 5. A prophet and messenger. 6. See also **Christ.**

MOHAMMED ALl 1. Can indicate dominance over circumstances or the environment. 2. Associated with individual expression and promotion. 3. May represent the expression of one's ego. 4. An inner conflict. See **Fight.** 5. You may also wish to see **People.**

MOLE 1. Associated with one who digs up dirt (i.e., attempts to undermine the activities or the reputation of another). See **Animals.** 2. One who burrows to protect oneself from emotions, others, or the environment. 3. You may also wish to see **Hole.**

MONASTERY 1. A spiritual haven, resting place, or place of safety. 2. That which is free from the outside material world. 3. A place of worship. See **Church.** 4. A spiritual community. 5. May be associated with religious vows: chastity, poverty, obedience, and service. 6. You may also wish to see **Monk.**

MONEY 1. That which is valuable or truthful (i.e., wealth, knowledge, love, etc.). 2. Something one possesses or desires to possess (an idea, an experience, power, etc.) that may be exchanged for something else. 3. Associated with the benefits or rewards of one's efforts. 4. Symbolic of success or the lack of it. See **Work.** 5. One's wealth, inner resources, or strength. 6. Could be associated with a storehouse of talents and abilities that are there for the taking. 7. Corresponds to a moneymaking proposition, idea, or experience. 8. Represents power, time, or energy. 9. The kind of money indicates its value: counterfeit money symbolizes that which is untrue, insincere, or worthless; borrowed money corresponds to something that belongs to another. 10. Metaphorically, in the money = to be a success. 11. May indicate energy and stability. 12. Suggestive of personal security and stability.   .

MONK 1. A spiritual presence, authority, or messenger. See also **Minister.** 2. Could represent spiritual safety or harmony. 3. One's own conscience or belief systems. 4. One who is involved in spiritual matters or pursuits. 5. May be symbolic of one who has isolated himself from others. 6. Can indicate something that explains spiritual laws. 7. Suggestive of discipline, chastity, and obedience. 8. Might correspond to the spiritualized masculine attributes. See **Phallus.** 9. Whatever one associates with monks will have a great impact on the associated symbolism. 10. See **People.**

MONKEY 1. Associated with one who mimics the activities of another. 2. May be associated with mischievousness and playfulness. 3. Metaphorically, don't monkey around with that = don't play with that; a monkey on one's back = a situation or a problem that must be dealt with, or an addiction. 4. Might also be associated with a lower intellect or an irrational behavior. 5. You may also wish to see **Animals.**

MONOPOLY 1. One's personal association with the game may have a great deal to do with the symbolism (i.e., relaxation, childhood, business, etc.). 2. Can correspond to how one plays the game of life. See **Game.** 3. Metaphorically, may be used as follows: to have a monopoly = to have complete control over a situation or an experience; to monopolize the conversation = to do all the talking.

MONORAIL 1. May represent tremendous focus, speed, and determination upon one's life journey. See **Journey.** 2. An established roadway. See **Road.** 3. That which directs one's journey. See **Train.** 4. Could correspond to a quick idea. 5. Being on the fast track of life.

MONSTER 1. Corresponds to irrational thoughts or behaviors. 2. One who is cruel or inhumane. 3. Associated with uncontrolled anger or rage. 4. Repressed or ignored portions of oneself. 5. Can represent one's own fears. 6. The outer personality attempting to hide one's true self or feelings. 7. An obstacle that must be faced or overcome. 8. Aspects of oneself at war with one another. See **Shadow.** 9. See also **People.**

MOON/MOONLIGHT ☽ 1. Associated with the emotions. 2. Represents the feminine aspects of oneself or the situation: feelings, receptivity, nurturing. See **Woman** and **Womb.** 3. Corresponds to the intuition or the unconscious. 4. Can represent desire, romance, yearning, or sexuality and passion. 5. Corresponds to cycles (psychological, physiological, human experience, planting, etc.). 6. Astrologically, associated with Cancer. See **Astrology.** 7. Associated with eighteen in the tarot. See **Tarot.** 8. Depending on imagery, you may also wish to see **Evening.**

MOP 1. Corresponds to that which needs to be mopped or cleaned (i.e., thoughts, patterns, habits, etc.). See **Clean.** 2. May correlate with small chores or ideas that need to be dealt with. 3. Might symbolize male sexuality. See **Phallus.** 4. Might indicate the need for literal housework.

MORGUE/MORTUARY 1. That which needs to be laid to rest; associated with that which has died. See **Funeral.** 2. The condition of the morgue may indicate something about oneself. See **Building.** 3. May indicate a storehouse of ideas or talents that have long been ignored or neglected. 4. See also **Death.**

MOSCOW 1. Can correspond to deception, cold (physical or emotional), the potential for freedom, etc. 2. Whatever one associates with the city will be highly significant. 3. May be associated with a foreign visitor or travel. 4. See also **Russia.**

MOSES 1. Associated with emancipation; the lawgiver. 2. Literally, that which was drawn from the water. See **Water.** 3. Corresponds to the deliverer of the Ten Commandments. See **Judaism.** 4. Can represent a spiritual messenger. See **Message/Messenger.**

MOSQUE 1. Associated with a Muslim house of worship. See **Temple** and **Islam.**

2. Can correspond to the need for religious discipline and spirituality.

MOSQUITO 1. That which feeds off oneself or others; irritants. 2. Corresponds to that which drains energies; that which is draining (i.e., the situation, another person, current thoughts, etc.). 3. See also **Bug.**

MOTEL 1. A temporary residence or state of mind. 2. May be associated with one's current situation, experience, or health. See **House.** 3. The appearance of the motel will have much to do with one's situation (i.e., luxurious or worn down). See **Building.** 4. May be associated with business, relaxation, or a discreet (perhaps illicit) relationship.

MOTH 1. That which puts holes in one's outer appearance. See **Bug.** 2. Can be associated with one who does damage in the dark. 3. A minor pest or irritant. 4. Could be a literal warning of moths.

MOTHER 1. Associated with the divine feminine and the unconscious. See **Woman.** 2. Often corresponds to that relationship you possess with your own mother (i.e., how your mother appears may be symbolic of your feelings toward her). 3. The mother is the feminine aspect of God and is receptive, compassionate, nurturing, etc., whereas the father embodies the masculine, which is energetic, forceful, and protective. 4. A deceased mother may indicate a message from another realm; see **Message/Messenger.** 5. That from whom life sprang forth. 6. Can represent the need to look after one's activities. 7. Metaphorically, to mother the situation = to take care of it. 8. Could indicate a suggestion or a warning in terms of your mother's welfare. 9. See also **People.**

MOUNTAIN 1. Represents higher states of

mental development. 2. Spiritual heights, understanding, or awareness. 3. A place where the physical/mental world can be viewed more clearly and understood. 4. A great challenge or obstacle that is to be overcome or an ambition that one has chosen. See **Cliff.** 5. Climbing a mountain symbolizes a new journey, life's direction, or the beginning of an experience. See **Journey** and **Ascend.** 6. Descending a mountain could mean the close of an experience, an obstacle successfully overcome, or the end of something. See **Descend.** 7. Metaphorically, making a mountain out of a molehill = making something sound worse, more difficult, or bigger than it really is. 8. Mount Olympus is the home of the mythical gods. See **Mythology (Roman and Greek).** 9. You may also wish to see **Direction.**

MOUSE 1. May be associated with mousiness or timidity. 2. Can correspond to that which is happening underfoot or unseen in one's own house. See **House.** 3. Toying with a mouse may be symbolic of teasing others or being domineering. 4. Can be associated with feelings of smallness or inadequacy. See **Size.** 5. Could be symbolic of one that has squealed (i.e., betrayed or told on). 6. You may wish to see **Animals.**

MOUTH 1. Can correspond to that which one is putting into themselves physically, mentally, or spiritually. See **Food.** 2. May be associated with words spoken. See **Teeth.** 3. That which may be used for positive or negative expression. 4. Metaphorically, having a big mouth = talking too much and/or speaking when one shouldn't be speaking; down in the mouth = a state of depression.

MOVIE 1. Watching one's life story or seeing the experience from another perspective. See **Drama.** 2. That which symbolizes the opinions, thoughts, or worldview of others. 3. The experiences or roles a movie star plays in life. See **Acting/Actor/Actress.** 4. Movie stars often symbolize whatever we think about in association with that star or one's own hopes and ambitions. See **Movie Star.**

MOVIE STAR 1. Often associated with the quality we think most about in regard to that person. See **People.** 2. May be indicative of our own need for personal recognition. 3. Could indicate a talent or an aspect of ourselves that has long been overlooked. 4. May also represent some aspect of a role played in a film. 5. You may also wish to see **Performance/Performers** and **Acting/Actor/Actress.**

MOVING 1. Can correspond to a change or progression in understanding or consciousness. 2. A change in one's situation or life's journey (i.e., a marriage, a promotion, etc.). See **Journey.** 3. Might be associated with a literal trip for work, personal activities, or a vacation. See **Trip.** 4. Could represent a literal move.

MOZART, WOLFGANG 1. Associated with musical talent or the ability to bring things together into a beautiful composition. See **Music.** 2. May be symbolic of Austria. 3. Could correspond to being taken away by one's own work or life. 4. May be associated with a foreign visitor or travel. 5. You may also wish to see **People.**

MUD 1. An obstacle, a minor difficulty, or a hindrance. 2. Associated with that which makes things unclear (misperceptions, emotions, or beliefs). 3. Can correspond to statements that are untrue or half-truths. 4. May be associated with problems in physical elimination systems. 5. Eating mud could be symbolic of putting inappropriate things in your system (physically, food or words; mentally, ideas or thoughts; or spiritually, soiled truths). See **Food.** 6. Muddy water may indicate an unclear situation or insight. See **Water.** 7. Biblically, can be associated with that which is apparently worthless being used for much good (i.e., Jesus healed blindness with mud, John 9:6); the building material of that which becomes brick (Exodus).

MUMMY 1. That which has been preserved or is unchangeable. 2. Can correspond to that which should have been dead or discarded and has been saved. See **Death.** 3. Could represent ancient secrets, wisdom, or mysteries. 4. See also **Egypt.** 5. Might deal with one's own mummy (mother). See **Mother.** 6. You may also wish to see **Corpse.**

MURDER 1. Associated with something you are trying to kill or dispose of, or that is trying to do away with you (i.e., aspects of self, a difficult experience, another person, repressed memories, etc.). 2. That which is destroyed or put to death. See **Death.** 3. Can correspond to the prevention or end of something. 4. Metaphorically, she got away with murder = her acts went unpunished or undiscovered. 5. Could indicate those portions of oneself that are at war or are being denied. See **Shadow.** 6. Might represent a crime or a wrongdoing. See **Crime/Criminal.**

MUSCLE 1. Can correspond to one's strength, stability, or balance. See **Body.** 2. The status of one's belief systems or foundation. 3. Metaphorically, to use muscle or to muscle someone = to use force in the situation.

MUSEUM 1. Storehouse of memories of past experiences. 2. Associated with an important or rare idea, experience, or relation-

ship. See **Antique.** 3. Can be the place where one keeps something extremely valuable. 4. See also **Building.** 5. Something that is old. See **Old.** 6. Depending on imagery, you may also wish to see **Dust.**

MUSIC 1. Corresponds to being in or out of harmony. 2. Associated with an idea or an experience that is in tune with oneself, one's environment, or the universe. 3. The ability to coordinate one's energy into a specific direction or purpose. 4. Cooperation with others. See **Orchestra.** 5. Spiritual insights or information manifest into materiality. 6. Can correspond to the harmony of one's own emotional outpourings. 7. You may also wish to see **Sing/Singer.**

MUSTACHE 1. May represent craftiness, virility, or sexuality. 2. May indicate the proliferation of ideas or creativity. See **Hair.** 3. Might be associated with facing oneself in the mirror. See **Face.** 4. That which one hides behind. See **Mask.** 5. Protecting oneself from the external environment or emotions.

MYTH 1. Associated with a story, a symbol, or an archetype with a meaning somehow greater and richer than its literal or historic truth. 2. A pattern of human experience with similarities across time and cultures. See **Archetype.** 3. A rich, symbolic story that attempts to relate a moral thought through its action, characterization, and plot development.

MYTHOLOGY 1. Associated with the study of myths—stories, symbolism, and archetypes—with a symbolic meaning greater and richer than the literal or historical truth. See **Myth.** 2. The stories of gods and archetypal legends that enable individuals to define and understand a sense of order out of human experience.

MYTHOLOGY (EGYPTIAN) 1. In ancient Egypt, each god was associated with specific skills or duties. Some of the principal gods are as follows.

Amun: The creator of all things. Often pictured with a dual–feathered crown.

Anubis: The god of judgment in the afterlife. Often pictured with the body of a man and the head of a jackal.

Hathor: The goddess of love and joy. Often portrayed as a cow or a woman with cow ears.

Horus: God of the sun and the sky. Often pictured as a falcon. The eye of Horus is associated with wisdom, insight, or intuition.

Isis: Goddess of fertility. Responsible for the civilization of humankind. Usually pictured as a woman with the sun over her head.

Khnum: The ram–headed god of creation. Creates and forms individuals on a pottery wheel.

Osiris: Teacher of agriculture and civilizer of humankind. Husband of Isis, god of the dead, and judge of the underworld.

Thoth: The god of invention, learning, time, and numbers. Often appears as an ibis bird, and is usually associated with the Greek god Hermes.

MYTHOLOGY (ROMAN AND GREEK) 1. In Greek Mythology (ruling atop Mount Olympus) the six great gods were as follows: Zeus, Poseidon, Hephaestus, Hermes, Ares, and Apollo; the six great goddesses were: Hera, Athena, Artemus, Hestia, Aphrodite, and Demeter. 2. The Roman counterparts of the twelve greatest deities were: Jupiter, Vesta, Minerva, Ceres, Diana, Venus, Mars, Mercury, Juno, Neptune, Vulcan, and Apollo.

3. Each god was associated with specific skills or duties. The twelve (and a few miscellaneous lesser gods) are as follows.

Apollo: Roman and Greek god of music and prophecy. The highest form of masculine beauty.

Ceres (Greek = Demeter): Goddess of agriculture and the fruits of the harvest.

Diana (Greek = Artemis): Goddess of chastity, the moon, and hunting.

Faunas (Greek = Pan): God of the fields and forest. Often associated with the flute.

Juno (Greek = Hera): The Supreme goddess; the goddess of marriage; wife of Jupiter, and second highest deity.

Jupiter or Jove (Greek = Zeus): The supreme god; in charge of all people and all other gods.

Mars (Greek = Ares): The god of war.

Mercury (Greek = Hermes): Messenger of the gods. The god of commerce, travel, and intrigue. Symbolized by wings attached to his ankles and helmet.

Minerva (Greek = Athena): Goddess of wisdom and the arts.

Neptune (Greek = Poseidon): The god of the sea.

Pluto: Roman and Greek god of the underworld. Also called Hades by the Greeks.

Saturn (Greek = Cronos): God of agriculture.

Uranus: Greek god of the heavens. Overthrown by his son Cronos.

Venus (Greek = Aphrodite): Goddess of love, beauty, and spring.

Vesta (Greek = Hestia): Goddess of the hearth and fire.

Vulcan (Greek = Hephaestus): God of metallurgy and fire.

1. *The fourteenth letter of the alphabet. 2. The Roman numeral for 90. 3. Chemically, the symbol for nitrogen. 4. In mathematics, a symbol for function. 5. In physics, the symbol for neutron. 6. Numerologically, equivalent to five. 7. In Greek, nu.*

911 1. An urgent situation, a problem, a horrible experience, or an emergency. 2. Could correspond to a literal warning. 3. That which has reached crisis proportions. 4. May be a precognitive warning of a possible situation, advising a different or a precautionary course of action. 5. Depending on imagery, you may wish to see **Police/ Police Station, Doctor,** or **Accident.** 6. Could correspond to the need for outside assistance. 7. Might represent an overwhelming but transformative experience. 8. Numerologically associated with eleven (9 + 1 + 1). See eleven in **Numerology.**

NAIL 1. That which will hold things together. 2. May symbolize the necessary ingredients of a new project, idea, or plan. See **Tool** and **Contractor.** 3. Metaphorically, can be used as follows: hitting the nail on the head = to do or to say something perfectly; it's nailed shut = it's over/closed; she was nailed = she was caught. 4. Liturgically, a symbol for the crucifixion. See **Crucifixion.** 5. For fingernails, see **Fingers.**

NAIL FILE 1. Suggests that one has free time on one's hands. 2. Could correspond to smoothing the rough edges off oneself. 3. You may also wish to see **Hand.** 4. Depending on imagery, might be associated with giving thought to the situation. 5.

Might represent the aggressive side of the feminine. See **Womb.**

NAKED 1. Can suggest feeling exposed or oversensitive. See **Nude.** 2. Corresponds to one who is showing off. 3. Losing one's facade. 4. Could correspond to the fear of being exposed or to doubts about one's self-worth. 5. Might represent the desire to let down your inhibitions. 6. Metaphorically, can be used as follows: to see something with the naked eye = for one to see it themselves; it's the naked truth = it's absolutely a fact. 7. You may also wish to see **Clothes** and **People.**

NAME 1. A name generally corresponds to whatever an individual first associates with the name; for example: oneself, a relative, a pun, a metaphor for an activity, famous names, a literal translation of the name, etc. 2. Hearing one's name is often associated with a message. See **Message/Messenger.** 3. Most characters are individual aspects of oneself, or aspects of oneself in relationship to that person or that activity. See **People.** 4. A name is associated with one's reputation, talents, and faults. See **Self.** 5. That which identifies one's individuality.

NATIVE 1. Represents the instinctive self or intuition. 2. Might indicate one's primitive nature. 3. See also **People.** 4. Depending upon the image of the surroundings, could be a representation of one's own environment (i.e., work) and symbolic of some aspect of that; for example: perhaps one needs to become a native (i.e., a more complete part of the team).

NAVEL 1. Associated with one's connection to one's mother. See **Mother.** 2. Might correspond to a birth or a new experience. See **Birth.** 3. You may also wish to see **Stomach.**

NAVY 1. Can correspond to order, power, discipline, or the relinquishment of personal will. 2. Associated with placing oneself subservient to a greater goal or good. 3. Can represent a warlike environment or situation. See **War.** 4. Might represent service or a spiritual journey. See **Boat, Journey,** and **Water.**

NAZI 1. Associated with the enemy. 2. Can represent an individual with whom one is having severe mental, emotional, and physical problems or burdens. 3. One who dominates and totally controls others. 4. Because of the insignia, may represent an X (i.e., an ex-spouse, ex-partner, etc.). 5. You may also wish to see **People.**

NECK 1. Can correspond to getting one's head on straight or to being a pain in the neck. 2. Associated with sticking one's neck out. 3. Metaphorically, can be used as follows: to risk one's neck = to do something dangerous; to neck with someone = to kiss or to make out; to wring one's neck = to reprimand or to punish. 4. If being choked, could indicate that one is feeling strangled in the situation.. 5. May be associated with one's willpower. See **Throat.** 6. You may also wish to see **Body.**

NECKLACE 1. Associated with one's willpower. 2. Can correspond to one's personal stature or current situation. See **Jewels/ Jewelry.** 3. That which an individual is carrying in life (i.e., ideas, problems, etc.). 4. You

may also wish to see **Noose.**

NEEDLE 1. That which pricks, pierces, or opens. 2. Could suggest sharp insight. 3. Getting the point. 4. Metaphorically, to needle something = to irritate it. 5. That which mends, stitches, or brings together.

NEIGHBOR 1. Associated with masculine or feminine aspects of one's own self. See **People.** 2. May correspond to that relationship one possesses with a neighbor. 3. Could indicate a suggestion or a warning in terms of your neighbor's welfare. 4. Someone or something near to you or that with which you have to live.

NEPTUNE ♆ 1. Corresponds to mysticism, mystery, and spiritual insight. 2. Associated with clairvoyance, genius, and sensitivity. 3. In Roman mythology, the god of the sea. See **Mythology (Roman and Greek).** 4. Eighth planet from the Sun; third largest planet in our solar system. Has a rotation year of 164.79 years. 5. Astrologically, associated with Pisces. See **Astrology.** 6. Metaphysically, associated with the second chakra (Lyden). See **Chakras.**

NET 1. That which prevents one from falling. 2. That which catches, supports, or traps. 3. Metaphorically, a safety net = that which prevents one from personal failure. 4. Depending on imagery, you may also wish to see **Fisherman/Fishing.**

NEW TESTAMENT 1. Spiritual truths or insights. 2. Associated with the Gospels. See **Gospel.** 3. Corresponds to the teachings of Jesus. See **Christ.** 4. You may also wish to see **Bible.** 5. Might be suggestive of grace, forgiveness, or turning the other cheek.

NEW YORK 1. Can correspond to high finance, business, the theater, overcrowding, or violence. 2. Whatever one associates with the city will be highly significant. 3. May indicate domestic travel.

NEWSPAPER 1. That which is of general or everyday interest. 2. A source of information, insight, or opinion. See **Library.** 3. Could represent a message or a personal insight; intuition. 4. Reading different portions of the paper are associated with different meanings. For example, reading the want ads symbolizes advice or desire to find a new job; reading the comics suggests the need or the desire for humor and laughter; reading the business section could indicate one's financial condition or specific advice. 5. You may also wish to see **Book.**

NIGHT 1. Associated with an ending, a completion, a dormancy, or a closing. See **Evening.** 2. Metaphorically, the difference between day and night = complete opposites (i.e., good and evil). 3. Could suggest a lack of clarity or insight. See **Dark.** 4. May indicate a period of dormancy. 5. Depending on imagery, might symbolize evil, error, or death. See **Evil** and **Death.** 6. You may also wish to see **Star** and **Moon/Moonlight.**

NIGHTMARE 1. Can represent that which one fears, is threatened by, or is running from. See **Run/Runner.** 2. May be associated with anxiety, apprehension, and uneasiness. 3. The inability to handle one's current experience. 4. Often, whatever one is fearful of is associated with something that needs to be faced in oneself. See **Shadow.** 5. That which one needs to face in conscious life, but one hasn't or won't, will often appear as a nightmare. 6. Nightmares can also occur in order to get the individual to remember the content of a specific image.

NILE RIVER 1. Associated with the flow of life. See **River.** 2. Could correspond to the body's own physical systems. 3. Symbolic of Egypt. See **Egypt/Egyptian.** 4. Could indicate going with the flow.

NINE 1. Associated with completion or wholeness. 2. See **Numerology.**

NOAH 1. Symbolic of one who oversees a cleansing or a transformation. See **Ark.** 2. Associated with the Great Flood. See **Flood.** 3. Biblically, corresponds to one who finds favor with God (Genesis 6). 4. Metaphysically, associated with one who is ready to undergo personal transformation or change.

NOBLE (MAN OR WOMAN) 1. Associated with dignity or fame. 2. Possessing grand ideas or qualities. 3. Could represent one's own higher self or spirituality. 4. May correspond to the noblest or best masculine or feminine traits. See **Man** or **Woman.** 5. Might indicate that which is too lofty. 6. Thinking highly of oneself. 7. See also **People.**

NOON 1. Can correspond to the pinnacle of day or the highest point of an experience. 2. May represent those things one does at noon or one associates with noon. 3. The appropriate timing. 4. Might symbolize the midpoint between ideas or experiences. 5. You may also wish to see **Day.**

NOOSE 1. Associated with a bad idea, decision, or outcome (i.e., that which will hang you). 2. May indicate one's hang-ups or attitudes and belief systems that keep hanging on. See **Hang.** 3. That which chokes, binds, or secures. See **Rope.** 4. An obligation or a responsibility that one finds difficult or that one does not desire (i.e., a relationship, a job, etc.). 5. You may also wish to see **Necklace.**

NORTH 1. Corresponds to wisdom and aging. 2. Metaphysically, associated with the higher self. 3. Can represent that which is unchanging. 4. In literature, may relate to goodness (i.e., Glinda the good witch in *The Wizard of Oz*). 5. See also **Direction.** 6. Can also symbolize that which is cold.

NORTH STAR 1. Can correspond to a clear insight or a spiritual direction. See **Direction.** 2. Gathering one's bearings. 3. Bright idea or one's highest ideal. See **Star.** 4. Could represent one's higher self or spiritual wisdom. 5. The guiding light for one's journey. See **Light** and **Journey.**

NOSE 1. Symbolizes putting one's nose into something where it may not belong or being nosy. 2. May represent that which smells (i.e., is not good or is unpleasant). 3. Metaphorically, can be used as follows: he's nosy = he's too inquisitive about things that are not his business; she paid through the nose = she paid too much; to follow your nose = to do what you think is best; under one's nose = in plain sight all along; putting someone's nose out of joint = to offend someone; to turn up one's nose = to be uninterested; to lead by the nose = to control someone; he won by a nose = he just barely won; right on the nose = exactly in the right spot or the exact amount; to look down the nose = to show disgust at something; don't cut your nose off to spite your face = don't do something that harms yourself later. 4. You may also wish to see **Face** and **Body.** 5. Might symbolize oneself. See **Self.**

NUDE 1. Can correspond to exposing oneself. See **Self.** 2. Being nude in a crowd can represent the desire to or the fear of baring everything to others. 3. Exposing that which should be hidden. 4. May be associated with one's true nature or the inner self without

the facade generally shown to the world. See **Clothes.** 5. Being laid bare to criticism or misunderstanding. 6. Can represent the desire to stop playing one's current role. 7. May be associated with vulnerability or humility. 8. An individual's fleshly nature or desires. 9. See also **Naked.**

NUMBERS 1. Generally, associated with the esoteric science of numerology. See **Numerology.** 2. Can be associated with specific dates, license numbers, the lottery, etc., providing insights into a situation, a relationship, possible precognition, etc. 3. Metaphorically, your number's up = your time is up, or the time is now.

NUMEROLOGY 1. The belief that everything is reducible to the essence of its numerical equivalent. 2. A mathematical truth that every combination of numbers when added together will always equal a digit between 1 and 9. For example: 637: $6 + 3 + 7 = 16$, and $1 + 6 = 7$; 9999: $9 + 9 + 9 + 9 = 36$, and $3 + 6 = 9$; 400: $4 + 0 + 0 = 4$. However, numbers that add up to eleven, twenty-two, or thirty-three are generally considered master numbers; see below. 3. Suggests that every letter of the alphabet can also be reduced to the energy of the number associated with it. For example: A, being the first letter, acts as a one; F, the sixth letter, corresponds to a six; Y, the twenty-fifth letter, corresponds to a seven $(2 + 5 = 7)$. 4. Words and names are also reducible in the same manner. For example: Woman $= 5 + 6 + 4 + 1 + 5$ (i.e., the numbers associated with the letters of *woman*) $= 21 = 3$; Robert $= 9 + 6 + 2 + 5 + 9 + 2 =$ the master number 33 as well as 6. 5. Practiced in ancient Egypt, Greece, and by Jewish mystics, it is the orderly understanding of the relationship and symbolism between numbers and the vibration and/or energy associated with them. 6. Each number has its own symbolic meaning, as follows.

Zero: 1. Associated with either the absence of anything or the containment of all that there is. 2. That which has neither beginning nor end. 3. See also **Circle.**

One: 1. Associated with the first; the beginning. 2. Corresponds to the active force or the male principle. See **Phallus.** 3. All other numbers are composed of combinations of one. 4. Associated with unity, individuality, or independence. 5. May be symbolic of God. 6. Corresponds to the first chakra. See **Gonads.**

Two: 1. Associated with duality or the division of the whole. 2. Can correspond to changeability, receptivity, or the feminine principle. See **Womb.** 3. Can represent opposites; for example: good and evil, light and dark. 4. Also associated with cooperation, union, and adaptability. 5. Symbolic of man and woman together. 6. Corresponds to the second chakra. See **Lyden.**

Three: 1. Corresponds to the trinity (the triune nature of God); the body, mind, and spirit; or the third dimension. 2. Associated with great strength, for it combines both the elements of one and two. 3. Represents synthesis and incorporation into the whole. 4. Can be symbolic of self–expression, joy, and diversification. 5. Corresponds to the third chakra. See **Adrenals.**

Four: 1. Associated with stability, materiality, service, and that which is of the earth. See **Earth**. 2. Can correspond to form and order. 3. May represent the four seasons, the four corners of the earth, the four winds, the four elements (air, earth, fire, and water), the four Gospels, or the Four Horsemen of

Revelation. 4. Metaphysically, corresponds to the four lower endocrine centers or to the fourth chakra alone. See **Thymus**.

Five: 1. Associated with change, new beginnings, or the five senses. 2. Symbolic of versatility, freedom, and resourcefulness. 3. Corresponds to the fifth chakra. See **Thyroid**.

Six: 1. Associated with symmetry, beauty, and harmony. 2. May be symbolic of the desire for community, groups, or a personal relationship. 3. Can represent human power or dominance. 4. Corresponds to the sixth chakra. See **Pineal**.

Seven: 1. Associated with spiritual forces. 2. Represents the most sacred of all numbers. 3. Can indicate perfection. 4. May be symbolic of introspection, meditation, or understanding. 5. Corresponds to the days of the week; the days of creation; the musical scales; the colors of the rainbow (see **Colors**); the seven endocrine centers, or the seventh chakra alone (see **Pituitary**). 6. Might be associated with the seven year itch and the desire for change.

Eight: 1. Associated with balance and satisfaction. 2. Can correspond to infinity, great strength, or great weakness. 3. Symbolic of good judgment. 4. May indicate financial well–being.

Nine: 1. Associated with completion or wholeness. 2. Corresponds to fulfillment or a completed transformation. 3. May be symbolic of compassion, universality, selflessness, or truth.

Ten: 1. Associated with completeness and strength. 2. Corresponds to a return to unity (1 + 0 = 1). 3. A new start or a new beginning. 4. May represent that which is human (i.e., ten fingers and ten toes). 5. That which is the same as one.

Eleven: 1. The first master number; mastery in the physical dimension. 2. Associated with courage and power. 3. May also correspond to spirituality and enlightenment. 4. When not brought to full manifestation, may simply be regarded as two (1 + 1 = 2).

Twelve: 1. Associated with cosmic order. 2. Symbolic of the wheel of life or the zodiac. See **Astrology**. 3. Corresponds to the twelve tribes of Israel. See **Jacob**. 4. Corresponds to the twelve apostles. 5. The twelve months of the year. 6. May simply be regarded as three (1 + 2 = 3).

Thirteen: 1. Can represent bad luck (i.e., Friday the thirteenth). 2. Also regarded as four (1 + 3 = 4).

Twenty-two: 1. The second master number; mastery in the mental/emotional dimension. 2. Associated with reason and diplomacy. 3. When not brought to full manifestation, may simply be regarded as four (2 + 2 = 4).

Thirty-three: 1. The third master number; mastery in the spiritual dimension. 2. Associated with Christ. See **Christ**. 3. Can represent spiritual consciousness through service. 4. Can correspond to self-sacrifice. 5. When not brought to full manifestation, may simply be regarded as six (3 + 3 = 6).

Forty: 1. Biblically, associated with cleansing, purification, trial, patience, the process of transformation, or humiliation (i.e., the Flood, forty years in the wilderness, forty days for Nineveh to reform, forty days of Jesus' temptation, etc.). 2. May also be regarded as four (4 + 0 = 4).

Seventy: 1. Biblically, associated with transition and the potential for human transformation (i.e., the number of Jewish elders, the number of Jesus' disciples). 2. May also be regarded as seven (7 + 0 = 7).

NUN 1. A spiritual presence, authority, or messenger. See also **Minister.** 2. Could represent spiritual safety or harmony. 3. One's own conscience or belief systems. 4. One who is involved in spiritual matters or pursuits. 5. May be symbolic of one who has isolated oneself from others. 6. Can indicate that which explains spiritual laws. 7. Suggestive of discipline, chastity, and obedience. 8. Might correspond to the spiritualized feminine attributes. See **Womb.** 9. Whatever one associates with nuns will have a great impact on the associated symbolism. 10. See also **People.**

NURSE 1. One who nurtures or comforts. 2. Associated with one's personal (internal) physician. See **Doctor.** 3. Might indicate a literal health message. 4. May correspond with one's own ability to help or heal others. 5. Metaphorically, to nurse a drink = to drink it slowly or to savor it. 6. See also **People.**

NUTS 1. Can correspond to being foolish or unusual. 2. A small idea or kernel of truth. 3. That which contains much more than itself when allowed to blossom and mature. See **Seed.** 4. Metaphorically, can be used as follows: here's the idea in a nutshell = here's the basics; I'm nuts about you = I'm in love with you; he's a nut = he's an idiot. 5. You may also wish to see **Food.**

1. *The fifteenth letter of the alphabet.* 2. *The Roman numeral for eleven.* 3. *Sometimes associated with zero.* 4. *Chemically, the symbol for oxygen.* 5. *Often associated with an expression of surprise or joy, as in, "Oh wow!"* 6. *Metaphysically, the ending, as in omega, or symbolizing a circle, eternity, or infinity.* 7. *In physics, the symbol for ohm.* 8. *Numerologically, equivalent to six.* 9. *In Greek, omicron and omega.*

O'HARA, SCARLETT 1. Associated with perseverance in spite of adversity. 2. Might symbolize the South. See **South.** 3. Could indicate that which will end or be *Gone with the Wind.*

OAR 1. To take part in a spiritual experience or journey. See **Water** and **Journey.** 2. Metaphorically, to put your oars in = to become involved with or to interfere. 3. Depending on imagery, you may also wish to see **Boat.**

OASIS 1. Corresponds to fertile ground (i.e., a good idea, a positive experience, possessing great timing, etc.). 2. Can represent a safe haven in the midst of adversity. 3. A bright spot in the middle of the wasteland. 4. Might indicate one's desire to be left alone. See **Hermit.** 5. Depending on imagery, you may wish to see **Earth, Plant** or **Water.**

OBELISK 1. May symbolize that which overcomes the earth. 2. Can represent male sexuality. See **Phallus.** 3. Might be associated with power. 4. Could correspond to a lofty ideal. See **Tower.** 5. Might be associated with Egypt. See **Egypt/Egyptian.**

OBSTRUCTION 1. Corresponds to an obstacle. 2. That which gets in one's way. 3. See also **Wall.** 4. May be associated with negative criticism, opinions, or prejudices.

OCEAN 1. The deepest reaches of the soul, the unconscious, or the emotions. See **Water.** 2. Associated with the source of all life. 3. Can correspond to spiritual depth. 4. Can represent any great quantity or meaningful experience. 5. An ocean journey symbolizes an emotional or spiritual experience. 6. Associated with the feminine. See **Womb.** 7. Might indicate a depth of insight or the intuition. 8. You may also wish to see **Boat** and **Journey.** 9. If there is bad weather in the imagery, see **Weather.**

OCTOPUS 1. Corresponds to attachment, involvement, or having a hand in the situation. See **Hand.** 2. That which branches out into many directions. 3. Might correspond to information from the unconscious. 4. Because of the number of tentacles, could represent eight. See eight in **Numerology.** 5. Might be associated with something that bites or draws life from another. 6. See also **Animals**.

ODOR 1. Can correspond to something that smells funny (i.e., not quite right, or out of place). 2. You may also wish to see **Nose.** 3. Could suggest the need for greater cleanliness for oneself, at home, or at work. 4. That which is garbage. See **Garbage.**

OFFICE 1. Associated with work or a working relationship. See **Work.** 2. Can correspond to one's duty or obligation. 3. The activity and appearance at the office will have a great deal to do with the symbolism. See **Building**. 4. Might suggest the need for personal discipline or the fact that one works too much. 5. One's own feelings about work, as well as the activity in the image (for example, if others are present), will have a great deal to do with the associated symbolism. 6. Depending on the imagery, you may also wish to see **People** and **Boss**.

OIL 1. Can indicate something is slick or well-greased. 2. That which is smooth. 3. Metaphorically, can be used as follows: to oil the machinery = to get things ready to do what you want them to do; to oil one's palms = to bribe someone; to strike oil = to become rich; burning the midnight oil = working or studying hard and late; pouring oil on the fire = to make things worse; to pour oil on troubled waters = to smooth things over. 4. Might correspond to that which is slippery. 5. May suggest that one needs to get rid of the friction.

OLD 1. That which has been used or has been available for a long time. 2. An old figure in a dream is generally a symbol of wisdom or guidance. See **Old Man/Old Woman**. 3. That which may no longer be of value. 4. See also **Antique**.

OLD MAN/OLD WOMAN 1. Associated with wisdom and insight through experience. 2. Often relates to an individual's own higher self or to subconscious information. 3. Frequently symbolizes a message from a wise source. 4. May be associated with a source of unlimited wisdom: a seer, a sage, a prophet, Christ, or God. 5. The fully realized self. See **Christ**. 6. Old lessons that need to be revisited or finally learned. 7. Could correspond to one's own past or future. 8. May

be indicative of karmic memory. See **Karma**. 9. Could represent facing one's own fears of growing old. 10. See also **People**.

OLD TESTAMENT 1. Spiritual truths or insights. 2. Associated with the Torah. See **Torah**. 3. You may also wish to see **Bible** and **Book**. 4. Might be suggestive of an eye for an eye.

OLIVE/OLIVE BRANCH 1. May suggest that which is bitter to swallow. 2. A sign of peace, tranquility, and healing. 3. Biblically, corresponds to the end of the Great Flood (Genesis 8:11). 4. You may also wish to see **Plant**.

OLYMPICS 1. Associated with an environment of competition (i.e., work). 2. The ultimate contest of skill and fitness. See **Sports**. 3. The Olympic torch symbolizes that which lights the way. See **Torch.** 4. You may also wish to see **Athlete.**

ONE 1. Associated with the first; the beginning. 2. See **Numerology.**

OPEN/OPENING 1. Could indicate receptivity. 2. Corresponds to that which is beginning to open up. 3. The beginning; the start of that which is enfolding. 4. Could suggest that one was becoming more open emotionally or to another's viewpoints. 5. You may also wish to see **Door.**

OPERATION 1. Might be associated with a project or a goal. 2. Corresponds to that which needs to be removed or cut out. 3. Could symbolize the opening of something (i.e., emotions that have been held in). 4. You may also wish to see **Cut.** 5. May indicate the need for some type of health or personal care. See **Doctor.**

ORANGE (COLOR) 1. Associated with energy and creativity. 2. See **Colors.**

ORANGE (FRUIT)/ORANGE JUICE 1. Often corresponds to the need for more orange juice, fruit, or vitamin C in one's diet. See **Food.** 2. Whatever is happening with the image is very important; for example: offering another individual a glass of orange juice could indicate friendship, sharing the fruits of the spirit, or the fact that you need to talk to the individual about a better diet. 3. May suggest one is in good health or needs to be in better health. 4. You may also wish to see **Fruit.**

ORCHARD 1. Associated with what one is cultivating in body, mind, or soul. 2. See **Field** and **Garden.** 3. May indicate that the field is ready for harvest. 4. Could be symbolic of one's talents, qualities, or ideas just ripe for the taking.

ORCHESTRA 1. Symbolic of people or activities working together in harmony. 2. Corresponds to an individual's emotional nature. 3. Could refer to the importance of music in life. See **Music.** 4. Might indicate the desire or the need for relaxation or harmony. 5. Depending on imagery, you may also wish to see **Dance.**

ORGY 1. Can correspond to excessive self-gratification. 2. May be associated with the misuse of energy or creative talents. 3. Metaphorically, it was a real orgy = it was a wild celebration or an overindulgence. 4. Might correspond to one's hidden desires. 5. May indicate a tremendous need for self-love or to be loved. 6. You may also wish to see **Sex** and **Naked.**

OSCAR 1. Associated with a reward, an honor, or an accomplishment. 2. Can correspond to being recognized by one's peers. 3. Might be in response to acting the part in a particular situation. See **Acting/Actor/ Actress.** 4. You may also wish to see **Movie Star.**

OSTEOPATH 1. Associated with one's spine. See **Back/Backbone.** 2. Could suggest that something is a pain in the back. 3. Might indicate something that is on one's back. 4. A literal suggestion to visit an osteopath. 5. You may also wish to see **Doctor** and **Bone.**

OUTLAW 1. Can correspond to that which is illegal, immoral, or unlawful. 2. Associated with taking advantage or being taken advantage of. 3. Something that is stealing one's ideas, energy, emotions, or vitality. 4. The villainous aspects of oneself. See **Villain.** 5. Someone who takes what is not theirs by force. 6. Might indicate that which is bent, unsavory, or immoral. 7. See also **People.**

OVEN 1. Can correspond to an idea or a creative solution that is cooking. See **Cook.** 2. May indicate that which is undergoing the process of transformation. 3. Might represent that which is undergoing fire or heat (i.e., close scrutiny). 4. Associated with female sexuality. See Womb. 5. You may also wish to see **Food.**

OVERCOAT 1. One's thoughts and attitudes. 2. Often indicates the outward personality one shows to the world. See **Clothes.** 3. Different types of coats are symbolic of various experiences; for example: wearing a raincoat = protecting your self from the emotions of others or from your own emotional upset; wearing a colored coat = types of emotions or attitudes one is dealing with (see **Colors**); wearing a fur coat = being insulated from your own or others' emotions. 4. Particular types of coats might be predictive of upcoming experiences, emotions, or literal weather patterns.

OWL 1. Can correspond to wisdom. 2. Clear vision and insight. See **Eyes.** 3. You may also wish to see **Bird.** 4. A silent observer.

OWN 1. One's body, higher self, or God. See **Self, Body,** or **God.** 2. That which one possesses (i.e., talents, strengths, weaknesses). 3. Metaphorically, can be used as follows: to come into one's own = to find one's respective place in life; he held his own = he was able to stand the criticism or inquiry; on one's own = independent or self-sufficient.

OX 1. Associated with strength. 2. Symbolic of patience and sacrifice. 3. Symbolic of hard work (i.e., a beast of burden). 4. A castrated bull. See **Bull.** 5. Might be associated with stubbornness. 6. You may also wish to see **Animals.**

OXYGEN 1. That which is necessary for life. 2. Could symbolize the breath of life. See **Air.** 3. Depending on imagery, might symbolize taking care of oneself, or the need to clear one's head. 4. An oxygen tank could indicate a possible health problem and the literal need to see a doctor, or making certain one possesses the necessary equipment and supplies.

P

1. *The sixteenth letter of the alphabet.* 2. *The Roman numeral for 400.* 3. *Chemically, the symbol for phosphorous.* 4. *In mechanics, the symbol for pressure or power.* 5. *Numerologically, equivalent to seven.* 6. *In genetics, a symbol for parental generation.* 7. *In Greek, pi.*

PAIN 1. Can correspond to hurt, sorrow, wrongdoing, or distress. 2. That which is labor-intensive or painstaking. 3. Metaphorically, can be used as follows: it pained her to participate = it wasn't easy for her; he is a pain = he is irritating. 4. To dream of someone in pain could represent that which may be true physically, mentally, or spiritually. 5. May be an indication of a literal physical problem. 6. You may also wish to see **Body** or **Wound.**

PAINT 1. The act of brushing up on appearances. 2. Metaphorically, can be used as follows: to paint the town red = to celebrate all over the place; painting a rosy picture = making things sound better than they are. 3. Might indicate that something has been covered up. 4. The color of the paint may be very significant. See **Colors.** 5. If someone is painting a room in a house, it may indicate cleaning up a portion of oneself, or acquiring a new aspect or talent. See **House.**

PALM (HAND) 1. Corresponds to oneself. See **Body.** 2. Depending on what the palms are doing, they can be associated with openness, victory, prayer, service, taking, giving, or pleading. 3. Metaphorically, can be used as follows: to cross one's palm = to offer a bribe; having an itchy palm = wanting

money; I palmed it off = I tricked someone else into taking it. 4. You may also wish to see **Hand.**

PALM (PLANT) 1. A symbol of victory, triumph, or joy. 2. Biblically, associated with Jesus' riding into Jerusalem on a donkey (John 12:13). 3. May represent that which is spiritual, holy, or worthwhile. 4. You may also wish to see **Plant.**

PANCAKES 1. Could indicate childish eating habits. See **Food.** 2. Might represent the need to eat breakfast. 3. That which is syrupy (i.e., false or too sweet).

PANTS 1. One's personal identity, philosophy, or direction. 2. That which one shows to the world. See **Clothes.** 3. Metaphorically, wearing the pants in the family = possessing the authority. 4. Can represent sexual feelings and desires. 5. You may also wish to see **Leg/Legless.**

PAPYRUS 1. Associated with an important message or insight. See **Message/Messenger.** 2. Represents a forgotten secret or ancient wisdom. 3. May be associated with religious doctrines or sacredness. 4. Associated with Egypt. See **Egypt/Egyptian.** 5. Might correspond to laws or customs. 6. You may also wish to see **Book.**

PARABLE 1. Associated with the New Testament and the teachings of Jesus. See **Jesus Christ** and **New Testament.** 2. A rich, symbolic story that attempts to relate a moral thought through its action, characterization, and plot development. See **Myth**. 3. You may also wish to see **Bible**.

PARACHUTE 1. Symbolic of escaping or deserting a situation. 2. Could indicate that which is being held back or that which needs to slow down. 3. An alternate plan needed to prevent falling (failing). 4. You may also wish to see **Sky** or **Airplane**.

PARADE 1. That which is on display for all the world to see. 2. To take part in a procession, a ceremony, or a showy exhibition. 3. Could be associated with a grand ego (i.e., parading one's talents before others).

PARADISE 1. Associated with perfection, great bliss, or joy. See **Heaven**. 2. A place of comfort, beauty, or spirituality. 3. Might represent that which is ideal or idealism. 4. Metaphorically, that's paradise = that's perfect.

PARAKEET 1. Associated with love birds (i.e., a close relationship). 2. May represent that which is caged. 3. Could symbolize that which is friendly or trainable. 4. See also **Bird**.

PARALYSIS 1. Often symbolizes one's own handicaps of criticisms, bad thoughts, or negative emotions toward others, for these paralyze the self. 2. Can represent the state of being powerless or feeling stuck in the situation. 3. Could indicate that which was numbed emotionally. 4. Helplessness. 5. See also **Body**.

PARENTS 1. Can correspond to an authority figure or one's higher self. 2. May indicate one's own feelings toward parents. See **Father** and **Mother**. 3. Associated with those who care for or may render assistance. 4. Corresponds to one's own source. 5. Might represent one's own qualities or faults as a parent. 6. Could indicate one's ultimate parent. See **God**. 7. You may also wish to see **People**.

PARIS 1. Can correspond to romance, creative expression, cuisine, or stuffiness. 2. Whatever one associates with the city will be highly significant. 3. May be associated with a foreign visitor or travel. 4. You may also wish to see **France**.

PARK 1. Can correspond to growth or recreation. See **Garden**. 2. That which one is currently cultivating. See **Field**. 3. You may also wish to see **Plant** or **Tree**.

PARKED 1. That which is rooted in place, stubborn, or unmoving. 2. Any parked vehicle may indicate a rest or a period of inactivity. 3. A parked airplane or one that cannot fly may correspond to plans that never got off the ground or plans that may be faulty. See **Airplane**. 4. Can correspond to putting everything in its place or having something temporarily stored. See **Garage**. 5. You may also wish to see **Road** and **Automobile**.

PARTY 1. Corresponds to a celebration, a recognition, or a reward. 2. Can represent one's social life or a lack of responsibility. 3. Something done with others for fun, enjoyment, and the benefit of all. 4. Metaphorically, can be used as follows: being a party to = being a part of the situation; the party line = the appropriate or published response; being a party man = a supporter of those in authority; she's a party animal = she loves to have fun. 5. May be indicative of a poor lifestyle or diet. See **Food**. 6. Associated with taking the time or needing to make time to enjoy life and relax. 7. Might correspond to avoiding responsibility or being lazy.

PASSENGER 1. Corresponds to allowing something to drive one's life. 2. Might indicate cooperation. 3. Depending on imagery, could suggest a period of rest or the need for rest in one's life. 4. May indicate a feeling of disassociation or disconnection from oneself, a particular situation, or life in general. 5. Could symbolize being taken for a ride, or going along for the ride. See **Ride**. 6. Refusing to take control or to take responsibility. 7. May represent one's physical body or current situation. See **Automobile**.

PASSOVER 1. A Jewish holiday commemorating the safety of the Hebrews and their release from Egypt. 2. Could indicate that which will pass or the act of being overlooked. 3. You may also wish to see **Lamb** and **Judaism**.

PASSPORT 1. Associated with permission. 2. Depending on imagery, could symbolize the necessity of entering or leaving a specific situation or relationship. 3. That which allows safe passage through the experience. 4. You may also wish to see **License**.

PAST 1. That which is over and done with. 2. Associated with something one cannot change. 3. Metaphorically, I wouldn't put it past her = there's a good chance she would do it. 4. Receding objects, the left side of a scene, or that which is antique or old are all symbols that may be associated with the past. 5. You may also wish to see **Time**.

PATH 1. Indicates direction or possible alternatives. 2. One's journey or current life experience. See **Journey**. 3. How one walks on the path may represent one's stature in life. 4. Symbolic of a course of action or conduct. 5. May indicate the need to be on the spiritual path. 6. You may also wish to see **Road**.

PATIENTS 1. Those portions of oneself that are ill, not quite well or whole, or need tending to. 2. May indicate one's ability to heal another. 3. Could be associated with the need for patience. 4. You may also wish to see **Nurse** or **Doctor**.

PAWN/PAWN SHOP 1. Trading something of value for something of less value. 2. Metaphorically, being used as a pawn = being used for someone's benefit or intention; giving up one's will. See **Puppet**. 3. Corresponds to that which has been pledged for something.

PAY 1. Associated with that which is due to or from another. 2. Corresponds to a recompense or a reward. See **Money.** 3. Metaphorically, to pay off = to bribe; to pay one's way = to take care of any cost; you'll pay = to swear revenge.

PEACH 1. Metaphorically, he's a real peach = he's a real nice guy. 2. Could indicate the need for more fruit in one's diet. 3. See also **Fruit.**

PEACOCK 1. Corresponds to pride, that which shows off, or thinking very highly of oneself. 2. Might indicate that which will enfold beautifully. 3. You may also wish to see **Bird** or **Animals.**

PEANUT 1. Metaphorically, she got it for peanuts = she bought it very cheaply. 2. You may also wish to see **Nuts.**

PEARL 1. Associated with great wisdom, the soul, or great faith. 2. May be symbolic of purity or beauty. 3. That which is made beautiful through hardship, irritation, an experience (i.e., a pearl of great price). 4. Metaphorically, to cast pearls before swine = to share something valuable with those who won't understand. 5. You may also wish to see **Jewels/Jewelry.**

PEGASUS 1. May represent a spiritual message. See **Horse.** 2. Can correspond to the ability of the spirit to transform the physical. 3. You may also wish to see **Mythology (Roman and Greek).**

PEN 1. One's ideas or experiences. 2. Used to express what an individual has been thinking. 3. May be associated with positive remarks or negative criticism. 4. Can represent the need to give or to accept a message. 5. May be a literal suggestion to write. See **Write.** 6. Symbolic of male sexuality. See **Phallus.** 7. See also **Letter.**

PENCIL 1. Same as pen; however, suggests a message that is not quite as important or permanent. 2. Can also indicate the need to make a point.

PENIS 1. Associated with the masculine and sexuality. 2. See **Phallus** and **Man.**

PENNY 1. Can correspond to that which is not worth very much. 2. Metaphorically, may be used as follows: a pretty penny = a lot of money; he turned an honest penny = he made the money legally. 3. Might be associated with good luck. 4. You may also wish to see **Money.**

PEOPLE 1. People usually represent various aspects of oneself. 2. A *person we know* either represents aspects of ourselves in relationship to that person or talents, qualities, or experiences that we associate with that person. 3. *Spiritual figures* (a minister, a religious figure, an angel) are often associated with one's higher self or spiritual wisdom. 4. *Authority figures* (police, a boss, a parent, etc.) can be symbolic of duty, disci-

pline, or the situation in which they reside (i.e., boss = work). 5. *Dreaming of a family member* often corresponds to the relationship one possesses with that individual (i.e., feelings toward the person, areas of the relationship that need to be worked on, etc.) or the dream could be a literal warning or suggestion regarding the individual's activities or welfare. 6. *A deceased relative* may indicate a message from another realm or a psychological issue that still needs to be addressed. 7. *Different types of people* are generally associated with their most outstanding trait or their occupation; for example: a wild man might suggest that we have allowed our temper to get out of control; a dentist (suggestive of teeth) could symbolize something that we've said or eaten and perhaps shouldn't have, especially if the dentist was pulling teeth; a cook might represent the fact that something is cooking (i.e., an idea); a contractor could be associated with what we're building. 8. *A movie star or famous individual* is often associated with the quality we think most about in regard to that person, or a well-known person could indicate our own need for personal recognition. A famous person may also be showing us a talent or an aspect in ourselves that has long been overlooked, or movie stars may represent some aspect of roles they've played in films. 9. *Groups of people* are often representative of our work, family life, or wherever else we may be involved in a group situation. 10. *Dark figures* generally symbolize dark aspects of oneself or one's own shadow. See **Shadow.** 11. *Male figures* can often represent the positive (i.e., determination, courage, etc.) or negative (i.e., aggression, dominance, etc.) masculine traits that one possesses in oneself. See **Phallus.** 12. *Female figures* can often represent the positive (i.e., intuitive, compassionate, etc.) or negative (i.e., indecisive, overly emotional, etc.) feminine traits that one possesses in oneself. See **Womb**. 13. *Foreign people* are generally parts of oneself that seem foreign (i.e., not integrated); they can correspond to what one thinks of individuals from that country (i.e., their most outstanding trait, quality, activity); or they may be indicative of a foreign visitor or travel. 14. Individuals may appear as bugs (irritants or that which has gotten under one's skin), they may appear in various types of clothing or attire, and they may be involved in any number of activities. Often the theme of what we see happening with the person in the dream will give us an indication that the very same theme needs to be addressed in ourselves or in our relationships with those around us. 15. You may also wish to see different types of people (i.e., see **Bag Lady**), different kinds of family relationships (i.e., see **Father**), as well as symbols of appearance (see **Clothes** or **Naked**). 16. See also **Man** or **Woman**.

PEPPER 1. That which is spicy, hot, or adds zest. 2. Could indicate one who adds hostility or aggression to the situation. 3. That which is pungent or flavorful. 4. May indicate a literal dietary suggestion (i.e., too much pepper). 5. You may also wish to see **Food**.

PERFORMANCE/PERFORMERS 1. Those who participate in the experience. See **Acting/Actor/Actress** and **Drama**. 2. May represent individual aspects of oneself. See **People**. 3. That which is acted upon or brought to fruition. 4. Can correspond to a display of one's own skills or talents. 5. May be associated with one acting the part. 6. You may also wish to see **Movie Star**.

PERFUME 1. Corresponds to that which makes something more pleasant than reality. 2. Associated with an individual's own talents, abilities, or image to the world. 3. Symbolizes how one expresses oneself to others. See **Clothes**. 4. May represent emotional outpouring or feelings. 5. To give a situation a pleasant aroma or a breath of fresh air. 6. You may also wish to see **Nose**.

PET 1. Associated with portions of oneself. See **Animals**. 2. Could correspond to pet projects. 3. Generally, whatever an individual associates with that particular pet will have a great deal to do with the symbolism; for an example using cats: an individual who loves cats may associate the symbol with love; someone who is allergic to cats may decide the symbol represents irritants that must be dealt with; and another person with no particular opinion may think that, because of the nature of cats, the symbol is indicative of independence. 4. Metaphorically, can be used as follows: she's the teacher's pet = she's the favorite; that's my pet peeve = that bothers me the most; they were petting = they were kissing. 5. May also suggest aspects that need to be tamed or trained or are already. 6. Dreaming of one's pet may literally be about that animal, providing insights into the pet's welfare or one's own feelings about the pet. 7. Having a pet on a leash could suggest that which was under another's control or influence. 8. See also specific types of pets; for example, see **Dog** or **Cat**.

PETALS 1. Can correspond to different aspects of the whole. See **Flowers**. 2. The flowering of one's talents or abilities. 3. May indicate vulnerable parts of the situation or oneself. 4. Could correspond to that which may be crushed.

PHALLUS 1. Associated with male sexuality. See **Man**. 2. Can correspond to the following positive traits: enterprising, logical, versatile, determined, etc. 3. Can correspond to the following negative traits: tactless, restless, bullying, aggressive, selfish, etc. 4. That which dominates or is forced into a situation. 5. Could indicate one's use of creativity. 6. Literal sexual feelings and drives. 7. May represent the forces of activity, endurance, and that which is outgoing. 8. Might symbolize the measure of one's desire or the lack of it for a particular situation. 9. One's own fears. 10. Could correspond to one's relationship with a male figure. 11. Associated with fire signs (**Aries, Sagittarius**, and **Leo**) and air signs (**Aquarius, Libra**, and **Gemini**) in astrology. See individual signs for additional positive and negative traits. 12. You may also wish to see **People**. 13. Might be associated with the gonads or first chakra. See **Gonads**.

PHARAOH 1. An authority figure. See **King**. 2. May represent insight, wisdom, control, or domination. You may wish to see **Phallus** or **Womb**, depending upon the individual's sex. 3, Could indicate a foreign or unexpected situation. 4. Might also symbolize Egypt. See **Egypt/Egyptian**.

PHILADELPHIA 1. Generally associated with liberty and independence. 2. Whatever one associates with the city will be highly significant. 3. The city of brotherly love. 4. May correspond to domestic travel.

PHOENIX (BIRD) 1. From Egyptian mythology, a beautiful bird that at death bursts into flames but rises from its own ashes. 2. A symbol of immortality and the soul. 3. Corresponds to a rebirth. See **Rebirth**. 4. That which destroys and rebuilds. 5. Liturgically, a symbol of the Resurrection. See **Resurrection**. 6. May be associated with higher spiritual wisdom. 7. You may also wish to see **Bird**.

PHOENIX (CITY) 1. Can correspond to retirement, heat, or the desert. 2. Whatever one associates with the city will be highly significant. 3. May correspond to domestic travel.

PHONE 1. Associated with gaining information or insight. 2. Corresponds to a message. See **Message/Messenger**. 3. Can represent telepathy or intuition. 4. Symbolic of how one listens or how one communicates with others. 5. Literal prediction of someone about to call or someone you need to call. 6. Might be associated with a relationship, an idea, or spoken words.

PHONOGRAPH 1. Associated with self-expression. See **Music**. 2. Could indicate playing the same song over and over again (i.e., revisiting the same situation repeatedly). 3. May correspond to harmony. 4. If a record is playing, it could indicate a particular cycle or the fact that the time has rolled around again. 5. You may also wish to see **Circle**.

PHOTOGRAPH 1. Corresponds to memories of experiences, ideas, or relationships. 2. Associated with recalling events with a more detached or objective perspective and gaining a clearer picture of what transpired. 3. Holding a representation of the picture (situation, experience, or person) in one's own hands. 4. To reexperience a situation that has transpired previously. 5. One's dreams coming to life. 6. May also be associated with karmic memory. See **Karma**.

PIANO 1. Associated with self-expression. See **Music** or **Sing/Singer**. 2. Can correspond to harmony or disharmony, depending upon the environment and the situation. 3. Could indicate discipline and study depending upon one's childhood association with the instrument. 4. Depending on the imagery, if the focus was upon piano keys, it might symbolize one's words. See **Teeth.**

PICNIC 1. That which is relaxing, romantic, a break, a family outing, a pleasure, or an experience outside the realm of one's normal routine. 2. Metaphorically, that was a picnic = that was easy. 3. You may also wish to see **Food.** 4. Could indicate ideas that are easy to take, or a pleasant encounter.

PICTURE 1. Can correspond to memories, ideas, or relationships. See **Photograph.** 2. Holding a representation of the picture (situation, experience, or person) in one's own hands. 3. That upon which one has focused attention. 4. May also be associated with karmic memory. See **Karma.**

PIE 1. Could indicate one's just desserts. 2. A temptation. 3. Metaphorically, can be used as follows: pie in the sky = that which is impossible; a piece of pie = something easy to take; she was pie–eyed = she was drunk. 4. May correspond to bad habits or the over-indulgence of physical appetites. 5 See also **Food.** 6. You may also wish to see **Crust.**

PIED PIPER 1. Could suggest the need for harmony and cooperation. See **Music.** 2. In literature, associated with Robert Browning's *Pied Piper of Hamelin* and being an obedient follower. See **Puppet.** 3. May correspond to any situation where there appears to be multiple followers and one leader. 4. Might also be associated with ridding one's surroundings of rats. See **Rat.**

PIER 1. Associated with the arrival of an important insight, a new situation, or a visitor. 2. May indicate a spiritual activity or experience. See **Boat** and **Water.** 3. Depending on the imagery, might suggest that one's ship has come in. 4. Metaphorically,

can be used as follows: one's peer = an equal; that which is docked = something that is shortened, lowered, or lessened. 5. Depending on the imagery, you may also wish to see **Shore, Bridge,** and **Journey.**

PIG 1. That which is greedy or filthy. 2. A person who hogs the show or makes themselves the center of attention. 3. Metaphorically, pigheadedness = being stubborn; they went whole hog = they went all out (i.e., extravagance); to buy a pig in a poke = to obtain something with little information or foresight; she was hog–wild = she was very excited. 4. Could be associated with one who is of low class morally or sexually. 5. May be symbolic of a poor diet, gluttony, or making a pig of oneself. 6. You may also wish to see **Animals.**

PILATE, PONTIUS 1. Associated with the inability to decide or the act of disavowing responsibility. 2. Could symbolize a ruling influence. See **King.** 3. Might indicate betrayal (i.e., depending upon what one associates with Pilate).

PILL 1. That which is unpleasant but must be swallowed. 2. Depending on the imagery, may be associated with healing or the desire to escape. 3. Metaphorically, can be used as follows: it's a bitter pill to swallow = it's a hard lesson; the Pill = birth control pills; she's a real pill = she's a very unusual person. 4. May be associated with literal warnings or advice regarding one's medication. 5. You may also wish to see **Vitamins.**

PILLOW 1. Can correspond to rest, relaxation, sleep, or sexual activity. See **Bed/ Bedroom.** 2. May be associated with a pleasant thought or situation. 3. Depending upon the imagery, might symbolize the need to take a rest or the fact that one is lazy.

PILOT 1. A divine messenger. See **Airplane.** 2. Corresponds to the one in charge of the journey. See **Journey.** 3. Could be associated with the higher self or soul. 4. Represents the one responsible for the experience and livelihood of those in the same situation. 5. The source of power and authority. 6. May be associated with a parental figure. 7. See also **People.**

PIMPLE 1. A blemish or irritation that has arisen. 2. Indicates that the situation has a blemish. 3. A problem that needs to be addressed. 4. Might also suggest a change in diet. 5. Could be associated with a literal health problem. 6. You may also wish to see **Face** and **Wart.**

PIÑATA 1. A symbol of celebration and joy. See **Party.** 2. That which contains value. 3. Associated with Mexico. See **Mexico.** 4. Depending on imagery, you may also wish to see **Animals.**

PINE 1. See **Tree.** 2. Metaphorically, an intense longing. 3. Associated with peace and serenity. 4. Could symbolize mental clarity.

PINEAL 1. A gland in the body. 2. Associated with the sixth endocrine center or chakra. 3. Relates to the self-realized individual or Christ. See **Christ.** 4. Metaphysically, corresponds to Mercury; also symbolized by a lamb or Christ. 5. In Revelation, it is represented by the Church of Philadelphia. 6. See **Chakras.**

PINK 1. Corresponds to the feminine, or higher love. 2. See **Colors.**

PINOCCHIO 1. A literary symbol of the immature, not fully developed self. 2. Metaphysically, associated with the soul's journey through life's experiences. See **Journey.**

3. May be associated with telling lies. 4. Could represent the process of self-realization and becoming whole. 5. Depending on one's personal association, might symbolize that which is hollow, wooden, or clumsy.

PIONEER 1. Associated with a journey into unexplored territory (i.e., a new idea, a new relationship, a new belief system, etc.). 2. One who prepares the way for others. 3. You may also wish to see **People.**

PIPE (SMOKING) 1. One's own association will greatly determine the symbolism; for example: may represent one's own father or grandfather. 2. Could correspond to introspection and thought. 3. That which goes up in smoke. See **Smoke/Smoking.** 4. Could indicate that which is smelly. 5. Might be associated with male sexuality. See **Phallus.** 6. Could be a warning regarding the inadvisability of smoking.

PIRATE 1. Can correspond to piracy (i.e., trying to take something illegally). 2. Associated with taking advantage or being taken advantage of. 3. Something that is stealing one's ideas, energy, emotions, or vitality. 4. See also **People.** 5. Someone who takes by force what belongs to others. 6. The villainous portions of oneself. See **Villain.**

PISCES ♓ 1. Twelfth sign of the zodiac, corresponding to February 19–March 20. 2. Associated with the following positive traits: humble, intuitive, spiritual, and receptive. 3. Associated with the following negative traits: impractical, vague, and secretive. 4. Astrologically, ruled by Neptune. See **Neptune.** 5. See also **Fish.** 6. A water sign. See **Water.** 7. See also **Astrology.**

PIT 1. May be associated with a trap or a

warning. 2. Could indicate a pitfall (i.e., a danger). 3. Might represent female sexuality. See **Womb.** 4. The feeling of being surrounded or hemmed in. See **Box.** 5. You may also wish to see **Prisoner, Earth,** and **Mountain.**

PITCHER (BASEBALL) 1. Association with communication, one's delivery, or the ability to pitch new ideas. 2. Can correspond to your capacity to deliver what was promised. 3. One's activities in a competitive field. See **Baseball** and **Sports.** 4. You may also wish to see **People.**

PITCHER (CONTAINER) 1. A container of ideas or emotions. 2. Depending upon what is in the pitcher, could be associated with a literal dietary suggestion. 3. The imagery will have a great deal to do with the symbolism; for example: drinking water from a pitcher could correspond to the need for more water in one's diet or to having one's spiritual thirst quenched; pouring something for another person may symbolize being generous or giving. 4. You may also wish to see **Drink.**

PITUITARY 1. A gland in the body. 2. Associated with the seventh endocrine center or chakra. 3. Relates to God's will or oneness. 4. Metaphysically, corresponds to Jupiter; also, symbolized by God (or an old wise man). 5. In Revelation, it is represented by the Church of Laodicea. 6. See **Chakras.**

PLANET 1. Corresponds to spiritual ideas. 2. Could be associated with faraway dreams. 3. The heavenly bodies in our solar system. 4. The planets (in order from the Sun) are as follows: Mercury, Venus, Earth, Mars, Jupiter, Uranus, Saturn, Neptune, and Pluto. 5. See also individual planets. 6. Might indicate bringing order out of chaos. 7. You may also wish to see **Sun/Sunlight, Moon/Moonlight, Star, Sky,** or **Mythology (Roman and Greek).**

PLANK 1. Associated with narrow-mindedness. 2. Can correspond to a dangerous and inevitable outcome. 3. Metaphorically, to walk the plank = to enter a no-win or dangerous situation. 4. Depending on imagery, you may also wish to see **Pirate.**

PLANT 1. Associated with a young idea or a new venture. 2. That which is alive, growing, thriving, or prospering. The condition of the plant will have a great deal to do with the symbolism. 3. Reaping what one has sown. See **Garden.** 4. Corresponds to that which is rooted in place. See **Roots.** 5. What one associates with the particular plant will have a tremendous effect upon the symbolism; for example: a daisy could indicate freshness, a rose could be associated with love or seeing things through rose-colored glasses; clover might symbolize good luck; cactus may correspond to a prickly situation; weeds often indicate negative thoughts or feelings; a weeping willow can suggest sorrow or deep emotions. 6. Metaphorically, a plant = a person who intends to swindle or mislead. 7. That which needs nurturing, care, and attention. 8. May indicate one's spiritual state. 9. Depending on imagery, you may also wish to see **Tree, Flowers, Vine, Weeds, Fruit,** or **Food.** 10. That which is green. See green in **Colors.**

PLANTATION 1. An enormous idea, duty, or responsibility. See **Field.** 2. Depending on imagery, could correspond to the surrendering of one's will to another. See **Slave.** 3. Might be associated with an intense situation or working environment. 4. You may also wish to see **Plant.** 5. If an enormous tobacco plantation, might suggest an overpowering smoking habit.

PLATFORM. 1. How one appears before others. See **Stage**. 2. That which is raised or elevated for all to see. 3. The condition of the stage may indicate the condition of the individual: physically, mentally, or spiritually. See **Body**. 4. Metaphorically, an individual's platform = the principles, goals, or ideals for which that person stands.

PLATYPUS 1. That which may appear silly and ridiculous. 2. See **Animals**. 3. Can be associated with Australia.

PLUMBING 1. Often a literal indication of the condition of one's own elimination systems. See **Body**. 2. The inability to release problems, thoughts, the situation, or emotions. See **House**. 3. Might represent how things are flowing. 4. Depending on imagery, may suggest that something is going down the drain. 5. You may also wish to see **Bathroom, Sink, Drain, Faucet, Tub**, or **Toilet**.

PLUTO ♇ 1. Corresponds to transformation, new beginnings, and rebirth. See **Rebirth**. 2. Associated with self-centeredness, and the potential for growth. 3. In Roman mythology, the god of the underworld. See **Mythology (Roman and Greek).** 4. Farthest planet from the Sun. Has a rotation year of 248.42 years. 5. Astrologically, associated with Scorpio. See **Astrology**.

POCKET 1. That which one has available to draw upon. See **Luggage**. 2. Can correspond to personal possessions or ideas. 3. Represents that which may be surrounded. 4. Metaphorically, can be used as follows: he's in the boss's pocket = he's under the boss's control; to pocket something = to take something that is not rightfully yours. 5. Can be symbolic of inner resources, memories, or talents. 6. Might correspond to receptivity or the feminine nature. See **Womb**.

POCKET WATCH 1. Can indicate that the timing is in one's own hands. 2. That which counts the passage of time or experiences. See **Time**. 3. Might suggest that for which one is waiting. 4. May also be associated with the circle. See **Circle**. 5. Depending on the imagery, you may also wish to see **Hand** and **Pocket**.

POISON 1. Associated with something harmful, detrimental, or dangerous. 2. Could correspond to being subject to dangerous circumstances. 3. May represent dietary warnings or be indicative of the accumulation of toxins within one's own system. 4. Attitudes, information, emotions, or beliefs that are harming oneself or others. 5. To influence wrongfully. 6. You may also wish to see **Food**.

POKER 1. May indicate how one plays the game of life. See **Game.** 2. Might symbolize the situation or experience one has been dealt. See **Cards.** 3. Could be associated with a partnership. 4. Metaphorically, a poker face = one that is hard to figure out (i.e., an expressionless face). 5. Might indicate a gamble. See **Gambling.**

POLICE/POLICE STATION 1. Corresponds to the law (man-made or universal). See **Law.** 2. Can represent one's own conscience. 3. That which provides regulation, safety, and moral guidelines. 4. Associated with keeping or the need for order and control. 5. Introducing into the situation that which tries to bring order out of disorder. 6. The clothing of the police officer may be important; for example: a plainclothes officer may indicate man-made laws; a uniformed police officer may be symbolic of spiritual, karmic, or universal laws. See **Clothes.** 7. A police station indicates that place from which law and order is maintained; could correspond to moral beliefs or the higher self. See **Building.** 8. You may wish to see **People.**

POLISH 1. Can correspond to making preparations for an activity, an experience, or a relationship. See **Clean.** 2. Metaphorically, she gave a polished performance = her performance was flawless. 3. Can correspond to that which is elegant, readied, or presentable.

POOL 1. Associated with peace and tranquility. 2. Could correspond to a spiritual source. 3. May indicate one's own feelings or emotions. 4. See also **Water.** 5. The condition of the water will have a great deal to do with the symbolism; for example: clear water may be associated with spirituality, wisdom, or that which is clean; cloudy water can indicate emotional problems or that which is unclear. 6. Might symbolize the need to pool the group's efforts. 7. Can correspond to one's current situation or experience. 8. Depending on imagery, you may wish to see **Swim.**

POPCORN 1. That which is light, airy, pleasant, unimportant, amusing, or playful. 2. One's own association with popcorn will have a great deal to do with the symbolism; for example: may be associated with the movies and relaxation or it could correspond to junk food. 3. You may also wish to see **Food.**

POPE 1. A spiritual presence or authority. See **Priest.** 2. Could indicate spiritual discipline or the need for it. 3. May represent the Catholic church. See **Church.** 4. One's own experience with organized religion will have a great deal to do with the symbolism.

5. Might symbolize earthly perfection. See **Christ.** 6. Associated with five in the tarot. See **Tarot.**

POPEYE 1. Associated with great strength, the need to eat spinach (or more vegetables), or being favored in a potential partnership or relationship. 2. Can correspond to the sea. See **Sea.** 3. Might be associated with the triumph of good over evil. 4. You may also wish to see **Sailor.** 5. Might be associated with one's own childhood.

PORCH 1. Can correspond to a new opening or a new opportunity. See **Door** and **House.** 2. Might suggest a temporary haven. 3. Could symbolize the act of being between two worlds or being on the edge of something. 4. See also **House.**

PORCUPINE 1. That which is prickly. 2. Could symbolize one's own defensiveness. 3. See **Animals.**

PORT 1. Associated with the arrival of an important insight, a new situation, or a visitor. 2. May indicate a spiritual activity or experience. See **Boat** and **Water.** 3. Depending on the imagery, might suggest that one's ship has come in. 4. Metaphorically, can be used as follows: that which is docked = something which is shortened, lowered, or lessened. 5. You may also wish to see **Shore** and **Journey.**

POTATO 1. The act of peeling potatoes may suggest punishment, humility, or discipline. 2. One's own association will have a great deal to do with the symbolism; for example: if an individual has a poor diet, it could indicate too many starches. 3. You may also wish to see **Food.**

PRAIRIE 1. Represents a wide-open expanse. 2. Could correspond to choices waiting to be made or new possibilities waiting to be planted. See **Plant.** 3. You may also wish to see **Field.**

PRAY/PRAYER 1. A spiritual request or admonition. 2. Associated with talking to God. See **God.** 3. Can correspond to a message. 4. Self-expression of one's inner self or higher self. 5. Might symbolize the need for more personal spiritual activity. 6. May be a literal warning that prayer is necessary for a situation or a person (i.e., a call to prayer). 7. You may also wish to see **Worship** and **Meditation.**

PRECOGNITION 1. Associated with previous knowledge or insight regarding a situation or a condition. See **ESP.** 2. Often one is forewarned of possible situations or experiences in order to make alternate choices or to be prepared when the condition actually occurs. 3. If an image is literally precognitive, one can only be expected to follow through on that which is practical, realistic, and feasible.

PREGNANCY 1. Often represents the birth of a new idea, a new development, or a new experience. See **Birth.** 2. That which is fertile or full of importance. 3. May be a literal indication of pregnancy. 4. Might suggest female sexuality. See **Womb.**

PREHISTORIC 1. Associated with the extinct or the outdated. See **Antique.** 2. Ideas that are no longer appropriate. 3. Metaphorically, he's a dinosaur = he is out of touch with contemporary thought. 4. May indicate one's own primitive nature. See **Beast.** 5. See also **Animals.**

PRESIDENT 1. Can correspond to one's own chief executive: God or one's higher

self. See **God.** 2. Might be a play on establishing a precedent. 3. Might indicate that you have the power of diplomacy, peace, or warfare (i.e., everything) in your own hands. 4. May be associated with the one responsible for everyone's experience and livelihood. 5. You may also wish to see **People.**

PRESLEY, ELVIS 1. The king of rock and roll. 2. Associated with music, entertainment, and movies. 3. One's own association with Elvis will have a great deal to do with the symbolism (i.e., the fifties, sixties, and seventies; growing up; musical talent; a prescription drug problem; etc.). 4. Might indicate one's own musical talent. 5. You may also wish to see **Music** or **Sing/Singer.**

PRESS (MEDIA) 1. Depending on imagery, could be associated with sensationalism, that which is of interest, or that which is newsworthy. 2. A source of information, insight, or opinion. See **Newspaper.** 3. May correspond to public opinion or your opinion of yourself. 4. Could be associated with the need to investigate, scrutinize, or gather additional facts.

PRESSED/PRESSURE 1. May symbolize emotional distress, pressure, an overpowering condition, stress, personal constraints, or unexpressed feelings and emotions. 2. Might correspond to the act of forcing someone into something, or of being forced. 3. Metaphorically, to be pressed into service = to have been impelled into an activity. 4. Suggests that immediate attention is required or there may be an explosion. See **Explosion.** 5. May literally indicate a literal health problem or high blood pressure.

PRIEST 1. A spiritual presence, authority, or messenger. See **Minister.** 2. Could represent spiritual safety or harmony. 3. One's own conscience or belief systems. 4. One who is involved in spiritual matters or pursuits. 5. Can indicate that which explains spiritual laws to others. 6. You may also wish to see **People** and **Church.**

PRINCE/PRINCESS 1. Can represent the untarnished, noble portion of yourself or another. 2. Depending on imagery, associated with the positive male/female qualities. See **Man** or **Woman.** 3. Metaphorically, can be used as follows: the guy's a real prince = he's a real nice guy; she's a princess = she's a precious little girl; she's a Jewish princess = she's really conceited and self-absorbed. 4. You may also wish to see **King** or **Queen.**

PRINTER 1. Associated with self-expression and communication. 2. May indicate a personal talent, or the need to communicate with someone. See **Write.** 3. A communication with one's inner self. 4. Could suggest the need for introspection and self-examination. 5. You may also wish to see **Computer.**

PRINTING PRESS 1. Associated with self-expression and communication. 2. That which is of general or everyday interest. See **Newspaper.** 3. A source of information, insight, or opinion. See **Library.** 4. May correspond to sending or receiving a message. See **Letter.** 5. You may also wish to see **Write** and **Book.**

PRISON 1. That which confines, surrounds, or penalizes. See **Wall.** 2. Losing individual freedom and will. See **Prisoner.** 3. That which has caused one to be trapped (i.e., habits, circumstances, a relationship, or one's environment).

PRISONER 1. Associated with one who is being controlled or trapped by circumstances, conditions, feelings, others, or the environment. 2. One who no longer enjoys personal freedoms. 3. Metaphorically, being a prisoner of love = losing independence because of your feelings toward another. 4. That part of oneself that is unable to see the outside world. See **Shadow.** 5. You may also wish to see **People.**

PRODIGAL SON 1. Associated with the journey of every soul. See **Journey.** 2. The individual seeker in life. 3. Corresponds to a parable of Jesus (Luke 15). See **Parable.** 4. Might be associated with the return of a relationship.

PROMOTION 1. Associated with making progress in one's life journey. See **Journey.** 2. To climb to a higher level of awareness or understanding. 3. May indicate the act of overcoming a situation or a difficulty. 4. Might correspond to a promotion or a rise in social or worldly position. 5. You may also wish to see **Mountain** and **Ladder.**

PROPELLER 1. That which allows something to get off the ground (i.e., an idea, a competent individual, etc.). 2. May symbolize that which is driving an activity forward. 3. Associated with that which assists flight. See **Airplane.** 4. Depending on imagery, might suggest an antiquated idea, project, or journey.

PROSTITUTE 1. To sell or debase oneself or to severely compromise one's principles. 2. Can correspond to exchanging one's services for low remuneration or for unworthy purposes. 3. See also **Sex.** 4. Might symbolize one's feelings of inadequacy, a poor self-image, or low self-esteem. 5. Could indicate misdirection of energies or just misdirection.

6. May indicate the corrupt side of the feminine (if female prostitute) or the masculine (if male prostitute). See **Womb** or **Phallus.** 7. May suggest a relationship that is loveless. 8. You may also wish to see **People.**

PSYCHIC 1. Corresponds to intuition, wisdom, foresight, or a message. See **Message/Messenger**. 2. Associated with one who is extremely sensitive or emotional. 3. Symbolic of information from beyond the material world (i.e., from the emotional/spiritual realms). See **ESP**. 4. You may also wish to see **People**.

PULL 1. Associated with something with which there is a strong connection, influence, struggle, or attraction. 2. Metaphorically, can be used in the following ways: to pull yourself up = to consider your needs only, or to get back on your feet; pull yourself together = regain your balance and composure; he pulled the wool over their eyes = he took advantage or tricked and deceived them; pulling through = overcoming a difficulty or challenge; she pulled it off = she made it happen; to pull apart/down = to find fault with or to ridicule. 3. Whatever is being pulled may indicate the symbolic meaning. For example, having one's teeth pulled suggests getting rid of gossip or negative comments regarding others; pulling a wagon could mean bringing one's message or purpose with one. 4. Depending on imagery, you may also wish to see **Wrestle.**

PULPIT 1. The place from which spiritual insights are delivered. See **Minister.** 2. Being on the pulpit indicates taking a stand or delivering one's own opinion. See **Platform.** 3. May be symbolic of the ability to teach or the need to be taught. 4. Could refer to those who are hearing a sermon. 5.

You may also wish to see **Church.**

PUPPET 1. Corresponds to one who is subject to the control, whims, or desires of another. 2. Suggestive of easy manipulation. 3. See **People.**

PURPLE 1. May represent honor, spiritual vision, or that which is extremely important. 2. See **Colors.**

PURSE 1. Associated with one's material resources or security. See **Money.** 2. Can correspond to one's identity. 3. That which carries one's ideas, resources, attitudes, or emotions. See **Bag.** 4. Metaphorically, can be used as follows: the size of the purse = how much money was involved. 5. May represent female sexuality. See **Womb.**

PURSUED 1. Can represent something that is chasing you (i.e., fears), that you are running from, or that you are pursuing. See **Run/Runner.** 2. May be associated with anxiety, apprehension, inferiority, or uneasiness. 3. The inability to handle one's current experience. 4. That which one is fearful of is often associated with something that needs to be faced in oneself. See **Shadow.** 5. A conflict between others or between portions of oneself. 6. Can correspond to an internal struggle. 7. You may also wish to see **Attack.**

PUS 1. That which is infected, wounded, or sore. 2. Could indicate degeneration. 3. May be a literal indication of ill health. See **Body.** 4. Can symbolize the fact that poisons are affecting one's system (i.e., negative thoughts, attitudes, or words). 5. You may also wish to see **Wound** or **Ill/Illness.**

PUZZLE 1. Can indicate something you are trying to solve; a puzzling situation. 2. Could correspond with putting the pieces of one's life together. 3. Might indicate that you do not yet possess all the pieces (i.e., viewpoints, facts, ingredients, etc.). 4. Metaphorically, it's a puzzle = it's confusing. 5. You may also wish to see **Game.**

PYGMALION 1. Associated with personal transformation and self–realization. 2. That which goes from poverty and neglect to personal fulfillment. 3. The realization of one's highest potential. 4. You may also wish to see **Phoenix (Bird)** and **People.**

PYRAMID 1. Often associated with ancient wisdom or spiritual initiation. 2. That which is solid, stable, supreme, or long–lasting. You may wish to see **Building.** 3. Might be associated with a pyramid scheme in investments. 4. May represent an inner spiritual source. 5. Symbolic of the spirit (the pinnacle of the structure) manifesting into the earth (the four corners of the base). See **Christ.** 6. Can be associated with a foreign visitor or travel. 7. You may also wish to see **Egypt/ Egyptian.**

Q

1. The seventeenth letter of the alphabet. 2. The Roman numeral for 500. 3. Numerologically, equivalent to eight. 4. In Greek, kappa.

QUAIL 1. Can correspond to that which shrinks, cowers, or trembles. 2. To lose heart or to become depressed. 3. See also **Bird**.

QUAKER 1. That which is shaken, frightened, or trembling. 2. Can correspond to a peacemaker. 3. Might symbolize a return back to spiritual basics. 4. Could represent that which is plain. 5. See **People**.

QUARANTINE 1. Associated with that which is off limits. 2. To be isolated or separated. 3. A warning. 4. That which is under strict control. 5. May indicate something is contagious. 6. You may also wish to see **Ill/Illness**.

QUARRY 1. Where one creates difficulties (see **Rock**) or foundations (see **Foundation**). 2. Associated with the creation of big ideas. 3. Can represent putting something out into the light (i.e., out where everyone can see it).

QUARTER/QUARTERS 1. Can represent a fourth or four equal parts. 2. Associated with very little money. See **Money**. 3. Might symbolize a new residence or place of work.

QUARTZ 1. Limited vision or insight (i.e., not as clear as crystal). 2. A receiver of energies. 3. That which is common and abundant. 4. Rose quartz is associated with the heart and healing. 5. You may also wish to see **Jewels/Jewelry**.

QUEEN 1. Corresponds to the ruling authority or the higher self. 2. Could represent a female authority figure, such as a boss, a mother, or a dominant female relationship. You may also wish to see **Woman**. 3. May be associated with a majestic or high ideal or principle; a dominant idea. 4. That which may provide nurturing, insight, and understanding. See **Womb**. 5. The female aspect of God. 6. Often that which rules the situation. 7. Corresponds to that which is elevated in stature. 8. See **People**. 9. Metaphorically, she's a queen = she's the best or the most beautiful; she acts like a queen = she thinks she's superior.

QUICKSAND 1. Unable to get a firm footing. See **Sink**. 2. Can correspond to the fact that you're on dangerous ground or that you're losing ground. 3. Associated with something that is sinking or failing. 4. May symbolize a poor foundation or base moral behavior. 5. A hopeless situation. 6. Indicates one is being engulfed by the situation or surroundings. 7. You may also wish to see **Sand**.

QUILL 1. Can correspond to one's ideas or experiences. 2. Used to express what an individual has been thinking. See **Pen**. 3. May indicate an old message or insight (i.e., from childhood). 4. You may also wish to see **Write.**

QUILT 1. Associated with personal security and comfort. 2. Can correspond to something that covers the situation. 3. Associated with that which one uses as a cover or outer appearance at home. 4. Separate pieces that may be brought together into a unified whole (with a little softness). 5. You may also wish to see **Bed/Bedroom.**

QUIZ 1. Corresponds to a test or a lesson. See **School.** 2. Associated with being questioned. 3. What is happening during the examination is significant; for example: not finding the testing room or the class could indicate that one feels lost in the situation; not knowing the answers may symbolize one's own uncertainties; not being ready suggests that you feel unprepared for your present condition; failure or a low grade is often associated with low self-esteem or personal insecurity. 4. Could suggest that one does not yet have all the answers or required information. 5. One's success at dealing with life's problems.

R

1. *The eighteenth letter of the alphabet.* 2. *Associated with schooling; the three R's: reading, writing, and arithmetic.* 3. *Numerologically, equivalent to nine.* 4. *In Greek, rho.*

RABBI 1. A spiritual presence, authority, or message. See **Minister.** 2. One who is involved in spiritual matters or concerns. 3. A teacher of wisdom. See **Teacher.** 4. Associated with the Jewish faith. See **Judaism.** 5. May represent the need to pay closer attention to the spiritual side of one's life. 6. Could correspond to one's own higher self. 7. You may also wish to see **Temple.**

RABBIT 1. Often associated with sexuality (i.e., to breed like rabbits). 2. Because of the shape of their ears, may correspond to listening or to the need to listen. See **Ears.** 3. Might be associated with burrowing oneself into hiding. See **Cave.** 4. Could indicate a literal dietary suggestion to eat more vegetables. 5. Might be associated with softness or vulnerability. 6. A tiny irritant (i.e., that which continuously nibbles at something). 7. In literature (*The Tortoise and the Hare*), corresponds to haste makes waste in comparison to that which is slow, methodical, and dependable. 8. See also **Animals.**

RACCOON 1. Because of their appearance, may be symbolic of one who is a robber or a thief. See **Burglar.** 2. Corresponds to one who operates at night (unseen but perhaps not quiet). See **Animals.**

RACE 1. The race or experience of life. See **Journey.** 2. To take part in a competition where one tries to finish first. See **Game.** 3. Could be associated with going too fast. See **Speed.** 4. Depending on imagery, you may also wish to see **Run/Runner** or **Automobile.**

RADIO 1. Associated with receiving or sending information or understanding over a distance. 2. Could represent intuitive insights or awareness from the higher self or subconscious. 3. May relate to receiving a message. See **Letter.** 4. The capacity to attune or tune into higher levels of awareness. 5. Might correspond to the body's own hearing mechanisms. See **Ears.** 6. Associated with information or insights that can be tuned into by anyone. 7. That which relates to entertainment, communication, or relaxation. See **Music.**

RAFT 1. May be associated with a temporary place of safety or isolation. 2. Can correspond to a solitary experience in one's life journey. 3. May represent a spiritual voyage. See **Boat.** 4. Could represent inadequate preparation, groundwork, foundation, or insight.

RAILROAD 1. An established roadway. See **Road.** 2. That from which one's journey is directed (i.e., intellect, experience, or the higher self). See **Train** and **Journey.** 3. Metaphorically, can be used as follows: he railroaded it through = he pushed it through quickly; she was railroaded = she was made the scapegoat. 4. Could indicate that which is on or off the track. See **Tracks.**

RAIN 1. Often associated with an outpouring of emotion. See **Weather.** 2. Depending on imagery, can correspond to a cleansing or an inundation. See **Flood.** 3. May indicate an unexpected turn of events (i.e., a picnic being rained out). 4. Could represent being showered with information, blessings, or insights. 5. Could be associated with the need to cleanse oneself physically, mentally, or emotionally. See **Shower.** 6. That which may be falling. See **Fall.** 7. Literally, could indicate the need to drink more water. 8. You may also wish to see **Water.**

RAINBOW 1. Symbolic of a covenant or a promise. See **Covenant.** 2. Biblically, associated with the Flood. See **Ark** and **Flood.** 3. That which identifies the location of a treasure. 4. May symbolize people of all walks of life, backgrounds, races, and religions. 5. Can signify the end of a problem, or the pot of gold after the storm. 6. A band of multicolored light; in order: red, orange, yellow, green, blue, indigo, and violet. See **Colors.**

RAINCOAT 1. That which isolates you from your emotions or the emotions of others. See **Clothes.** 2. One's outward emotional nature or attitudes. See **Coat.** 3. Might represent the fact that one needs to be more isolated from the emotional outpourings of others. 4. Could be a literal indication that it is going to rain.

RAISIN 1. Can correspond to that which is dried, preserved, or aged. 2. May be associated with fruitfulness. See **Grapes.** 3. Might be a literal dietary suggestion for more fruit in one's diet. See **Fruit.**

RAM 1. Associated with power, strength, leadership, determination, and drive. 2. Can correspond to selflessness, sacrifice, or homage to God. See **Lamb** and **God.** 3. Might represent the act of forcing or pushing something into place. 4. To plunge or to stuff. 5. Slang for forcing an idea to be accepted by someone else. 6. Might be symbolic of sexuality or drive. 7. Astrologically, one of the twelve signs of the zodiac. See **Aries.** 8. See also **Animals.** 9. Might be associated with male aggression or domination. See **Phallus.** 10. In ancient Egypt, the ram was the god of creation. See **Mythology (Egyptian).**

RAPE 1. Corresponds to being forced into submission. 2. An aggressive assault against one who is in a position of vulnerability. 3. That which is taken by force. 4. Could be a literal warning to take precautionary measures. 5. May be associated with anything violated, dominated, plundered, or destroyed. 6. You may wish to see **Attack.**

RASH 1. That which causes an irritation. 2. Indicates that the situation has a blemish. 3. Corresponds to a problem that needs to be addressed. 4. Might also suggest a change in diet. 5. Could be associated with a literal health problem or allergy. 6. Might also indicate that something is being attempted or decided too hastily. 7. You may also wish to see the area of the body in which the rash occurs. See **Body.** 8. That which covers the situation. See **Skin.**

RAT 1. Can correspond to one who is cruel, immoral, or irritating. 2. May be symbolic of dirt, disease, or filth. 3. Could correspond to inappropriate and unseen activities occurring in one's environment (i.e., work or home). See **Mouse.** 4. Metaphorically, can be used as follows: I smell a rat = I sense there's an unseen problem or hidden intrigue; he's a rat = he's not a nice guy. 5. You may also wish to see **Animals.**

RAVEN 1. A predatory bird. See **Bird.** 2. Can correspond to an uncontrollable hunger or desire (i.e., ravenous). 3. Might be associated with an ill omen, bad luck, or a death. 4. Biblically, a sign of God's promises and the interconnectedness of God's creation (ravens fed Elijah by the brook; I Kings 17:4).

READ 1. The need, desire, or act of gaining additional information and insights. 2. Associated with study, relaxation, or learning. See **Book.** 3. Metaphorically, can be used as follows: you need to read between the lines = you need to look closely to see what is really there; she read what she wanted into it = she decided for herself what it meant. 4. If the imagery contains literal words, may be a message or intuitive information. 5. You may also wish to see **School.**

REBIRTH 1. Corresponds to a new beginning, a fresh start, a reawakening, or a regeneration. See **Resurrection.** 2. May be associated with reincarnation. See **Reincarnation.** 3. A second chance. 4. May symbolize a transformation.

RECEIPT 1. Can correspond to having paid one's dues or having fulfilled an obligation. 2. Associated with an acknowledgment for the receipt of payment. 3. Might symbolize the fulfillment of karmic debt. See **Karma.** 4. You may also wish to see **Money.**

RECEPTION 1. A formal function or social gathering. 2. May correspond to a celebration, a recognition, or a reward. See **Party.** 3. Might symbolize a partnership, a new beginning, or a relationship. See **Birth** and **Marriage.**

RECIPE 1. Associated with gathering all of the necessary ingredients for an activity, an idea, or a project. 2. Could correspond to

that which is cooking (i.e., in the works). See **Cook.** 3. Might indicate literal dietary suggestions. See **Food.**

RECURRING DREAMS/IMAGES 1. Often occur in response to information in one's conscious life that has been repeatedly neglected, overlooked, or intentionally ignored. 2. May be a precognitive warning of a possible situation, advising a different or a precautionary course of action. 3. Associated with one's own unresolved physical, mental, or spiritual issues. 4. You may also wish to see **Precognition.**

RED 1. Associated with energy, trouble, misunderstanding, anger, or lust. 2. See **Colors.**

REFORM SCHOOL 1. Suggests the necessity of reform, behavior modification, or discipline. 2. Might indicate something in need of reform. 3. Could be associated with the lessons and education provided by daily life. 4. May correspond to being controlled or the need to be controlled by others, circumstances, conditions, feelings, or the environment. See **Prisoner.** 5. You may also wish to see **School.**

REFRIGERATOR 1. Where one stores, preserves, chills, or keeps things static. 2. Could indicate the act of being chilly or cool toward others. 3. Might indicate sexual frigidity. See **Freeze/Freezer.** 4. That which is untouched by the external environment.

REINCARNATION 1. The belief that an individual goes through a series of lifetimes and experiences as a means of becoming a better person. 2. Metaphysically, it is the process whereby a soul achieves wholeness. 3. Associated with the memories of one's past and how they impact upon the present. See **Karma.** 4. Reincarnation images are often associated with foreign places; historical scenes, activities, or attire; and things that are old (i.e., old, dusty books; an old library; antiques; etc.). See **Historical Clothing/ Settings.**

REINS 1. Can indicate the need to slow down, to restrain an individual, or to restrain oneself. 2. Metaphorically, can be used as follows: he needs to be given free rein = he needs total freedom; she wanted to keep a rein on the situation = she wanted to keep some control over the situation. 3. Associated with a horse. See **Horse.**

RELATIVES 1. Often corresponds to the relationship one possesses with that individual (i.e., feelings toward the person, areas of the relationship that need to be worked on, etc.). See specific family relationships; for example, see **Mother.** 2. Often corresponds to various aspects of oneself. 3. May represent aspects of ourselves in relationship to that person or talents, qualities, or experiences that we associate with that person. 4. A deceased relative may indicate a message from another realm or a psychological issue that still needs to be addressed. 5. A parental figure can represent the need to look after one's activities. 6. Might indicate a literal suggestion or a warning in terms of the person's welfare. 7. Metaphorically, it's all relative = it's all important, connected, or meaningful. 8. See also **People.** 9. You may also wish to see **Child, Man,** or **Woman,** depending upon the individual's age and sex.

REM 1. Corresponds to rapid eye movement sleep, a period of sleep when an individual is dreaming. 2. You may also wish to see **Dream.**

REMODELING/RENOVATING 1. Can

symbolize areas of one's life that are being altered, changed, rebuilt, revived, or transformed. 2. Depending on imagery, might correspond to portions of yourself or your situation that are in need of repair. See **Repair.** 3. You may also wish to see **Contractor.**

REPAIR 1. That which is in need of attention. 2. Depending on imagery, might correspond to portions of yourself or your situation that are in need of repair. 3. The act of undergoing transformation. 4. You may also wish to see **Contractor.** 5. See also whatever is being repaired; for example: see **Automobile, House, Body,** etc.

REPRODUCE 1. That which multiplies, expands, or procreates. 2. Associated with sex. See **Sex.** 3. That which creates an exact replica of itself. See **Mirror.** 4. Might correspond to that which is repeatable, copied, or duplicated.

RESTAURANT 1. Associated with where one is fed or nurtured physically, mentally, or spiritually. 2. Corresponds to the sustenance that you are allowing others to prepare for you. 3. Could be associated with the literal need to become more aware of personal dietary habits. 4. A place where you may buy anything you desire to feed yourself. See **Food.** 5. Can correspond with relaxation or socializing. 6. The appearance of the restaurant will have a great deal to do with the quality of what you are feeding yourself. See **Building.** 7. You may also wish to see **Store.**

RESURRECTION 1. Corresponds to a new beginning, a fresh start, a reawakening, or a regeneration. 2. Associated with transformation and spiritual rebirth. 3. Liturgically, corresponds to the ability of the divine to raise that which is dead back to life. 4. Metaphysically, the power of the spirit to awaken the physical to its highest potential. See **Christ.** 5. Metaphorically, to resurrect something = to reconsider it. 6. You may also wish to see **Phoenix (Bird).**

RETIREMENT 1. Can correspond to old age, the achievement of one's goals, or literal retirement. See **Old.** 2. May indicate feelings of uselessness. 3. Might be associated with an involuntary dismissal or the act of being fired. 4. Could suggest the need for more rest and relaxation. 5. You may also wish to see **Work.**

REVELATION 1. An insight, awareness, or inner knowing. See **ESP.** 2. A disclosure or message of that which is unknown. 3. You may also wish to see **Letter.**

REVELATION, BOOK OF 1. Associated with John's visions, dreams, and imagery while he was in exile. 2. Liturgically, symbolic of the Apocalypse, Judgment Day, and the Second Coming. 3. Metaphysically, corresponds to John's awakening consciousness as he tuned into the reaches of his own higher self. See **Christ.** 4. The frequent symbology of seven in the Book of Revelation is associated with the Chakras. See **Chakras.** 5. The symbology of the churches is as follows:

Church of Ephesus: Associated with the gonads, patience, abandonment, the white horse, and the first seal.

Church of Smyrna: Associated with the Lyden, suffering, insincerity, the black horse, and the second seal.

Church of Pegamos: Associated with the adrenals, faithfulness, stumbling blocks (challenges), the red horse, and the third seal.

Church of Thyatira: Associated with the thymus, charity, fornication, the pale horse, and the fourth seal.

Church of Sardis: Associated with the thyroid, few not defiled, imperfection, the souls of the perfect slain, and the fifth seal.

Church of Philadelphia: Associated with the pineal, open door (expectancy), no faults, the earthquake, and the sixth seal.

Church of Laodicea: Associated with the pituitary, that which is lukewarm, the silence, and the seventh seal.

6. Additional miscellaneous symbology of John's attunement while in meditation is as follows:

Angel: Corresponds to spiritual intelligence and wisdom.

Armageddon: Symbolic of the conflict between good and evil within self.

Babylon: Associated with selfish ideals, earthly pleasures, and self-gratification.

Beast: Selfishness, self-centeredness, animal instincts.

Book of Life: Collective unconscious or akashic record.

Crown of Life: Symbolic of the state of perfection.

Eyes of Flame: Corresponds to perception.

Feet of Brass: Understanding.

Four and Twenty Elders: Refers to the twenty-four cranial nerves that lead to the body's five senses.

Four Beasts: Desires of the four lower chakras (self-gratification, self-preservation, sustenance, and propagation).

Golden Girdle: Associated with worth.

In the Spirit: In meditation.

Jezebel: Corresponds to the misdirection of creative energies.

Lamb: Christ consciousness manifested in the earth.

Morning Star: Associated with the state of perfection and illumination before the Fall.

New Jerusalem: New state of awareness.

New Heaven: Perfected state of consciousness.

Reins: Method of control.

Sea of Glass: Corresponds to the stilled emotions.

Seven Churches: Symbolic of the seven spiritual centers: Ephesus = Gonads; Smyrna = Lyden; Pergamos = Adrenals; Thyatira = Thymus; Sardis = Thyroid; Philadelphia = Pineal; Laodicea = Pituitary.

Seven Golden Candlesticks: Same symbology as the seven churches, but includes the power of mind within each chakra.

Seven Heads and Seven Crowns: Rebellious and selfish urges in control of the body's chakras.

Seven Seals: Endocrine centers in normal closed state.

Seven Stars: Associated with the subconscious control points of each spiritual center.

Synagogue of Satan: Unperfected aspects of self.

Two-Edged Sword: The awareness and power from attunement may be applied constructively or destructively depending upon the will.

White Hair: Symbolic of wisdom.

White Raiment: State of purity.

7. You may also wish to see **Numerology** and **Bible**.

RIBBON 1. That which can decorate or tie. 2. May symbolize an honor or a recognition. See **Medals**. 3. Can correspond to freedom, a celebration, or a relationship. 4. Often associated with one's own use of ribbons; for example: it may indicate the arrival of a gift; a blue ribbon often symbolizes the birth of a baby boy (pink = girl). 5. The color and type of ribbon will have a great deal to do with the imagery; for example: a yellow ribbon might suggest a homecoming; a baby ribbon could indicate literal or figurative birth (see **Birth**); a black ribbon may be associated with death. 6. You may also wish to see **Clothes** and **Colors**.

RIDE 1. The act of going on or being taken on a journey. See **Journey**. 2. Metaphorically, can be used as follows: being taken for a ride = to be cheated or deceived; she decided to ride it out = she decided to follow the experience through to the finish; the boss rode him hard = the boss criticized or reprimanded him; going along for the ride = joining with or cooperating with others. 3. Associated with being delivered, transported, or conveyed. 4. Going for a ride with someone may indicate that you have allowed another to take control of the current situation. 5. Riding something or someone may suggest a thing or person over which you have control. 6. Depending on imagery, you may also wish to see **Passenger**. 7. See also the vehicle being ridden; for example: see **Car**.

RIFLE 1. Can correspond to imposing one's views or will onto others. 2. Associated with violence or aggression. 3. Represents that which can cause injury. 4. Could represent being overly defensive or the need to become defensive. 5. May indicate an aggressive male nature. See **Phallus**. 6. That which causes fear. 7. Metaphorically, can be used as follows: to rifle through something = to search through it haphazardly; it was rifled = it was stolen. 8. You may also wish to see **War**.

RIGHT 1. Associated with the future, that which is fixed, something conservative, and the east. 2. Often associated with the conscious parts of oneself. 3. May indicate a proper choice, good judgment, or a correct direction. See **Direction**. 4. However, one who is right-brained is generally intuitive, irrational, and receptive. 5. May be associated with the masculine side of oneself. See **Man** and **Phallus**. 6. Metaphorically, can be used as follows: in one's own right = self-reliance; right away = immediately; the problem was righted = the problem was fixed; right on = an affirmative exclamation.

RING 1. Corresponds to a relationship, an agreement, a commitment, or a bond. See **Jewels/Jewelry**. 2. Whatever is happening to the ring is highly significant; for example: losing the ring could symbolize a loss of the relationship, or a literal possibility of losing the jewelry; missing a stone in one's wedding ring might suggest one is feeling like something is missing from one's marriage, or a literal sign that the stone is loose; etc. 3. You may also wish to see **Circle**.

RIPE 1. That which is ready for use or harvest. 2. Can be associated with perfect timing. 3. Could represent that which is developed and mature. 4. Metaphorically, a ripe old age = an elderly individual. 5. You may also wish to see **Plant**.

RITUAL 1. May be associated with habits, patterns, dogmas, or one's routine. 2. Could correspond to formality, procedural dictates, or one's systematic approach to spirituality and religion.

RIVER 1. Associated with a flow of spirit, information, or insight. See **Water**. 2. May be associated with the flow of one's own energies or elimination systems. 3. Can correspond to the passage of time. 4. That which divides people, ideas, or the environment. 5. May be associated with one's life path or direction. See **Direction** and **Road**. 6. Metaphorically, to send someone down the river = to betray or to take advantage of him. 7. Could indicate cooperation (i.e., going with the flow).

ROACH 1. Can correspond to a real pest. See **Bug**. 2. May symbolize an area of one's life that is literally or metaphorically dirty. 3. Could indicate the need for a cleanup physically, mentally, and spiritually. 4. Might symbolize an unseen irritant. 5. Depending on one's personal association, may also symbolize marijuana or hallucinogenic drugs.

ROAD 1. Associated with the journey of life. See **Journey**. 2. May indicate the direction one is pursuing. See **Direction**. 3. Often corresponds to an individual's destiny. 4. Types of roads indicate particular experiences; for example: a fork in the road or a crossroads = potential choices; a dirty road = you may be on the wrong path; a rocky road = your journey could be filled with obstacles for the time being. 5. See also **Street**.

ROADBLOCK 1. That which stands in one's path. 2. An obstacle that must be overcome or gone around. 3. A possible warning sign regarding one's current direction. 4. See also **Wall**.

ROBBER 1. Can correspond to trying to take something illegally. 2. Associated with taking advantage or being taken advantage of. 3. Something that is stealing one's ideas, energy, emotions, or vitality. 4. See also **People.**

ROBIN 1. Associated with regeneration and rebirth (i.e., the robin is the harbinger of spring). 2. See **Bird.**

ROCK 1. Difficulties that need to be overcome or gone around. 2. Corresponds to a sturdy foundation. 3. Rocks in the road represent obstacles in one's path. See **Road.** 4. That which is ageless or ancient. 5. Associated with permanence or sturdiness. 6. Could represent emotional aloofness or the inability to change or open up. 7. Symbolic of that which is of the earth or materiality. See **Earth.** 8. Metaphorically, that which is on the rocks = that which is in great financial difficulty, or that which comes with ice; a rock = a diamond (see **Jewels/Jewelry**). 9. Liturgically, associated with the church.

ROLLER COASTER 1. May be symbolic of ups and downs in one's present circumstance, finances, or relationship. 2. Depending on one's personal association, might be related to something that thrills or frightens. 3. Might be symbolic of sexual activity. See **Sex.** 4. Metaphorically, she's got me on an emotional roller coaster = she puts me through all kinds of emotional extremes.

ROME 1. Corresponds primarily to whatever an individual thinks of Rome (i.e., associated with ancient civilizations, romance, expressive emotions, the Vatican, etc.). 2. May be indicative of a foreign visitor or travel. 3. Could be pun on the tendency for one to be detached, wandering, or cheating on a relationship (i.e., Roman = roaming).

ROOF 1. Associated with higher or spiritual thoughts. See **House.** 2. Can relate to physical, mental, emotional, or spiritual security. 3. May correspond to that which covers the situation or the environment. 4. Metaphorically, to raise the roof = to make a loud noise or disturbance or to complain. 5. You may also wish to see **Head.**

ROOM 1. Often represents aspects of one's own self. See **House.** 2. Whatever is occurring in the room as well as the characters that are present (see **People**) will have a great deal to do with the symbolic meaning.

ROOSTER 1. Indicates it is time for one to wake up to the situation. 2. Associated with a male chicken; one who is afraid. See **Chicken.** 3. See also **Cock.** 4. You may also wish to see **Animals.**

ROOTS 1. Suggestive of a deep-rooted condition, belief, or problem. 2. May indicate a strong foundation. See **Foundation.** 3. Might symbolize that which draws life from its surroundings. 4. Metaphorically, can be used as follows: that's at the root of the issue = that's the real core; she put down roots = she decided to settle down. 5. Depending on imagery, might correspond to a literal health condition and the need to see a doctor. 6. You may also wish to see **Plant.**

ROPE 1. That which ties, binds, connects, or secures. 2. Could correspond to unified strength or that which pulls things together. 3. Depending upon imagery, might represent dangling someone by a thread. See **Puppet.** 4. Metaphorically, can be used as follows: she knows the ropes = she knows what she's doing; he's at the end of his rope = he cannot handle any more problems or stress; the boss was roped into the project = the boss was persuaded. 5. May be associated with a way out of the situation. 6. Might symbolize that which can cause a hang-up. See **Hang.**

ROSARY 1. Associated with prayer. See **Prayer.** 2. Corresponds to a state of worship. 3. You may also wish to see **Meditation.**

ROSE 1. Can correspond to love and romance. 2. May be associated with harmony. 3. Metaphorically, a rose by any other name = that being referred to is as beautiful, delicate, or as pleasing as a rose. 4. See also **Flowers.**

ROUND 1. That which is without beginning or end (i.e., that which continues endlessly). 2. Can correspond to that which is whole, complete, or eternal. See **Circle.** 3. Metaphorically, to make one's rounds = to travel a specific course of action or activity.

ROUND TABLE 1. Associated with King Arthur's knights. 2. Corresponds to wholeness, the aspects of man, the signs of the zodiac, the circle, etc. See **Circle.** 3. Symbolic of cooperation, unity, and teamwork. 4. You may also wish to see **Table.**

RUBBER 1. That which is adaptable, cooperative, or able to withstand pressure and return to its previous form. 2. That which insulates one from the environment. See **Clothes.** 3. Metaphorically, a rubber = a condom.

RUBBISH 1. A mess, disorder, or something that is no longer worthwhile. 2. Associated with worthless or discarded ideas, talents, statements, people, etc. 3. Metaphorically, rubbish = nonsense.

RUG 1. A foundation; that which is under consideration. See **Carpet.** 2. Associated with an independent or separate idea or experience. 3. You may also wish to see **Floor.**

RULER 1. Can correspond to that which measures, guides, or draws the line. 2. Associated with parameters and guidelines. See **Law.** 3. Depending on imagery, might symbolize the act of behaving in a very straightforward manner and/or the need to become more relaxed.

RUN/RUNNER 1. Associated with that part of oneself that is running away from something. 2. Can correspond to the deliverer of a message or insight. 3. Indicates participation in some type of a race. See **Race.** 4. That which moves swiftly. 5. Represents orchestrated motion, movement, and mobility. 6. Metaphorically, used in the following ways: to run into someone = to meet by chance; being run down = the state of exhaustion or submission; it runs in her blood = it's part of who she is; a run-in = an argument; taking a run for your money = involved in some type of competition; it's in the running = it's a possibility. 7. Independent and solitary focus. 8. May literally suggest the need for physical exercise. See **Exercise.** 9. Might indicate a hurried state of mind or the act of trying to catch up. 10. Could be associated with being under a lot of pressure and stress. 11. You may also wish to see **Sports.**

RUNES 1. An esoteric belief system suggesting that two simultaneous and seemingly unrelated events may be causally and meaningfully connected. See **Synchronicity.** 2. Characters, symbols, or hieroglyphs associated with specific meanings and subject to interpretation much like imagery or a dream. 3. A tool for gaining an objective perspective of one's inner reality. 4. You may also wish to see **I Ching.**

RUSSIA I. Corresponds primarily to what-ever an individual associates with Russia or Russians (i.e., communism, cold, oppression, vodka, the good of the many taking prece-dence over the few, etc.). 2. May be indica-tive of a foreign visitor or travel. 3. Could be a pun on the fact that one is hurrying (i.e., Russian = rushing). 4. Metaphorically, one who plays Russian roulette = one who plays with danger.

RUST I. That which is neglected, ignored, spoiled, aged, or forgotten. 2. Can corre-spond to something that requires immedi-ate attention. 3. Might suggest that which is no longer necessary. See **Antique.** 4. Might indicate an old appearance, personality, or manner that needs to be removed.

S

1. The nineteenth letter of the alphabet. 2. The Roman numeral for seven or seventy. 3. Chemically, the symbol of sulfur. 4. In English, used as a word ending to denote plural or possessive. 5. Numerologically, equivalent to one. 6. In Greek, sigma.

SABBATH 1. A day of rest. 2. Associated with Sunday in most sects of Christianity (Saturday in some), Saturday in Judaism, and Friday in Islam. 3. The day set aside for worship and prayer. See **Worship.** 4. A covenant of our relationship with God (Exodus 31: 16). See **Covenant.**

SACRIFICE 1. Associated with giving up a part of oneself. 2. A surrender to a higher authority or power. 3. Could symbolize the need to surrender one's lower self or negative traits to one's higher self or positive traits. 4. Metaphorically, I sold it at a sacrifice = I sold it for less than it was worth; to sacrifice the ball = intentionally bunting for the benefit of another member of the team. 5. You may also wish to see **Kill** and **Death.**

SAD 1. One of the four basic emotions (glad, mad, sad, and scared). See **Emotion.** 2. May be associated with activities or interactions causing one to be unhappy, depressed, sorrowful, or melancholy. 3. Metaphorically, that was a sad performance = that was a very poor performance.

SAFE 1. Can represent security, protection, secrecy, or locking away a particular situation or emotion. 2. The place of one's talents and abilities. 3. Can indicate that which is safely set aside or stored. .See **Closet.** 4.

Might be associated with the storehouse of one's memories or experiences. 5. That which is mysterious or hidden. 6. Can correspond to that which has value. See **Money.** 7. Might be symbolic of female sexuality. See **Womb.** 8. You may also wish to see **Vault.**

SAFETY 1. Freedom from harm, danger, or disaster. 2. Could be a literal indication of what one must do in order to be free from harm. 3. Might suggest that one has no need to be anxious or worried.

SAGITTARIUS ♐ 1. Ninth sign of the zodiac, corresponding to November 22–December 21. 2. Associated with the following positive traits: sincere, adaptable, optimistic. 3. Associated with the following negative traits: careless, tactless, prone to exaggeration. 4. Astrologically, ruled by Jupiter. See **Jupiter.** 5. See **Centaur.** 6. A fire sign. See **Fire.** 7. See also **Astrology.**

SAILING 1. Associated with a spiritual journey or experience. See **Boat** and **Journey.** 2. Depending on imagery, that which is an easy, enjoyable, or relaxing experience; or that which is a harsh, treacherous, or dangerous experience. 3. May be associated with the need to enjoy life rather than racing through it, or going with the flow. 4. Could indicate the need for more relaxation and recreation. 5. Metaphorically, smooth sailing = free from any obstacle. 6. You may also wish to see **Water.**

SAILOR 1. One who is upon life's journey. See **Journey.** 2. May indicate the status of one's own spiritual search. See **Water.** 3. Depending on imagery, might symbolize smooth or rough sailing. 4. One who is not navigating, only along for the ride. 5. See **People.** 6. You may also wish to see **Boat.**

SAINT 1. Representative of spirituality. 2. A messenger of spirit. See **Message/Messenger.** 3. Can correspond to truth, wisdom, or guidance. 4. Sometimes is symbolic of a coming birth or death of an individual or a situation/opportunity. 5. Metaphorically, he's a saint = he's a wonderful person. 6. You may also wish to see **People.**

SALAD 1. Often associated with literal dietary recommendations. See **Food.** 2. Could indicate a pleasing combination of ideas that will be beneficial. 3. Lettuce may symbolize money or could be encouraging delegation and cooperation (i.e., let us).

SALT 1. Associated with making something more palatable. 2. That which preserves. 3. Metaphorically, can be used as follows: he's an old salt = an old sailor, or he's someone who has been around for a long time; salty humor = a sharp wit; she's the salt of the earth = she's a very upstanding person; take it with a grain of salt = believe it with a little skepticism and objectivity; to rub salt in the wound = to make things even worse. 4. Could suggest the need to add spice to one's life. 5. May be a literal dietary suggestion regarding too much salt (i.e., eating a plate of salt). 6. Might be associated with the need to become more conscious in one's activities (i.e., smelling salts). 7. Throwing salt over one's shoulder is associated with keeping away evil influences. 8. Biblically, associated with Lot's wife (Genesis 19:26). 9. You may also wish to see **Food.**

SAMSON 1. An archetype of strength. 2.

Could indicate physical strength under spiritual direction. 3. May indicate blindness. 4. Might be associated with the loss of ideas (i.e., Samson had his head shaved). 5. See also **Hair** or **Baldness.**

SAND 1. The passage (sands) of time. See **Time.** 2. That which is eternal. 3. See **Desert.** 4. That which gets into one's shoes (i.e., tiny irritants that get in the way of where one is going). 5. Biblically, the sand relates to the descendants of Abraham (see Genesis 32:12). 6. Associated with ancient time or, in an hourglass, time running out. 7. Could correspond to the edge of consciousness. See **Beach.** 8. Might be associated with unsure footing or an unstable foundation. 9. You may also wish to see **Shore.**

SANDAL 1. Symbolic of a journey, an independent idea, or a lone experience. 2. See also **Shoes.** 3. You may also wish to see **Feet.** 4. Might be suggestive of a temporary experience.

SARAH 1. Biblically, may symbolize spiritual regeneration. 2. Might be associated with patience. 3. Could represent the birth of a new idea. 4. Might correspond to an unexpected pregnancy. See **Birth.**

SATAN 1. Can correspond to one's lowest nature or base materiality. 2. The personification of evil. See **Evil.** 3. Temptation. 4. Could represent the dark side of one's nature (i.e., hatred, jealousy, etc.). 5. The shadow part of oneself. See **Shadow.** 6. Wickedness. 7. Liturgically, associated with Lucifer, the chief of the fallen angels. See **Devil.** 8. May be symbolic of harsh words, unkind thoughts, or that which is oppressive. 9. See also **People.**

SATURN ♄ 1. Could correspond to determination and perseverance. 2. Associated with starting over, cleansing, sudden changes, or a rebirth. 3. In Roman mythology, the god of agriculture. See **Mythology (Roman and Greek).** 4. Sixth planet from the Sun; second largest planet in our solar system; recognized by the rings of Saturn. Has a rotation year of 29.5 years. 5. Astrologically, associated with Capricorn and Aquarius. See **Astrology.** 6. Metaphysically, associated with the first chakra (gonads). See **Chakras.**

SATYR 1. Associated with Greek mythology; that which is part human and part goat. See **Goat.** 2. May indicate an oversexed male. 3. You may also wish to see **People, Animals,** and **Mythology (Roman and Greek).**

SAVAGES 1. Portions of oneself that are at war. See **Shadow.** 2. Could represent any group environment and the negative interpersonal relationships. 3. That which is primitive or that which focuses upon personal survival. 4. Associated with being uncivilized, ill-tempered, or inhumane. See **Beast.** 5. See also **People.**

SCAFFOLD 1. Associated with something that is undergoing construction, change, or renovation. See **Contractor.** 2. Could be associated with something that needs to be improved, updated, or given a new face (i.e., appearance). 3. A temporary support or framework. 4. Might symbolize one's skeletal system. See **Skeleton.**

SCALDED 1. Symbolic of a hot or a burning issue. See **Burn.** 2. Metaphorically, to be scalded = to get into trouble. 3. Can be associated with extreme anger, frustration, or irritation. 4. Might indicate suppressing one's emotions. 5. Depending on imagery, you may also wish to see **Fire.**

SCALES (FISH) 1. That which covers the situation. 2. The spiritual portions of oneself. 3. A shiny idea. 4. Could represent that which appears brilliant but is a little slippery. 5. Associated with spiritual protection or defense. See **Armor** and **Clothes.** 6. See also **Fish.**

SCALES (METHOD OF WEIGHING) 1. Metaphor for judgment, balance, or decision. 2. Corresponds to worthiness or unworthiness. 3. Metaphorically, to turn the scales = to achieve a decision in one's own favor. 4. Astrologically, one of the twelve signs of the zodiac. See **Libra.**

SCALP 1. Associated with thinking and ideas. See **Head** and **Hair.** 2. See also **Body.** 3. Metaphorically, may be associated with being cheated, or the act of taking advantage of someone.

SCAR 1. Associated with that which has been blemished, wounded, or marred. See **Wound.** 2. Can correspond to a problem or difficulty resulting from past behavior, activity, thoughts, or emotions. 3. Represents the memory of a past experience. 4. That which blemishes the current situation (i.e., old thought patterns). 5. Can be associated with that which has lasting impact. 6. May indicate the inability to release old emotions or thoughts. 7. You may also wish to see **Body.**

SCARAB 1. Associated with rebirth, prosperity, resurrection, abundance, long life, and good luck. 2. Symbolic of Egypt. See **Egypt/Egyptian.** 3. You may also wish to see **Bug** and **Beetle.**

SCARECROW 1. Can correspond to something that has a frightening appearance but is actually harmless. 2. May be associated with a partial being or someone who is not all there. 3. Can indicate the need to stand guard or to be on guard, at least for the sake of appearance. 4. In literature, associated with one's own search for inner wisdom and enlightenment (i.e., *The Wizard of Oz*). 5. See also **People.** 6. You may also wish to see **Brain.**

SCARED 1. One of the four basic emotions (glad, mad, sad, and scared). See **Emotion.** 2. May be associated with activities or interactions causing one to be afraid, startled, anxious, or frightened. 3. Metaphorically, he was able to scare up a little business = he found or produced some business.

SCARLET LETTER 1. In literature, associated with adultery (Hawthorne's *The Scarlet Letter*). 2. Can correspond to compromising one's principles or, to selling oneself. See **Prostitute.** 3. Might be associated with the letter A. 4. Might be associated with the color red. See **Colors.**

SCHOOL 1. Associated with the lessons and education provided by daily life. 2. Can correspond to the need or the opportunity to expand one's thoughts, education, or consciousness in a particular situation. 3. What one has to teach to others or what one needs to learn from others. See **Teacher.** 4. Awareness or knowledge from a higher realm. 5. May be symbolic of unresolved issues or experiences from the past. 6. That which can provide discipline to the untrained or immature mind. 7. That which brings unrelated individuals together for a common goal. See **Building.** 8. Can symbolize one's own thirst for knowledge. 9. Metaphorically, a school of fish = a large group of fish that swim together in unison. See also **Test.** 10. Often associated with one's current situation or working environment.

SCISSORS 1. Can correspond to one's own cutting or hostile remarks or activities. 2. Could indicate what needs to be cut out of one's life, activities, or interactions. 3. Associated with that which may be harming or cutting oneself. 4. Can represent a severing or a death. See **Death.** 5. The desire to cut loose from that which binds. 6. To be released from a situation or a relationship. 7. Two independent activities or individuals that, when brought together, may accomplish something that neither may do individually; a union. 8. May be associated with feeling cut off from others or from the surrounding environment. 9. Associated with aggressive male sexuality. See **Phallus.**

SCORPIO ♏ 1. Eighth sign of the zodiac, corresponding to October 23–November 21. 2. Associated with the following positive traits: persistent, discerning, possessing powerful emotions. 3. Associated with the following negative traits: jealous, overly introverted, stubborn. 4. Astrologically, ruled by Pluto and Mars. See **Pluto** and **Mars.** 5. See **Scorpion.** 6. A water sign. See **Water.** 7. See also **Astrology.**

SCORPION 1. Associated with danger; possessing a poisonous sting. 2. Slang for an offensive or annoying person. 3. May correspond to that which is hurtful, bitter, or stinging. 4. Biblically, refers to a whip with spikes. 5. Astrologically, one of the twelve signs of the zodiac. See **Scorpio.**

SCRATCH 1. That which digs, scrapes, or mars. 2. That which is erased or canceled. 3. To err. 4. Metaphorically, can be used as follows: they've only scratched the surface = they've just barely started; she needs to start from scratch = she needs to start over. 5. May be associated with the name of the devil. See **Devil.**

SCREAM 1. A message of extreme pain, anger, or frustration. 2. A shrill or dishar-monious form of expression. 3. Metaphor-ically, that was a scream = that was very funny. 4. May suggest that one is not feeling heard by others. 5. You may also wish to see **Hear.**

SCREW 1. Associated with joining things together. 2. Metaphorically, can be used as follows: she was screwed out of the raise = she was cheated; he has a screw loose = he's not all there mentally; they went off to screw = to have sex; she put the screws on = she put on the pressure.

SCREWDRIVER 1. That which tightens, loosens, joins, or turns. See **Screw.** 2. Can correspond to building an idea; making that which is mental become material. See **Con-tractor.** 3. May represent male sexuality. See **Phallus.** 4. You may also wish to see **Tool.**

SCROLL 1. An important message. See **Message/Messenger.** 2. Represents a for-gotten secret or ancient wisdom. 3. Associ-ated with religious doctrines or sacredness. 4. Rabbinically, represents the five books of Moses; the Torah. 5. Corresponds to laws or customs. 6. You may also wish to see **Book.**

SEA 1. The deepest reaches of the soul, the unconscious, or the emotions. See **Water.** 2. Associated with the source of all life. 3. Can correspond to spiritual depth. 4. Can repre-sent any great quantity or meaningful ex-perience. 5. A sea journey could symbolize an emotional or spiritual experience. See **Journey.** 6. Associated with the feminine. See **Womb.** 7. Might, indicate a depth of in-sight or intuition. 8. You may also wish to see **Boat** and **Sailing.** 9. If there is bad weather, see **Weather.**

SEARCH 1. May be associated with one's life journey. See **Journey.** 2. That which is being or needs to be examined. 3. Could in-dicate self-examination. 4. May suggest un-discovered aspects of oneself. See **House.**

SEASHELL 1. May be associated with inner thoughts or the inner self. 2. Can represent the environment one crawls into for per-sonal protection or safety. 3. That which comes from the source (i.e., the sea). See **Water.** 4. Potential ideas or truths. 5. Ideas, individuals, or activities we may encounter in everyday life. 6. The outer covering or personality shown to the world. See **Clothes** and **Mask.**

SEASONS 1. Corresponds to the appropri-ate or appointed timing. 2. The seasons are associated with the orbit of the earth in re-lationship to the sun:

Fall (or Autumn): The end of an age, ex-perience, or idea. The onslaught of change *or* aging. Corresponds to Sep-tember 21 to December 21.

Spring: A new beginning. A fresh start. That which begins to thrive or prosper. Corresponds to March 21 to June 21.

Summer: The best time. Associated with relaxation, harvest, and warmth: Cor-responds to June 21 to September 21.

Winter: A time of endings. A period of dormancy. Could represent rest or age-less wisdom. Corresponds to Decem-ber 21 to March 21.

3. Associated with the right timing for a spe-cific activity; for example: the seasons of planting. 4. Metaphorically, for a season = for a while; in good season = when the time is right. 5. Could also correspond literally to the specific timing when something will happen or is expected.

SEDUCED 1. To give in to temptation. 2. The act of allowing oneself to be manipulated, lured, or controlled by another. See **Puppet**. 3. Metaphorically, he was seduced into buying it = he was persuaded to buy it. 4. Might correspond to a repressed desire. 5. You may also wish to see **Sex**.

SEED 1. The embryonic form of an idea; thought, relationship, or project. 2. That which contains much more within itself when fully developed and allowed to blossom. 3. Associated with the source or the beginning of anything. 4. Can correspond to that which needs to be sowed, disseminated, or planted. See **Plant**. 5. Biblically, associated with faith or the word of truth. 6. The storehouse of the past from which the future springs forth. 7. Can indicate new beginnings. See **Birth**. 8. Physical, mental, or spiritual children. 9. May correspond to the seed of one's loins; male = sperm, female = eggs. 10. Metaphorically, can be used as follows: he's a bad seed = he's a bad influence; it went to seed = it deteriorated. 11. See also **Garden.** 12. May be associated with karmic memory. See **Karma**.

SELF 1. Corresponds to one's personal identity. 2. May indicate one's qualities, faults, and thoughts. 3. How we see ourselves or how others see us. 4. Associated with one's reputation, individuality, talents, and faults. See **Name**. 5. One's naked self. See **Naked**. 6. You may also wish to see **Shadow, People**, and **Man** or **Woman**.

SEMESTER 1. Associated with a period of learning. See **School**. 2. May be a literal indication of a period of time. 3. You may also wish to see **Time**.

SENSES 1. Associated with the five conscious sensory systems of the body: taste, smell, hearing, touch, and sight. 2. Additional senses include feelings and intuition. See **ESP**. 3. You may also wish to see **Eyes, Ears, Hand, Nose**, and **Mouth**.

SERPENT 1. May represent energy, wisdom, temptation, or power. See **Snake**. 2. See also **Animals**.

SERVANT 1. One who submits to the employ, will, or activities of another. See **Puppet**. 2. Corresponds to devotion, loyalty, assistance, or dedication. 3. May represent the inner call to focus one's own abilities or ideas in the direction of a goal or an idea. 4. Associated with one who would be of service. See **Christ**. 5. See also **People**.

SERVE 1. To assist a greater good or goal. 2. Associated with making one's own will subservient to another person or a specific goal. See **Servant**. 3. Corresponds to carrying out duties or activities due to one's commitment, beliefs, emotional involvement, or servitude. 4. Metaphorically, at one's service = readied to provide assistance.

SEVEN 1. Associated with spiritual forces. 2. Represents the most sacred of all numbers. 3. See **Numerology**.

SEX 1. May correspond to creativity, love, reproduction, or self-gratification. 2. May indicate a close relationship or the need to develop a unified relationship. 3. Can correspond to one's own sexual desires, fears, or frustrations. 4. Associated with energy. 5. See also **Bed/Bedroom**. 6. You may also wish to see **Phallus** or **Womb**.

SHACK 1. A dilapidated idea, situation, or physical condition. See **House**. 2. Can correspond to a neglected physical condition, state of mind, or spiritual life and environment. 3. Metaphorically, to shack up with someone = to live together in a sexual relationship.

SHADE 1. Corresponds to that which is partially hidden, incompletely revealed, or not fully understood. See **Dark**. 2. Could symbolize one's own feelings of being in the dark (i.e., unable to comprehend the situation). 3. Might be associated with one's own shadow. See **Shadow**. 4. Depending upon the imagery, could relate to a place of safety from the heat.

SHADOW 1. A portion of oneself that is partially hidden, denied, or concealed. 2. Psychologically, the repressed, ignored, frustrated, forgotten, or dark side of one's inner nature. See **Unconscious**. 3. Corresponds to that portion of one's inner emotional personality that is projected out to others, causing one to perceive one's own personal issues and shortcomings in other people rather than in oneself. 4. That which is clouded, hard to grasp, or just beyond clear vision. See **Shade**. 5. Might be associated with negative issues, feelings, or emotions. 6. The outer personality attempting to cover one's inner self. See **Beast**. 7. That which is mysterious and hard to grasp. 8. Might represent a half-truth. 9. Could correspond to a faint image or message of that which is to come; a vague indication, omen, or symbol. 10. Metaphorically, to be in the shadow of someone or something = to be so alike and/or harmonious as to be nearly indistinguishable one from the other. 11. Might represent a foreboding sense of darkness, danger, or mystery. 12. See also **People**. 13. You may also wish to see **Subconscious**.

SHAKESPEARE, WILLIAM 1. Associated with communication, especially writing. See **Write**. 2. Could represent an important

message. 3. May be symbolic of one's own career calling (i.e., a writer). 4. May represent England. 5. May be associated with a foreign visitor or travel.

SHAMAN 1. A holy man or woman, spiritual presence, authority, or messenger. See **Holy Man/Holy Woman**. 2. Might be associated with one's own higher self. See **Wise Man/Wise Woman**. 3. One who utilizes the realm of spirits and the subconscious in the healing process. See **Healer**. 4. Could correspond to a spiritual witch doctor. See **Wizard**. 5. You may also wish to see **People**.

SHAMPOO 1. Symbolic of clearing, changing, or improving one's mind. See **Hair**. 2. Can correspond to pondering an idea or a project; i.e., thinking it over in one's head. 3. To rid oneself of old thoughts, habits, ideas, or patterns. 4. May represent preparing for new thoughts or establishing the foundation for an open mind. 5. An attempt to rid oneself of a relationship.

SHARK 1. That which is treacherous or dangerous. 2. Might suggest the need to be ready for an unexpected attack. 3. Metaphorically, a shark = a cheat or a swindler, or one who is extremely adept in one's field. 4. Associated with an evil fish. See **Fish**.

SHAVE 1. May indicate one's desire to be sexually pleasing to the opposite sex. 2. Can correspond to improving one's appearance. 3. You may also wish to see **Hair**.

SHEEP 1. Associated with those who are easily led. See **Lamb**. 2. May indicate that one has been fleeced (i.e., cheated). 3. May be suggestive of being on the spiritual path. See **Shepherd**. 4. You may also wish to see **Animals**.

SHELL 1. Metaphorically, can be used as follows: come out of your shell = don't be so shy and withdrawn; she had to shell it out = she had to pay for it. 2. Can represent the environment one crawls into for personal protection or safety. See **Seashell**. 3. The outer covering or personality one shows to the world. See **Mask**.

SHEPHERD 1. One who takes charge of the situation or experience. 2. Associated with an individual who may bring various ideas or people together into a unified group. 3. Biblically, associated with Jesus. See **Christ**. 4. Metaphorically, to shepherd the situation = to guide, to nurture, or to direct. 5. See also **People**.

SHERIFF 1. Can represent one's own conscience. 2. Associated with lawfulness, regulation, safety, or moral guidelines. See **Police/Police Station**. 3. May correspond to keeping order or the need for control. 4. You may also wish to see **Law**.

SHIELD 1. That which protects or insulates from the environment. See **Armor**. 2. Could be associated with one's words or thoughts. 3. May indicate a battle. See **War**. 4. You may also wish to see **Wall**.

SHIP 1. Corresponds to one's life journey. See **Journey**. 2. Associated with a spiritual voyage or experience. See **Boat**. 3. Can represent a talent, a thought, or an idea that is available for one's use. 4. Literally, may be symbolic of a real journey, vacation, or trip. 5. Metaphorically, waiting for one's ship to come in = waiting for one's good fortune. 6. That which is to be carried abroad. 7. In ancient Egypt, a boat was used for the journey into the afterlife. 8. Might be associated with one who is beginning to explore the realms of spirit or the unconscious. 9. See also **Water**.

SHIPWRECK 1. A potential disaster on one's life journey. See **Journey**. 2. Could indicate a negative emotional confrontation or experience. 3. Depending upon the imagery, you may also wish to see **Weather**. 4. May correspond to an accident. See also **Accident**.

SHIRT 1. The outer personality shown to others. See **Clothes**. 2. One's own thoughts, ideas, or occupation. 3. That which we have put on in everyday life (i.e., thoughts, emotions, fears, ideas, etc.). 4. Metaphorically, can be used as follows: losing one's shirt = to experience a severe financial setback; keep your shirt on = be patient. 5. A white shirt may symbolize a white-collar position or an executive position; a blue shirt may symbolize a blue-collar position or a laborer's position. 6. Biblically, to give one's shirt to another means to provide service, tithes, or assistance to another.

SHIVA 1. In Hinduism, the god of fertility, reproduction, power, transitions, and destruction. See **Hinduism**. 2. One of the Hindu trinity (Brahma, Shiva, and Vishnu). 3. Often symbolized by the phallus. See **Phallus**.

SHOEMAKER 1. Associated with one who helps formulate a plan, an idea, or a sturdy foundation. See **Shoes** and **People**.

SHOES 1. May represent an individual's beliefs, ideas, occupation, foundation, principles, direction, perspective, etc. See **Clothes**. 2. Associated with one's current direction, identity, or journey. See **Direction** and **Journey**. 3. That which insulates oneself from daily life. 4. Metaphorically, can be used as follows: to be in another's shoes = to experience life from another person's perspective; to have the shoe on the other foot

= to experience the situation from a different viewpoint; to fill someone else's shoes = to take his place. 5. Different portions of the shoe may be symbolic of different meanings; for example: the tongue could symbolize one's words; the sole might indicate one's principles or morals, the covering may indicate an outer appearance or an idea. 6. You may also wish to see **Feet** and **Walk.**

SHOOT 1. To attempt to wound, to kill, or to maim. See **Kill.** 2. To put an end to something. 3. Metaphorically, can be used as follows: the boss shot down the idea = the boss verbally attacked it; she shot off her mouth = she said things that should not have been said; his plan was shot through with holes = there were too many problems with it; she shot up the ladder = she rose very quickly. 4. Often associated with verbal aggression or arguments. See also **Gun.**

SHOP 1. Corresponds to choices, making decisions, and having options. 2. May be symbolic of one's business, possibilities, potential ideas, etc. 3. Metaphorically, can be used as follows: they talked shop = they had a business discussion; she set up shop = she started her business. 4. You may also wish to see **Store.**

SHORE 1. The edge of consciousness between emotions or spirit (water) and the physical world (sand). See **Sand** and **Water.** 2. Could be associated with relaxation, calm, joyfulness, or solitary reflection. 3. That which borders levels of one's consciousness or the various aspects of an experience.

SHORT/SHORTS 1. Associated with one's personal identity, philosophy, or direction. See **Clothes** and **Pants.** 2. May indicate that which is not yet grown up or is immature. See **Small.** 3. Metaphorically, can be as fol-

lows: it came up short or fell short = it didn't do what was expected; she was short-changed = she's not very intelligent; being a little short = being low on money; he's short-tempered = he's quick to become angry; that's a shortcut = a quicker direction. 4. Could represent baring oneself or one's direction for public scrutiny. 5. Might correspond to relaxation or the state of being unprepared. 6. You may also wish to see **Leg/Legless.**

SHOULDERS 1. Can correspond to the ability to support oneself or others or to take on responsibilities. See **Arm.** 2. Metaphorically, can be used as follows: to rub shoulders = to associate with famous people; she gave him the cold shoulder = she ignored him; put your shoulder to the wheel = put some effort into it; straight from the shoulder = a very frank discussion; to cry on someone's shoulder = to tell someone your problems. 3. You may also wish to see **Body.**

SHOUT 1. A loud outburst or cry. See **Scream.** 2. Metaphorically, to shout someone down = to talk so loudly that they cannot be heard. 3. Can correspond to words that created quite an uprising. 4. You may wish to see **Mouth.**

SHOWER 1. To be cleansed of old ideas or experiences. 2. Could correspond to an outpouring of some kind, especially emotional. See **Water.** 3. The need to be cleansed of one's current situation or state of mind. See **Clean.** 4. Might correspond to the act of getting rid of prejudices or that which is no longer necessary. 5. Could be a literal symbol of the need for or the act of some type of physical, mental, or spiritual cleansing. 6. Metaphorically, can be used as follows: to take a shower = to suffer a loss; he needs a cold shower = he needs to cool off sexually.

7. You may also wish to see **Nude.**

SHOWING OFF 1. Can correspond to being vain or attempting to draw attention to oneself. 2. Could indicate the need for closer self-examination. See **Nude.** 3. Might indicate that persona we wish the world to see. See **Performance/Performers.**

SHRINK 1. To recoil, cower, or decrease in amount. 2. To lose importance or stature. See **Size.** 3. Whatever is shrinking will have a great deal to do with the symbolism; for example: a shrinking heart may correspond to losing interest in a loved one or it could indicate a physical problem; a shrinking plate could suggest that one is eating too much.

SICKLE 1. May be associated with death. See **Death.** 2. Might correspond to heavy or arduous labor. 3. A hammer and sickle can represent the former Soviet Union (i.e., communism). 4. May correspond to sowing and reaping. See **Plant** and **Karma.**

SIDEWALK 1. Could symbolize one who watches from the sidelines. 2. May indicate one's current path or direction. See **Path.** 3. Might be associated with having a firm footing or a clear sense of direction. 4. You may also wish to see **Walk.**

SIGN 1. A message; often the sign is a literal indication of what one must do (i.e., a stop sign indicates that you stop what you're doing; a yield sign suggests you give in to the wishes of another; go means it's okay to proceed, etc.), but it could have a metaphorical meaning, too. See **Message/Messenger** or **Metaphor.** 2. That which you're supposed to pay attention to. 3. That which may be viewed by anyone. 4. Metaphorically, can be used as follows: to sign something over = to give it away; to sign off = to stop speaking.

5. Depending on imagery you may wish to see **Colors.** 6. Might represent an astrological sign. See **Astrology.**

SIGNATURE 1. Associated with the self. See **Self.** 2. Could correspond to ownership or acceptance. 3. One's personal identity. See **Name.** 4. Depending on imagery, you may wish to see **Write.** 5. Might suggest a prescription or a course of action.

SILHOUETTE 1. Corresponds to the outline or the overview rather than the individual pieces that create the whole. 2. May be associated with looking at things from a limited, one-dimensional perspective. 3. Could represent the dark, shadowy side of a situation or a person. See **Shadow.** 4. You may wish to see **Ghost.**

SILVER 1. Associated with money, prestige, and position. 2. Biblically, a symbol of betrayal (Matthew 26:14–16). 3. See **Colors.**

SING/SINGER 1. Can correspond to self-expression or harmony. 2. May suggest the need to be more joyful. 3. Might be a literal indication of one's own talent. 4. Could indicate the desire to speak out in such a way that others will listen. 5. You may wish to see **Music.**

SINK 1. May symbolize one's emotions or eliminations (i.e., holding them in). See **Plumbing.** 2. Depending on imagery, may suggest that something is going down the drain. See **Drain.** 3. You may also wish to see **Water.**

SINKING 1. May be associated with losing one's footing in a situation. 2. Being engulfed by the experience or your surroundings. See **Quicksand.** 3. Can correspond to depression. 4. Might indicate danger. 5. You may also wish to see **Descend.**

SISTER 1. Often represents one's own relationship or feelings toward a sister, either literal or symbolic. 2. Can indicate a youthful part of oneself (younger sister) or a wiser part (older sister). See **Girl.** 3. A close relationship with one who is like a sister. 4. Could indicate a suggestion or a warning in terms of your sister's welfare. 5. A younger sister might correspond to one's inner child (see **Child**), or one's shadow (see **Shadow**). 6. See also **People.**

SIX 1. Associated with symmetry and harmony. 2. See **Numerology.**

SIZE 1. Associated with the magnitude, importance, or condition of an activity, a person, a memory, an experience, etc. 2. A large object may be that which one associates with being important or that makes one feel overwhelmed. See **Large.** 3. A large object can also represent that which is before oneself or in the future. 4. A small object can correspond to something that is overlooked, considered insignificant, or that is underdeveloped. See **Small.** 5. A small object can also represent that which is behind oneself or in the past. 6. That which is shrinking corresponds to that which is lessening in importance. See **Shrink.** 7. That which is growing is suggestive of that which is becoming more important. See **Grow.** 8. Something thin may be associated with a meager idea, plan, or situation. It could also represent a personal desire for weight loss. See **Thin.** 9. Something fat can correspond to that which is excessive, overly pronounced, or very productive; or it could symbolize one's poor self–image. See **Fat.** 10. Metaphorically, to size up a situation = to assess the situation.

SKATE 1. Can be associated with freedom, smooth sliding, or gliding through any difficulty. See **Sliding/Slipping.** 2. Might correspond to being on thin ice (i.e., in a potentially disastrous or harmful situation). 3. May indicate skill and agility. 4. You may also wish to see **Sports, Ice,** and **Journey.**

SKELETON 1. That which is the supporting framework. See **Bone.** 2. Can indicate that something needs to be further fleshed out. 3. Metaphorically, having a skeleton in one's closet = having a family secret one wishes kept hidden. 4. May be associated with death or the end of something. 5. You may also wish to see **Back/Backbone** and **People.**

SKI 1. Can be associated with freedom, smooth sliding, or gliding through any difficulty. See **Sliding/Slipping.** 2. Corresponds to being under one's own power. 3. May indicate skill and agility. 4. You may also wish to see **Sports** and **Snow.**

SKIN 1. Associated with the self. See **Self.** 2. Corresponds to one's situation or the environment in which one lives. 3. May symbolize one's sensitivity or lack of it. 4. Metaphorically, can be used as follows: give me some skin = slap my palm; by the skin of one's teeth = just barely; a skin game = a swindle; a skinflint = a very cheap person; it's no skin off her back = it won't affect her; save your skin = save yourself; he's thick-skinned = he's not sensitive. 5. You may also wish to see a corresponding part of the body; for example, see **Back/Backbone.** 6. See also **Body.**

SKULL 1. Can be associated with a warning, thievery (i.e., pirates), or danger. 2. May suggest that more thought is required. You may wish to see **Head.** 3. Metaphorically, having a thick skull = one who is dimwitted. 4. May be associated with death or the end of something. 5. See also **Skeleton.**

SKUNK 1. Might represent a stinky situation or that which creates a real stink. See **Nose.** 2. That which is repulsive. 3. What's driving you away. 4. Metaphorically, can be used as follows: to skunk someone = to have beaten them at an activity; he's a skunk = he's an offensive or unusual individual. 5. Because of its color, may correspond with that which is seen as right or wrong, black or white. 6. See also **Animals** and **Smell.**

SKY 1. Can indicate the sky is the limit or where your sights are. 2. Associated with higher thought or spirituality. 3. The condition of the sky will have a great deal to do with the symbolism; you may also wish to see **Weather.** 4. That which is heavenly or heaven-sent. See **Heaven.** 5. Metaphorically, out of the clear blue sky = it happened unexpectedly; the sky is the limit = anything is possible. 6. You may also wish to see **Air.**

SKYSCRAPER 1. May correspond to great heights, financial stability, a lofty goal, or an enormous project. 2. The appearance of the skyscraper will have much to do with the imagery. See **Building.** 3. Might be associated with one's higher self or inner wisdom. 4. That which is strong or domineering. 5. That which rises above the situation or the surrounding environment. See **Mountain.** 6. Could be associated with an ascent (i.e., a raise, spiritual progress, gaining a new level of awareness, etc.). See **Ascend.**

SLAVE 1. Can correspond to one who is completely dominated by the will of another. See **Puppet.** 2. One who is without personal freedom. 3. Associated with one who submits to the employ, will, or activi-

ties of another. See **Servant**. 4. Metaphorically, she works like a slave = she works continuously (voluntarily or involuntarily).

SLEEP 1. Associated with being unconscious to the external environment. 2. Could correspond to the need for more rest. 3. Might indicate laziness. 4. You may wish to see **Bed/Bedroom**. 5. In literature, associated with *Sleeping Beauty*, the internal feminine waiting to be awakened. See **Woman**. 6. You may also wish to see **Dreaming**.

SLEEPING BEAUTY 1. In literature, associated with the archetypal female just waiting to be awakened. 2. Can correspond to the positive feminine traits that may be brought to the surface (i.e., compassion, sensitivity, intuition). See **Woman**. 3. Might indicate laziness.

SLIDING/SLIPPING 1. Depending on imagery, may be associated with smooth sailing, freedom, or losing control of oneself or the situation. 2. Could indicate the need to watch where you are going. 3. Might represent gliding through an experience. 4. Possible warning of a tricky situation. 5. Metaphorically, can be used as follows: to let something slip = to say something that should not have been said; he slipped up = he made a mistake; she slipped one over on us = she tricked us; they gave us the slip = they got away. 6. May be associated with one who is backsliding. 7. Depending upon what is slipping, you may wish to see **Walk** or **Drive**.

SLOT MACHINE 1. Can correspond to taking a gamble. See **Gambling**. 2. Often associated with Las Vegas, See **Las Vegas**. 3. Might indicate wasting one's money or resources.

SMALL 1. Can be associated with feelings of smallness or inadequacy. See **Size**. 2. That which is underdeveloped or in the growing stages. See **Seed**. 3. Can correspond to that which is insignificant, minuscule, or hardly worth the effort. 4. Might indicate that which is in the past.

SMELL 1. A bad smell can correspond to that which is unpleasant, unfair, or stinks. 2. A good smell might suggest that which is good, positive, or fair. 3. Depending on imagery, could indicate one who is overly inquisitive or a spy. See **Nose**. 4. One of the five senses.

SMILE 1. Corresponds to joy, happiness, or satisfaction. 2. That which is favorable. 3. A sign of welcome or approval. 4. You may also wish to see **Face, Laugh**, or **Mouth**.

SMOKE/SMOKING 1. That which goes up in smoke. 2. Can indicate a lack of clarity or insight. 3. Associated with a smoke screen. 4. May be a literal warning about smoking. 5. Metaphorically, to smoke something out = to force it into the open. 6. You may also wish to see **Air, Clouds/Cloudy**, or **Cigar/Cigarette**.

SNAKE 1. May represent wisdom, energy, temptation, or power. 2. Often associated with healing, enlightenment, mysticism, or medicine (i.e., the caduceus is a winged staff with two serpents and is symbolic of the medical profession). 3. Can represent harmful or threatening conditions, emotions, or individuals. See **Animals.** 4. A snake biting its tail can symbolize wholeness, self-realization, and the eternal. See **Circle** and **God.** 5. May be associated with temptation, sex, and physical desires. 6. Metaphorically, a snake in the grass = a person or a situation that is dangerous although it may appear

harmless or hidden. 7. Associated with pure and creative energy (i.e., in mysticism, the symbol for the kundalini). 8. May correspond to one who is treacherous or deceitful. 9. That which may transform itself (i.e., shedding skin). 10. Biblically, associated with the Fall of man. See **Adam.** 11. May be symbolic of male sexuality. See **Phallus.**

SNEAK 1. Can correspond to something that you want kept secret or undetected by others. 2. An unknown portion of oneself. See **Shadow.** 3. You may also wish to see **Hide.**

SNORKEL 1. Could be associated with being overwhelmed or engulfed by one's experience or emotions. See **Swim.** 2. Depending on imagery, may correspond to a spiritual journey. See **Journey.** 3. You may also wish to see **Water.**

SNOW 1. Associated with frozen or unchanging emotions. See **Weather.** 2. Often represents purity. 3. Can indicate emotions that have completely overpowered or covered a situation. 4. Feeling left out in the cold. 5. You may also wish to see **Ice.**

SOAP 1. Could indicate the need for a cleansing (physically, mentally, or spiritually). See **Bath** or **Wash.** 2. Metaphorically, can be used as follows: to soft-soap someone = to flatter them; to stand on one's soapbox = to give one's personal opinion. 3. Whatever one is doing with the soap is very significant; for example: washing your mouth indicates that you said something that you ought not to have said; washing your hands could imply guilt or giving up on the situation, etc. 4. You may also wish to see **Clean.**

SODA POP 1. Depending upon the imagery, may be a literal dietary suggestion that one is consuming too much soda. 2. Because of the bubbles, associated with that which is under pressure or bottled up (i.e., emotions). 3. Depending on imagery, you may also wish to see **Bubbles.**

SOLDIER 1. Corresponds to one who is in the employ of a higher authority or purpose. 2. Can be associated with duty. 3. Associated with fighting for what's right. See **War.** 4. Metaphorically, he's a good little soldier = he does whatever he's told. See **Puppet.** 5. May be associated with an aggressive male nature. See **Phallus.** 6. See also **People.**

SOLITAIRE 1. May correspond to being alone, lonely, or independent. 2. Symbolic of the situation or experience one has dealt oneself. See **Cards.** 3. Might indicate how one plays the game of life. See **Game.**

SOLOMON 1. Associated with wisdom and justice. See **Judge.** 2. Could symbolize absolute authority. 3. Might symbolize the manifestation of spirituality on the earth (i.e., he built the temple).

SON 1. Often suggests aspects of that relationship you possess with your own son (i.e., how your son appears may be symbolic of your attitude and feelings toward him). 2. Could indicate a suggestion or a warning in terms of your child's welfare. 3. Associated with that childish part of oneself. See **Child.** 4. Metaphorically, favorite son = the favored male in any group; son of a gun = exclamation of surprise. 5. May be symbolic of youthful masculinity. See **Man.** 6. That part of yourself that may still need direction. 7. See also **People.** 8. Might represent the Son of God. See **Christ.**

SONG 1. Associated with music and har-

mony. See **Music.** 2. Metaphorically, can be used as follows: she got it for a song = she purchased it very cheaply; he gave the boss a song and dance = he gave the boss excuses. 3. See also **Sing/Singer.**

SORCERER/SORCERY 1. That which is enchanted, magical, or mysterious. 2. Bringing other levels of reality into the physical. 3. May indicate the process of making ideas come to fruition. 4. See **Witch** or **Wizard.** 5. You may also wish to see **People.**

SORE 1. That which is bothersome (physically, mentally, or spiritually). See **Wound.** 2. Could indicate an irritant that has gotten under one's skin. 3. Associated with something wounded or bruised. 4. Representative of sadness or sorrow. 5. Metaphorically, can be used as follows: she was sore = she was angry; that project is sorely advised = it is not a good idea; he sorely needs money = he really needs money.

SOUL 1. Associated with the spiritual part of oneself. 2. The higher self or the perfectly realized inner self. 3. That which is immortal, selfless, loving, compassionate, and godlike. See **Christ.** 4. The true inner individuality of a person. See **Self.** 5. Might correspond to that part of oneself that is apart from the physical body. See **Ghost.** 6. Metaphysically, associated with one's spiritual nature, the journey of the soul, and the attainment of self-awareness through experience. See **Journey.** 7. Metaphorically, she sold her soul = she became subservient to another (i.e., giving up her own aspirations and goals).

SOUP 1. Could be a literal dietary recommendation. See **Food.** 2. Might be precognitive regarding the possibility of approaching illness (i.e., seeing oneself eating chicken soup). 3. Metaphorically, can be used as follows: the car has really been souped up = the car has been turned into a racing car; they're all in the soup = they're all in the problem together; the sky was as thick as soup = there was a lot of fog. 4. That which promotes healing.

SOUTH 1. Corresponds to the body and sexuality. 2. Metaphysically, associated with the lower self. 3. May indicate materiality or past experience. 4. Associated with the Confederacy. 5. See also **Direction.**

SPACE 1. That which is above the earth. See **Sky.** 2. The universe that is without limits, encompassing all possibilities. See **Universe.** 3. Might suggest an appropriate waiting period between events. 4. See also **Air.**

SPACE SHIP 1. Could indicate an unusual or an alien idea. See **Alien.** 2. That which is out of place or from another environment. 3. Associated with a message from another realm or another level of the mind. See **Message/Messenger.** 4. May be associated with a foreign or an unknown activity or experience. 5. A lofty idea or project. See **Airplane.**

SPADE 1. Can correspond to that which is sterilized or no longer productive. 2. A tool for digging or uncovering something buried. 3. Might suggest the need to cultivate oneself. See **Field.** 4. Metaphorically, to call a spade a spade = say exactly what you think. 5. Associated with a suit (often the highest; i.e., trump) in playing cards. See **Cards.** 6. Sometimes, the ace of spades is considered the card of death or disaster.

SPAIN 1. Corresponds primarily to whatever an individual thinks of Spain or the Spanish (i.e., associated with discovery, dancing, the Mediterranean, war, etc.). 2. May be indicative of a foreign visitor or travel.

SPEECH 1. Can indicate one's sincerity, integrity, quality of voice, professional mannerisms, etc. 2. Associated with communicating one's thoughts, words, or feelings. 3. May be suggestive of a literal message. See **Message/Messenger.** 4. Might be associated with how one hears or is heard by others. See **Hear.**

SPEED 1. Associated with acceleration. 2. Going too fast symbolizes getting out of control in certain aspects of life. 3. The need to slow down in life. 4. Could be associated with too much sugar or alcohol in the system. See **Food.** 5. If too slow, something is impeding energy or movement or it could indicate poor dietary habits. 6. You may also wish to see **Automobile.**

SPIDER 1. That which lures and traps. See **Bug.** 2. Associated with one who spins a web of deceit, intrigue, or falsehood. See **Web.** 3. Can be a warning sign of entrapment. 4. Might be symbolic of widowhood or death. See **Death.** 5. Depending on imagery, you may also wish to see **Bite.**

SPINE 1. Associated with strength and the ability to carry one's load. 2. That which one has on their back. See **Back/Backbone.** 3. Where one gets support (the condition of the back may be very symbolic of the kind of support one is getting). 4. Metaphorically, can be used as follows: he is spineless = he is unable to speak up or take a position about anything. 5. You may also wish to see **Skeleton.**

SPIRIT/SPIRITS 1. Associated with one's true nature or inner self. See **Soul.** 2. The motivating influence or force that permeates a specific activity. 3. That which is somewhat illusory to the material world. See **Ghost.** 4. May be associated with spirits (i.e., liquor). See **Alcohol.** 5. Might correspond to that which is animated. 6. The underlying force of everything. 7. Liturgically, associated with the Word of God or the Holy Spirit. See **God.**

SPIT/SPITTOON 1. Suggests something unpleasant that is ejected from one's mouth (i.e., harsh words). 2. Could correspond to insults. 3. A spittoon is that which contains the useless or the discarded. See **Garbage.** 4. You may also wish to see **Mouth.**

SPOON 1. Corresponds to one's dietary habits. 2. Could represent stirring things up. 3. Associated with receiving or giving information in small doses. 4. Metaphorically, can be used as follows: to be born with a silver spoon in one's mouth = to have good luck or fortune; spooning = to kiss or make out; to be spoon fed = to be given small doses or to be treated like a child; he spoons it out = he gives it out (i.e., criticism). 5. The condition of the spoon may be symbolic of one's current station in life. 6. You may also wish to see **Eat.**

SPORTS 1. Associated with the game of life. See **Game.** 2. Often symbolic of one's own group activities (i.e., work, family, etc.). 3. The activity in the imagery may display one's own propensity or lack of it for cooperation, teamwork, sportsmanship conduct, winning and losing, etc. 4. May indicate the act of competing with oneself. 5. Might be suggestive of exercise, relaxation, or getting out of one's normal routine. 6. May represent one's physical health (i.e., stamina, endurance, etc.). 7. Metaphorically, may be used as follows: she's a real sport = she's really easy to

get along with; he just made sport of it = he just made fun of it; they're just poor sports = they don't like to lose; she sported a new coat = she wore a new coat. 8. You may also wish to see **Baseball** or **Football.**

SPOT 1. That which is not pure, whole, or without blemish. 2. Metaphorically, can be used as follows: it needs a spot check = it needs to be examined; X marks the spot = it's right here; I spotted her some money = I gave her some money. 3. You may also wish to see **Colors.**

SPOTLIGHT 1. Pay attention to that which is highlighted. 2. Associated with that which is important. 3. See **Light** or **Lamp.** 4. Corresponds to the ability or the need to focus on the real situation or problem. 5. Metaphorically, that was in the spotlight = everybody noticed it. 6. Might suggest that all eyes are watching you. 7. Could correspond to the need to investigate or scrutinize.

SPRING 1. Associated with the time of new beginnings, projects, or ideas. See **Seasons.** 2. Metaphorically, to spring at or on = to acquire very quickly, or to move toward; to spring a leak = to start leaking suddenly; to spring from jail = to get out of jail. 3. Life after a period of dormancy.

SQUARE 1. Can correspond to one who is out of touch with contemporary life. 2. That which is symmetrical, equal, balanced, and direct. 3. That which is elementary and practical. 4. Metaphorically, can be used as follows: she's been squared away = she's been taken care of; he's a square peg in a round hole = he's in the wrong place (i.e., doesn't fit in); that's fair and square = that treats everyone equally; they're going to square off = they're getting ready to argue; three square meals a day = three wholesome and complete meals. 5. Might be associated with the four elements: air, earth, fire, and water 6. Could be associated with four in numerology. See **Numerology.** 7. You may also wish to see **Box.**

SQUASH 1. Metaphorically, to squash something = to silence, suppress, beat, or squeeze. 2. Depending on imagery, might indicate the fact that one is retaining water or emotions. 3. You may also wish to see **Vegetables.**

SQUIRREL 1. Can be associated with high energy and speed. 2. Might represent the act of saving or hoarding. 3. Metaphorically, he's squirrelly = he's a wimp. 4. See also **Animals.**

STAGE 1. That which is shown to the outside world. See **Acting/Actor** and **Actress Performer.** 2. The condition of the stage may indicate the condition of the individual physically, mentally, or spiritually. See **Body.** 3. Associated with something about to go public. See **Platform.** 4. May represent one's need or desire to be the center of attention. 5. Where one's state of mind is currently focused. 6. Corresponds to that which is currently being organized, planned, or thought out. 7. Metaphorically, he always takes center stage = he always tries to be in the center of attention or he always makes it appear as though he's the most important.

STAIRS 1. Associated with rising or descending to another level (i.e., in consciousness, awareness, success, spiritually, etc.). Depending on imagery, see **Ascend** or **Descend.** 2. Can correspond to the need to take life one step at a time, or to the fact that one has missed a step. 3. May suggest a journey to the higher self or higher mind. 4. You may also wish to see **House.**

STAMP 1. May represent the need to send a message or to communicate. 2. That which is crushed or held down. 3. A distinguishing symbol or mark indicating ownership. 4. Metaphorically, to rubber-stamp something = to give it automatic approval (i.e., without even looking at it). 5. You may wish to see **Letter.**

STAPLE/STAPLER 1. That which holds or binds things together or shut. 2. May indicate a necessary aspect or ingredient. 3. You may wish to see **Desk.**

STAR 1. Can represent dreams, aspirations, ideals, or hopes. 2. Associated with omens or messages, especially from a higher realm. See **Message/Messenger.** 3. Metaphorically, a star = someone who has excelled tremendously or someone who is the center of attention (see **People**); to thank one's stars = to be grateful for one's situation or experience; stars and stripes = the United States. 4. Associated with that which is brilliant or exceptional. 5. A five-pointed star can symbolize the physical senses, human experiences, or the human body. 6. A six-pointed star may represent Judaism. (See **Star of David.**) 7. A seven-pointed star can correspond to the spiritual centers or chakras. See **Chakras.** 8. Liturgically, a nine-pointed star may represent the fruits of the spirit: love, joy, peace, long-suffering, gentleness, goodness, faith, meekness, and temperance (Galatians 5:22–23); or, the trifold nature of God, man, or the third dimension. 9. That which is bright. 10. A falling star can correspond to a death, a demotion, or a descent. See **Death** and **Descend.** 11. A rising star can represent a bright idea, a favored person, or a promotion. See **Ascend.** 12. Biblically, a star corresponds to the birth of Christ. See **Christ.** 13. Associated with seventeen in the tarot. See **Tarot.** 14. See also individual numbers corresponding to the number of points of the star. See **Numerology**.

STAR OF DAVID 1. Associated with Judaism. See **Judaism**. 2. Can represent a specific destiny or a chosen people/experience. 3. The six points of the two interwoven triangles represent the six days of Creation. 4. See also **Star**.

STARCH 1. Can correspond to that which is stiff and unmoving. 2. Could indicate one who is stuffy or too formal. 3. You may also wish to see **Laundry**. 4. If one is eating starch, it might suggest that one's diet is either lacking or overly abundant in starch.

STARFISH 1. Could correspond to spiritual pursuits or ideals. 2. Might suggest dreams or aspirations. See **Star**. 3. May be associated with regeneration or self-healing. 4. Because of the number of arms, may be representative of five. See **Numerology**. 5. You may also wish to see **Fish** and **Water**.

STATUE 1. That which is immobile, immovable, and unchanging. 2. May be symbolic of someone who has been put on a pedestal. 3. Corresponds to that which has been raised up on a platform. See **Platform**. 4. Goals, aspirations, or wishes. 5. A part of oneself that is lifeless. 6. The physical manifestation of an idea. 7. The desire to make immortal and unchanging a thought, a dream, a wish, an emotion, or a person. 8. That which is unaffected by the outside environment.

STATUE OF LIBERTY 1. Associated with the United States of America. 2. Symbolic of liberty, freedom, independence, and hope. 3. May correspond to new beginnings, dreams, or insights. 4. May indicate domes-

tic travel. 5. You may also wish to see **Statue**.

STEAL 1. To take that which does not belong to you. See **Thief**. 2. Metaphorically, can be used as follows: she stole a glance at him = she looked at him when he wasn't watching; you've stolen my heart = I've fallen in love with you (perhaps unexpectedly); he stole home = in baseball, he scored when the other team wasn't expecting it.

STEAM 1. Associated with the release of pent-up aggressive emotions or words. 2. The transformation of one substance to another. 3. Could correspond to water vapor (i.e., a spiritual essence). See **Water**. 4. You may also wish to see **Smoke/Smoking**.

STEEL 1. That which is solid, firm, immovable, and lasting. 2. Could indicate strong convictions. 3. Might be a pun on the act of stealing. 4. You may also wish to see **Iron.**

STEERING WHEEL 1. Corresponds to that which controls one's direction. See **Direction.** 2. Having someone else drive your vehicle might be associated with giving the control of your life to another. See **Automobile.** 3. Associated with where one is being taken for a ride.

STEPS 1. Usually associated with progression (ascension) or regression (descension). See **Stairs** or **Ladder**. 2. Can correspond to one's life journey. See **Journey.** 3. Metaphorically, can be used as follows: she's out of step = she's not acting in accord with the rest of us; step by step = one segment at a time; step up to the bench = approach the bench; watch your step = watch what you're doing or where you're going; he stepped down = he resigned; we're stepping out today = we're going out together today (i.e., a date). 4. Can symbolize doing things in order. 5. You may also wish to see **Walk.**

STEREO 1. Can correspond to being in the midst of everything. 2. May symbolize balance and harmony. 3. Suggestive of self-expression. 4. You may also wish to see **Music.**

STETHOSCOPE 1. Associated with that which measures love or emotional outpouring. 2. Can measure the health of one's emotions, relationships, or physical well-being. 3. Corresponds to rhythms, especially of the spiritual life. 4. Could be a literal suggestion to slow down, watch your pace, or to see a doctor. 5. You may also wish to see **Heart.**

STICK 1. The type of stick is highly significant; for example: a staff may symbolize leadership; a wand could indicate limitless possibilities; a pointed stick might represent a sharp remark; a spear could symbolize a warlike environment, etc. 2. Could be associated with the staff of life. 3. Metaphorically, can be used as follows: to stick to or by = to remain firm in one's principles or support; they live in the sticks = they live in the country; to stick with = to stand by, or to make someone else pay; to stick up = to rob; to be stuck on = to have a crush on someone; sticks and stones = things that are more harmful than words. 4. May correspond to male sexuality. See **Phallus.**

STILL 1. Associated with alcohol. See **Alcohol.** 2. Can correspond to that which is bottled up (i.e., emotions). 3. Could indicate something in the process of development, fermentation, or distillation (i.e., an idea). 4. That which is illegal or unlawful.

STOCKINGS 1. May be associated with

ideas, principles, or direction. See **Shoes** and **Feet.** 2. You may also wish to see **Clothes.**

STOMACH 1. Associated with digestion and assimilation (i.e., food, ideas, emotions, etc.). 2. Metaphorically, can be used as follows: she doesn't have the stomach for it = she can't handle it. 3. Can correspond to acceptance (good assimilation) or rejection (upset stomach) of an idea or an experience. 4. May literally symbolize diet. You may wish to see **Food.** 5. Could symbolize personal constitution. 6. See also **Body.** 7. Might be associated with the adrenals or third chakra. See **Adrenals.**

STONE 1. A symbol of power and foundation. See **Rock.** 2. For a listing of precious stones and jewels, see **Jewels/ Jewelry.** 3. That which is ageless, timeless, or eternal. 4. Metaphorically, to cast the first stone = the first to criticize or pass judgment; leaving no stone unturned = doing everything that can be done; a stone's throw = very close in proximity. 5. Biblically, to sentence to death. See **Kill.**

STOP 1. Associated with a message. See **Message/Messenger.** 2. Might correspond to danger, the need for personal caution, or the indication to stop what you are doing. See **Danger.** 3. Depending on imagery, you may wish to see **Traffic Light** or **Sign.**

STORE 1. A place where one might buy any need, idea, or possibility (i.e., physical: literal diet or food for thought; mental: a new image or attitude; spiritual needs: where to search next in one's journey). 2. What one is accustomed to providing for oneself (i.e., old thoughts, attitudes, ideas, etc.). You may also wish to see **Building** and **Shop.** 3. Being in an old-fashioned store could represent ideas that are outdated or, if they appear to be antiques, they could be very valuable. See **Antiques.** 4. Metaphorically, in store = that which is available or the resulting consequences.

STORK 1. Associated with a new beginning or birth. See **Birth.** 2. Could indicate the arrival of a new project, idea, or activity. 3. You may also wish to see **Bird.**

STORM 1. Challenges or difficulties. 2. Represents an emotional or mental state of mind. See **Weather.** 3. An environmental (i.e., work, home, etc.) upheaval, outbreak, or disturbance of some kind. 4. Can correspond to anger and aggression.

STOVE 1. Can correspond to an idea or a creative solution that is cooking. See **Cook.** 2. May indicate that which is undergoing a process of transformation. 3. Metaphorically, putting something on the back burner = setting it aside for a time. 4. Might represent that which is undergoing fire or heat. See **Fire.** 5. Can symbolize continuous labor (i.e., slaving over a hot stove).

STRANGER 1. Often corresponds to those portions of oneself that have been ignored, overlooked, or suppressed. See **Shadow.** 2. That which is unusual, unfamiliar, or unexpected. 3. Could correspond to being alienated from oneself or from another. 4. An unknown aspect (talent, trait, etc.) of oneself. 5. Might suggest alienation, withdrawal, or divorce. 6. You may also wish to see **People.**

STRAW 1. Can correspond to that which is meaningless or worthless. 2. Metaphorically, grasping at straws = trying anything to succeed, regardless of its uselessness. 3. A field of straw could suggest a harvest. See **Field** and **Plant.** 4. A drinking straw may symbolize

that which one uses to suck up. See **Drink**.

STRAWBERRY 1. Associated with an individual's own feelings for or experiences with strawberries. 2. May be a dietary recommendation for more fruit in one's diet. See **Fruit** and **Food**. 3. May indicate a sweet and perhaps harmless temptation.

STREET 1. Represents one's current situation, experience, or journey. See **Journey**. 2. See also **Road**. 3. Metaphorically, the man in the street = the average person. 4. The condition of the street and one's direction may have a great deal to do with the symbology; for example: a street full of holes may indicate one's current plan is full of holes; taking a right turn may suggest you're doing the right thing (whereas left may connote wrong), etc.

STRING 1. Metaphorically, can be used as follows: stringing someone along = playing with them emotionally; to pull some strings = to make things happen through another's influence; she's on a string = she does what she's told; he has a shoestring budget = he has very little money. 2. May suggest that which binds or connects. 3. Can correspond to the feeling of being tied up in knots. See **Knot**. 4. You may also wish to see **Rope**.

STRIPES 1. Associated with that which is subject to change (i.e., loyalty, commitment, etc.) or variety, whereas a solid color may indicate consistency or permanence. See **Colors**. 2. May represent one's current status in life or achievement (i.e., a general's stripes). See **Clothes**. 3. That which identifies, surrounds, or covers.

SUBCONSCIOUS 1. That portion of mental activity that is just beneath the surface of conscious awareness. 2. Can correspond to one's inner self. 3. Often the level of personal images, symbols, sleep, and dreams. See **Symbol/Symbolism**. 4. The storehouse of one's feelings, fears, emotions, dreams, hopes, and aspirations. 5. Associated with the inner self. See **Self**. 6. Can correspond to the deeper reaches of the body, the mind, or the soul. 7. You may also wish to see **Unconscious**.

SUBTERRANEAN 1. Associated with the deeper reaches of the body, the mind, or the soul. See **Subconscious**. 2. That which is hidden just beneath the surface. 3. May be associated with the animal, basic, or dark part of one's nature. See **Shadow**.

SUBWAY 1. May correspond to a journey in understanding, or to one's present situation or experience. 2. Can symbolize a subconscious insight or a source of information. 3. May indicate tunnel vision. See **Tunnel**. 4. Might symbolize that which is being done in the dark, undercover, or secretly. 5. You may also wish to see **Train** and **Journey**.

SUFFER 1. That which is painful or hard to bear. 2. Could indicate one's inner emotional state or torment. 3. Associated with one who is in agony over the current situation or environment.

SUGAR 1. That which is enjoyable, pleasing, easy to take, tempting, or fattening. 2. May correspond to having too much sugar in one's diet. See **Food**. 3. Could indicate one's just desserts. 4. Might be associated with insincere flattery. 5. Can correspond to the need to be sweeter.

SUICIDE 1. Can correspond to the fact that your current situation (i.e., attitudes, work, home, life in general) is killing you. See **Kill**. 2. May be a literal warning of an individual's

state of mind or emotional condition, prompting the dreamer to be of some aid so that the experience need not occur. 3. Might correspond to an obvious failure (i.e., a project that is suicide). 4. Could indicate those parts of oneself that are at war with one another. 5. You may also wish to see **Death**.

SUIT 1. One's duty, occupation, or state of mind. See **Uniform**. 2. Can correspond to one's professional appearance or talents. See **Clothes**. 3. May be associated with how others see you. 4. One's thoughts and attitudes, especially related to work. See **Work**.

SUMMER 1. Associated with the time of harvest, fulfillment, maturity, the height of success, tremendous growth, or great development. See **Seasons**. 2. Corresponds to a period of perfection. 3. Can be representative of fun, relaxation or the need for it, vacation, etc. 4. Metaphorically, Indian summer = a mild, tranquil period, generally later in the year or later in one's life.

SUN/SUNLIGHT ☉ 1. That which gives life, light, illumination, energy, and meaning. 2. Corresponds to the brightest heavenly body, message, or idea. 3. Metaphorically, one's place in the sun = being in the limelight or being in a great position; under the sun = within the whole world. 4. The spiritual force manifesting in the earth. See **God** and **Christ**. 5. That which is distributed equally to all (i.e., God's love for his children). 6. Can represent success, achievement, and happiness. 7. May correspond to peace and tranquility. 8. May be associated with masculine energy and the active principle or force. See **Man** and **Phallus**. 9. Could indicate a literal suggestion to be in the outdoors, to get some sun, rest and relaxation, etc. 10. Associated with nineteen in the tarot.

See **Tarot.** 11. You may also wish to see **Astrology.**

SUNRISE 1. The dawning of a new idea, a new cycle in one's life, a new relationship, or a new possibility. 2. May symbolize the beginning of enlightenment. 3. A new insight or a beginning. 4. Can correspond to a rebirth, a spiritual birth, or a literal birth. See **Birth.** 5. Might correspond to the spring of one's life. See **Seasons.** 6. See also **Sun/Sunlight.**

SUNSET 1. The closing of a period in one's life, the end of an experience, or the end of a relationship. 2. May correspond to the fall of one's life. See **Seasons.** 3. Might correspond to a literal death. 4. See also **Sun.**

SUPERMAN 1. Can correspond to the higher self or one's ultimate potential. 2. The fully self-realized individual. See **Christ.** 3. Associated with a lofty goal or ideal. See **Flying.** 4. Might represent a literal super man. 5. You may also wish to see **Man** and **People.**

SURGERY 1. Corresponds to that which needs to be removed or cut out. 2. Might be associated with a project or a goal (i.e., an operation). 3. Could symbolize the opening of something (i.e., emotions that have been held in). 4. You may also wish to see **Cut.** 5. May indicate the need for some type of health or personal care. 6. You may also wish to see **Doctor.**

SURRENDER 1. The act of submission or giving up. 2. To yield to another's will, desire, or intentions. See **Puppet.** 3. Might be suggestive of the need for cooperation.

SWALLOW 1. Can indicate that which is easy or difficult to swallow (i.e., accept). 2.

May be associated with eating. See **Eat.** 3. Depending on imagery, you may also wish to see **Throat.**

SWAN 1. Symbolic of peace, tranquility, or serenity. 2. May be associated with personal transformation or the realization of selfhood (i.e., the *ugly duckling* became a swan). 3. Can be symbolic of the soul. 4. See also **Animals** and **Bird.**

SWASTIKA 1. A bent cross representing Nazi Germany or Hitler (when the wheel of the cross moves clockwise), or evil. See **Nazi.** 2. An ancient religious symbol (when the wheel moves counterclockwise) used by the Greeks, early Christians, Hindus, and American Indians. 3. You may also wish to see **Cross.**

SWEATER 1. Associated with thoughts and attitudes. See **Coat.** 2. Often indicates the outward personality one shows to the world. See **Clothes.** 3. That which insulates the self from emotions or others. 4. Might be a literal indication of upcoming weather patterns or the need to dress more warmly.

SWEEP 1. Associated with doing a cleaning (physically, mentally, or spiritually); or, that which should be swept away. See **Broom.** 2. Metaphorically, can be used as follows: making a clean sweep = starting over, or winning everything. 3. Can represent the need to clean up one's act.

SWELLING 1. Corresponds to that which is swollen, sore, irritated, or infected. See **Infection.** 2. May indicate that which is under pressure (emotional or physical). See **Pressure.** 3. Metaphorically, he has a swollen head = he's very egotistical.

SWIM 1. Associated with being engulfed in

spirituality, emotions, feelings, creative ideas, a goal, or a project. See **Water.** 2. Corresponds to that which is in fluid motion. 3. May be a literal suggestion for exercise. See **Exercise.** 4. The attitude of the swimmer is highly significant; for example: struggling in the water may indicate being in something over one's head; feeling relaxed and assured could represent feeling confident in one's present situation. 5. Could be the act of submerging oneself in any activity from spirituality to sexuality. 6. The appearance of one's swimming environment will have a great deal to do with the imagery. See **Pool.**

SWORD 1. Can correspond to aggression, hostility, or forced dominance. 2. That which cuts, divides, separates, or wounds. 3. That which is two-edged or two-sided. See **Scissors.** 4. Can represent an aggressive male figure. See **Phallus.** 5. Associated with power, domination, or authority. 6. May indicate the need to be protected or the fear of being attacked. 7. Associated with a struggle with oneself, a situation, another, or the environment. 8. Corresponds to a weapon of war. 9. You may also wish to see **War.**

SYMBOL/SYMBOLISM 1. That which represents or stands for something else entirely. See **Metaphor.** 2. A representation of an experience, an image, an activity, a thought, or an individual. See **Imagery.** 3. Associated with a pattern or symbol of human experience that is significant across time and cultures. See **Archetype.** 4. The language of the brain. 5. Psychologically, associated with the collective unconscious: a ready-made system of images, emotions, fears, instincts, and beliefs attached to the human psyche from birth and influencing an individual's perception.

SYMPHONY 1. Symbolic of people or activities working together in harmony. 2. Corresponds to an individual's emotional nature. 3. Could refer to the importance of music in life. 4. Might indicate the desire or the need for relaxation. 5. You may also wish to see **Music.**

SYNAGOGUE 1. Associated with worship, study, and tradition. See **Temple.** 2. Corresponds to the Jewish faith. See **Judaism.**

SYNCHRONICITY 1. The belief that two simultaneous and seemingly unrelated events may be causally and meaningfully connected. 2. A Jungian proposition that suggests all activities may be subject to the fourth-dimensional parameters of time, space, causality, and synchronicity. 3. A meaningful and timely coincidence. 4. You may wish to see **I Ching, Runes,** and **Tarot.**

1. The twentieth letter of the alphabet. 2. The Roman numeral for 160. 3. Referring to shape, as in a T square. 4. In English, used as a suffix to form past tense (as in slept) or to form a contraction as in 'twas (it was). 5. Numerologically, equivalent to two. 6. In Greek, tau.

TABLE 1. Associated with putting things out in the open. 2. Can symbolize that which lies before you. 3. Metaphorically, can be used as follows: to turn the tables = to reverse the situation; putting one's cards on the table = to express oneself in a situation; come to the table = a gathering place for cooperation and communication; that's been tabled = that's been postponed. 4. May correspond to one's work (desk), one's spirituality (altar), one's family (dining table), etc. 5. That which is on the table will have a great deal to do with the symbolism. 6. You may also wish to see **Food**.

TACK 1. May be a play on words suggestive of using more diplomacy in one's dealings with others (tact). 2. Could indicate a temporary connection or agreement. 3. That which joins things together. 4. Metaphorically, that's tacky = that's unsuitable or shabby.

TACKLE 1. That which has been seized or grabbed hold of. 2. To take part in the game. See **Game**. 3. Associated with being involved in the situation. 4. You may also wish to see **Sports**. 5. Fishing tackle could indicate necessary equipment or a spiritual search. See **Fisherman/Fishing**. 6. You may also wish to see **Box**.

TAIL 1. Can correspond to the end of something. 2. Could symbolize making an ass of oneself. 3. Might suggest looking at the reverse side of the situation. 4. Metaphorically, can be used as follows: he turned tail and ran = he disappeared from the situation; her tail was between her legs = she felt bad or felt beaten; you're pulling my tail = you're joking with me; he tailed behind = he came last. 5. Could indicate that which was in the past. 6. You may also wish to see **Animals**.

TAKEOFF 1. Associated with rising above the situation or the experience. See **Flying**. 2. An airplane taking off may represent an idea or a plan whose time has come. 3. Might represent a closing, a departure, or the end of a relationship. 4. See also **Airplane**.

TALL 1. Associated with one's stature, one's appearance, or one's elevation. 2. May correspond to what one thinks of oneself, or what one thinks of others. 3. Metaphorically, a tall tale = an exaggerated or an unbelievable tale. 4. Can correspond to that which is big (i.e., an obstacle, a problem, a reward, an idea, etc.). 5. Could be associated with pride. 6. You may also wish to see **Size** and **Ascend**.

TALMUD 1. Associated with Judaism and includes the Mishnah text and the Gemara commentary. See **Judaism**. 2. Can correspond to laws, instruction, and teachings. 3. Literally means to learn. 4. You may also wish to see **Torah**.

TAOISM 1. The philosophy of Lao–tse (sixth century B.C.). 2. Associated with the belief that perfection, goodness, and godliness is all around, and one must learn to attune oneself to the *Tao* (the way) in order to let that ultimate reality flow through oneself spontaneously. 3. Primary religious text is the *Tao Te Ching*. 4. Corresponds to selflessness, simplicity, emotionlessness, and inward focusing. 5. Associated with the philosophy that one may not learn *Tao*, one may only practice *Tao*.

TAPE RECORDER 1. Associated with hearing and the need to remember or recall verbal communication. See **Hear**. 2. Can correspond to memories of experiences, ideas, or relationships. 3. Associated with recalling events or the need to recall events with a clear picture of what transpired. 4. To reexperience a situation that has transpired previously. 5. May also be associated with karmic memory. See **Karma**.

TAPESTRY 1. Can correspond to a visual representation of one's life story or one's soul journey. See **Journey**. 2. May represent one's higher self, inner creativity, or subconscious mind. 3. Could be symbolic of karmic memory. 4. Depending on the imagery (i.e., where the tapestry is located and how it is used), you may also wish to see **Wall**, **Curtain**, or **Floor**.

TAR 1. May be representative of one's own associations with tar (i.e., a roadway or direction under construction; that which creates a real mess). 2. Metaphorically, to be tar and feathered = the act of being reprimanded and humiliated. 3. The imagery will have a great deal to do with the meaning; for example: walking on hot tar could suggest going in a dangerous direction; putting one's hands into a bucket of tar might indi-

cate reaching into areas one doesn't belong, etc. 4. You may also wish to see **Road**.

TAROT 1. Associated with the belief that ancient esoteric cards may give individuals an objective tool for self–study, evaluation, and insight. 2. A tool for obtaining inner guidance through the use of symbolism, attunement, and synchronicity (i.e., the fact that two simultaneous and seemingly unrelated events may be causally and meaningfully connected; see **Synchronicity**). 3. A system of seventy–eight cards consisting of archetypes of human emotion and experience from which one may gain clearer personal insights regarding oneself. 4. The cards are separated into twenty–two major arcana (corresponding to the Hebrew letters of the alphabet) and fifty–six minor arcana (from which modern–day playing cards descend; see **Cards**). 5. The major arcana are as follows.

> ***Zero or Twenty-two: The Fool:*** Associated with being at the crossroads on one's journey and the possibility of discovering one's true fate. Corresponds to the possibility of great luck and the fulfillment of one's wishes.
> ***One: The Magician:*** Represents the search for the knowledge that makes all things possible. Suggests that faith, willpower, and determination rightly placed in God will lead one in the proper direction.
> ***Two: The High Priestess:*** Can correspond to great inspiration and intuition. Associated with a period of introspection and contemplation rather than action.
> ***Three: The Empress:*** Symbolic of personal growth and success in all areas of one's life. Can indicate the qualities of love, beauty, and understanding.
> ***Four: The Emperor:*** Associated with rea-

son, experience, and personal knowledge. Corresponds with a time of taking independent and practical action.

Five: The Hierophant (Pope): Represents the search for truth, advice, or knowledge. Suggests the possibility of change, personal healing, and being open to new interests and a new outlook in life.

Six: The Lovers: Can correspond to a time of important decisions and choices to be made. Associated with deciding what one truly desires at a soul level and making creative and spiritual choices accordingly.

Seven: The Chariot: Symbolic of the need to exercise self-discipline in order to find success. Can indicate the necessity of harnessing one's energies, intellect, and spiritual activities to be truly disciplined.

Eight: Strength: Associated with personal responsibility and the need to meet all situations one has created with love and patience. Corresponds to pulling together one's personal fortitude in the face of any obstacle.

Nine: The Hermit: Represents the necessity of withdrawing from one's normal activities (i.e., a vacation, a time of introspection, etc.). Suggests that such a move will place one in closer attunement with available wisdom and guidance.

Ten: The Wheel of Fortune: Can correspond to a change in one's situation for the better. Associated with the need to make prudent and wise decisions at this point in one's life, leading toward an even brighter future.

Eleven: Justice: Symbolic of the need to trust in oneself and to take control of one's own destiny. Can indicate the necessity of being cautious in taking another's advice, for one's own expe-

riences are the better teacher.

Twelve: The Hanged Man: Associated with the need to move beyond one's usual thoughts and activities. Corresponds to the possibility of tapping into higher levels of meditation, wisdom, and spirituality.

Thirteen: Death: Represents the process of change, rebirth, and personal transformation. Suggests that one release the past, allowing openness to the new possibilities of the future.

Fourteen: Temperance: Can correspond to harmony and balance or the need to nurture these attributes. Associated with the need to slow down, refrain from impulsiveness, and pursue all things with patience.

Fifteen: The Devil: Symbolic of an overindulgence in the material side of life. Can indicate the need for caution in pursuit of the external things of the earth and a greater focus on that which is inward, spiritual, or selfless.

Sixteen: The Tower: Associated with the inevitable change in one's current situation, health, or personal relationships. Corresponds to the need to let go of the past and trust the awakening awareness of one's inner guidance.

Seventeen: The Star: Represents the possibility of rewards, success, and future accomplishments. Suggests that one will receive external help, assistance, and guidance or help from one's higher self.

Eighteen: The Moon: Can correspond to uncertainty and the possibility of change. Associated with the need for caution and the use of one's own inherent intuitive abilities.

Nineteen: The Sun: Symbolic of opportunities coming up that need to be pursued cautiously. Can indicate great happiness and personal fulfillment.

Twenty: Judgment: Associated with discernment, personal introspection, and reflection. Corresponds to the need to break free of old thought patterns and to become objective about one's current situation.

Twenty-one: The World: Represents personal fulfillment and the completion of current activities. Suggests the ability to proceed in any desired direction.

6. You may also wish to see **Numerology.** 7. The minor arcana are separated into four suits of fourteen cards: king, queen, knight, page, ten, nine, eight, seven, six, five, four, three, two, and Ace.

Wands (also clubs or scepters) are associated with energy, distinction, or opposition.

Ace of Wands: Summer, new beginnings, growth.

Two of Wands: Perseverance, achievement with patience, dominion.

Three of Wands: Teamwork, success though proper use of talents and strengths.

Four of Wands: Achievement, harvest, and harmony.

Five of Wands: Possible strife, competition, or change.

Six of Wands: Victory, successful end, or continuous improvement.

Seven of Wands: Courage, determination, the need to make decisions and rely on inner strength.

Eight of Wands: Approaching changes or goal; acceleration in activities.

Nine of Wands: The need for determination, resolve, preparation, and application.

Ten of Wands: Oppressive situation or wrong use of energies.

Page of Wands: Associated with a fair-haired messenger or child; may relate to energy, distinction, or opposition.

Knight of Wands: Associated with a young man; change.

Queen of Wands: Mature woman, magnetic personality.

King of Wands: Mature man, friendly, great leader, business success.

Cups (also hearts or goblets) are associated with love, pleasure, cooperation, or happiness.

Ace of Cups: Spring, productivity, fresh starts.

Two of Cups: Cooperation, reciprocity, or possible conflict in a relationship.

Three of Cups: Happiness and fulfillment, but the need to avoid overindulgence.

Four of Cups: Dissatisfaction, boredom, needing change.

Five of Cups: Loss, deep sorrow, breakup, or the desire to get away.

Six of Cups: New situation or environment, happiness from the past.

Seven of Cups: Lots of choices and possible ideas; the need to make a decision.

Eight of Cups: Discontent with materiality; the need for spiritual fulfillment and meaning.

Nine of Cups: Success, well-being, one's wishes come true.

Ten of Cups: New relationship, personal fulfillment, happiness is in one's future.

Page of Cups: Associated with a medium-haired messenger or child; may relate to love, pleasure, happiness, or cooperation.

Knight of Cups: Associated with a young man; struggle.

Queen of Cups: Mature woman, intuitive and imaginative.

King of Cups: Mature man, subtle, very empathetic or two–faced.

Swords (also spades) are associated with struggle, trouble, or difficulty.

Ace of Swords: Fall, conquest, or harvest.

Two of Swords: Indecision, the need for balance and cooperation.

Three of Swords: Sorrow, disappointment, tears, or separation.

Four of Swords: A period of rest; positive change is approaching.

Five of Swords: Deception, intrigue, and selfishness.

Six of Swords: Difficult situation ending; possibility of a literal journey or a journey in understanding.

Seven of Swords: Instability, only partial success; the need to obtain additional information or advice.

Eight of Swords: Indecision and confusion; the need to rest from worry and fear.

Nine of Swords: Anxiety, tragedy, or misery.

Ten of Swords: Unhappiness and depression; a sense of loss and misery.

Page of Swords: Associated with a darker haired messenger or child; may relate to struggle, trouble, or difficulty.

Knight of Swords: Associated with a young man; domineering or vengeful.

Queen of Swords: Mature woman, keen intelligence, familiar with personal struggle, may be a sympathetic ear.

King of Swords: Mature man, full of ideas, may be good counselor; possibility of being overbearing or distrustful.

Pentacles (also diamonds, disks, or coins) are associated with money, education, or business.

Ace of Pentacles: Winter, material gain, wealth.

Two of Pentacles: The need for harmony, decisiveness, and organization.

Three of Pentacles: Indication of activity, work, and financial gain.

Four of Pentacles: Earthly concerns, strong authority.

Five of Pentacles: Time of reflection, determination, and taking care of the situation or oneself.

Six of Pentacles: Prosperity, generosity, one's just rewards; the need to be recognized for one's labors.

Seven of Pentacles: Possible change and delay, but eventual success; the need for patience.

Eight of Pentacles: Skill, stability, determination in achieving material goals.

Nine of Pentacles: Financial security but feeling incomplete; the need to focus on spirituality.

Ten of Pentacles: Wealth and prosperity; the need for new motivation.

Page of Pentacles: Associated with a messenger or child (hair of any shade); may relate to money, education, or business.

Knight of Pentacles: Associated with a young man; laborious or lazy, patient, and deliberate.

Queen of Pentacles: Mature woman, very successful, creative, generous, charming, and moody.

King of Pentacles: Mature man, friendly, steady, dependable, and successful.

TATTOO 1. Can correspond to a symbol, a sign, or an insignia. See **Medals**. 2. A permanent mark or blemish. See **Scar**. 3. May be associated with belonging to a group or an experience. 4. That which appears on one's skin. See **Skin**.

TAURUS ♉ 1. Second sign of the zodiac, corresponding to April 20–May 20. 2. Associated with the following positive traits: dependability, endurance, practical in business matters. 3. Associated with the following negative traits: possessive, stubborn, obsessive. 4. Astrologically, ruled by Venus. See **Venus**. 5. See **Bull**. 6. An earth sign. See **Earth**. 7. See also **Astrology**.

TAXI 1. Corresponds to that which one is allowing to drive one's life. 2. May indicate a feeling of disassociation or disconnection from oneself, a particular situation, or life in general. 3. May represent one's physical body or current situation. See **Automobile**. 4. Could symbolize being taken for a ride.

TAYLOR, ELIZABETH 1. Generally corresponds to one's personal association (i.e., beauty, temptation, acting, etc.). 2. May be indicative of marriage. See **Marriage**. 3. You may also wish to see **Movie Star**.

TEA 1. Could indicate the need to stay awake (i.e., alert) in the situation. 2. How the tea is pictured is very significant; for example: receiving a very tiny glass or cup could indicate that one needs to cut back on consumption. 3. May represent the need to become more energized. 4. Whatever one's personal associations are with tea are significant (i.e., relaxation, socializing, hospitality, a break, a stimulant, etc.). 5. You may also wish to see **Food**.

TEACHER 1. Anyone or anything that aids one's development. 2. Associated with an authority figure or one who gives advice or counsel. 3. Corresponds to the ability to teach or the need to be taught. 4. One who is critical or testing. 5. A lesson or experience. 6. Associated with one who shows how something can be done. 7. See also **People**.

8. You may also wish to see **School** and **Test**.

TEAR 1. Associated with sadness. See **Cry**. 2. Can correspond to the welling up of any emotion (i.e., great happiness, joy, sympathy, sadness, etc.). 3. That which cleanses one's eyes or vision. See **Eyes**.

TEETH 1. Symbolic of one's words; what one says. 2. False teeth symbolizes false words or saying something one doesn't really believe. 3. Baby teeth represent immature words or the need to become more mature. 4. Metaphorically, can be used as follows: getting one's teeth into it = getting involved; he showed his teeth = he became angry. 5. Could literally correspond to eating or dietary habits. See **Food**. 6. Wearing braces may symbolize the need to restrain or straighten one's words. 7. You may also wish to see **Mouth** and **Body**.

TELEGRAM 1. A message, idea, or insight of value. See **Message/Messenger**. 2. Could correspond to information from another source, person, or the intuition. 3. Might be associated with a death. See **Death**. 4. The arrival of a new opportunity, experience, or perspective. 5. May be suggestive of self–expression or the need to express oneself.

TELEPHONE 1. Associated with gaining information or insight. 2. Corresponds to a message. See **Message/Messenger**. 3. Can represent telepathy or intuition. 4. Symbolic of how one listens or how one communicates with others. See **Hear**. 5. Literal prediction of someone about to call or someone you need to call. 6. Might be associated with a relationship, an idea, or words spoken.

TELESCOPE 1. The ability to see far off (i.e., that which is coming, the future). 2. Associated with detecting future trends. 3. Corresponds to great vision; being a visionary. See **Vision**. 4. Possessing clear insight. 5. Oversensitivity to things that are not that large; making something big out of something small. 6. You may also wish to see **Eyes**.

TELEVISION 1. Associated with receiving information, insights, or understanding over a distance. 2. Could represent intuitive insights or awareness from the higher self or the subconscious. 3. May relate to receiving a message. See **Message/Messenger**. 4. The capacity to tune into higher levels of awareness. 5. Might correspond to the body's own seeing mechanisms. See **Eyes**. 6. Associated with information or insights that can be tuned into by anyone. 7. That which relates to entertainment, news, communication, or relaxation. 8. May be associated with one who spends too much time in front of the television.

TEMPLE 1. Associated with spiritual forces; the dwelling place of spirituality, the soul, or higher wisdom. 2. May correspond to safety and security from the outside world. 3. May represent spiritual community. 4. Symbolic of one's religious or personal beliefs or childhood association with religion. 5. Can represent one's entire being: physically, emotionally, mentally, and spiritually. 6. The condition of the building may give indications into one's present life, beliefs, or condition. See **Building.** 7. The spiritual facade we present to the world. 8. Corresponds to that which gives assistance in one's own spiritual life. 9. Place of worship. 10. Where spiritual forces impinge upon the conscious mind or the material. 11. May indicate spiritual initiation.

TEN 1. Associated with completeness and strength. 2. See **Numerology.**

TEN COMMANDMENTS 1. The laws of God; universal laws. See **God.** 2. May also be a message regarding one's need for more spiritual conduct. See **Message/Messenger.** 3. See also **Bible.** 4. Might indicate the need to take stock of one's current situation or lifestyle. 5. For a listing of the Ten Commandments, see **Judaism.** 6. You may also wish to see **Moses.**

TENT/TEPEE 1. Associated with a changeable or temporary idea, relationship, emotion, or physical body. See **House.** 2. May correspond to that which is Native American. See **Indian.** 3. That which may be moved by oneself. See **Luggage.** 4. For nature lovers, could be indicative of rest, relaxation, or getting back to nature. 5. Because of shape, may be associated with the triangle. See **Triangle.**

TERMITE 1. Corresponds to that which gnaws, irritates, destroys, or undermines. See **Bug.** 2. Could be a literal indication of termites. 3. Might be associated with hidden worries or fears.

TERROR 1. Associated with extreme anxiety, apprehension, fear, or uneasiness. 2. The inability to handle one's current experience. 3. Often whatever people fear is associated with something they need to face in themselves. See **Shadow.** 4. Metaphorically, that child is a terror = the child is uncontrollable. 5. Depending upon the imagery, it might be a literal warning of some kind.

TEST 1. Corresponds to a test or a lesson. See **School.** 2. Associated with being questioned. 3. What is happening during the examination is significant; for example: not finding the testing room or the class could indicate that one feels lost in the situation; not knowing the answers may symbolize one's own uncertainties; not being ready suggests unpreparedness for a present condition; failure or a low grade is associated with low self-esteem or insecurity. 4. Could suggest that one does not yet have all the required information. 5. Success at dealing with life's problems. 6. Often associated with a current challenging experience or situation in life. 7. Metaphorically, that was a real test = that was a real challenging experience or a real trial to undergo.

THEATER 1. The stage of life. See **Drama.** 2. Associated with the scene or the environment of a particular situation or experience. 3. Metaphorically, good theater = good drama or a lively experience.

THEOLOGY 1. The study of God, spirituality, and the interconnection of humankind with the universe. See **God.** 2. Could correspond to the need to be more involved in spiritual pursuits. 3. Depending upon the imagery, might suggest that one is studying spirituality but not applying what one knows. See **School.**

THERMOMETER 1. Can correspond to the temperature of one's emotional state of mind. 2. That which registers changing conditions or a changing environment. 3. Can represent the calculation of opinion, judgment, or criticism. 4. May be a literal indication to watch one's health.

THIEF 1. Can correspond to trying to take something illegally. 2. Associated with taking advantage or being taken advantage of. 3. Something that is stealing one's ideas, energy, emotions, or vitality. 4. See also **People.** 5. Someone who takes what is not his by force. 6. The villainous portions of oneself. See **Villain.**

THIGH 1. That which gives support or strength; the upper portion of the leg. See **Leg/Legless.** 2. Biblically, may correspond to making an oath or a promise. 3. Could be associated with one's direction. See **Direction.**

THIN 1. Associated with a poor idea, plan, or situation. See **Size.** 2. Could indicate one's personal desire for weight loss. 3. Metaphorically, your comments are a little thin = they're flimsy. 4. May be a literal indication of a dietary deficiency. 5. Can correspond to that which is meager or weak, physically, mentally, or spiritually.

THIRST 1. The desire, yearning, or craving for something. 2. Being thirsty for water (i.e., spirit) may correspond to the need for spiritual activities in one's life. 3. You may also wish to see **Drink.**

THE THORN BIRDS 1. Associated with desire and forbidden or unrequited love. 2. Might correspond to Australia. 3. Could correspond with suffering for a higher cause.

THORNS 1. May indicate a prickly or dangerous situation. 2. An undesirable experience or thought. 3. Could be associated with dangers, difficulties, or obstacles. 4. A crown of thorns is associated with suffering and the crucifixion. See **Crucifixion.** 5. Depending on imagery, you may also wish to see **Plant.**

THREE 1. Corresponds to the Trinity (the triune nature of God); the body, mind, and spirit; or the third dimension. 2. See **Numerology.** 3. You may also wish to see **Triangle.**

THRESHOLD 1. That which is on the verge of one's experience (i.e., an idea, an event, a relationship, etc.). 2. An entrance or doorway. See **Door.** 3. You may also wish to see **House.**

THROAT 1. Associated with one's voice, words, and ability to communicate. 2. Corresponds to one's personal will and willpower or lack of it. 3. Metaphorically, can be used as follows: she rammed it down his throat = she forced him into accepting her opinion or letting her have her way; he had a lump in his throat = he was filled with emotion; the boss cut his throat = the boss did him in; he jumped down her throat = he gave her an emotional reprimand. 4. Can be associated with sticking one's neck out. See **Neck**. 5. Might represent having to swallow one's words. 6. Corresponds to the thyroid or fifth chakra. See **Thyroid**. 7. You may also wish to see **Body**.

THUMB 1. Often corresponds to being under someone's control (i.e., being under one's thumb) or controlling another. See **Puppet**. 2. Metaphorically, can be used as follows: she's all thumbs = she's very clumsy with her hands; thumbs down = no; thumbs up = yes; to thumb your nose = to think you are above or better than the activity or the person; thumbing a ride = hitchhiking; he's got a green thumb = he's good with growing plants. 3. You may also wish to see **Body**.

THUNDER 1. An important or unexpected message. 2. Often associated with situational, mental, or emotional states. See **Weather**. 3. You may also wish to see **Explosion/Explosive**.

THYMUS 1. A gland in the body. 2. Associated with the fourth endocrine center or chakra. 3. Representative of human love. 4. Metaphysically, corresponds to Venus; also may be symbolized by the eagle. 5. In Revelation, it is represented by the Church of Sardis. 6. See **Chakras**.

THYROID 1. A gland in the body. 2. Associated with the fifth endocrine center or chakra. 3. Relates to human or divine will. 4. Metaphysically, corresponds to Uranus; also may be symbolized by the Holy Spirit. 5. In Revelation, it is represented by the Church of Thyatira. 6. See **Chakras**.

TICK 1. Associated with an irritant, that which is sucking the life out of you, or something biting. See **Bug**. 2. Could indicate that which is ticking you off.

TICKET 1. One's passage, entry, chance, or permission into the experience. See **License**. 2. Receiving a police ticket corresponds to breaking some type of a personal, man-made, or universal law. See **Law**. 3. Metaphorically, that's the ticket = that's perfect. 4.. May be associated with a literal warning to change one's habits or to exercise caution.

TIE 1. Associated with mental or emotional ties. 2. Corresponds to one's appearance or the need to look one's best. See **Suit**. 3. Associated with male energy. See **Phallus**. 4. Could indicate a joining or a relationship. See **Knot**. 5. Might also indicate a karmic tie. See **Karma**. 6. You may also wish to see **Clothes**.

TIGER 1. Associated with aggression, strength, stalking, and ferocity. See **Animals**. 2. Could symbolize negative or aggressive feminine attributes (i.e., spite, gossip, sexual dominance, etc.). See **Woman**. 3. Metaphorically, a tiger = a cruel person. 4. You may also wish to see **Cat**.

TIGHT 1. That which is snug, a close call, secure, or barely passable. 2. Metaphorically, he's tight-fisted = he's extremely cheap. 3. If clothing is too tight, it may suggest that one's belief system is no longer adequate or that one is not suited for the present situation or experience. See **Clothes.**

TIGHTROPE 1. Corresponds to a dangerous or an unstable situation, experience, or relationship. 2. May indicate an overly dependent connection (i.e., a tight rope). See **Rope.** 3. Associated with the need to do a balancing act. 4. Depending on imagery, you may also wish to see **Acrobat.**

TIME 1. That in which individuals have the opportunity to schedule events and their life journey. See **Journey;** 2. That which accounts for the passage of one experience to another. 3. Metaphorically, can be used as follows: she's behind the times = she's out of touch with the current situation; he's just killing time = he's just wasting time or waiting; they had the time of their lives = they had one of their most enjoyable experiences. 4. Can be associated with clocks, calendars, sand, an old man, etc. 5. May correspond to the appropriate timing for an activity, event, relationship, or change. 6. May be associated with whatever one does at the specific time being indicated.

TIN 1. That which is bendable, changeable, and malleable. 2. Can correspond to that which preserves, protects, coats, or envelops something to keep it away from the external environment.

TIN MAN 1. In literature (i.e., *The Wizard of Oz*), associated with a search to get in touch with or to come to terms with true emotions and feelings. 2. See also **People.** 3. You may also wish to see **Heart.**

TOAD 1. Can be associated with enchantment, uncleanliness, or unconscious knowledge. 2. Might indicate an enchanted prince. 3. That which can leap over hurdles. 4. Metaphorically, he's a toad = he's an unwanted, a

disgusting, or an unsuitable person. 5. You may also wish to see **Water, Fish,** and **Animals.**

TOES 1. An extension of one's foot (i.e., principles, stance, etc.). See **Feet.** 2. Metaphorically, can be used as follows: he toed the line = he did his duty or behaved appropriately; she's on her toes = she's very capable; to dip one's toe in the water = to become involved, perhaps cautiously. 3. May be associated with balance and direction. See **Direction.** 4. You may also wish to see **Shoes.**

TOILET 1. May be associated with one's lower self, moral depravity, lack of cleanliness, or the need to eliminate something. See **Plumbing.** 2. Going to the bathroom in public may symbolize the need to release or confess old ideas, grudges, or emotions, or it may suggest feeling a lack of privacy. See **Bathroom.** 3. May simply be the subconscious mind acting out the body's desire to go to the bathroom. 4. Might be associated with literal physical elimination problems. 5. You may also wish to see **Urinate** or **Defecate.**

TOMB 1. May represent one's lower self or sexuality. 2. Could be associated with the unconscious or the subconscious mind. See **Unconscious** or **Subconscious.** 3. If dark and dreary, could indicate that which is dead, useless, or buried. See **Grave.** 4. If lighter in appearance, might be associated with knowledge, wisdom, or intuition. See **Vault.** 5. Depending upon imagery, could correspond to hidden talents. 6. Biblically, associated with the Resurrection. See **Resurrection.**

TONGUE 1. Associated with speech. See **Teeth.** 2. Can correspond to eating or that which is in one's mouth. 3. Symbolic of self-expression. 4. Metaphorically, can be used as follows: hold your tongue = watch what you say, or stop talking; she has a silver tongue = her words are beautiful and perhaps false; it's on the tip of my tongue = I just can't quite remember. 5. Biblically, the gift of tongues is associated with the Holy Spirit. 6. You may also wish to see **Mouth.**

TOOL 1. An implement, instrument, or machine one uses in order to perform some work or labor. 2. The appearance of the tools will have a great deal to do with the symbolism; for example: using a rusted saw might suggest something that can't quite cut it; a shiny new hammer and nail could indicate the ability to drive home one's point, etc. 3. Might indicate the need to prepare oneself with the proper equipment. 4. Depending upon the shape and the activity of the tool, may be associated with aggression and male sexuality. See **Phallus.** 5. You may also wish to see **Contractor** or to see names of individual tools. For example, see **Hammer.**

TOOTHBRUSH 1. Can correspond to the need to clean up one's words. See **Teeth.** 2. May literally be associated with bad breath and personal hygiene. 3. Could symbolize the need to see a dentist. 4. You may also wish to see **Mouth.**

TORAH 1. Rabbinically, associated with the first five books of the Bible (the books of Moses, the Pentateuch); may represent Jewish literature in its entirety, including the Talmud. See **Judaism** and **Talmud.** 2. Corresponds to laws or customs. 3. An important message. See **Message/Messenger.** 4. May represent ancient wisdom. See **Book.** 5. Symbolic of religious doctrines or sacredness. See **Bible.**

TORCH 1. Associated with that which illuminates the darkness (i.e., vision or insight). 2. Could represent wisdom or enlightenment. 3. One who leads or lights the way. 4. Could symbolize a vision or a visionary. See **Vision.** 5. You may also wish to see **Light** and **Fire.**

TORNADO 1. Corresponds to major challenges in one's life experience. 2. Associated with emotional problems and upsets. 3. Might indicate mental illness or a breakdown. 4. Could be a literal indication of a tornado. 5. See **Weather.**

TORTURE 1. Associated with great pain, revenge, or control. 2. Can correspond to emotional anguish or distress. 3. A torture chamber could symbolize a situation, a condition, or a relationship that has one trapped in a great deal of pain or anguish. 4. Depending on imagery, you may also wish to see **Wound.**

TOURIST 1. May symbolize a temporary activity, experience, situation, or encounter. 2. Might indicate the need for a change in scenery, personal habit patterns, or simply the desire for a vacation. See **Travel.** 3. Associated with a journey to an unfamiliar destination or an unknown part of oneself, or the arrival of a guest. 4. You may also wish to see **People.**

TOWER 1. A lofty ideal. 2. Could be associated with one's higher self or inner wisdom. 3. That which is strong or domineering. 4. The appearance of the tower will have a great deal to do with the meaning. See **Building.** 5. That which rises above the situation or the surrounding environment. 6. Could be associated with an ascent or descent (i.e., a raise, a demotion, spiritual progress, spiritual regression, gaining a new level of awareness, etc.). Depending on imagery, see **Ascend** or **Descend.** 7. Associated with sixteen in the tarot. See **Tarot.** 8. You may also wish to see **Mountain.**

TOWER OF BABEL 1. Biblically, represents confusion. 2. Metaphysically, symbolic of the lower self attempting to rise above the higher self. 3. Corresponds to disaster. 4. The inability of individuals to understand one another or to communicate. 5. You may also wish to see **Tower.**

TOY 1. Associated with joy or playfulness. 2. Can correspond to childhood. See **Child.** 3. Represents trivial pursuits that occupy one's time and attention. 4. Might correspond to immaturity. 5. Metaphorically, to toy with someone = to play with a person's emotions.

TRACKS 1. If railway, associated with a fixed journey or an established path. See **Railroad.** 2. If footsteps or hoofprints, corresponds to who or what one is presently following. 3. You may also wish to see **Footprints, Road,** or **Journey.**

TRAFFIC LIGHT 1. Associated with a message. See **Message/Messenger.** 2. The color of the light has a great deal to do with the meaning; for example: red = danger or the need to stop; yellow is associated with caution; green is an okay or a go. Depending on imagery, see **Go, Stop,** or **Yield.** 3. You may also wish to see **Colors** and **Sign.**

TRAIN 1. Can correspond to the journey of life. See **Direction** or **Journey.** 2. May be associated with one's present condition or state of mind. See **Automobile.** 3. Metaphorically, a train of thought = the direction or flow of ideas; to train for something = to prepare; one who has been railroaded = someone who has been mistreated. 4. May be a literal indication of travel, especially to a place of one's own past. 5. Could indicate the controlling force in one's present situation (i.e., who's driving the train). 6. What's occurring with the train is very significant; for example: a missed train may indicate a missed opportunity; a steady train could be symbolic of following the proper course of events; a derailed train might indicate a lost sense of direction or a state of confusion or depression.

TRAMPOLINE 1. Depending on imagery, could indicate an idea or an activity that will enable one to reach new heights. See **Flying.** 2. That which will prevent you from falling or failing. 3. Associated with that which is a little jumpy, nerve-racking, or unstable. See **Jump.**

TRANSLUCENT 1. Associated with something that allows light or vision to pass through. See **Light** and **Window.** 2. The ability to see clearly what lies beyond. 3. Could be associated with being visionary. See **Vision.**

TRAP 1. Can correspond to being tricked or misled. 2. May represent a pitfall, an obstacle, a literal warning, or the need to be cautious. 3. Associated with a loss of one's personal freedom. 4. Represents the feeling or fear of being trapped in a situation or a relationship. 5. That which is holding you back (ideas, perceptions, beliefs, other people, a situation, etc.). 6. You may also wish to see **Prisoner.**

TRASH 1. That which has caused a mess, is disorderly, or is no longer worthwhile. 2. Associated with discarded ideas, talents, statements, people, etc. 3. Metaphorically, trash = that which is worthless or that which is morally degrading.

TRAVEL 1. Can correspond to one's life

journey. See **Journey.** 2. Might be associated with a literal trip for work, personal activities, or a vacation. See **Trip.** 3. May be symbolic of a journey in understanding or in stature (i.e., a promotion or demotion). 4. Might literally represent a possible move.

TREASURE 1. One's wealth, inner resources, or strength. See **Money.** 2. Could be associated with a storehouse of talents and abilities that are there for the taking. 3. Biblically, associated with the desire of one's heart (Matthew 6:21). 4. Depending on imagery, you may also wish to see **Pirate.**

TREATY 1. Corresponds to a reconciliation or a peaceful outcome. 2. Might indicate an alliance or an unexpected partnership. 3. Could be suggestive of a relationship. See **Marriage.**

TREE 1. Corresponds to the ability to bring great ideas into common language. 2. That which is grounded, stable, and sturdy, or that which flourishes and rises above the environment. 3. Metaphorically, can be used as follows: to be up a tree = to be cornered; to pine away = to have great and unrelenting sadness. 4. Types of trees can be symbolic of different meanings (generally what you associate with their fruit or the tree itself); for example: an apple tree can be symbolic of temptation, growing up (mom or grandma), or patriotism; an oak generally symbolizes strength, maturity, and wisdom; a pine is associated with mental forces at rest, faith, or death (i.e., a pine box). 5. May be associated with great depth and height. 6. Can symbolize knowledge and belief systems. 7. That which is stable and well-rooted. See **Roots.** 8. Symbolic of that which connects the heavens with the earth. 9. Biblically, the Tree of Knowledge = the forbidden fruit that led to the Fall of man. See **Adam.** 10. Liturgically, a tree can be symbolic of the cross. 11. In Buddhism, a tree may symbolize enlightenment. 12. You may also wish to see **Plant** and **Grow**.

TRIAL 1. The act of being judged, being too judging, or judging oneself. See **Judge**. 2. Could correspond to being convicted of a crime or a misdeed. 3. Metaphorically, that's a real trial = that's a real difficulty, or that's a real test.

TRIANGLE 1. Could correspond to the individual aspects of oneself: physical, mental, and spiritual. 2. Associated with the numerological value of three. See **Numerology**. 3. That which is geometric, three-sided, or pyramidal. 4. Liturgically, represents the Trinity (Father, Son, and Holy Spirit). 5. Might correspond to a relationship triangle.

TRICYCLE 1. A childish activity, journey, or thought. 2. Associated with motion or movement. See **Bicycle**. 3. Depending on imagery, may indicate the need for balance (training wheels), additional insight, or greater maturity.

TRINITY 1. Associated with the triune nature of God (Father, Son, and Holy Spirit). See **God**. 2. May correspond to the body, mind, and spirit. 3. You may also wish to see three in **Numerology**.

TRIP 1. May be associated with one's life journey or destiny. See **Journey**. 2. Can correspond to a change in direction, thought processes, environment, surroundings, or situation. 3. May be symbolic of an actual journey. 4. Could correspond to the need to pay attention to or to watch one's current situation or direction. 5. Might indicate a need for a change in scenery, personal habit patterns, or simply the desire for a vacation. 6. You may also wish to see **Travel**.

TROLL 1. Depending on one's personal as-sociation, can represent that which blocks one's passageway, a little evil, a thief, or that which is enchanted. 2. Can correspond to one who is attracted to individuals much younger than oneself. 3. You may also wish to see **Dwarf**.

TROPHY 1. Corresponds to a reward, a rec-ognition, or an accomplishment. 2. Might suggest a job well done. 3. You may also wish to see **Medals**.

TROUBLE 1. A warning of a possible mis-take, danger, or risk. 2. May indicate the need for caution. 3. That which is at risk. 4. Often a literal indication of that which is transpir-ing behind the scenes, perhaps suggesting alternative plans or choices.

TROUT 1. May be associated with spiritual wisdom or insight. See **Fish**. 2. Could cor-respond to the need to relax or to take it easy. 3. You may also wish to see **Water**.

TRUCK 1. That which can carry people, be-longings, ideas, etc. 2. May be associated with oneself, one's work, or one's current situation. See **Car.** 3. Depending upon the imagery, could indicate taking portions of oneself (i.e., hopes, ideas, activities) in the same direction; a truckload of vegetables can be a message to eat more vegetables. 4. May cor-respond to one's life journey. See **Journey**.

TRUMPET 1. Associated with a message or a warning or that which is proclaimed loudly. See **Message/Messenger.** 2. Could indicate one's egotistical behavior (i.e., blow-ing one's horn). 3. May be associated with music and harmony or disharmony. See **Music.** 4. Liturgically, associated with a call to worship or the Day of Judgment and Res-urrection.

TUB 1. To be cleansed of old ideas or ex-periences. 2. Could correspond to an emo-tional situation. See **Water** and **Plumbing.** 3. The need to be cleansed of one's current situation or state of mind. See **Clean.** 4. Might correspond to the act of getting rid of prejudices or that which is no longer nec-essary. 5. Could be a literal indication of the need for or the act of some type of physical, mental, or spiritual cleansing. 6. Metaphor-ically, can be used as follows: to take a bath = to suffer a heavy financial loss; every tub must stand on its own bottom = every ac-tivity must support itself. 7. You may also wish to see **Nude.**

TUMOR 1. That which has gotten under one's skin. 2. Can correspond to that which is irritating, unsightly, or feeds off itself. 3. May indicate holding on to a problem or a bad situation. 4. Might represent self-criti-cism or punishment, or those negative as-pects of oneself that one has refused to part with. 5. See also **Body.** 6. May symbolize emotional distress or pressure. 7. Could in-dicate a literal health problem.

TUNNEL 1. A light tunnel is associated with passing into higher levels of consciousness. 2. A dark tunnel corresponds to a dark situ-ation, experience, or passageway. 3. May in-dicate tunnel vision. 4. Metaphorically, there's light at the end of the tunnel = this experience is almost over. 5. Could be asso-ciated with receiving information from one's subconscious. 6. Might symbolize female sexu-ality. See **Womb.** 7. That which protects, en-closes, or conceals. 8. You may also wish to see **Cave.** 9. Wherever the tunnel is may have a great deal to do with the symbolism; for ex-ample: a tunnel passing through a moun-tain may correspond to one's way through a difficult situation or obstacle; a tunnel un-der the water can indicate a spiritual journey.

TURBAN 1. Associated with an idea. 2. That which is mysterious or intriguing to the mind. 3. Symbolic of what is on one's mind. 4. May represent an individual's occupation or involvement. See **Clothes**. 5. May be symbolic of receiving a foreign idea or a visitor. 6. Could indicate foreign travel.

TURKEY 1. Metaphorically, can be used as follows: something that's a turkey = something that isn't very positive or desirable; let's talk turkey = let's be up front. 2. Because of Thanksgiving, may be associated with the act of being or the need to be thankful. 3. Might be associated with one's diet. 4. You may also wish to see **Bird**.

TURTLE 1. Associated with age and longevity. 2. That which is slow, methodical, and dependable. 3. Corresponds to that which is introverted and may withdraw into its shell. See **Shell**. 4. Could indicate the need to go more slowly and carefully, or the fact that one is moving too slowly. 5. In literature (*The Tortoise and the Hare*), corresponds to slow, methodical, and dependable traits being superior to that which is hasty and inconsistent. 6. See also **Animals**.

TUXEDO 1. May correspond to formality, looking one's best, or the importance of appearances. See **Clothes**. 2. One's personal association will have a great deal to do with the imagery; for example: a tuxedo could remind you of weddings, funerals, celebrations, etc. 3. You may also wish to see **Suit**.

TV 1. See **Television**. 2. Can correspond to receiving information, insights, or understanding over a distance.

TV HOST/HOSTESS 1. Associated with the television. See **Television**. 2. Often corresponds to whatever one thinks about the host/hostess, game show, etc. 3. You may also wish to see **People**.

TWELVE 1. Associated with cosmic order. 2. Symbolic of astrology. See **Astrology**. 3. See **Numerology**.

TWILIGHT 1. Associated with enchantment, mystery, or that which is concealed. 2. The period between sunset and night and between sunrise and full day. See **Sunrise** and **Sunset**. 3. Depending on imagery, you may also wish to see **Moon/Moonlight**. 4. See also **Dark**.

TWINS 1. Can represent two sides. 2. Associated with another choice in the matter. 3. Metaphorically, receiving twice what was expected. 4. To be separated from oneself. 5. To dream of twins while pregnant could be taken literally. 6. Can correspond to being two-faced. 7. Astrologically, one of the twelve signs of the zodiac. See **Gemini**.

TWO 1. Associated with duality or the division of the whole. 2. See **Numerology**.

TWO-FACED 1. Associated with betrayal, lies, or deceit. 2. Corresponds to one who is hypocritical. 3. Presenting the opinion (or face) one thinks is appropriate to the situation in spite of one's true feelings or beliefs. See **Mask**.

TYPEWRITER 1. Associated with self-expression and communication. 2. May indicate a personal talent or the need to communicate with someone. See **Write**. 3. A communication with one's inner self. 4. Could suggest the need for introspection and self-examination.

1. The twenty-first letter of the alphabet. 2. Historically (prior to the eighteenth century), a variant of V. 3. Referring to the shape of an object. 4. Chemically, the symbol for uranium. 5. Numerologically, equivalent to three. 6. In Greek, upsilon.

UFO 1. Associated with a message from another realm (i.e., one's higher self). 2. A lofty idea or project. 3. Could correspond to an unknown or unbelievable outcome. 4. That which is spacey. 5. If the UFO appears threatening, may be associated with angry or negative thoughts or emotions. 6. You may also wish to see **Airplane.**

UGLY 1. That which is unpleasant to look at. 2. May be symbolic of a negative activity or behavior in oneself. 3. Metaphorically, she's ugly when she wants to be = she can be cross and angry when she wants. 4. In literature, *The Ugly Duckling* is the story of personal transformation and coming into one's own.

ULCER 1. That which festers, eats away, or bothers you. 2. Associated with warring with oneself and one's thoughts and emotions. See **Body.** 3. Can be associated with that which is open, vulnerable, unhealing, or constantly irritating. 4. Could literally correspond to poor dietary habits. 5 You may also wish to see **Stomach.**

UMBRELLA 1. That which protects you from your own emotions or the emotions of others. See **Rain.** 2. One's outward emotional nature or attitudes. 3. Might represent the fact that one needs to be more isolated

from the emotional outpourings of others. 4. Associated with preparedness or the need to be prepared. 5. Could be a literal indication that it is going to rain. 6. You may also wish to see **Clothes.**

UMPIRE 1. The final authority in the rules of the game. See **Sports.** 2. That which makes quick and final decisions or judgments between various points of view. 3. May be symbolic of one's higher self or inner wisdom. 4. Can correspond to one's fairness, judgment, or analysis of oneself or others. See **Judge.** 5. You may also wish to see **People.**

UNBALANCED 1. Could symbolize that which is unfair, unjust, or unstable. 2. May be associated with a physical, mental, or spiritual instability or health problem. 3. That which is inequitable. 4. Metaphorically, he's unbalanced = he's mentally unstable.

UNCONSCIOUS 1. That portion of mental activity that is unknown to the conscious mind. 2. Psychologically, the totality of all thoughts, impulses, and desires that influence one's behavior. 3. The repressed, ignored, frustrated, forgotten, or dark side of one's inner nature. See **Shadow**. 4. May be associated with the unknown aspects of oneself. 5. In psychology, the collective unconscious is the storehouse of symbols and archetypes. See **Symbol/Symbolism**. 6. See also **Subconscious**.

UNDERGROWTH 1. Associated with activity, productivity, and life that is occurring just beneath the surface. See **Plants**. 2. May correspond to productive ideas and mental processes. 3. The appearance of the undergrowth will have a great deal to do with the symbolism; for example: dark, viny, treacherous undergrowth could indicate old thoughts, habits, and patterns that get in the way of one's thinking. 4. May be associated with the health of one's unconscious mind. 5. You may also wish to see **Roots**.

UNDERTAKER 1. May represent the end of an idea, an experience, a project, or a relationship. See **Death** and **Corpse**. 2. One who thrives on death, disaster, or others' misfortunes. 3. Something that buries or discards that which is no longer necessary. 4. You may also wish to see **People**.

UNDRESS 1. To expose oneself to others. See **Nude**. 2. Associated with baring one's feelings, emotions, or setting aside one's personality. 3. To discard one's inhibitions, fears, beliefs, or morals. 4. Might correspond to sexual desires. 5. You may also wish to see **Clothes**.

UNFAITHFUL 1. Associated with breaking one's promises, vows, principles, or ethics. 2. Could reflect one's fears. 3. Might be a literal indication that someone is being untrue, dishonest, or sneaky.

UNHAPPY 1. That which makes one sad or that which causes an undesirable outcome. 2. Could be a reflection of one's own mental state. 3. May suggest the need for a fresh perspective or the need to cultivate more joy in one's life. 4. See **Emotion**.

UNICORN 1. Symbol of purity, virginity, and that which is pristine. 2. Associated with ancient mysteries or knowledge. 3. Symbolizes the imagination, the mysterious, the

enchanted, or the magical. 4. Can correspond to spiritual freedom or a spiritual message. 5. Liturgically, an early symbol of Christ. See **Christ**. 6. May be associated with one's higher self. 7. You may also wish to see **Animals**.

UNIFORM 1. Associated with one's duty, occupation, or state of mind. See **Clothes**. 2. Can represent power or authority. 3. That which is uniform, unchanging, static, or consistent. 4. Can be symbolic of a shared or similar interest with others or the desire for community and to be joined with others. 5. May correspond to teamwork. See **Sports**. 6. Might be associated with fairness and balance. See **Balance**. 7. Depending upon the uniform, could be associated with an authority or a parental figure.

UNITED STATES 1. Associated with freedom, democracy, liberty, power, equality, and worldly success. 2. Could correspond to lawfulness and justice. 3. May be symbolic of bureaucracy. 4. Might be associated with domestic travel.

UNIVERSE 1. The totality of all that exists; the absolute. See **God.** 2. The limitless range of potentials and possibilities. 3. May correspond to a message from the higher self or the higher mind. See **Heaven.** 4. You may also wish to see **Planet** and **Astrology.**

UNIVERSITY 1. A place of higher learning. 2. Associated with the lessons and education provided by daily life. 3. Can correspond to the need or the opportunity to expand one's own thoughts, education, or consciousness in a particular situation. 4. What one has to teach to others or what one needs to learn from others. See **Teacher.** 5. Awareness or knowledge from a higher level. 6. May be symbolic of unresolved issues or experiences from the past. 7. That which can provide discipline to the untrained mind. 8. That which brings unrelated individuals together for a common goal (i.e., work may be seen as a university where one might learn cooperation, human interaction, and teamwork). 9. Can symbolize one's own thirst for knowledge. 10. You may also wish to see **Building** and **Test.** 11. Often associated with one's current situation or working environment.

UNLOCK 1. Can correspond to a new possibility, a hidden part of oneself that is about to come to the surface, an opening in understanding, or a change of mind. 2. That which is revealed or brought out into the open. 3. Whatever one is unlocking will have a great deal to do with the imagery; for example: unlocking a treasure chest could symbolize beginning to use one's hidden store of talents or ideas; unlocking a door may indicate a new dirction or a change in understanding. 4. Depending on imagery, you may also wish to see **Door, Lock,** or **Key.**

UNPACK 1. Associated with bringing things out into the open that have been stored. 2. Can correspond with deciding to stay in one's current situation. 3. May represent the baggage (experiences, ideas) an individual has available or needs to get rid of (i.e., habits, attitudes). 4. You may also wish to see **Luggage.**

UNPOLISHED 1. That which needs to be cleaned or refurbished. See **Clean.** 2. Associated with something that lacks refinement. 3. Can correspond to something that has not yet reached its full potential. 4. May represent an unhealthy or immature portion of one's life, physically, mentally, or spiritually. 5. Metaphorically, she's a little unpolished = she's not quite as able as she needs to be. 6. Depending on imagery, you

may also wish to see **Dirt.**

UNTIE 1. Associated with loosening, unbinding, releasing, or freeing a portion of oneself (i.e., attitudes, beliefs) or one's connection to or overdependence on something or someone. 2. Might correspond to solving a complicated or tangled problem. 3. You may also wish to see **Loose.**

URANUS ♅ 1. Can correspond to going to extremes, or to possessing intuition and insight. 2. Associated with the unconventional, the unusual, and the unexpected. 3. In Greek mythology, the first ruler of the heavens. See **Mythology (Roman and Greek).** 4. Seventh planet from the Sun. Has a rotation year of 84 years. 5. Astrologically, associated with Aquarius. See **Astrology.** 6. Metaphysically, associated with the fifth chakra (Thyroid). See **Chakras.**

URINATE 1. To spoil with a part of oneself. 2. To cleanse one's impurities: physically, mentally, or spiritually. 3. Done in public, it is often associated with showing off, making a mistake, or doing something one shouldn't have done. 4. See also **Bathroom.** 5. Could indicate the need to release toxins or impurities from one's physical, mental, or spiritual systems. 6. Something in the urine might correspond to a health problem. 7. May be a literal need to urinate.

URN 1. Corresponds to that which is put out for decoration or display. See **Vase.** 2. Whatever one associates with an urn will have a great deal to do with the imagery (i.e., a container for ashes is associated with death; a Roman vase symbolizes ancient knowledge or wisdom; a receptacle for flowers suggests one's inner spiritual beauty, etc.). 3. Might be representative of feminine sexuality. See **Womb.**

1. The twenty-second letter of the alphabet. 2. The Roman numeral for five. 3. Referring to the shape of an object, as in V-shaped. 4. A symbol for victory or peace. 5. Chemically, the symbol for vanadium. 6. Numerologically, equivalent to four.

VACATION 1. A time of relaxation and freedom. 2. May correspond to the need to rest from one's normal routine. 3. Might be in recognition of a job well done. 4. Could correspond to a literal vacation. 5. Whatever one associates with vacations will have a great deal to do with the symbolism. 6. Might be associated with one who constantly rests from certain responsibilities. 7. You may also wish to see **Trip**.

VACCINATION 1. That which makes one immune, insusceptible, or safe from a problem, an illness, or a situation. 2. Might be associated with painful and yet necessary and perhaps even helpful experience. 3. You may wish to see **Needle** and **Doctor**.

VACUUM 1. May correspond to the need to clean up one's environment, one's thoughts or emotions, one's situation, or one's activities. 2. Could indicate the need for physical, mental, or spiritual housecleaning. See **Clean**. 3. Might suggest the act of sucking up to someone.

VAGINA 1. Associated with the feminine and sexuality. 2. See **Womb** and **Woman**.

VALENTINE 1. Corresponds to love, romance, or infatuation. 2. May be associated with one's desires or inner feelings. 3. Could

indicate the possibility of a close relationship with another. 4. Might correspond to the need to communicate one's emotions. 5. You may also wish to see **Letter**. 6. Depending on imagery, you may wish to see **Heart**.

VALLEY 1. Can correspond to a time of ease, security, and happiness between life's challenges and hurdles (i.e., hills or mountains). 2. Depending upon imagery, might indicate depression or a low point in one's life. 3. A time of wide-open possibilities in one's life journey. See **Journey**. 4. Might be associated with female receptivity or sexuality. See **Womb**. 5. Biblically, associated with the Twenty-third Psalm and God's presence in the midst of adversity.

VALVE 1. May indicate the need to release emotional distress, pressure, or an overpowering condition. See **Pressure**. 2. That which controls the flow of energy, water, or emotions. See **Hose**. 3. Might be associated with a literal heart problem.

VAMPIRE 1. Associated with something that sucks or drains one's life, emotions, energy, or patience (i.e., the situation, another person, current thoughts, etc.). 2. That which feeds off others, another's ideas, or someone else's talents. 3. You may also wish to see **People**.

VAN 1. That which can carry people, belongings, ideas, etc. 2. May be associated with oneself, one's work, or one's current situation. See **Car**. 3. Depending on imagery, could indicate some type of a group endeavor or journey (i.e., several people in the van); may be associated with getting all of the various portions of oneself (i.e., hopes, ideas, activities) headed in the same direction, etc. 4. May correspond to one's life journey. See **Journey**.

VANILLA 1. Can indicate that which is plain, bland, or usual. 2. Might indicate the need for more creativity, spice, or zest. 3. The routine or ordinary. 4. Of course, if vanilla is an individual's favorite flavor, it could be associated with that which is tasty, enjoyable, or worthwhile. 5. You may also wish to see **Food**.

VASE 1. Representative of the feminine. See **Womb**. 2. Associated with a container for one's creativity, talents, or soul. 3. Corresponds to that which is put out for decoration or display. 4. Historically, that which is sculptured with a great deal of time, precision, and effort.

VAULT 1. Associated with knowledge or wisdom from another source. 2. Could correspond to hidden talents. See **Safe**. 3. May represent the unconscious or subconscious mind. See **Unconscious** or **Subconscious**. 4. Depending on imagery, might represent one's lower self, sexuality, untapped wisdom, or intuition. 5. Might correspond to karmic memory. See **Karma**. 6. You may also wish to see **Box**.

VCR 1. Corresponds to memories of experiences, ideas, or relationships. 2. Associated with recalling events or the need to recall events with a clear picture of what transpired. 3. Depending upon what one associates with VCRs, could symbolize a problem or an experience that one does not know how to work. 4. To reexperience a situation that has transpired previously. 5. May also be associated with karmic memory. See

Karma. 6. You may also wish to see **Television**.

VEGETABLES 1. Often corresponds to literal dietary suggestions. 2. Could indicate the need for less aggression (i.e., meat) in one's life. 3. May be associated with something that feeds and nourishes one's body, mind, or soul. See **Food**.

VEHICLE 1. Associated with oneself or one's journey through life. See **Journey**. 2. What one may use to carry oneself, others, or personal belongings (i.e., luggage, thoughts, beliefs, attitudes, etc.). 3. You may also wish to see the type of vehicle; for example, see **Automobile**, **Train**, **Boat**, or **Airplane**.

VEIL 1. That which conceals or disguises the truth. 2. Suggests that one needs to look beyond what one thinks is there, for the truth is hidden. 3. May be symbolic of hiding the real self. See **Shadow**. 4. See also **Face**. 5. You may also wish to see **Clothes.** 6. Might indicate one's own intuitive abilities. 7. Could be associated with shyness, humility, or low self-esteem. 8. Might correspond to the various levels of one's mind (i.e., the veil between the conscious and subconscious).

VEIN 1. That which provides one's life force; the source of life. 2. Metaphorically, a vein of truth = a direct line of truthful information. 3. Could indicate one's mood, health, or stress level. 4. You may also wish to see **Body.**

VELVET 1. Associated with luxury, wealth, or smoothness. 2. Could correspond to smooth talk or putting on a display of empathy. 3. You may wish to see **Clothes.** 4. See also **Colors.**

VENTRILOQUIST 1. Can correspond to controlling or speaking for another. See

Puppet. 2. Might suggest putting words in someone else's mouth or having words put in your mouth. 3. You may also wish to see **People.**

VENUS ♀ 1. Corresponds to love, beauty, companionship, and music. 2. Associated with emotions and femininity. 3. In Roman mythology, the goddess of love. See **Mythology (Roman and Greek).** 4. Second planet from the Sun; brightest planet in our solar system. Has a rotation year of 225 days. 5. Historically called Hesperus, as the evening star, and Lucifer, as the morning star. 6. Astrologically, associated with Taurus and Libra. See **Astrology.** 7. Metaphysically, associated with the fourth chakra (thymus). See **Chakras.**

VERMIN 1. That which is irritating, filthy, feeds off others, or causes trouble. See **Bug.** 2. Metaphorically, they're all a bunch of vermin = they're all disgusting.

VERTEBRAE 1. Associated with one's support, personal image, or stature. See **Back/Backbone.** 2. Might correspond to courage or self-worth. 3. You may also wish to see **Skeleton.**

VEST 1. Often indicates the outward personality one shows to the world. See **Coat.** 2. One's thoughts and attitudes. See **Clothes.** 3. Because it covers the chest area, may be associated with one's heart or emotions. See **Heart.**

VESTIBULE 1. Corresponds to the entrance of a church. See **Church.** 2. May indicate the need to enter into spiritual activity or to become recommitted to it. 3. You may also wish to see **Door.**

VET 1. That which may tend to one's animal instincts or nature. See **Animals.** 2. Depending upon the imagery, may be a literal indication to take one's pet to the vet. See **Pet.** 3. You may also wish to see **Doctor.**

VICTIM 1. Associated with one who feels victimized or taken advantage of. See **Attack.** 2. That which is being sacrificed by another or by oneself. 3 You may also wish to see **People.**

VICTORIAN 1. Associated with modesty. 2. Depending on imagery, can correspond to being conservative, prudish, bigoted, etc. 3. May be symbolic of that which is old yet valuable. See **Antique.** 4. Those portions of self (i.e., ideas, thoughts, activities) that are outmoded or outdated.

VIDEO CASSETTE RECORDER 1. See **VCR.** 2. Associated with memories of activities or situations.

VIDEO GAMES 1. Associated with mental focus and involvement. 2. Depending on one's personal association, may indicate that too much time is being spent in this activity. 3. The mental games with which one is involved. See **Game.**

VILLAGE 1. One's community, environment, or current situation. 2. Could be associated with various aspects of oneself. 3. Depending upon the imagery, might be representative of group activities (i.e., work) and teamwork or the lack of it. See **Sports.** 4. You may also wish to see **Building.**

VILLAIN 1. Corresponds to the perpetrator of evil, intrigue, deception, or criminal activity. See **Evil.** 2. Might be associated with the villainous aspects of oneself (i.e., bad thoughts, negative attitudes, harsh words, etc.). 3. May be associated with the hidden side of oneself. See **Shadow.** 4. Depending on the imagery, you may also wish to see **Thief.** 5. See also **People.** 6. Associated with taking advantage or being taken advantage of. 7. Might indicate that which is bent, unsavory, or immoral.

VINE. 1. Associated with one's thoughts, ideas, aspirations, habits, patterns, interests, desires, emotions, etc. 2. The imagery of the symbolism has a great deal to do with the meaning (i.e., is a new idea thriving or is an old belief system choking out new possibilities?). See **Plant.** 3. You may also wish to see **Garden.**

VINEGAR 1. That which is sour, acidic, harsh, or hard to take. 2. Metaphorically, she's vinegary = she's harsh or has a sour disposition. 3. Liturgically, associated with the crucifixion (John 19). 4. See **Food.**

VIOLENCE 1. Associated with fighting and aggression. See **Fight.** 2. Can indicate extreme anger, frustration, or conflict with oneself or others. 3. Might correspond to an aggressive male nature. See **Phallus.** 4. The act of being forced, dominated, or punished. 5. Might be indicative of something that has been repressed (i.e., guilt, anger, emotions, etc.). 6. You may also wish to see **Attack.**

VIOLET (COLOR) 1. Generally associated with spirituality. 2. See **Colors.**

VIOLET (FLOWER) 1. One's spiritual gifts, talents, or qualities. See **Flowers.** 2. Could be symbolic of a new growth or interest in spirituality.

VIOLIN 1. Can correspond to romance or harmony. 2. Might be associated with a sob story, 3. Could indicate one's ability to create harmony on one's own. 4. That which

one can do alone. 5. You may also wish to see **Music.**

VIRGIN 1. Symbolic of purity, newness, and inexperience. 2. Corresponds to modesty. 3. Can represent the undiscovered, as in the virgin forest, or the first, as in a virgin voyage. 4. A processed substance that has been obtained without the use of heat; for example, cold-pressed olive oil. 5. Astrologically, one of the twelve signs of the zodiac. See **Virgo.** 6. Depending on imagery, you may also wish to see **Woman.**

VIRGIN MARY 1. The feminine side of spirituality. 2. Archetype for the divine mother or feminine. See **Mother** and **Woman.** 3. A spiritual messenger. See **Message/Messenger.** 4. The feminine counterpart of Christ. See **Christ.**

VIRGO ♍ 1. Sixth sign of the zodiac, corresponding to August 23–September 22. 2. Associated with the following positive traits: modest, analytical, clean, neat, tidy. 3. Associated with the following negative traits: overly critical, a worrier, too conventional. 4. Astrologically, ruled by Mercury. See **Mercury.** 5. See **Virgin.** 6. An earth sign. See **Earth.** 7. See also **Astrology.**

VISHNU 1. In Hinduism, the divine preserver. See **Hinduism.** 2. The supreme god of the Hindu trinity (Brahma, Shiva, and Vishnu). 3. Often symbolized by a beautiful individual with four arms standing atop a winged beast. 4. Believed to have incarnated on earth as Krishna, Jesus, and others.

VISION 1. May correspond to insights, awareness, or information from one's higher self. 2. Seeing that which will come to pass. See **ESP.** 3. The act of clear seeing. See **Eyes.** 4. May be associated with a dream, imagery, an inner knowing, etc. 5. Metaphorically, she's a vision of loveliness = she's very beautiful. 6. A glimpse into other levels of reality or other levels of the mind.

VISITOR 1. Associated with a messenger, an unknown or unexpected part of oneself, or a guest. 2. May symbolize a temporary activity or encounter coming into one's experience. 3. Depending on imagery, may symbolize the arrival of an unexpected guest (i.e., a baby). See **Baby.** 4. You may also wish to see **People.**

VITAMINS 1. Could correspond to literal dietary suggestions. 2. May indicate the need to reinforce or care for oneself physically, mentally, or spiritually. 3. Might be associated with a literal indication of one's susceptibility to illness or colds. 4. You may also wish to see **Pill** and **Food.**

VOICE 1. Can indicate one's sincerity, integrity, quality of voice, professional mannerisms, etc. 2. Associated with communicating one's thoughts, words, or feelings. 3. May be suggestive of a literal message. See **Message/Messenger.** 4. Might be associated with how one hears or is heard by others. See **Hear.** 5. One's personal voice is associated with the self. See **Self.** 6. Metaphorically, can be used as follows: he voiced his opinion = he stated his opinion; they were with one voice = they agreed with one another. 7. Might be symbolic of one's own conscience.

VOLCANO 1. May correspond to anger, pent-up emotions, or the possibility of an emotional eruption. 2. Might symbolize one's suppressed fears, or those repressed things that have never been resolved. 3. In-

ner turmoil or confusion. 4. May be associated with a dangerous obstacle or hurdle. See **Mountain.** 5. You may also wish to see **Explosion/Explosive.**

VOMIT 1. May symbolize that which is hard to stomach. 2. A repulsive idea, thought, activity, or situation. 3. Can correspond to ejecting from oneself that which is foul, undesirable, or toxic (i.e., one's words). 4. Depending upon the imagery, could be associated with that which makes one sick; for example: eating a particular food beforehand could suggest that which wasn't good for you; eating a letter might indicate that one's words were foul, sickening, or harsh. 5. Might correspond with one's true feelings in spite of what one actually said. 6. Associated with something that is making one ill, physically, mentally, or spiritually. You may also wish to see **Ill/Illness.**

VOTING 1. To express one's opinion, ideas, or self, especially in a group activity. 2. Suggestive of the need to speak one's mind. 3. May be associated with the approval or disapproval of one's higher self. 4. You may also wish to see **Voice.**

VOW 1. A promise or a contract. 2. Could be calling to mind wedding vows, a partnership, or any promise. 3. May represent a proposal or a cooperative venture. See **Marriage.** 4. If a spiritual vow, see **Monk** or **Nun.**

VULTURE 1. Associated with death or that which is dying. See **Death.** 2. See also **Bird.** 3. Metaphorically, a vulture = an individual who preys upon others (sexually or otherwise), their possessions, and/or their weaknesses.

1. The twenty-third letter of the alphabet. 2. Chemically, the symbol for tungsten. 3. Numerologically, equivalent to five.

WADE 1. Can be associated with testing the waters of an idea or a situation. See **Water.** 2. May be symbolic of walking through or crossing a situation or experience. See **Walk.** 3. Might symbolize a spiritual journey. See **Journey.** 4. A movement forward with some degree of difficulty. 5. May indicate childhood or youthful memories. 6. May represent caution or introversion.

WAIST 1. Associated with one's personal image, self-esteem, or stomach. See **Body** and **Stomach.** 2. Depending on imagery, might suggest the need for restraint or control of oneself. See **Belt.** 3. May be associated with one's dietary habits and the desire to lose weight. 4. Depending on imagery, you may also wish to see **Fat** or **Thin.** 5. Might be a pun on that which is a waste. 6. That which comes in the middle.

WAIT 1. Can correspond to waiting for the arrival of an experience, a new situation, a relationship, or insights into one's current situation. 2. Could indicate the need for openness, receptivity, or relaxation. 3. Depending on imagery, could also be associated with inactivity or laziness. 4. You may also wish to see **Anticipation.**

WAITER/WAITRESS 1. Can be associated with taking or giving orders or being of service. See **Servant.** 2. Could indicate one's own attitude about assisting others. 3. May

symbolize what one is waiting for. 4. The attitude of the waiter or waitress and those being waited on will have a great deal to do with the symbolism; for example: remaining friendly during a lunch rush could correspond to one's ability to remain optimistic during stressful situations, or it may be a suggestion to try it; having a waitress stand around with no tables might indicate your own desire to serve but perhaps you haven't yet found the appropriate channels; ordering something that is not available could symbolize the need to make another choice. 5. See also **People.** 6. You may also wish to see **Restaurant.**

WALK 1. Associated with one's current activities, situation, state of mind, or journey. See **Journey.** 2. Can correspond to taking one step at a time. See **Steps.** 3. One's course of action or conduct. 4. Metaphorically, can be used as follows: she walked out on me = she left me; he walked off the job = he quit suddenly; you walk a fine line = you're getting very close to being in trouble. 5. The condition of the ground upon which one is walking will have a great deal to do with the meaning; for example: a bumpy path may suggest minor difficulties or problems; a fork in the road represents the fact that you need to make a choice or a decision. 6. You may also wish to see **Road.**

WALL 1. Symbolic of an obstacle that stands in the way or that must be overcome. 2. May represent a protective barrier, shelter, or boundary. See **Box.** 3. Associated with some type of barrier (emotional, mental, or physical), a limit, or a problem. 4. Can correspond to the experience of being confined. See **Prison.** 5. Metaphorically, can be used as follows: up against a wall = few options remain, or the moment of truth; off the wall = very unusual or crazy; hitting one's head against the wall = going nowhere. 6. That which divides or separates. 7. A crack in the wall may represent stubborn old patterns, emotions, or belief systems that are crumbling. 8. You may also wish to see **Fence.**

WALLET 1. Associated with one's material resources or security. See **Money.** 2. May be associated with what one values (i.e., relationships, time, resources, spirituality, etc.). 3. Might represent a reward or a recognition. 4. Can correspond to one's personal identity. 5. Could be associated with having someone in your back pocket. 6. May represent male sexuality. See **Phallus.**

WALTZ 1. Corresponds to a rhythmic movement or to step out with precision. 2. May suggest the dance of life. See **Journey.** 3. To join in partnership with an individual or a group. 4. To work together harmoniously; may suggest the need for harmony and cooperation. 5. May symbolize the need to watch your step.

WAND 1. May represent untapped and limitless potential. 2. That which can accomplish anything. See **Magic.** 3. Can correspond to having all that is required within one's own hands. 4. Might be associated with male sexuality. See **Phallus.**

WAR 1. A conflict between others or portions of oneself. See **Fight.** 2. An environment of hostility, aggression, and oppression. 3. Can correspond to an internal struggle. 4. Often associated with retaliation for previous thoughts, words, or actions. 5. May in-

dicate the need to consciously deal with problems that are struggling at the unconscious level. 6. Could be associated with the need to fight for what's right. 7. Depending on the time period and imagery, you may also wish to see **Historical Clothing/Settings, People,** or **Shadow.**

WARDEN 1. Associated with being in charge of unruly portions of oneself. See **Shadow.** 2. May correspond to the desire to control one's outer environment, relationships, or activities. 3. Might indicate the fact that one feels isolated from the outside world. See **Prison.** 4. You may also wish to see **People** and **Police/Police Station.**

WARRIOR 1. Associated with fighting for what's right. See **Soldier** and **War.** 2. Metaphorically, he's a good warrior = he's a good or dependable worker. 3. Can correspond to complete determination and commitment. 4. May be associated with an aggressive male nature. See **Phallus.** 5. See also **People**.

WART 1. Can correspond to that which is irritating, unsightly, or that which feeds off itself. 2. May indicate holding onto a problem or a bad situation. 3. Might represent self-criticism or punishment. 4. Could symbolize those blemishes in oneself that one has refused to part with. 5. See also **Body**.

WASH 1. That which has been or needs to be cleansed, purified, scrubbed, or washed. See **Bath.** 2. May correspond to the physical, mental, or spiritual portions of oneself. 3. What is being washed is very significant; for example: washing clothes may symbolize changing attitudes or one's consciousness; washing a car may indicate the need to change one's personal appearance; washing one's mouth is symbolic of having said something that one shouldn't have said.

4. Metaphorically, can be used as follows: I wash my hands of it = I want no part in it, or I give up; he's all washed up = he's a failure; it will all come out in the wash = it will be discovered later. 5. You may also wish to see **Soap** and **Water**.

WASHINGTON, D.C. 1. Associated with freedom, democracy, power, and the United States of America. 2. Could correspond to lawfulness and justice. 3. May be symbolic of bureaucracy. 4. Might be associated with domestic travel. 5. One's personal association will have a great deal to do with the symbolism.

WASHINGTON, GEORGE 1. The father of our country. See **Father**. 2. Associated with independence, liberty, and freedom. 3. Might correspond to the need to tell the truth. 4. You may also wish to see **United States**.

WASTE 1. That which is worthless, offensive, or immoral. 2. Can correspond to those things you have discarded or that need to be discarded (i.e., ideas, opinions, attitudes, etc.). 3. Might also be calling to mind those things that one inadvertently threw away and shouldn't have, or the fact that one wastes too much. 4. Could indicate a rotten diet or food that has been wasted. 5. Might be associated with one's stomach (i.e., especially the image of a garbage disposal). 6. Could also be symbolic of the lower sex drive. 7. Metaphorically, to lay something to waste = to destroy it. 8. You may also wish to see **Food**.

WATCH 1. That which counts the passage of time or experiences. See **Clock** and **Time**. 2. Might suggest the actual timing of an event. 3. May indicate the necessity of being alert. 4. Depending on imagery, might correspond to one's own timeliness.

WATCHDOG 1. Corresponds to one who is keeping a watchful eye on a person, a place, or the situation. 2. Might suggest the need to be on guard. See **Guard**. 3. See also **Dog**.

WATER 1. Associated with the source of all life, sustenance, understanding, or wisdom. 2. The embodiment of spirituality or spiritual wisdom. 3. May represent emotions, the unconscious or subconscious, or the soul. 4. Associated with a spiritual or a life journey. See **Journey** and **Boat**. 5. The type of water could be symbolic of particular feelings, moods, and desires; for example: clear water may indicate clarity of insight or vision; dirty or muddy water might represent an unclear situation, clouded emotions, feelings, or understanding. 6. Associated with the feminine. See **Womb**. 7. Can correspond to the passage of time, a new birth, or a death. 8. That which is willing to flow. See **Sailing**. 9. What one is doing with the water is very significant; for example: drinking water may symbolize the literal need to drink more water or the fact that one is having or needs to have their spiritual thirst quenched; pouring water on someone else could suggest that you are dowsing their enthusiasm or that one too frequently uses the individual as an emotional release. 10. Can represent the need for physical, mental, or spiritual cleansing, or renewal. 11. That which reflects one's image, experience, or the situation. See **Mirror.** 12. Biblically, associated with baptism or spiritual rebirth. See **Christ**. 13. Metaphorically, out of hot water = out of trouble; keeping one's head above water = barely keeping afloat financially or personally; to make water = to urinate; making one's mouth water = having a great desire for. 14. One of the four elements (air, earth, fire, and water). See **Elements.** 15. Can correspond to the astrological water signs: **Pisces, Cancer,** and **Scorpio.** See individual signs for traits. 16. You may also wish to see **River, Ocean, Rain,** and **Fish.**

WATERFALL 1. Can be associated with the flow of one's emotions, ideas, insights, etc. See **River.** 2. Could symbolize a spiritual flow, a cleansing, or the process of healing. 3. Might represent the passage of time. See **Time.** 4. Depending on imagery, may symbolize purity, that which is pristine, that which is in its natural state, or that which is dangerous or treacherous. 5. Might represent God's continuous involvement (or flow) in creation, nature, or beauty. 6. Could indicate the need for rest, relaxation, or solitude. 7. Could be associated with the need to cleanse oneself physically, mentally, or emotionally. See **Shower.** 8. A source of energy, spirit, wisdom, or enlightenment. See **Water.** 9. You may also wish to see **Fall.**

WAVE 1. Often associated with arrivals or departures. 2. Could indicate the beginning or the ending of either a situation or a relationship. 3. You may also wish to see **Hand.**

WAVES 1. Associated with periods of intense or swelling emotions. 2. Can correspond to the ups and downs of emotions or feelings. 3. That which may be unstable or wavering. 4. See also **Water.** 5. You may also wish to see **Weather.**

WEAPON 1. That which one uses to harm, injure, or kill another; that which one uses to protect oneself. See **Kill.** 2. Usually associated with words, actions, thoughts, or deeds; for example: poking someone with a knife might suggest that you are prodding them or that you are cutting them off. See **Knife.** 3. Sharp-pointed weapons can correspond to an aggressive male behavior. See **Phallus.** 4. Exploding weapons are often

symbolic of holding in one's emotions. See **Explosion/Explosive.** 5. That which is used for fighting. See **Fight.** 6. You may also wish to see **War.**

WEATHER 1. Generally corresponds to an individual's emotional or mental states. 2. Can be associated with the natural rhythms and cycles of life. 3. Specific weather conditions often indicate particular traits, opportunities, emotions, or challenges. For example:

> *Avalanche:* A shattering and overwhelming experience or the breakup of internal forces.
>
> *Clouds, Fog,* or *Mist:* Inability to see clearly, generally due to cloudy feelings, emotions, perceptions, or understanding.
>
> *Hurricanes* or *Tornadoes:* Major challenges, emotional problems, perhaps even mental illness.
>
> *Ice:* That which is frozen, frigid, detached, or on thin ice.
>
> *Rain:* Overcome or cleansed by emotions. Can represent spiritual healing or purification. Heavy rain could indicate being overwhelmed by the situation or by one's own mental state.
>
> *Snow:* May indicate a cold-hearted nature or remaining frozen in one's own perception, state of mind, or emotions. Could also represent purity in the midst of a storm.
>
> *Storms:* Symbolic of mental challenges, arguments, disagreements, or environmental challenges and conditions.
>
> *Thunder* and *Lightning:* May be associated with quick and uncontrollable outbursts. Could also correspond to an important message or flashes of insight or intuition from one's higher self.
>
> *Wind:* Often represents the flow of

thoughts, emotions, or events. Could indicate the movement of spirit or a message from one's higher self.

4. Maintaining your calm in the midst of weather conditions generally suggests inner peace and balance or even acceptance of the situation. However, it may also be associated with being too detached or unfeeling toward other individuals or the situation. 5. You may also wish to see **Seasons** and **Spring, Summer**, **Fall**, or **Winter**.

WEATHERMAN 1. One who maintains stability in the midst of any circumstance. 2. Associated with one who controls or forecasts the environment (i.e., surroundings, emotions, people). 3. You may also wish to see **Weather** and **People**.

WEB 1. That which lures and traps. 2. Can be a warning sign of entrapment. 3. Could be associated with a web of intrigue (i.e., a scheme) or danger. 4. Might be symbolic of widowhood or death. See **Death**. 5. See also **Bug** and **Spider**.

WEDDING 1. A joining together. 2. Might indicate a literal wedding. 3. May be associated with a union, a partnership, a promise, a commitment, or a reconciliation. 4. Could symbolize the integration of two parts of oneself. See **Shadow**. 5. See also **Marriage**.

WEDDING RING 1. Can correspond to a relationship, a partnership, or an amicable union. 2. May also indicate a literal wedding. 3. You may also wish to see **Ring** and **Jewelry**.

WEEDS 1. Associated with unwanted or negative thoughts, ideas, or a bad situation. 2. Can correspond to one's neglect of a sit-uation or a relationship. See **Garden**. 3. That which threatens (or chokes) the desired result. 4. Can indicate problems or obstacles that need to be removed. 5. See also **Plant**.

WEEP 1. Corresponds to the release of emotions. 2. May indicate a severe disappointment. 3. Might symbolize a cleansing. 4. To lament the situation in your life or to feel sorry for what you have done. 5. You may also wish to see **Eyes**.

WELL 1. That which is a natural spring of water. See **Water**. 2. Associated with making a wish. See **Magic**. 3. A source of energy, healing, vitality, or sustenance.

WEST 1. Associated with the setting sun; the end of a situation or an experience. 2. May also indicate an adventure (i.e., the settlers moved toward the western frontier). 3. The place of spirituality. 4. See also **Direction**. 5. Might be associated with the right. See **Right**.

WHALE 1. Could represent an enormous spiritual undertaking or journey. See **Fish**. 2. Metaphorically, can be used as follows: that was a whale of an idea = that was a great idea; that was a whale of a story = an exaggerated or good story. 3. May be associated with oneself (i.e., a mammal). 4. You may also wish to see **Animals**.

WHEAT 1. May be associated with the staff of life. See **Bread**. 2. Could indicate specific dietary recommendations or allergies. See **Food**. 3. Might indicate the need for harvesting what one has sown. See **Plant**. 4. You may also wish to see **Seed**.

WHEEL 1. Corresponds to motion or activity. 2. Associated with that which steers a motor vehicle. See **Steering Wheel**. 3. Represents cycles of activity that come around in their turn. 4. Biblically, associated with a heavenly message (Ezekiel 1). 5. In Eastern thought, corresponds to the wheel of the law, cause and effect, or karma. See **Karma.** 6. Taking the wheel could indicate the need to take control of the situation. See **Automobile.** 7. Might be associated with the wheel of fortune.

WHEELCHAIR 1. Might indicate a portion of oneself that is handicapped or disabled. See **Handicap.** 2. Depending on imagery, might suggest a smooth ride through the experience. 3. Might correspond to the inability to stand on one's own feet (i.e., support or believe in oneself). See **Feet.** 4. Could be associated with one's feeling of being dominated or pushed around. 5. May correspond to the need to be cautious in one's activities or an injury could be the result. 6. That which may give support. See **Leg/Legless.**

WHIP 1. Associated with being whipped into shape. 2. Could indicate one's own feelings of personal chastisement. 3. May indicate one's anger directed toward another. 4. Can be associated with lashing out at others verbally. 5. May represent being dominated (i.e., being a whipping boy), or being dominant and aggressive toward others. 6. May correspond to male sexuality. See **Phallus.**

WHISKEY 1. May correspond to physical overindulgence or habits. See **Food.** 2. That which causes the loss of physical consciousness or personal inhibitions. See **Drunk.** 3. Can represent something that is making the individual intoxicated or overcome. 4. Associated with a desire to escape reality or to force relaxation through artificial means. 5. May be a pun on partaking of the spirit. 6. See also **Alcohol.**

WHISPER 1. Can be associated with one's own "still small voice" within. 2. Depending on one's normal speech pattern, could indicate the need to speak up for oneself or that you need to speak more gently in order to be heard. 3. May be associated with a secret. 4. You may also wish to see **Voice.**

WHISTLE 1. A message, a warning, or a call to become alert. 2. Metaphorically, can be used as follows: I need to wet my whistle = I need a drink. 3. Might indicate approval of one's appearance or action.

WHITE 1. Generally associated with purity, virginity, innocence, and holiness. 2. See **Colors.**

WHITE HOUSE 1. Symbolic of the United States, politics, or the president. See **President.** 2. Can represent one's own house or living situation. See **House.** 3. May be associated with Washington, D.C., or the possibility of domestic travel. 4. Might correspond to one's own chief executive (i.e., God, one's higher self, or one's boss).

WIDOW/WIDOWER 1. Can correspond to being alone, abandoned, or isolated. 2. May be associated with one's fears. 3. Could mean that one is killing a relationship. See **Death.** 4. Might suggest that the current situation or experience has outlived its usefulness. 5. Might be a literal indication of death. 6. The desire to be free from one's current situation. 7. You may also wish to see **Husband** or **Wife.**

WIFE 1. Often suggests literal aspects of the relationship one possesses with one's own spouse. 2. How your wife appears may be symbolic of your attitude and feelings toward her. 3. Could indicate a suggestion or a warning in terms of your wife's welfare. 4.

Can correspond to new insights into your wife's behavior, attitudes, or opinions. 5. May indicate how your conscious inter- actions are affecting her physically, mentally, or spiritually. 6. Might be associated with the feminine part of oneself. See **Woman.** 7. May also represent a close personal rela- tionship with any female, especially if one isn't married. 8. Might be a literal indication of marriage. 9. You may also wish to see **Womb** and **People.**

WIG 1. A phony or false idea, belief, atti- tude, or opinion. See **Hair.** 2. That which is not true about oneself or one's belief sys- tem. 3. Might symbolize attempting to take credit for someone else's ideas. 4. You may also wish to see **Head.**

WIGWAM 1. Associated with a changeable or temporary idea, relationship, emotion, or physical body. See **House.** 2. May corre- spond to that which is Native American. See **Indian.** 3. That which may be moved by oneself. See **Luggage.** 4. For nature lovers, could be indicative of rest, relaxation, or get- ting back to nature.

WILD BEAST/MAN/WOMAN 1. Associ- ated with uncontrolled anger or rage. 2. A repressed or ignored portion of oneself. 3. Psychologically, an individual's shadow. See **Shadow.** 4. Can represent one's own fears. 5. See also **Beast, Man,** or **Woman.** 6. The emotionally upset part of oneself. 7. You may also wish to see **People.**

WILDERNESS 1. Depending on the type of wilderness, that which is uncivilized, un- cultivated, or unexplored or that which is desolate, deserted, and uninhabitable. See **Jungle** or **Plant.** 2. That which is infertile, bleak, or abandoned (i.e., no talents, no ideas, and no insights). 3. Being caught with-

out the proper insight or equipment. 4. May also correspond to that which is primitive and unruly. 5. Might indicate emotional iso- lation. See **Island.**

WIND 1. Represents flow of emotions, thoughts, or events. See **Weather.** 2. Can be indicative of spiritual insight or a message from the higher self. 3. Metaphorically, can be used as follows: she took the wind out of my sails = she got rid of my enthusiasm, or she stopped the whole thing; he needs to get his second wind = he needs a rest; to break wind = to have gas.

WIND CHIMES 1. May be associated with one's ability to maintain harmony in the midst of emotional situations or problems. 2. Could indicate a message of forthcoming problems or opportunities. 3. Might corre- spond to music. See **Music.** 4. Depending on imagery, you may also wish to see **Wind** and **Weather.**

WINDMILL 1. That which can be used for power or for grinding. 2. Can be associated with that which is inexpensive and indus- trious. 3. The condition of the windmill will have a great deal to do with whether the symbol is positive or negative. See **Build- ing.** 4. In literature, associated with fighting enemies that do not exist (i.e., *Don Quixote*).

WINDOW 1. Associated with sight, aware- ness, attitudes, or that which you present to the world. See **Vision.** 2. Can correspond to an opening or a different perspective. 3. The shape, size, color, number of panes, and whether or not the window is opened or closed is very important; for example: a closed window can be symbolic of not look- ing beyond one's current circumstances or environment; a stained glass window may indicate spiritual vision or insight; a foggy window may suggest a clouded perspective, or the need to get new glasses. 4. How one sees the outside world. See **Eyes.** 5. Curtains on the window indicate either opening or closing a portion of one's life or a death. See **Curtain.** 6. If the window is in a door, it's generally associated with a new insight into oneself or a new experience one is about to enter into. See **Door.** 7. You may also wish to see **Glass.**

WINE 1. Generally associated with the spirit. 2. Can correspond to relaxation or the need for it. 3. Depending on imagery, may indicate success, romance, or a celebration. 4. You may also wish to see **Alcohol** and **Food.**

WINGS 1. May represent a spiritual journey, insight, or a messenger. See **Airplane** and **Angel.** 2. Can be associated with the soul. 3. Might indicate that one is about to take flight or soar. See **Flying.** 4. Could suggest the need to rise above one's current situation. 5. Metaphorically, I'll wing it = I'll just figure out how to do it while I'm doing it.

WINK 1. Associated with partial vision, flirting, or sending a message. 2. Metaphorically, she took forty winks = she took a nap. 3. See also **Eyes.**

WINTER 1. Associated with the ending of an experience, project, life, or a relationship. See **Seasons.** 2. May represent ageless wisdom. 3. Corresponds to dormancy and rest. 4. Could be associated with a waiting period prior to a new start or a rebirth. 5. Corresponds to the north. 6. A time of decline, coldness, or adversity. 7. The last possible chance for any harvest. 8. Associated with hibernation. 9. You may also wish to see **Snow** and **Cold.**

WISE MAN/WISE WOMAN 1. Wisdom and insight through experience. 2. Often relates to an individual's own higher self or to subconscious information. 3. Frequently symbolizes a message from a wise source. See **Message/Messenger.** 4. May be associated with a source of unlimited wisdom: a seer, a sage, a prophet, Christ, or God. 5. Associated with the three wise men (astrologers) at the birth of Jesus. See **Christ.** 6. The bearer of lessons that need to be revisited or finally learned. 7. Could correspond to one's own past or future. 8, May be a messenger of karmic memory. See. **Karma.** 9. See also **People.** 10. You may also wish to see **Teacher.**

WITCH 1. Associated with magic, the manifestation of the subconscious into the material world, and the supernatural. 2. That which is enchanted, magical, or mysterious. 3. Can be a good witch and positive (i.e., bringing one's gifts of the spirit into manifestation), or a bad witch and negative (i.e., attempting to control others or the environment for selfish purposes). 4. May be symbolic of intuition and the feminine attributes of the subconscious. See **Woman.** 5. That which is bewitching or charming. 6. Might be associated with the witchy (i.e., negative or bitchy parts of oneself). 7. See also **Wizard**. 8. Metaphorically, they're a real witch = they're really negative or hard to deal with. 9. You may also wish to see **People** and **Magic.**

WITNESS 1. Can correspond to that part of oneself that possesses an objective perspective of one's activities or one's past. 2. May be associated with a testimony or a memory of what transpired. 3. Might symbolize karmic memory. See **Karma.** 4. You may also wish to see **Photograph.**

WIZARD 1. Associated with magic, the manifestation of the subconscious into the material world, and the supernatural. 2. That which is enchanted, magical, or mysterious. See **Witch.** 3. May be symbolic of wisdom and the masculine attributes of the subconscious. See **Man.** 4. May represent untapped and limitless potential. 5. Can be a good wizard and positive (i.e., associated with wisdom and mentoring), or a bad wizard and negative (i.e., associated with evil and controlling others). 6. That which can accomplish anything. 7. May correspond to mysticism or ancient knowledge. 8. Could be symbolic of the conscious mind trying to dominate the unconscious. 9. May indicate the process of making ideas come to fruition. 10. Metaphorically, that guy is a wizard = that guy is really intelligent. 11. You may also wish to see **People** and **Magic.**

WOLF 1. Can be associated with anger, aggression, domination, or base sexuality. 2. Metaphorically, can be used as follows: the wolf's at the door = things are very bad in this situation; the guy is a wolf = he's lecherous, or he's totally dominant in business affairs; she wolfed it down = she ate it very quickly; to cry wolf = to issue a false alarm. 3. You may also wish to see **Animals.**

WOMAN 1. Associated with the individuality of oneself. 2. Corresponds to the feminine side of one's nature. 3. Possibly corresponding to feminine traits (i.e., compassion, intuition, sensitivity, receptivity, and tenderness). See **Womb.** 4. Can represent the emotional, intuitive, family, or maternal instincts. 5. Different types of women can be associated with different meanings; for example: an old woman symbolizes wisdom or experience; a wild woman is associated with uncontrollable aspects of oneself or an emotional nature; a

young woman suggests youthfulness, naïveté, or inexperience. 6. The age of the woman may also correspond to a feminine aspect of oneself or one's projects of about the same age. 7. You may also wish to see **People** and **Girl.**

WOMB 1. Associated with female sexuality. See **Woman.** 2. That which is receptive to a situation. 3. Could indicate one's use of creativity. 4. Literal sexual feelings. 5. May represent the forces of reproduction, compassion, and receptivity. 6. Might symbolize whether or not one is blocked or has the desire for a particular situation. 7. One's own fears. 8. Can correspond to the following positive traits: sympathetic, intuitive, patient, loving, etc. 9. Can correspond to the following negative traits: moody, possessive, critical, rigid, etc. 10. Associated with both water signs (**Pisces, Cancer,** and **Scorpio**) and earth signs (**Taurus, Virgo,** and **Capricorn**) in astrology. See individual signs for additional positive and negative traits. 11. You may also wish to see **People.** 12. Might be associated with the gonads or first chakra. See **Gonads.**

WOODS 1. Associated with multiple ideas, possible directions, or limitless outcomes. See **Forest** and **Tree.** 2. May represent new possibilities or something constructive about to occur. 3. Could indicate becoming lost in one's own state of mind. 4. Whatever the individual associates with being in the woods will be very significant; for example: being lost, enjoying nature, relaxing, etc. 5. Metaphorically, we're not out of the woods yet = we're still in trouble. 6. You may also wish to see **Plant.**

WOOL 1. That which is soft, comforting, and warm. You may also wish to see **Sheep** and **Blanket.** 2. Metaphorically, to pull the wool over someone's eyes = to trick them.

WORK 1. Generally corresponds to one's present occupation. 2. One's own feelings about work as well as the activity in the image (for example: if others are present, if it is a stressful situation, or if you feel useful) will have a great deal to do with the associated symbolism. 3. Can correspond to one's duty or obligation (i.e., actual work, family, a project, etc.). 4. May suggest either the need for personal discipline or the fact that one works too much. 5. Former places of employment are often associated with similar attitudes, emotions, people, and experiences that one is still attempting to learn from in the present. 6. May be associated with working out a problem from any aspect of life. 7. Metaphorically, can be used as follows: to make quick work of = to take care of something quickly; to work it off = to sober up; give me the works = give me a little bit of everything. 8. May be symbolic of success or the lack of it. See **Money.** 9. Might correspond to working out or working on a problem, a situation, or a relationship. 10. The activity and appearance at the office will have a great deal to do with the symbolism. See **Building.** 11. One's present situation or environment. 12. Depending on the imagery, you may also wish to see **People** and **Boss.**

WORLD 1. May correspond to that place where one resides or the situation one is in the midst of. 2. Might be associated with that which is usual, mundane, material, earthly, or sensual. See **Earth.** 3. Can represent the great mother. See **Mother.** 4. Associated with the totality of all that exists in one's possible experience. 5. Metaphorically, can be used as follows: she's on top of the world = everything is going great for her; it's out of this world = it's fantastic. 6. Might be as-

sociated with that which is worldly rather than spiritual. 7. Associated with twenty-one in the tarot. See **Tarot.** 8. You may also wish to see **Universe.**

WORLD WAR I OR II 1. May represent that which wars against itself. See **War.** 2. Could indicate an inner struggle. 3. Associated with an aggressive or hostile situation. See **Fighting.** 4. You may also wish to see **Historical Clothing/Settings.**

WORM 1. Associated with a despicable person or that which gnaws, crawls, or slithers. See **Bug.** 2. Might be associated with fishing or bait. See **Fishing** and **Bait.** 3. Metaphorically, can be used as follows: she wormed it out of me = she got the information; it's a can of worms = it's a big problem; he wormed out of it = he got out of having to do it. 4. Might correspond to death and decay. See **Death.** 5. That which is earthy. See **Earth.** 6. A worm in food is associated with temptation or that which is not healthy for you.

WORN 1. That which is damaged by use, worry, or age. 2. Can correspond to being no longer usable in its present condition. 3. If clothing is worn, it may be associated with a part of one's outer personality that needs to be addressed, mended, or replaced. See **Clothes.**

WORRIED 1. May represent another situation with which one is concerned. 2. Associated with restlessness and worry. 3. Might be associated with eager anticipation. 4. You may also wish to see **Emotion.**

WORSHIP 1. Corresponds to one's spiritual or devotional life. See **Prayer** and **Meditation.** 2. May indicate the need to listen to one's higher self. 3. Might be associated with that which one craves, desires, or yearns. 4. Could indicate what one has made most important in one's life. See **Idol.** 5. Associated with the need to spend more time in spiritual activities.

WOUND 1. May be associated with an injury to oneself or others (physically, mentally, or spiritually). 2. The portion of the body that has been wounded may give you an indication of the problem; for example: a wounded chest could symbolize problems or hurts in the emotional area; a wounded back might symbolize that you have been knifed in the back or have done the same to another. 3. You may also wish to see types of wounds; for example, see **Broken, Cut,** or **Scratch.** 4. Surface wounds can represent words and feelings or they may be associated with a literal health condition. See **Body** and **Skin.**

WRAPPING PAPER 1. Associated with a gift, a present, or one's hidden talent. See **Gift.** 2. Could indicate a special message. See **Message/Messenger.** 3. Might indicate being wrapped up in the situation. 4. Can correspond to a facade or that which covers the real situation. 5. Could suggest the need to finish what you are doing (i.e., wrapping things up). 6. You may also wish to see **Box.**

WREATH 1. May be associated with a celebration, an honor, Christmas, a victory, a birth, or a death. 2. Corresponds to a message. See **Message/Messenger.** 3. You may also wish to see **Door** or **Window,** depending upon where the wreath is displayed.

WRECK 1. Corresponds to a disaster, a problem, a bad situation, or a horrible experience. 2. The type of accident has a great deal to do with the symbolism; for example:

a car wreck is often associated with a warning about one's body, diet, stress level, or situation (see **Automobile**); a plane wreck might indicate a spiritual problem (see **Airplane**); a shipwreck could indicate a problem with one's current life journey (see **Journey**). 3. May be a literal warning suggesting alternate plans, doing what one can do to prevent the incident, etc. 4. Metaphorically, can be used as follows: he's a wreck = he's in very bad shape physically, mentally, emotionally, or spiritually.

WRESTLE 1. Can be associated with wrestling with one's own emotions, ideas, desires, or thoughts. 2. Associated with the contest between different portions of oneself (i.e., physically, mentally, or spiritually). See **Shadow.** 3. A struggle with someone or something at work, home, or in the present situation. See **Fighting.** 4. To pull away or to try to extract oneself from an experience. 5. May correspond to the struggle between various portions of one's mind (conscious, subconscious, or higher self).

WRINKLES 1. May be associated with wisdom, experience, gentleness, hardship, or age. 2. Metaphorically, that gives it a different wrinkle = that provides additional insight into the situation. 3. You may also wish to see **Age** and **Old Man/Old Woman.**

WRIST 1. Associated with an obligation or a commitment. 2. Depending on imagery, may correspond to that which has hold of oneself. 3. See also **Body.** 4. You may also wish to see **Bracelet.**

WRITE 1. Associated with self-expression and communication. 2. To send or to receive a message. See **Letter.** 3. May indicate a personal talent or the need to communicate with someone. 4. Metaphorically, can be used as follows: she wrote it off = she forgot it; he was written up = he received notoriety or he got into trouble; let it be written = see that it's accomplished. 5. A communication with one's inner nature or higher self. 6. Could suggest the need for introspection and self-examination. 7. Might be a pun on the need to set things right. 8. You may also wish to see **Pen.**

WRONG WAY 1. A message, warning, or sign about one's direction. 2. Suggestive of the need for a different course of action; 3. You may wish to see **Sign** or **Journey.**

#

1. *The twenty-fourth letter of the alphabet.* 2. *The Roman numeral for ten.* 3. *Referring to the shape of an object.* 4. *Referring to the correct spot or the place for an individual's signature, as in X marks the spot.* 5. *An abbreviation for Christ, as in Xmas.* 6. *Chemically, the symbol for xenon.* 7. *Mathematically, an unknown quantity or the sign for multiplication.* 8. *Numerologically, equivalent to six.* 9. *In Greek, xi.*

XMAS 1. Representative of Christmas. See **Christmas.** 2. Might suggest that one has taken the Christ out of Christmas.

X RAY 1. Associated with the ability to see through a person, an obstacle, or an experience. 2. Corresponds to enhanced vision. See **Vision.** 3. Representative of a photograph that reveals the entire picture. See **Photograph.** 4. Might correspond to one's intuition or ESP. See **ESP.** 5. You may also wish to see **Eyes.**

XYLOPHONE 1. Associated with a musical instrument. See **Music.** 2. Symbolic of the ability to bring together different pieces, individuals, or experiences into a harmonious whole.

Y

1. *The twenty-fifth letter of the alphabet.* 2. *The Roman numeral for 150.* 3. *Referring to the shape of an object.* 4. *Chemically, the symbol for yttrium.* 5. *Mathematically, an unknown quantity.* 6. *A suffix used to denote familiarity, as in daddy or Bobby.* 7. *Numerologically, equivalent to seven.* 8. *In Greek, upsilon.*

YACHT 1. A new idea, attitude, change, or direction. See **Boat.** 2. A pleasurable experience or message. 3. May be symbolic of taking it easy or the need to relax. 4. You may also wish to see **Water** and **Sailing.**

YAHWEH 1. Associated with the Hebrew name for Jehovah. See **God.** 2. May represent the Jewish faith. See **Judaism.**

YANG AND YIN 1. Corresponds to the active male (yang) and the passive female (yin) life energies. See **Phallus** and **Womb.** 2. Associated with duality: life and death, summer and winter, good and evil, etc. 3. Together, may represent personal fulfillment, the achievement of selfhood, perfect balance, or spiritual transformation. See **Christ.**

YANKEE 1. Associated with a Union soldier in the Civil War. 2. Corresponds to the inhabitants of New England and/or the northern states. 3. May be symbolic of any native or inhabitant of the United States. 4. May represent independence, liberty, or prosperity. 5. See **United States.** 6. Depending upon one's personal background, may be associated with the unusual or the enemy. 7.

You may also wish to see **Historical Clothing/Settings.**

YARD 1. Corresponds to one's current situation, environment, state of mind, or occupation. See **Garden** and **House.** 2. That which is enclosed or surrounded on all sides. See **Fence.** 3. Associated with a particular industry or business (i.e., shipyard, lumberyard). 4. You may also wish to see **Field.**

YARDWORK 1. Depending on personal association, can correspond to personal responsibility, discipline, or that which is tedious and ongoing. 2. Could correspond to the need to get one's activities, environment, thoughts, or life in order. 3. You may also wish to see **Yard.**

YARN 1. Metaphorically, associated with an exaggerated story. 2. The fiber that holds itself together. 3. Could correspond to strands of an idea or personalities that may come together in a single project. 4. See also **String** and **Rope.**

YAWN 1. Associated with that which is boring. 2. May correspond to personal fatigue or depletion. See **Sleep.** 3. Can be symbolic of the repetition of that which has gone or been stated before. 4. You may also wish to see **Mouth**.

YEAR 1. Corresponds to time, the passage of time, or increments of time. 2. Can represent memories. See **Photograph**. 3. May represent any cycle or evolutionary period. 4. Associated with twelve months. See **Cal-**

endar. 5. You may also wish to see **Numerology**. 6. The number of years may be symbolic of an activity or a person of about the same age.

YEARN 1. Associated with being filled with desire, longing, or grief. 2. Can correspond to an inner urge for direction. See **Direction** and **Journey**. 3. You may also wish to see **Cry**.

YEAST 1. Associated with something that leavens or infiltrates the whole. 2. Can correspond to disruption, fermentation, or agitation. 3. That which gives the increase. See **God**. 4. Can be symbolic of being uplifted or raising one's ideas, thoughts, or sights to a higher level. 5. May represent tiny ideas that could grow to fruition. 6. You may also wish to see **Bread**.

YELL 1. Symbolic of an important message, warning, or idea. See **Message/Messenger**. 2. That which aroused one from a current state of mind or present situation. 3. Associated with the desire to be heard or one's inability to hear. See **Hear**. 4. You may also wish to see **Scream**.

YELLOW 1. Generally associated with intelligence and power. 2. See **Colors**.

YELLOW BRICK ROAD 1. In literature, associated with the soul's journey to self-realization and enlightenment (*The Wizard of Oz*). 2. The attainment of wisdom through personal experience. 3. One's personal direction and path. 4. See also **Road**.

YIELD 1. Associated with a message. See **Message/Messenger**. 2. May be associated with the need for relinquishment, submission, or personal caution. 3. Represents the need for cooperation and integration with the needs of others. 4. Could be symbolic of the return or the potential dividends. 5. Depending on imagery, you may wish to see **Traffic Light** or **Sign**.

YODEL 1. To sing loudly or abruptly. See **Sing/Singer**. 2. To attempt personal harmony. 3. May be symbolic of Switzerland or Austria.

YOGA/YOGI 1. Associated with meditation, focused thought, and discipline. See **Meditation**. 2. May correspond to self-mastery or the need for self-mastery. 3. May be symbolic of the need to focus one's thoughts, energies, or attention. 4. Could indicate the need for greater spiritual discipline. 5. That which links various levels of reality (i.e., the conscious mind with the infinite). 6. A Yogi could be symbolic of one's own higher self. 7. You may also wish to see **Wise Man/Wise Woman.**

YOKE 1. The state of being connected, united, or involved in an activity, relationship, or process. See **Rope**. 2. Associated with something that can bind things together forcibly (i.e., emotions, commitment, duty, guilt, etc.). 3. Can correspond to bondage or service. 4. May represent the state of marriage. See **Marriage.** 5. May be associated with an ox or bull. See **Bull.**

YOLK 1. The inner portion or principal substance. See **Seed**. 2. That which may come out of its shell. 3. See also **Egg.**

YOUNG/YOUTH 1. That which is immature or in the early portion of life. See **Child.** 2. Corresponds to that which is not yet developed. 3. Symbolic of that which is fresh and uncorrupted. 4. The symbol of a youth with an old man can signify the transformation of the old to the new; the rising and setting sun; or the arrival of the new year and the passing of the old year.

YULE 1. Corresponds to Christmas. See **Christmas.** 2. Originally (until the Middle Ages) associated with the winter solstice. 3. Yule symbols (i.e., yule log, yule fire) will often have meanings associated with one's own memories of the season.

1. *The twenty-sixth letter of the alphabet.* 2. *The Roman numeral for 2000.* 3. *Mathematically, an unknown quantity.* 4. *Numerologically, equivalent to eight.* 5. *In Greek, zeta.*

ZACHARIAH 1. Associated with one who was healed due to faith and obedience. 2. Metaphysically, corresponds to the idea that God has never forgotten any individual.

ZEBRA 1. Associated with a messenger with stripes, perhaps bearing a distinctive message. See **Stripes**. 2. Can represent freedom and the wild. 3. May indicate that which is in a cage. See **Prisoner**. 4. You may also wish to see **Horse** and **Animals**.

ZEN 1. A branch of Buddhism. See **Buddhism**. 2. The system of thought and spirituality that suggests that existence is all there is; that which exists cannot be adequately described by words, but can only be experienced. 3. Corresponds to transcendence, personal experience, and individual meditation rather than dogma or scripture.

ZEPPELIN 1. Can represent a buoyant message. See **Airplane**. 2. A new idea or an idea that has resurfaced. 3. That which brings peace, struggle, or change. 4. Might indicate the earthly attempting to conquer the spiritual. 5. You may also wish to see **Balloon**.

ZERO 1. Corresponds to either the absence of anything or the containment of everything. See **Numerology**. 2. May be associated with absolute zero (centigrade) and freezing temperatures. 3. Metaphorically, to zero in = to focus attention upon. 4. You may also wish to see **Circle**.

ZIGZAG 1. Associated with quick, sharp changes in thought, opinion, or direction. See **Direction**. 2. Could correspond to the need to make a lasting decision. 3. Might indicate one who is extremely confused.

ZINC 1. That which coats, impregnates, or protects. 2. See also **Iron**.

ZIPPER 1. That which fastens or joins together. 2. Could represent sexual desires either being exposed or repressed. 3. What one is doing with the zipper would be symbolic of the meaning; for example: closing a zipper could indicate pulling the ends (of a project, idea, or experience) together; unzipping one's outfit may symbolize sexual desire, etc. 4. You may wish to see the name of the garment to which the zipper is attached; for example, see **Coat**. 5. See also **Clothes**.

ZODIAC 1. The twelve equal parts of the heavens, divided into astrological signs. 2. See individual signs or **Astrology**. 3. May indicate the range of inner possibilities. 4. You may also wish to see **Heaven** or **Planet.**

ZOMBIE 1. Corresponds to that which has been dead and discarded suddenly being placed under the influence of another; an animated corpse. See **Puppet** and **Death.**

2. Could represent an idea that was killed and should have remained dead, suddenly resurfacing. 3. That which is intellectually dull. 4. You may also wish to see **Corpse.**

ZOO 1. Can correspond to various parts of one's own self: personality, talents, ideas. See **Animals.** 2. Represents those wild portions of an individual that are viewed publicly. 3. Metaphorically, the place is a zoo = a state of disorder, disarray, and/or chaos.

ZOROASTRIANISM 1. Associated with the religion begun by Zoroaster based, in part, upon the writings of the Zend–Avesta. 2. Emphasis is upon good works and good thoughts. 3. Belief in the immortality of the soul, the war between good and evil, the existence of an afterlife, and the supremacy of God: Ahura Mazda. 4. Although originally begun in Persia, most Zoroastrians now reside in India and call themselves Parsees.

Personal Symbols

Personal Symbols

Personal Symbols

Personal Symbols

Personal Symbols

Personal Symbols

References and Recommended Reading

Ackroyd, Eric. *A Dictionary of Dream Symbols.* A Blandford Book: London. 1993.

Cayce, Edgar (readings). *Dreams and Dreaming. Volumes I and II,* and *Meditation, Volume I.* Association for Research and Enlightenment, Inc.: Virginia Beach, Virginia. 1974, 1976.

Cirlot, J. E. *A Dictionary of Symbols.* Philosophical Library, Inc.: New York. 1971.

Connolly, Eileen. *Tarot: A New Handbook for the Apprentice.* Newcastle Publishing Company: North Hollywood, California. 1990.

Crisp, Tony. *Do You Dream?* Neville Spearman: London. 1971.

de Laszlo, Violet S., ed. *Psyche & Symbol: A Selection from the Writings of C. G. Jung.* Doubleday & Company: New York. 1958.

Hickey, Isabel M. *Astrology: A Cosmic Science.* Fellowship House: Waltham, Massachusetts. 1970.

Holy Bible. King James Version.

Javane, Faith, and Dusty Bunker. *Numerology and the Divine Triangle.* Whitford Press: West Chester, Pennsylvania. 1979.

Lineman, Rose, and Jan Popelka. *Compendium of Astrology.* Para Research/Schiffer Publishing, Ltd.: West Chester, Pennsylvania. 1984.

Parker, Derek, and Julia Parker. *The Compleat Astrologer.* Bantam Books: New York. 1981.

Rodriguez, Magaly del Carmen. *Creative Imaging Work.* Privately published. 1988/89.

Sechrist, Elsie. *Dreams: Your Magic Mirror.* Warner Books: New York. 1974.

Shelley, Violet. *Symbols and the Self* A.R.E. Press: Virginia Beach, Virginia. 1986.

Smith, Huston. *The Religions of Man.* Harper & Row, Publishers, Inc.: New York. 1965.

Stalnaker, Leo. *Mystic Symbolism in Bible Numerals.* C & R Anthony, Inc.: New York. 1956.

Tanner, Wilda B. *The Mystical, Magical, Marvelous World of Dreams.* Sparrow Hawk Press: Tahlequah, Oklahoma. 1988.

Unity School of Christianity. *Metaphysical Bible Dictionary.* Unity Village, Missouri. 1931.

Van de Castle, Robert L. *Our Dreaming Mind.* Ballantine Books: New York. 1994.

Webster's New Universal Unabridged Dictionary. Simon & Schuster: New York. 1979.

Whittemore, Carroll E., ed. *Symbols of the Church.* Abingdon Press: New York. 1959.

Wing, R. L. *The I Ching Workbook.* Doubleday & Company: New York. 1979.

A.R.E. PRESS

The A.R.E. Press publishes books, videos, and audiotapes meant to improve the quality of our readers' lives–personally, professionally, and spiritually. We hope our products support your endeavors to realize your career potential, to enhance your relationships, to improve your health, and to encourage you to make the changes necessary to live a loving, joyful, and fulfilling life.

For more information or to receive a free catalog, call:

1–800–723–1112

Or write:

A.R.E. Press
215 67th Street
Virginia Beach, VA 23451–2061

DISCOVER HOW THE EDGAR CAYCE MATERIAL CAN HELP YOU!

The Association for Research and Enlightenment, Inc. (A.R.E.®), was founded in 1931 by Edgar Cayce. Its international headquarters are in Virginia Beach, Virginia, where thousands of visitors come year-round. Many more are helped and inspired by A.R.E.'s local activities in their own hometowns or by contact via mail (and now the Internet!) with A.R.E. headquarters.

People from all walks of life, all around the world, have discovered meaningful and life-transforming insights in the A.R.E. programs and materials, which focus on such areas as personal spirituality, holistic health, dreams, family life, finding your best vocation, reincarnation, ESP, meditation, and soul growth in small-group settings. Call us today at our toll-free number:

1–800–333–4499

or

Explore our electronic visitors center on the Internet: **http://www.edgarcayce.org.**

We'll be happy to tell you more about how the work of the A.R.E. can help you!

A.R.E.
215 67th Street
Virginia Beach, VA 23451–2061